C000163457

Traction Recognition

Colin J. Marsden

PUBLISHING

First published 2007
Reprinted 2009
Second edition published 2011
This Third edition first published 2014

ISBN 978 0 7110 3792 2

All rights reserved. No part of this book may be reproduced or transmitted in any form or by any means, electronic or mechanical, including photocopying, recording, scanning or by any information storage and retrieval system, on the internet or elsewhere, without permission from the Publisher in writing.

© Ian Allan Publishing Ltd 2014

Published by Ian Allan Publishing.

An imprint of Ian Allan Publishing Ltd, Hersham, Surrey KT12 4RG.
Printed in Bulgaria

Visit the Ian Allan Publishing website at www.ianallanpublishing.com

Copyright
Illegal copying and selling of publications deprives authors, publishers and booksellers of income, without which there would be no investment in new publications. Unauthorised versions of publications are also likely to be inferior in quality and contain incorrect information. You can help by reporting copyright infringements and acts of piracy to the Publisher or the UK Copyright Service.

Above: *First Great Western currently operates a fleet of 17 Class 150/1 sets; 15 are formed as two-car sets and two are three-car units with a Class 150/2 vehicle marshalled in the middle. The sets are allocated to Bristol and Exeter depots and operate alongside Class 150/2 and 153 sets on local and branch line services. Set No. 150122 is seen at Penzance awaiting departure with a stopping service to Exeter on 17 July 2013.* **CJM**

Introduction

Welcome to the 2014 edition of the Ian Allan *ABC Traction Recognition*, the all-encompassing enthusiasts' guide to the present fleet of locomotives, diesel multiple and electric multiple units and now coaching stock operating over the main-line rail network in the UK.

It does not seem possible that is almost 35 years ago since I first authored the predecessor series of this title 'Motive Power Recognition' and 'Rolling Stock Recognition', which at that time had one entire book covering each of the three basic traction types and a separate volume covering coaching stock.

During that period, we have seen the UK rolling stock fleet change beyond belief, with a level of standardisation in both locomotive and multiple unit types, and a massive reduction in the number of locomotives and a substantial increase in the number of multiple unit trains.

As in the past, *ABC Traction Recognition* is arranged in five main chapters, colour coded for your convenience: blue for locomotives, red for diesel multiple units, green for electric multiple units, and brown for coaching stock, and a new section for this edition covering UK depots is coloured mustard.

Each chapter is broken down in Total Operations Processing System (TOPS) class order. Each class has a full technical description giving the basic dimensions, capacities, outputs and, if passenger carrying, the number of seats. The technical information has been supplied by the lease owners and train operators, supported by visual checks where possible. As with all such works, some conflicts of information exist, especially in terms of local modifications, which render differences. In the main the information provided is for the core fleet.

Unlike in the BR days, where just a handful of exterior liveries were to be found, today hundreds of different colour schemes are prevalent. *ABC Traction Recognition* has tried to show as many as possible of these colours, but it is not possible to show all variations and modifications.

In traditional 'Recognition' style many numerated illustrations showing position and identity of front end, underside or, in the case of locomotives, internal equipment positions are included. For a few classes detailed illustrations of equipment have also been included.

Sadly in 2014 the UK no longer has any workshops offering a new build of diesel or electric locos, with fleet owners now having to look to overseas suppliers for their needs. In terms of diesel locos Electro Motive Diesels and General Electric based in the USA dominate the market, with Spanish builder Vossloh now building the Class 68s for Direct Rail Services.

Following UK rail privatisation in the mid-1990s, most operators sought to replace their inherited rolling stock fleets, improving the travelling environment, and lowering operating costs. This was quickened by the Government's demand that slam-door passenger stock had to be phased out as quickly as possible.

A number of builders bid for these very lucrative contracts with Canadian-owned Bombardier Transportation and German-owned Siemens being the principal winners, both producing huge numbers of new trains over the last 20-25 years. The Bombardier (née Adtranz/ABB) trains have been built mainly in the UK at Derby with some production in Belgium, while the Siemens products have all been built in Germany or Austria.

Since the publication of the last edition of *Traction Recognition* in 2011 some new classes have emerged and entered service; most recently this has included Vossloh Class 68s, GE Class 70s, and Bombardier Class 377 and 387s. In the future we can look forward to many new classes and fleets, including the first of the InterCity Express Project (IEP) HST replacement trains Class 800 and 801 built by Hitachi in County Durham, extra Eurostar Class 374 sets, Class 700 EMUs for the Thameslink project being built by Siemens and the Bombardier-built Class 345s for CrossRail.

Refurbishment of many older trains will also take place following cascading from the introduction of new trains, which will include Class 319s transferring to Northern Rail.

The compilation of *Traction Recognition* would not have been possible without the assistance of the train builders, lease companies and train operators, many of which have answered numerous e-mails about the technical specifications and details of their products. The acquisition of illustrations to show as many different types, modifications, liveries and parts as possible has not been easy and I am very grateful for the assistance of many, most notably Antony Christie, Bill Wilson and Nathan Williamson who have gone out of their way to assist.

I do hope that as a reader of *ABC Traction Recognition* you will enjoy its pages and content.

I welcome any technical updates, new illustrations, detail changes or comments from readers. These should be addressed to me via the publishers or sent with an illustration by e-mail to cjmarsden@btopenworld.com .

Colin J. Marsden
July 2014

Class 08

Sub-class:	08/0	08/9
TOPS number range:	08001-08958 (08077-08956)	08993-08995
Previous number ranges:	13000-13366, D3000-D4192	(From main fleet)
Former class codes:	DEJ4, then D3/2, 3/1	08/0
Built by:	BR workshops Derby, Crewe, Darlington, Doncaster, Horwich	BR Landore
Years introduced:	1953-1959	1985-1987
Wheel arrangement:	0-6-0	0-6-0
Weight:	49.6-50.4 tonnes	49.8 tonnes
Height:	12ft8⅝in (3.88m)	11ft 10in (3.60m)
Length:	29ft 3in (8.91m)	29ft 3in (8.91m)
Width:	8ft 6in (2.59m)	8ft 6in (2.59m)
Wheelbase:	11ft 6in (3.50m)	11ft 6in (3.50m)
Wheel diameter:	4ft 6in (1.37m)	4ft 6in (1.37m)
Min curve negotiable:	3 chains (60.35m)	3 chains (60.35m)
Engine type:	English Electric 6KT	English Electric 6KT
Engine output:	400hp (298kW)	400hp (298kW)
Power at rail:	260hp (194kW)	260hp (194kW)
Tractive effort:	35,000lb (156kN)	35,000lb (156kN)
Cylinder bore:	10in (250mm)	10in (250mm)
Cylinder stroke:	12in (300mm)	12in (300mm)
Maximum speed:	15mph (25km/h)	15mph (25km/h)
Brake type:	Originally Vacuum, some later Dual or Air	Dual or Air
Brake force:	19 tonnes	19 tonnes
Route availability:	5	5
Heating type:	Not fitted	Not fitted
Multiple coupling type:	Not fitted (See notes)	Not fitted
Main generator type:	EE801-8E or E801-14E	EE801-8E or E801-14E
Aux generator type:	90V locos - EE736-2D or EE736-4E 110V locos - EE906-3D	EE736-2D or EE736-4E
Traction motor type:	EE506-6A or EE506-7C	EE506-6A
No of traction motors:	2	2
Gear ratio:	Overall - 23.9:1, First train - 82:15, Second train - 70:16	Overall - 23.9:1, First train - 82:15, Second train - 70:16
Fuel tank capacity:	668gal (3,036lit)	668gal (3,036lit)
Lub oil capacity:	45gal (204lit)	45gal (204lit)
Sanding equipment:	Pneumatic	Pneumatic
Present owners:	Various	DBS Finance
Present operators:	DBS, Freightliner, Wabtec, FGW, NRL, Alstom, HNRC, EMT, EUS, BAR, GBR, WCR, LNW, WAB, RIV, KBR, LMI, MRL, BOM, RVE and NYM	DBS
Special fittings:	Some locos – Radio, TPWS, Buck-eye couplers, high-level air pipes 08948 – Scharfenberg coupler 08495/605/701/706/735/757/784/804/879/ 888 – remote control equipment, 08738/939 fitted with multiple control for ECR	Some locos — Radio
Sub-class variations:	Standard loco, a descendant of LMS design	Locomotives modified from Class 08/0 with reduced cab height for use on BPGV line in West Wales

Fact File

Based on the pre-War LMS design of 0-6-0 diesel-electric shunting locomotive, 1,193 locos of this design were built for British Railways between 1952 and 1962. The design became the 'standard' heavy shunting loco for the UK and operated in all areas, except where limited clearance or axle restrictions were imposed.

The fleet was gradually reduced in size over the years as yards and the need for pilot locos reduced. In 2014 less than 200 remain active for the mainstream operators, with fewer than 150 authorised for Network Rail operation.

A number of locomotives are now owned by the private sector and used within industry, while a huge number have been preserved.

Originally all were painted in BR black or green livery; this changed to BR blue from the late 1960s. After privatisation many new liveries were applied to reflect ownership.

A number of DBS-operated locos are now fitted for remote control equipment and many locos have local modifications. ■

Above: *Although more than 1,000 BR 'standard' Class 08 shunting locos were built, only a handful remain, with most shunting now performed by train locos. EWS liveried No. 08482 is seen from its cab end. This is a standard loco, fitted with air brake equipment and limited end lighting. A cast nameplate is fitted in the standard position, attached to the side of the battery box. Equipment positions (also applicable to Class 09) A: Radiator/ cooler group, B: Vacuum exhauster box (disused), C: Removable roof sections, D: Engine compartment, E: Fuel shut- off valve, F: Battery box, G: Battery isolating switch, H: Milometer, I: Fuel tank, J: Driving cab, K: Sandbox, L: Fuel filler port.* **Nathan Williamson**

Right Middle: *All but a handful of standard 0-6-0 shunting locos now only sport air brakes, as a very limited number of vacuum braked vehicles still remain in service. Air brake fitted No. 08624 displays Freightliner green and yellow livery with standard 'wasp' warning ends.* **Richard Lillie**

Right Bottom: *Passenger operator First Great Western operates a fleet of nine Class 08s for depot pilot work. Some are fitted with drop-head knuckle couplers allowing attachment to HSTs, some have equipment to allow main line operation and all have headlights. No. 08641 in BR blue is shown.* **Nathan Williamson**

Above: *The three low-cab profile Class 08/9s were modified from standard height locos for operation on the BPGV line is West Wales. These locos are still in operation with DB-S. No. 08995 is viewed at Westbury from its low-cab profile end. Note the smaller end windows and less body end above the windows to roof height.*
Nathan Williamson

Left Middle: *Displaying the latest First Great Western livery and sporting 'wasp' colours on the front edge of the compressor box and fuel tank, No. 08836 is seen at Paddington with the empty stock from the overnight sleeping car train from Penzance, awaiting departure to Old Oak Common. This loco is equipped for main line operation.*
Antony Christie

Left Bottom: *Passenger operator East Midlands Trains has a fleet of five Class 08s on its books to provide depot pilotage duties, mainly involving HST stock; for this reason, the locos are fitted with drop-head knuckle couplers. Four of the five locos sport full Stagecoach EMT blue livery. No. 08690 David Thirkill is seen from its radiator end inside Leeds Neville Hill depot. Note the large central headlight.* **Ron Cover**

Right: *Two Class 08 standard shunting locos are operated by London Midland for depot pilot duties at Tyseley and Soho depots. There work mainly involves shunting vehicles or units which are unable to power themselves. One loco, No. 08616, is painted in a version of London Midland livery and used at Tyseley, while the Soho-allocated loco No. 08805 is painted in former BR rail blue. Drop-head knuckle couplers are fitted.*
John Stretton

Right: *When Eurostar train sets of Class 373 entered service in the mid 1990s, a method of shunting either power cars or passenger stock was required, thus requiring a vehicle which was fitted with a suitable Dellner style auto coupler. As no 'off-the-shelf' loco was available, Eurostar UK funded the conversion of No. 08948 to have drop-head couplers and an air drying system, together with revised draw-gear. Originally the loco was based at North Pole depot in west London, but after the UK base for Eurostar stock transferred to Temple Mills, the '08' was transferred to this depot, where this view was recorded in spring 2014.*
Antony Christie

Right: *A large number of Class 08s have, after withdrawal from mainstream operators, been purchased by either preservationists or the private sector for hire use to train operators or industrial operators. The established hire operator Harry Needle Railway Co has a significant number of operational Class 08s and offers these for hire. These locos are maintained in a first class condition and several carry the HNRC yellow and grey livery.*
Norman E. Preedy

Right: *The industrial company Knorr Bremse Rail owns both Wolverton and Glasgow Works and operates a small fleet of Class 08s, two locos being based at each establishment. The locos at Wolverton carry a unique Knorr Bremse livery, while the Glasgow locos carry two-tone grey, as illustrated on No. 08730.* **Bill Wilson**

Class 09

Sub class:	09/0	09/1	09/2
TOPS number range:	09001-09026 (09002-026)	09101-09107 (09101-107)	09201-09205 (09201-204)
Previous number range:	D3665-71, D3719-21, D4099-114	Rebuilt from Class 08	Rebuilt from Class 08
Former class codes:	DEJ4, then 3/1	Class 08	Class 08
Built by:	BR Darlington/Horwich	RFS Kilnhurst	RFS Kilnhurst
Years introduced:	1959-1962	1992-1993	1992-1993
Wheel arrangement:	0-6-0	0-6-0	0-6-0
Weight:	50 tonnes	50 tonnes	50 tonnes
Height:	12ft 8⅝in (3.88m)	12ft 8⅝in (3.88m)	12ft 8⅝in (3.88m)
Length:	29ft 3in (8.91m)	29ft 3in (8.91m)	29ft 3in (8.91m)
Width:	8ft 6in (2.59m)	8ft 6in (2.59m)	8ft 6in (2.59m)
Wheelbase:	11ft 6in (3.50m)	11ft 6in (3.50m)	11ft 6in (3.50m)
Wheel diameter:	4ft 6in (1.37m)	4ft 6in (1.37m)	4ft 6in (1.37m)
Min curve negotiable:	3 chains (60.35m)	3 chains (60.35m)	3 chains (60.35m)
Engine type:	English Electric 6KT	English Electric 6KT	English Electric 6KT
Engine output:	400hp (298kW)	400hp (298kW)	400hp (298kW)
Power at rail:	269hp (201kW)	269hp (201kW)	269hp (201kW)
Tractive effort:	25,000lb (111kN)	25,000lb (111kN)	25,000lb (111kN)
Cylinder bore:	10in (250mm)	10in (250mm)	10in (250mm)
Cylinder stroke:	12in (300mm)	12in (300mm)	12in (300mm)
Maximum speed:	27½mph (34km/h)	27½mph (34km/h)	27½mph (34km/h)
Brake type:	Dual	Dual	Dual
Brake force:	19 tonnes	19 tonnes	19 tonnes
Route availability:	5	5	5
Heating type:	Not fitted	Not fitted	Not fitted
Multiple coupling type:	Not fitted	Not fitted	Not fitted
Main generator type:	EE801-13E or EE801-14E	EE801-13E or EE801-14E	EE801-13E or EE801-14E
Aux generator type:	EE906-3D	EE906-3D	EE906-3D
Traction motor type:	EE506-10C	EE506-10C	EE506-10C
No of traction motors:	2	2	2
Gear ratio:	Overall - 23.9:1 First train - 82:15 Second train - 70:16	Overall - 23.9:1 First train - 82:15 Second train - 70:16	Overall - 23.9:1 First train - 82:15 Second train - 70:16
Fuel tank capacity:	668gal (3,037lit)	668gal (3,037lit)	668gal (3,037lit)
Cooling water capacity:	140gal (636lit)	140gal (636lit)	140gal (636lit)
Lub oil capacity:	45gal (204lit)	45gal (204lit)	45gal (204lit)
Sanding equipment:	Pneumatic	Pneumatic	Pneumatic
Present operator:	GBR, DBS, LOG, HNR, SOU	DBS	DBS, LNW
Special fittings:	Some locos - Radio, Headlight, TPWS	Some locos - Radio, Headlight, TPWS	Some locos - Radio, Headlight, TPWS
Sub-class variations:	Higher-speed version of standard Class 08 originally allocated to the former BR Southern Region	Modified from standard Class 08, using 110V electrical equipment	Modified from standard Class 08, using 90V electrical equipment

Left: Owned by Transport for London (TfL) Class 09 No. 09007 is restored to 1960s BR green livery with a 'lion holding wheel' logo on its batterybox sides. The loco also sports its 1957 series running number of D3671. The loco is based at Willesden depot and used to shunt Class 378 stock as required. The loco has high level duplicate air pipes and has had its vacuum brake equipment removed. Since its BR shunting days on the Southern Region, some revision has been made to front marker/tail lights with just two of the original four remaining.
Antony Christie

Above: *The National Railway Museum at York owns and operates Class 09/0 No. 09017 which is used for powering passenger rides and the provision of shunting power at the museum. In its 'preserved' condition the loco now sports maroon livery with NRM branding and has some extra electrical conduit on the ends. The loco has lost its high level duplicate air connections, but retains dual brake capability; an important factor is shunting heritage stock within the museum.*
Norman E. Preedy

Right: *Class 09 cab end equipment layout, also applicable to Class 08 locomotives. A: Main reservoir air pipe (yellow), B: Position for vacuum pipe (removed), C: Air brake pipe (red), D: Lifting socket in buffer beam (one of two), E: High-level duplicate main reservoir and brake pipe (controlled by single valve), F: End marker/ tail lights.* **CJM**

Note: One Class 09/0 operates for Southern, based at Brighton, and DB-S operates one member of Class 09/0, 09/1 and 09/2 for freight operations and pilot duties.

The 26 members of the original Class 09 fleet were built for BR Southern Region use and had a higher top speed of 27½ mph (34km/h).

The design incorporated waist-height air connections for coupling to SR EMU and DEMU stock of the 1951-66 designs. After the need for '09s' diminished on the SR, the fleet found deployment around the entire network.

In 1992-93 when modernisation of the shunter fleet was on the cards, two small batches of Class 09s were modified from Class 08s with new equipment and a higher top speed of 27½mph. These conversions did not have waist-height air connections and were operated by the freight sector.

Many locos are now withdrawn, while some operate for other businesses including GBRf, Southern and London Overground. ■

Class 20

Sub-class:	20/0	20/3	20/9
TOPS number range:	20001-20227	20301-20315	20901-20906
1957 BR number range:	D8000-D8199, D8300-D8327 series	20047/084/127/120/095/ 131/128/187/075/190/ 102/042/194/117/104	20101/060/083/041/ 225/219
Former class codes:	D10/3, then 10/3	20/0	20/0
Built by:	English Electric, Vulcan Foundry or Robert Stephenson & Hawthorn	Rebuilt: Brush Traction or RFS Doncaster	Rebuilt: Hunslet Barclay
Years introduced:	1957-1968	1995-1998 (as 20/3)	1989 (as 20/9)
Wheel arrangement:	Bo-Bo	Bo-Bo	Bo-Bo
Weight:	73 tonnes	73 tonnes	73 tonnes
Height:	12ft 7⅝in (3.85m)	12ft 7⅝in (3.85m)	12ft 7⅝in (3.85m)
Length:	46ft 9¼in (14.26m)	46ft 9¼in (14.26m)	46ft 9¼in (14.26m)
Width:	8ft 9in (2.67m)	8ft 9in (2.67m)	8ft 9in (2.67m)
Wheelbase:	32ft 6in (9.90m)	32ft 6in (9.90m)	32ft 6in (9.90m)
Bogie wheelbase:	8ft 6in (2.59m)	8ft 6in (2.59m)	8ft 6in (2.59m)
Bogie pivot centres:	24ft 0in (7.31m)	24ft 0in (7.31m)	24ft 0in (7.31m)
Wheel diameter:	3ft 7in (1.09m)	3ft 7in (1.09m)	3ft 7in (1.09m)
Min curve negotiable:	3.5 chains (70.40m)	3.5 chains (70.40m)	3.5 chains (70.40m)
Engine type:	English Electric 8SVT Mk2	English Electric 8SVT Mk2	English Electric 8SVT Mk2
Engine output:	1,000hp (746kW)	1,000hp (746kW)	1,000hp (746kW)
Power at rail:	770hp (574kW)	770hp (574kW)	770hp (574kW)
Tractive effort:	42,000lb (187kN)	42,000lb (187kN)	42,000lb (187kN)
Cylinder bore:	10in (220mm)	10in (220mm)	10in (220mm)
Cylinder stroke:	12in (350mm)	12in (350mm)	12in (350mm)
Maximum speed:	75mph (121km/h)	75mph (121km/h)	60mph (97km/h)
Brake type:	Vacuum, later dual	Air	Air
Brake force:	35 tonnes	31 tonnes	35 tonnes
Route availability:	5	5	5
Heating type:	Not fitted (through piped)	Not fitted	Not fitted
Multiple coupling type:	Blue star	DRS system	Blue star
Main generator type:	EE819-3C	EE819-3C	EE819-3C
Aux generator type:	EE911-2B	EE911-2B	EE911-2B
ETS generator type:	Not fitted	Not fitted	Not fitted
Traction motor type:	EE526-5D or EE526-8D	EE526-8D	EE526-8D
No of traction motors:	4	4	4
Gear ratio:	63:17	63:17	63:17
Fuel tank capacity:	380gal (1,727lit)	1,080gal (4,909lit)	380-1,040gal (1,727-4,727lit)
Cooling water capacity:	130gal (591lit)	130gal (591lit)	130gal (591lit)
Lub oil capacity:	100gal (455lit)	100gal (455lit)	100gal (455lit)
Sanding equipment:	Pneumatic	Pneumatic	Pneumatic
Special fittings:	Snowplough brackets	Snowplough brackets	Snowplough brackets
Present operator:	GBR, HNRC, IND, PRI	DRS, HNRC	GBR, HNRC
Sub-class variations:	Standard as-built locos. Some locos authorised for use on Network Rail.	Refurbished locos for DRS. Modified cab equipment.	Modified from Class 20/0 sold to Hunslet Barclay, then DRS, now HNRC/GBR.

Fact File

The BR standard Type 1, later Class 20, built as a direct result of the BTC 1955 Modernisation Plan and introduced from 1957, is one of the most robust and reliable diesel-electric loco classes ever built.

A total of 228 locos were built over an 11-year period, with members operating on the Eastern, London Midland and Scottish Regions.

With the run-down of diesel classes from the late 1970s, the vast majority of Class 20s were withdrawn. However, the 1990s expansion of the private rail sector saw a huge number of locos pass to further operational ownership; six locos were sold to Hunslet Barclay of Kilmarnock to operate weedcontrol trains. Private ownership expanded when BNFL's rail division Direct Rail Services (DRS) purchased a fleet and refurbished them for flask and general freight traffic.

Today, more than 55 years after first introduction, a number of Class 20s are still in daily operation, working for DRS, GBRf and several 'spot-hire' companies such as Harry Needle Railroad Company (HNRC). A large number of the fleet have also been saved by the preservation movement as these locos are ideal power for small branch line operations.

It looks like this design of single cab loco will be around for at least another 10 years. ∎

Above: *Class 20 equipment positions. A: No. 2 end, B: No. 1 end, C: Compressor and traction motor fan compartment, D: Radiator compartment, E: Engine compartment, F: Generator compartment, G: Traction motor blower compartment, H: Secondary fuel tank (some locos only), I: Battery box with air reservoir behind, J: Fuel filler port, K: Light cluster unit (tail/head/marker), L: Headlight, M: Warning horn (behind grille), N: Sandbox, O: Engine control air pipe (white), P: Main reservoir air pipe (yellow), Q: Air brake pipe (red), R: DRS style multiple control jumper socket. On this example, No. 20307, the original vacuum brake and blue star multiple equipment has been removed. This loco is now withdrawn.* **CJM**

Below: *In 2014, Direct Rail Services operates a fleet of eight Class 20/3s based at Carlisle for general freight operations, and all are now painted in 'Compass livery'. The ever popular fleet is frequently requested for railtour duties as demonstrated in this view of Nos. 20308 and 20303 passing Dawlish with a Kingswear to Crewe charter service.* **CJM**

Left: *The Class 20/3 locos converted for Direct Rail Services received an upgraded driving cab, with modern switch gear and improved positioning of equipment. The cab of No. 20302 is illustrated. A: Cab-cab radio handset, B: Cab-cab call button, C: Loudspeaker, D: NRN radio handset, E: NRN radio, F: Windscreen wiper valve, G: Handbrake wheel, H: Warning lights, I: AWS indicator, J: Traction ammeter, K: Brake pipe pressure gauge, L: Bogie brake cylinder gauge, M: Speedometer, N: Light switches, O: Lights indicator, P: Headlight flasher, Q: AWS reset button, R: Sand apply button, S: Light switches, T: Main reservoir pressure gauge, U: Master switch, V: Power controller, W: Cooker.* **CJM**

Below: *In 2012 GB Railfreight had a need for Class 20s to fulfill a contract to haul new London Underground stock between Bombardier Derby and Old Dalby or the LUL network. The company hired locos in a deal with HNRC and two locos of the contract, No. 20901 and 20905, were repainted by Barrow Hill in full GBRf livery. The locos used for this contract are also fitted with 'trip cock' apparatus for operating over the LU controlled lines in the Chiltern network. Nos. 20901/905 are seen near Wichnor Junction leading a rake of London Transport 'S' stock.* **Antony Christie**

Right: *Class 20 cab-front end equipment. A: Two-tone warning horns behind grille, B: Radio aerial, C: Windscreen washers, D: DRS-style multiple control jumper socket (cable stowed inside locomotive when not in use), E: Group Standard light cluster, tail, head and marker lights, F: Main reservoir pipe (yellow), G: Engine air control pipe (white), H: Air brake pipe (red), I: Coupling shackle and hook.*
Brian Garrett

Below: *Two main line certified Class 20s, Nos. 20142 and 20189, were in April 2014 repainted in a new Balfour Beatty blue and grey livery. The pair, seen passing Kidsgrove on delivery from Crewe to Derby, will be used to power part of the new Great Western electrification train. These locos are fitted with dual brakes and blue star multiple control equipment.*
Cliff Beeton

Class 31

Sub-class:	31/1	31/4	31/5
TOPS Number range:	31101-31327	31400-31469	31507-31569
1957 BR number range:	D5518-D5862	From Class 31/1 fleet	From Class 31/4 fleet
Former class codes:	D14/2, then 14/2	31/1	31/4
Built by:	Brush, Loughborough	Modified by BR	Modified by BR
Years introduced:	1958-1962	As 31/4 - 1970-1985	As 31/5 - 1990-1994
Wheel arrangement:	A1A-A1A	A1A-A1A	A1A-A1A
Weight:	107-111 tonnes	107-111 tonnes	107-111 tonnes
Height:	12ft 7in (3.84m)	12ft 7in (3.84m)	12ft 7in (3.84m)
Length:	56ft 9in (17.30m)	56ft 9in (17.30m)	56ft 9in (17.30m)
Width:	8ft 9in (2.67m)	8ft 9in (2.67m)	8ft 9in (2.67m)
Wheelbase:	42ft 10in (13.05m)	42ft 10in (13.05m)	42ft 10in (13.05m)
Bogie wheelbase:	14ft 0in (4.27m)	14ft 0in (4.27m)	14ft 0in (4.27m)
Bogie pivot centres:	28ft 10in (8.79m)	28ft 10in (8.79m)	28ft 10in (8.79m)
Wheel diameter:	Powered - 3ft 7in (1.09m) Pony - 3ft 3½in (1m)	Powered - 3ft 7in (1.09m) Pony - 3ft 3½in (1m)	Powered - 3ft 7in (1.09m) Pony - 3ft 3½in (1m)
Min curve negotiable:	4.5 chains (90.52m)	4.5 chains (90.52m)	4.5 chains (90.52m)
Engine type:	English Electric 12SVT	English Electric 12SVT	English Electric 12SVT
Engine output:	1,470hp (1,096kW)	1,470hp (1,096kW)	1,470hp (1,096kW)
Power at rail:	1,170hp (872kW)	1,170hp (872kW)	1,170hp (872kW)
Tractive effort:	31102-110 42,000lb (187kN) 31128-319 35,900lb (160kN)	35,900lb (160kN)	35,900lb (160kN)
Cylinder bore:	10in (250mm)	10in (250mm)	10in (250mm)
Cylinder stroke:	12in (300mm)	12in (300mm)	12in (300mm)
Maximum speed:	31101-116 - 80mph (129km/h) 31117-327 - 90mph (145km/h)	90mph (145km/h)	90mph (145km/h)
Brake type:	Vacuum, modified to Dual	Dual	Dual
Brake force:	49 tonnes	49 tonnes	49 tonnes
Route availability:	5	6	6
Heating type:	Steam - Spanner Mk 1 (removed)	Electric, index 66, dual heat Spanner Mk 1	Electric - isolated
Multiple coupling type:	Blue star	Blue star	Blue star
Main generator type:	Brush TG160-48	Brush TG160-48	Brush TG160-48
Aux generator type:	Brush TG69-42	-	-
Aux ETS alternator type:	-	Brush BL100-30	Brush BL100-30
Traction motor type:	Brush TM73-68	Brush TM73-68	Brush TM73-68
No of traction motors:	4	4	4
Gear ratio:	31101-31116 - 64:17 31117-31327 - 60:19	60:19	60:19
Fuel tank capacity:	530gal (2,409lit)	530gal (2,409lit)	530gal (2,409lit)
Cooling water capacity:	156gal (709lit)	156gal (709lit)	156gal (709lit)
Lub oil capacity:	110gal (500lit)	110gal (500lit)	110gal (500lit)
Boiler water capacity:	600gal (2,727lit) (if fitted)	600gal (2,727lit) (if fitted)	-
Boiler fuel capacity:	100gal (455lit) (if fitted)	100gal (455lit) (if fitted)	-
Sanding equipment:	Pneumatic	Pneumatic	Pneumatic
Present operator:	NRL, RVE, BAR	NRL, RVE, NRL	PRE
Sub-class variations:	Basic locomotives	Locos fitted with electric train supply (ETS)	31/4s with ETS isolated

Note: Locomotives numbered lower than D5530 (31112) and selectively between D5531 and D5561 (31113 and 31143) had disc train reporting equipment. All other locos had a roof-mounted headcode/marker light boxes.

Fact File

This is another of the classes built as a direct result of the 1955 British Transport Commission (BTC) Modernisation Plan, the Brush Type 2, later BR Class 31. Over the years several derivatives have been introduced during the fitting of electric train supply.

Following withdrawal by BR a number were sold to private operators, and today Rail Vehicle Engineering, DCR, BAR and Network Rail are the main operators.

The Network Rail locos are painted in yellow livery and operate track test trains, while the RVEL locos can be found virtually anywhere on the network powering freight, charter or 'spot-hire' services, including Network Rail. The DCR and BAR locos operate freight and engineering duties.

The Class 31s are popular with preservation groups and a number are to be found restored and in frequent use on the larger preserved lines.

After original construction in the late 1950s the entire fleet was re-engined with English Electric units, replacing the original Mirrlees engines. ■

31/6
31601-31602
From Class 31/1 fleet
31/1
Modified by Fragonset
As 31/6 - 1999
A1A-A1A
107-111 tonnes
12ft 7in (3.84m)
56ft 9in (17.30m)
8ft 9in (2.67m)
42ft 10in (13.05m)
14ft 0in (4.27m)
28ft 10in (8.79m)
Powered - 3ft 7in (1.09m)
Pony - 3ft 3½in (1m)
4.5 chains (90.52m)
English Electric 12SVT
1,470hp (1,096kW)
1,170hp (872kW)
35,900lb (160kN)

10in (250mm)
12in (300mm)
60mph (97km/h)

Dual
49 tonnes
5
Through wired

Blue star
Brush TG160-48
Brush TG69-42
-
Brush TM73-68
4
60:19

530gal (2,409lit)
156gal (709lit)
110gal (500lit)
-
-
Pneumatic
BAR
Class 31/1 fitted with through
ETS control and cabling to enable
operation at remote end of trains

Above: *A handful of the 1950s vintage Brush Type 2s are still in service, mainly for Network Rail until newer vehicles are made available. Class 31/1 No. 31105, an example without a roof headcode display, is shown from its No. 2 end painted in Network Rail yellow.* **John Stretton**

Below: *Later-built Brush Type 2s, later Class 31s, were fitted with a four character route indicator display, which from the mid-1970s fell out of use and is now plated over. Some of the Class 31s operated by Network Rail undertake specific roles for the track and infrastructure inspection teams and are fitted with special front end lights and filming equipment. Sprouting an array of different headlights and recording equipment, No. 31285 is illustrated from its No. 2 end at Paignton.*
Antony Christie

Right: *Another main line operator of Class 31s is Devon & Cornwall Railway, which operates 'spot hire' for infrastructure contracts. Here Class 31/4 No. 31452 is seen in DCR green livery powering the RailVac train, a train which DCR usually powers. The Class 31/4 sub-class was formed of standard locos fitted with electric train supply.*
Nathan Williamson

Traction Recognition

Left: *Brush Type 2 Class 31 front end equipment positions. Main items are the same for all sub-classes. 1: Original four character route display, now sporting two fixed beam marker lights, 2: Tail light, 3: Headlight, 4: Blue star multiple control jumper receptacle, 5: Blue star multiple control jumper cable, 6: Main reservoir air pipe (yellow) with engine control air pipe (white) adjacent, 7: Air brake pipe (red), 8: Vacuum brake pipe, 9: Coupling hook and shackle. No. 31190 (D5613) is illustrated painted in mock 1960s green with a yellow warning panel; this loco is operated by British American Railways.* **Antony Christie**

Below: *To allow for the provision of electric train supply (ETS) a number of standard Class 31/1 locomotives were refurbished at BREL Doncaster and fitted with a train supply alternator. To identify these locos from the non or steam heat fitted examples, the locos were renumbered in the 314xx series. The locos were also visually identifiable by the provision of ETS jumpers and receptacle on the buffer beam. Painted in Network Rail yellow, No. 31465 is illustrated from its No. 1 or cooler group end. This locomotive has had its original front communicating door sealed and its original footholds removed.* **Nathan Williamson**

Above: *In 1999, two standard Class 31/1s were modified to enable attachment at the remote end of a Class 31/4 powered train and have the ability to switch on or off the electric train supply of the rear loco. For this operation standard ETS jumper cables and a remote heat 'on' and heat 'off' panel in the driving cab were installed. The locos were reclassified as Class 31/6 and numbered 31601 and 31602. Both are now owned by Devon & Cornwall Railways and No. 31601 is illustrated from its No. 2 end.* **Nathan Williamson**

Below: *In mid-2014, a total of 27 Class 31s were preserved; in the main these are operational and show a diverse selection of liveries. No. D5830 (31297/31463) operating on the Great Central Railway has been restored to a golden ochre livery, applied to one loco No. D5578 (31160) for a trial period in 1960.* **Antony Christie**

Class 33

Sub-class:	33/0	33/1	33/2
TOPS Number range:	33001-33065	33101-33119	33201-33212
BR 1957 number range:	D6500-D6585	Random from 33/0 fleet	D6586-D6597
Former class codes:	D15/1, later 15/6	-	D15/2, later 15/6A
Southern Region code:	KA	KB	KA-4C
Built by:	Birmingham RC&W	Birmingham RC&W	Birmingham RC&W
Years introduced:	1960-1962	1965-1966	1962
Wheel arrangement:	Bo-Bo	Bo-Bo	Bo-Bo
Weight:	77 tonnes	78 tonnes	77 tonnes
Height:	12ft 8in (3.86m)	12ft 8in (3.86m)	12ft 8in (3.86m)
Length:	50ft 9in (15.47m)	50ft 9in (15.47m)	50ft 9in (15.47m)
Width:	9ft 3in (2.81m)	9ft 3in (2.81m)	8ft 8in (2.64m)
Wheelbase:	39ft 0in (11.89m)	39ft 0in (11.89m)	39ft 0in (11.89m)
Bogie wheelbase:	10ft 0in (3.04m)	10ft 0in (3.04m)	10ft 0in (3.04m)
Bogie pivot centres:	29ft 0in (8.84m)	29ft 0in (8.84m)	29ft 0in (8.84m)
Wheel diameter:	3ft 7in (1.09m)	3ft 7in (1.09m)	3ft 7in (1.09m)
Min curve negotiable:	4 chains (80.46m)	4 chains (80.46m)	4 chains (80.46m)
Engine type:	Sulzer 8LDA28A	Sulzer 8LDA28A	Sulzer 8LDA28A
Engine output:	1,550hp (1,156kW)	1,550hp (1,156kW)	1,550hp (1,156kW)
Power at rail:	1,215hp (909kW)	1,215hp (909kW)	1,215hp (909kW)
Tractive effort:	45,000lb (200kN)	45,000lb (200kN)	45,000lb (200kN)
Cylinder bore:	11.02in (270mm)	11.02in (270mm)	11.02in (270mm)
Cylinder stroke:	14.17in (360mm)	14.17in (360mm)	14.17in (360mm)
Maximum speed:	85mph (137km/h)	85mph (137km/h)	85mph (137km/h)
Brake type:	Dual	Dual	Dual
Brake force:	35 tonnes	35 tonnes	35 tonnes
Route availability:	6	6	6
Heating type:	Electric - index 48	Electric - index 48	Electric - index 48
Multiple coupling type:	Blue star	Blue star, 27 way 1951-66 EMU jumpers	Blue star
Main generator type:	Crompton Parkinson CG391-B1	Crompton Parkinson CG391-B1	Crompton Parkinson CG391-B1
Aux generator type:	Crompton Parkinson CAG193-A1	Crompton Parkinson CAG193-A1	Crompton Parkinson CAG193-A1
ETS generator type:	Crompton Parkinson CAG392-A1	Crompton Parkinson CAG392-A1	Crompton Parkinson CAG392-A1
Traction motor type:	Crompton Parkinson C171-C2	Crompton Parkinson C171-C2	Crompton Parkinson C171-C2
No of traction motors:	4	4	4
Gear ratio:	62:17	62:17	62:17
Fuel tank capacity:	750gal (3,410lit)	750gal (3,410lit)	750gal (3,410lit)
Cooling water capacity:	230gal (1,046lit)	230gal (1,046lit)	230gal (1,046lit)
Lub oil capacity:	108gal (491lit)	108gal (491lit)	108gal (491lit)
Sanding equipment:	Pneumatic	Pneumatic	Pneumatic
Special fittings:		Buck-eye couplers, waist-height connections, Weymouth tramway light socket	Slow Speed Control
Owner/Operator:	WCR, PRE	PRE	CR, PRE
Sub-class variations:	Basic locomotive	Fitted with push-pull control equipment to operate with post-1951 EP EMU stock	Locos built to narrower Hastings line profile

Fact File

One of the most versatile locos built was this batch of 98 BRCW Type 3s, designed for the BR Southern Region to replace steam traction from the main lines.

The fleet was fitted with electric train supply from new, with the last 12 constructed to the narrower 'Hastings' body profile to allow operation over the restricted clearances of the Tonbridge-Hastings line.

In 1965-66 when electrification of the Waterloo-Bournemouth line was progressing, 19 members of the standard fleet were modified to allow push-pull operation with post-1951-built EMU stock. These locos became the highly sought-after Class 33/1 fleet.

At privatisation in the 1990s the majority of the fleet had been withdrawn. Several entered preservation and others continue to operate for West Coast Railway. All operational locos now have TPWS and OTMR. ∎

Above: *Just three of the popular ex-Southern Region Birmingham RC&W Type 3 'Crompton' locos remain in main line operation. These dual brake and electric heat locos have a high reliability rate and are fitted with dual position driving controls, enabling the loco to be operated from either side of the cab. Now preserved on the South Devon Railway, No. 33002 is seen in its BR days painted in general freight grey at Woking. Equipment positions (applicable to all sub classes) are: A: Sand box, B: Brake cylinder, C: Cab foot steps, D: Electrical control cubicle position, E: Lifting point, F: Brake cylinder, G: Exhaust port, H: Sand box, I: Position of generator group, J: Battery box, K: Fuel tank, L: Power unit position, M: Fuel tank filler port, N: Cooler group.* **CJM**

Right: *Viewed from its No. 1 end showing the A side, narrow-bodied Class 33/2 No. 33207 painted in West Coast Railway maroon is seen at Eastleigh, complete with a set of three-section miniature snowploughs.* **Antony Christie**

Below: *The same locomotive, No. 33027, is now viewed showing the B side, again from the No. 1 or cooler group end. Both sides have four glazed windows and one equipment door. The loco is seen passing Millbrook Freightliner terminal on 6 March 2014 hauling a Class 108 from Swanage to Eastleigh Works.* **Antony Christie**

Sub-class:	37/0 & 97/3	37/3	37/4
TOPS number range:	37001-37308 , 97301-97304¤	37330-37383	37401-37431
1957 BR number range	D6600-D6999	From main fleet	From main fleet
Former class codes:	D17/1, then 17/3	37/0	37/0
Built by:	English Electric, Vulcan Foundry or Robert Stephenson & Hawthorn	-	-
Refurbished by:	-	BR Depots	BREL Crewe
Years introduced:	1960-1965 , 97/3 - 2008	1988-1995	1985-1986
Wheel arrangement:	Co-Co	Co-Co	Co-Co
Weight:	102-108 tonnes	102-108 tonnes	107 tonnes
Height:	Between 12ft 9⅛in and 13ft 0¾in (3.89m-3.96m) #	Between 12ft 9⅛in and 13ft 0¾in (3.89m-3.96m) #	13ft 0¾in (3.96m)
Length:	61ft 6in (18.74m)	61ft 6in (18.74m)	61ft 6in (18.74m)
Width:	8ft 11⅝in (2.73m)	8ft 11⅝in (2.73m)	8ft 11⅝in (2.73m)
Wheelbase:	50ft 8in (15.44m)	50ft 8in (15.44m)	50ft 8in (15.44m)
Bogie wheelbase:	13ft 6in (4.11m)	13ft 6in (4.11m)	13ft 6in (4.11m)
Bogie pivot centres:	37ft 2in (11.32m)	37ft 2in (11.32m)	37ft 2in (11.32m)
Wheel diameter:	3ft 7in (1.09m)	3ft 7in (1.09m)	3ft 7in (1.09m)
Min curve negotiable:	4 chains (80.46m)	4 chains (80.46m)	4 chains (80.46m)
Engine type:	English Electric 12CSVT	English Electric 12CSVT	English Electric 12CSVT
Engine output:	1,750hp (1,304kW)	1,750hp (1,304kW)	1,750hp (1,304kW)
Power at rail:	1,250hp (932kW)	1,250hp (932kW)	1,254hp (935kW)
Tractive effort:	55,500lb (245kN)	56,180lb (250kN)	57,440lb (256kN)
Cylinder bore:	10in (250mm)	10in (250mm)	10in (250mm)
Cylinder stroke:	12in (300mm)	12in (300mm)	12in (300mm)
Maximum speed:	As built 90mph (145km/h) Modified 80mph (129km/h)	80mph (129km/h)	90mph (145km/h)
Brake type:	Vacuum, later dual	Dual	Dual
Brake force:	50 tonnes	50 tonnes	50 tonnes
Route availability:	5	5	5
Heating type:	Steam, later removed	Not fitted	Electric - index 30
Multiple coupling type:	Blue star	Blue star	Blue star
Main generator type:	EE822-10G, EE822-13G or EE822-16J	EE822-10G	-
Main alternator type:	-	-	Brush BA1005A
Aux generator type:	EE911/5C	EE911/5C	-
Aux alternator type:	-	-	Brush BA606A
ETS alternator type:	-	-	Brush BAH701
Traction motor type:	EE538-1A	EE538-1A	EE538-5A
No of traction motors:	6	6	6
Gear ratio:	53:18	53:18	59:16
Fuel tank capacity:	890gal (4,046lit)	890gal (4,046lit)	1,690gal (7,682lit)
Cooling water capacity:	160gal (727lit)	160gal (727lit)	160gal (727lit)
Lub oil capacity:	120gal (545lit)	120gal (545lit)	120gal (545lit)
Sanding equipment:	Pneumatic	Pneumatic	Pneumatic
Special fittings:	97/3 - ERTMS	CP7 bogies	Some locos - RETB
Operator:	37 - HNR, PRE, DRS, WCR COL. 97/3 -NRL	-	PRE, DRS, COL
Sub-class variations:	Basic locomotive, fitted with steam heating, now removed	Fitted CP7 bogies	Refurbished loco fitted with electric train supply and CP7 bogies
Notes:	¤ ERTMS trials locos # Depending on body style	# Depending on body style	

37/5	37/6	37/7	37/9
37503-37521, 37667-37699	37601-37612	37701-37899	37901-37906
From main fleet	From main fleet	From main fleet	From main fleet
37/0	37/5	37/0	37/0
-		-	-
BREL Crewe	BRML Doncaster	BREL Crewe	BREL Crewe
1986-1987	1994-1996	1986-1987	1986-1987
Co-Co	Co-Co	Co-Co	Co-Co
107 tonnes	106 tonnes	120 tonnes	120 tonnes
13ft 0¾in (3.96m)	13ft 0¾in (3.96m)	13ft 0¾in (3.96m)	13ft 0¾in (3.96m)
61ft 6in (18.74m)	61ft 6in (18.74m)	61ft 6in (18.74m)	61ft 6in (18.74m)
8ft 11⁵/₈in (2.73m)	8ft 11⁵/₈in (2.73m)	8ft 11⁵/₈in (2.73m)	8ft 11⁵/₈in (2.73m)
50ft 8in (15.44m)	50ft 8in (15.44m)	50ft 8in (15.44m)	50ft 8in (15.44m)
13ft 6in (4.11m)	13ft 6in (4.11m)	13ft 6in (4.11m)	13ft 6in (4.11m)
37ft 2in (11.32m)	37ft 2in (11.32m)	37ft 2in (11.32m)	37ft 2in (11.32m)
3ft 7in (1.09m)	3ft 7in (1.09m)	3ft 7in (1.09m)	3ft 7in (1.09m)
4 chains (80.46m)	4 chains (80.46m)	4 chains (80.46m)	4 chains (80.46m)
English Electric 12CSVT	English Electric 12CSVT	English Electric 12CSVT	Mirrlees MB275T §
1,750hp (1,304kW)	1,750hp (1,304kW)	1,750hp (1,304kW)	1,800hp (1,340kW)
1,250hp (932kW)	1,250hp (932kW)	1,250hp (932kW)	1,300hp (940kW)
55,590lb (247kN)	55,500lb (245kN)	62,000lb (276kN)	62,680lb (279kN)
10in (250mm)	10in (250mm)	10in (250mm)	10¼in (275mm)
12in (300mm)	12in (300mm)	12in (300mm)	12¼in (305mm)
80mph (129km/h)	90mph (145km/h)	80mph (129km/h)	80mph (129km/h)
Dual	Air	Dual	Dual
50 tonnes	50 tonnes	50 tonnes	50 tonnes
5	5	7	7
Not fitted	Through wired	Not fitted	Not fitted
Blue star	Blue star, plus DRS	Blue star	Blue star
-	-	-	-
Brush BA1005A	Brush BA1005A	Brush BA1005A@	Brush BA1005A
-	-		-
Brush BA606A	Brush BA606A	Brush BA606A	Brush BA606A
-	-		
EE538-5A	EE538-5A	EE538-5A	EE538-5A
6	6	6	6
59:16	59:16	59:16	59:16
1,690gal (7,682lit)	1,690gal (7,682lit)	1,690gal (7,682lit)	1,690gal (7,682lit)
160gal (727lit)	160gal (727lit)	160gal (727lit)	160gal (727lit)
120gal (545lit)	120gal (545lit)	120gal (545lit)	120gal (545lit)
Pneumatic	Pneumatic	Pneumatic	Pneumatic
		'Heavy-weight locos'	Development locos
DRS, WCR, PRE	DRS	DRS, WCR	PRE
Refurbished standard freight locos	Refurbished locos, for Nightstar and Eurostar tractor use. Fitted with special jumpers. Sold to DRS and fitted with cabtop-mounted marker lights	Refurbished heavy-weight freight locos	Refurbished heavy-weight freight locos, fitted with experimental power units
		@ 37796-37803 have GEC G564AZ	§ 37905-906 fitted with Ruston RK270T

Above: *A number of the early 1960s-built English Electric Type 3 Class 37s are still in traffic on the national network operated by Direct Rail Services, West Coast Rail, Colas, Network Rail and HNRC. In addition a large number are preserved. Several of the original Class 37/0s are in service numbered in the 370xx, 371xx, 372xx and 373xx range. Today, most have been modified in terms of front end bodywork and the vast majority are now air brake fitted only. Direct Rail Services is the largest operator and the illustration of No. 37038 at Gloucester represents the standard loco. This example has been heavily modified with Group Standard head/marker/tail lights and a roof mounted marker light. A DRS style multiple control jumper receptacle is on the nose end and the buffer beam valance has been removed. The loco is viewed from its No. 1 or cooler group end.* **Norman E. Preedy**

Below: *Class 37 bodyside equipment positions, applicable to all members of Class 37. 1: No. 1 end, 2: No. 2 end, 3: Nose section housing traction motor blower and vacuum brake exhauster (if fitted), 4: Main electrical compartment, 5: Power unit and generator/alternator compartment, 6: Cooler group radiator with fan assembly on roof, 7: Nose section housing traction motor blower and air compressor, 8: Fire system activation handle, 9: Brake connection, 10: Radiator water filler port, 11: Lubricating oil filler port, 12: Main fuel tanks with filler between, 13: Fuel tank gauge, 14: Sandbox filler port, 15: Brake cylinder, 16: Hinged roof section providing access to engine, 17: Nose section hinged access doors.* **CJM**

Over 300 English Electric Type 3s or Class 37s were built by English Electric between 1960 and 1965 and originally allocated to all BR regions except the Southern.

As time progressed, the fleet reached all parts of the UK network and became one of the most reliable diesel classes ever built.

By the mid-1980s major refurbishing commenced with 31 examples fitted with electric train supply for passenger operations and a significant number refurbished for freight service with an alternator replacing the original generator.

At privatisation EWS, now DBS, took over the majority of locos, but all have now been disposed of to other operators. In 2014 Colas became an operator taking over some previously preserved locos.

Direct Rail Services and the private traction sector now maintain a sizeable fleet for freight, charter and 'spot-hire' use.

The preservation movement has managed to save a large number of locos from the cutter's torch with many superbly restored in various era liveries. ∎

Above: *In the mid-1980s a batch of 31 standard Class 37s were refurbished at BREL Crewe and fitted with an electric train supply alternator to operate with the increasing number of electric heated passenger vehicles. The modified locos were classified Class 37/4 and can be recognised by the addition of ETS cables on the nose ends. Now operated by Direct Rail Services No. 37402 is illustrated with its No. 1 end on the left.* **CJM**

Right: *Class 37 driving cab layout. A: Radio telephone handset, B: Auto brake valve, C: Straight air brake valve (loco only), D: Windscreen wiper valve, E: Windscreen wiper motor, F: On Train Monitoring Recording (OTMR) equipment, G: Cab radio, H: Warning lights (indicating engine stopped, wheelslip, or general fault), I: Desk light dimmer switch, J: Speedometer, K: Main ammeter giving indication of output from generator or alternator, L: Brake pipe gauge, M: Vacuum brake gauge, N: Brake cylinder pressure, O: Train length button, P: Automatic Warning System (AWS) reset button, Q: Sand application button, R: Headlight switch, S: Slave loco cut-out switch, T: Main reservoir pressure gauge, U: Slow speed control (SSC) switch, V: Engine start button (stop button below), W: Switches for nose end compartment light, cab heat (x 2), X: Slow speed control speedometer, Y: Master switch, key socket and power controller, Z: Warning horn valve. The cab illustrated is from Class 37/7 'heavyweight' No. 37718.* **CJM**

Above: *In 1994-95 12 Class 37/5s were rebuilt at Doncaster Works into Class 37/6s to operate diesel legs of Eurostar UK overnight passenger services, operating with generator cars. However, the 'Nightstar' business was abandoned and the Class 37/6s became spare. Eventually Direct Rail Services took on the entire fleet and rebuilt them, removing UIC train heating equipment and fitting DRS style jumpers and Group Standard light clusters. The 12 locos operate both freight and charter passenger services and can operate in multiple with other DRS multiple fitted locos. No. 37610 is seen at Crewe Gresty Bridge depot from its No. 1 or cooler group end.* **CJM**

Left: *Standard Class 37 front end layout, showing the later type of loco built with a central four-character route display. The loco shown is a Class 37/4 with electric train supply (heat). A: Warning horns, B: Cab radio aerial, C: Marker lights (in original headcode box), D: Red rear marker light, E: Sandbox filler, F: Fire pull handle, G: Electric train supply jumper socket, H: Electric train supply jumper cable, I: Headlight, J: Blue star electro-pneumatic multiple control jumper cable, K: Vacuum pipe, L: Coupling, M: Air brake pipe (red), Main reservoir pipe (yellow), Engine control air pipe (white), N: Main reservoir pipe (yellow), Engine control air pipe (white).* **CJM**

Right: *Front end detail of Direct Rail Services Class 37/6 showing the revised features, including triangulation marker lights, Group Standard light clusters and revised jumpers. A: High-level marker light, B: Warning horns behind grilles, C: Former marker light positions, D: Group Standard light clusters (marker, head and tail lights), E: DRS-type multiple control jumper socket, F: RCH-style jumper cable (now removed), G: UIC jumper cable (now removed), H: Train supply on/off switches (now removed), I: Fire system activation handle, J: Sandbox filler port, K: Electric train supply jumper receptacle, L: Electric train supply jumper cable.* **CJM**

Right Middle: *In June 2014 a pair of Class 37/7s emerged from overhaul by Boden Rail, Washwood Heath for hire-company Europhoenix. The first to emerge, No. 37884 is seen carrying full Europhoenix livery. The two Europhoenix Class 37/7s were locos returned to the UK from a DB-S hire comtract with GIF in Spain. It is the intention of Europhoenix to hire the pair to a UK operator, but if this can not be found, they may go overseas.* **John Tuffs**

Right Bottom: *In 2008 four Class 37s were rebuilt for Network Rail and reclassified as Class 97/3 in the departmental classification system. The locos were to power engineering works trains and three were modified with European Rail Traffic Management System (ERTMS) in-cab ETCS (European Train Control System) level 2 equipment which was to be tested on the Cambrian line. The locos were fully refurbished and returned to traffic in full Network Rail yellow livery. The locos based at Derby can be found powering track and infrastructure test trains as well as further ERTMS trials. No. 97304 is seen at Newton Abbot.* **Antony Christie**

Traction Recognition

Class 43 – HST

Locomotives

TOPS number range:	43002-43198, 43206-43484
Built by:	BREL Crewe
Refurbished:	Brush Traction, Loughborough
Years introduced:	1976-1982
Refurbished:	2006-2009
Wheel arrangement:	Bo-Bo
Weight:	70.25 tonnes
Height:	12ft 10in (3.91m)
Length:	58ft 5in (17.80m)
Width:	8ft 11in (2.72m)
Wheelbase:	42ft 4in (12.90m)
Bogie wheelbase:	8ft 7in (2.62m)
Bogie pivot centres:	33ft 9in (10.29m)
Wheel diameter:	3ft 4in (1.02m)
Min curve negotiable:	4 chains (80.46m)
Brake force:	35 tonnes
Engine type:	East Midlands Trains - Paxman 12VP185
	FGW, AXC, East Coast, Network Rail, Grand Central - MTU 16V4000 R41R
Engine output:	Paxman 12VP185 - 2,100hp (1,565kW) at 1,500rpm
	MTU 16V4000 R41R - 2,250hp (1,678kW) at 1,500rpm
Power at rail:	1,770hp (1,320kW)
Tractive effort:	17,980lb (80kN)
Cont tractive effort:	10,340lb (46kN)
Cylinder bore:	12VP185 - 7¾in (196mm)
	MTU4000 - 6½in (165mm)
Cylinder stroke:	12VP185 - 7½in (190mm)
	MTU4000 7½in (190mm)
Maximum speed:	125mph (201km/h)
Brake type:	Air
Route availability:	5
Bogie type:	BP16
Heating type:	Electric - three phase 415V
Multiple coupling type:	Within type
Main alternator type:	Brush BA1001B
Traction motor type:	Brush TMH68-46 - all except 43124-152 - GECG417AZ
No. of traction motors:	4
Gear ratio:	59:23
Fuel tank capacity:	1,030gal (4,682lit)
Cooling water capacity:	163gal (741lit)
Lub oil capacity:	75gal (341lit)
Sanding equipment:	Not fitted
Luggage capacity:	1.5 tonnes, increased to 2.5 tonnes
Special fittings:	Automatic Train Protection on all FGW power cars
	43013/014/065/067/068/080/084/123 fitted with nose end buffing gear
Owners:	Porterbrook, Angel Trains, First Group
Operators:	FGW, EMT, Arriva XC, East Coast, Grand Central, NRL

Fact File

The High Speed Train or HST is without doubt the most successful high speed diesel powered passenger train in the world. Built in the mid-70s as a 'stop-gap' until advanced passenger trains were introduced, the 196 power cars soon formed the backbone of the BR InterCity fleet.

Originally operated on the Western, Eastern, Scottish and London Midland Regions, the sets passed into the private sector in 1996 owned by Porterbrook and Angel leasing companies, working for Great Western, Great North Eastern Railway, Virgin Trains and Midland Mainline.

By 2011, following franchise changes and redeployment, the fleet is now operated by First Great Western, East Midlands Trains, East Coast, Arriva CrossCountry and Grand Central.

In recent years major refurbishment has been undertaken on most power cars and all except EMT vehicles have MTU engines.

In the early years of this century, a New Measurement Train (NMT) was formed of modified HST vehicles to operate track assessment at speeds of up to 125mph. This set, owned by Network Rail, is painted yellow.

Since their introduction just three Class 43s and a handful of passenger vehicles have been withdrawn following collisions. ∎

Above: *Class 43 HST power car equipment positions. A: Original position of inner end driving compartment (removed), B: Air reservoirs, C: Luggage van sliding door, D: Cooler grille roof fan, E: Cooler group side radiator panels, F: Battery box, G: Battery isolating switch, H: Fuel tank, I: Engine position, J: Air compressor (other side), K: Exhaust port, L: Alternator position, M: Fire alarm pull handle. N: Hinged roof hatches for access to power unit. Equipment positions apply to all operators' power cars.* **CJM**

Right: *First Great Western has a fleet of 119 Class 43 power cars allocated to Laira, Old Oak Common and Landore depots. All are refurbished with revised front ends and MTU power units. No. 43010 is seen at Newton Abbot from the non-driving side.* **CJM**

Below Right: *Inner end connection of Class 43 power cars. A: Emergency end power car door, B: Buck-eye auto-coupler, C: HST control jumper, D: Central door locking jumper, E: Main reservoir pipe (yellow), F: Air brake pipe (red), G: Emergency lamp bracket.* **CJM**

Below: *Front end layout of Class 43 power cars. A: Forward facing CCTV camera (not all operators), B: Dual marker/tail light, C: Headlight, D: Two-tone warning horn (behind grille), E: Emergency coupler (behind hinged flap).* **CJM**

Above: *CrossCountry Trains operates a fleet of 10 Class 43 power cars, with usually six being in traffic at one time. The cars are fully refurbished using MTU engines and sport the latest light clusters. Allocated to Edinburgh Craigentinny, No. 43207 is illustrated near Teignmouth.* **CJM**

Left and Below: *A number of HST power cars carry cast nameplates, and a small selection of styles are illustrated. Anticlockwise from left:* MTU Power. Passion. Partnership *applied to No. 43020,* 11 Explosive Ordnance Disposal Regiment Royal Logistic Corps *applied to FGW No. 43087,* Deltic 50 1955-2005 v *carried by East Coast No. 43367 and* In Support of Help for Heroes *as carried by East Midlands Trains No. 43076.* **CJM, Antony Christie**

Above and Right: *East Coast has a fleet of 32 Class 43s allocated to Edinburgh Craigentinny. These carry a mix of East Coast all over grey and East Coast branded National Express style livery. All cars are refurbished and have MTU power units and are all fitted with forward facing cameras. No. 43316 is seen above carrying East Coast grey, while on the right No. 43320 demonstrates the East Coast branded National Express colours. A new livery will be launched when the EC franchise is re-let. Both:* **CJM**

Above: *Open Access operator Grand Central has a fleet of six Class 43 power cars; these are all refurbished and now have the HST standard MTU power unit. All six have buffer draw gear, being part of the batch of 10 converted to act as surrogate DVTs for East Coast duties when the Class 91s were being introduced. The GC cars are based at Heaton and work on the Sunderland/Bradford to London route. No. 43467 is illustrated passing northbound through Doncaster.* **CJM**

Above: *East Midlands Trains, owned by Stagecoach, has a fleet of HSTs to operate on its London St Pancras to Nottingham and Sheffield routes. The vehicles, based at Leeds Neville Hill, are technically refurbished but retain Paxman VP185 prime movers. The cars are painted in the Stagecoach blue swirl livery style. These vehicles retain the original six light front end display with a marker, head and tail light on each side. Power car No. 43045 is seen passing Mill Hill Broadway.* **Nathan Williamson**

Below: *East Midlands Trains has 24 Class 43s at its disposal, which in normal circumstances operate on the St Pancras to Nottingham corridor, with the operator's Class 222s working on the Sheffield route. Vehicle No. 43061 is seen at London St Pancras International in spring 2014 awaiting departure to Nottingham.* **Antony Christie**

Right: *Network Rail operates three Class 43 power cars, based at Heaton. A pair are deployed on the New Measurement Train and the third is usually spare. Two of the vehicles, Nos. 43013/014, are buffer fitted. All three are refurbished with MTU power units and the latest light clusters. Special camera slots are positioned on the front ends above the horn grille and these are the only HSTs to have a roof mounted marker light. The New Measurement Train is seen led by No. 43013 at Dawlish on 26 July 2013.* **CJM**

Below: *HST driving cab (FGW vehicle illustrated) 1: Main reservoir pressure gauge, 2: Bogie brake cylinder pressure gauge, 3: Air brake pipe pressure gauge, 4: AWS indicator and alarm, 5: Speedometer, 6: Speaker, 7: Ammeter, 8: Cab-train telephone, 9: Vigilance device isolation switch, 10: Driver's reminder appliance isolation switch, 11: Fire system pressure alarm, 12: Fire system activation button, 13: ATP data entry, 14: Cab air conditioning controls, 15: Warning horn valve, 16: AWS reset button, 17: Master switch with key socket in top, 18: Brake test switch, 19: Power controller, 20: Engine stop/start indicator, 21: Engine stop button, 22: Cab-train buzzer, 23: Cab buzzer alarm, 24: Gauge dimmer switch, 25: Spare, 26: Wheel slip light, 27: Engine start button, 28: Locked axle warning light, 29: Blank, 30: Blank, 31: Great Western ATP controls, 32: Brake controller, 33: Fire alarm test button, 34: AWS operational light, 35: Parking brake 'on' button, 36: Parking brake alarm, 37: Parking brake indicator, 38: Parking brake 'off' button, 39: Emergency brake plunger, 40: Hazard warning light button (flashing headlghts), 41: Electric Train Supply 'off' button, 42: Train supply indicator, 43: Train supply 'on' button, 44: Driver's reminder appliance (DRA), 45: General fault light, 46: Driver's safety device pedal, 47: Windscreen wash and wipe switch, 48: TPWS panel, 49: Headlight switch, 50: Engine room (body) light switch, 51: Cab light switch, 52: Electric Train Supply indicator dimmer, 53: Demister switch, 54: Desk light switch, 55: Taillight switch driver's side, 56: Tail light switch (non driving side), 57: Marker light switch.* **CJM**

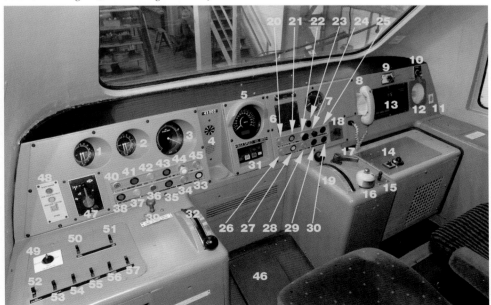

Sub-class:	47/0	47/3	47/4
TOPS number range:	47001-47299	47300-47379, 47981	47401-47665
1957 BR number range:	D1521-D1998	D1782-D1900	Random from fleet
Former class code:	27/2	27/2	27/2
Built by:	Brush, Loughborough and BR Crewe Works	Brush, Loughborough and BR Crewe Works	Brush, Loughborough and BR Crewe Works
Years introduced:	1962-1965	1964-1965	1962-1987
Wheel arrangement:	Co-Co	Co-Co	Co-Co
Weight:	111-121 tonnes	114 tonnes	120-125 tonnes
Height:	12ft 10⅜in (3.92m)	12ft 10⅜in (3.92m)	12ft 10⅜in (3.92m)
Length:	63ft 6in (19.35m)	63ft 6in (19.35m)	63ft 6in (19.35m)
Width:	9ft 2in (2.79m)	9ft 2in (2.79m)	9ft 2in (2.79m)
Wheelbase:	51ft 6in (15.69m)	51ft 6in (15.69m)	51ft 6in (15.69m)
Bogie wheelbase:	14ft 6in (4.42m)	14ft 6in (4.42m)	14ft 6in (4.42m)
Bogie pivot centres:	37ft 0in (11.28m)	37ft 0in (11.28m)	37ft 0in (11.28m)
Wheel diameter:	3ft 9in (1.14m)	3ft 9in (1.14m)	3ft 9in (1.14m)
Min curve negotiable:	4 chains (80.46m)	4 chains (80.46m)	4 chains (80.46m)
Engine type:	Sulzer 12LDA28C	Sulzer 12LDA28C	Sulzer 12LDA28C
Engine output:	2,580hp (1,924kW)	2,580hp (1,924kW)	2,580hp (1,924kW)
Power at rail:	2,080hp (1,551kW)	2,080hp (1,551kW)	2,080hp (1,551kW)
Tractive effort:	60,000lb (267kN)	60,000lb (267kN)	60,000lb (267kN)
Cylinder bore:	11in (270mm)	11in (270mm)	11in (270mm)
Cylinder stroke:	14in (350mm)	14in (350mm)	14in (350mm)
Maximum speed:	95mph (153km/h) later 75mph (121km/h)	95mph (153km/h) later 75mph (121km/h)	95mph (153km/h)
Brake type:	Dual or air	Dual or air	Dual or air
Brake force:	61 tonnes	61 tonnes	61 tonnes
Route availability:	6	6	7
Heating type:	Steam, later removed	Not fitted	Electric - index 66, some fitted with dual heatir
Multiple coupling type:	Not fitted, some later with DRS system	Not fitted	Not fitted, some later with DRS system
Main generator type:	Brush TG160-60 Mk2, TG160-60 Mk4 or TG172-50 Mk1	Brush TM172-50 Mk1A	Brush TG160-60 Mk2, TG160-60 Mk4 or TG172-50 Mk1
Aux generator type:	Brush TG69-20 or Brush TG69-28Mk2	Brush TG69-20	Brush TG69-20 or Brush TG69-28Mk2
ETS Alternator type:	-	-	Brush BL100-30
Traction motor type:	Brush TM64-68	Brush TM64-68 Mk1	Brush TM64-68
No of traction motors:	6	6	6
Gear ratio:	66:17	66:17	66:17
Fuel tank capacity:	720-1,221gal (3,273-5,550lit)	720-1,221gal (3,273-5,550lit)	720-1,295gal (3,273-5,887lit)
Cooling water capacity:	300gal (1,364lit)	300gal (1,364lit)	300gal (1,364lit)
Lub oil capacity:	190gal (864lit)	190gal (864lit)	190gal (864lit)
Sanding equipment:	Not fitted	Not fitted	Not fitted
Owners:	Various	Various	Various
Operators:	WCR, RIV	WCR	WCR, RIV, DRS, FLT, NRM
Sub-class variations:	Original locomotives built with steam train heating, many later converted to electric heating; all remaining are devoid of train heat equipment. (Some classified as 47/2 with air brakes only)	Locomotives built without provision for train heat - freight only locos. (Some classified as 47/2 fitted with air brakes)	Constructed with either dual (steam and electric) or electric train heating
Notes:	Engine output originally 2,750hp		

The Class 47 or Brush Type 4 fleet was the single largest class of diesel locomotive ever built in the UK, with 512 examples being constructed between 1962 and 1965 as the second generation of UK main line diesel power.

The fleet operated to all corners of the UK network powering passenger and freight services and over the years became one of the most reliable fleets to operate the BR/National Network.

47/7	47/7	47/4 (47/8)
47701-47717	47721-47793	47798-47799 47801-47854, 47971-47976
From Class 47/4 fleet	From Class 47/4 fleet	From Class 47/4 fleet
-	-	-
Rebuilt BREL Crewe	Modified by BR depots	Rebuilt BREL Crewe or BR depots
-	-	-
1979-1984	1993-1995	1989-1995
Co-Co	Co-Co	Co-Co
119 tonnes	119-121 tonnes	124 tonnes
12ft 10⅜in (3.92m)	12ft 10⅜in (3.92m)	12ft 10⅜in (3.92m)
63ft 6in (19.35m)	63ft 6in (19.35m)	63ft 6in (19.35m)
9ft 2in (2.79m)	9ft 2in (2.79m)	9ft 2in (2.79m)
51ft 6in (15.69m)	51ft 6in (15.69m)	51ft 6in (15.69m)
14ft 6in (4.42m)	14ft 6in (4.42m)	14ft 6in (4.42m)
37ft 0in (11.28m)	37ft 0in (11.28m)	37ft 0in (11.28m)
3ft 9in (1.14m)	3ft 9in (1.14m)	3ft 9in (1.14m)
4 chains (80.46m)	4 chains (80.46m)	4 chains (80.46m)
Sulzer 12LDA28C	Sulzer 12LDA28C	Sulzer 12LDA28C
2,580hp (1,924kW)	2,580hp (1,924kW)	2,580hp (1,924kW)
2,080hp (1,551kW)	2,080hp (1,551kW)	2,080hp (1,551kW)
60,000lb (267kN)	60,000lb (267kN)	60,000lb (267kN)
11in (270mm)	11in (270mm)	11in (270mm)
14in (350mm)	14in (350mm)	14in (350mm)
95mph (153km/h)	95mph (153km/h)	95mph (153km/h)
Dual or air	Dual or air	Dual or air
61 tonnes	61 tonnes	61 tonnes
7	6	6
Electric - index 66	Electric - index 66	Electric - index 66
Not fitted - TDM wired (47714 Green circle system)	Not fitted - TDM wired	Not fitted (47971-47976 fitted with Blue star system)
Brush TM172-50 Mk1A	Brush TM172-50 Mk1A	Brush TG160-60 Mk2, TG160-60 Mk4 or TG172-50 Mk1
Brush TG69-20 or Brush TG69-28Mk2	Brush TG69-20 or Brush TG69-28Mk2	Brush TG69-20 or Brush TG69-28Mk2
Brush BL100-30	Brush BL100-30	Brush BL100-30
Brush TM64-68 Mk1	Brush TM64-68	Brush TM64-68
6	6	6
66:17	66:17	66:17
1,295gal (5,887lit)	1,295gal (5,887lit)	1,295gal (5,887lit)
300gal (1,364lit)	300gal (1,364lit)	300gal (1,364lit)
190gal (864lit)	190gal (864lit)	190gal (864lit)
Not fitted	Not fitted	Not fitted
Various	Various	Various
Pres	WCR, DRS, Pres	Pres
Converted 47/4s with an early RCH push-pull system for use on the Edinburgh to Glasgow high speed service	Modified 47/4s with RCH Time Division Multiplex push-pull equipment for use with trains formed of PCV sets on Royal Mail duties under the 'Railnet' scheme	Locomotives refurbished for passenger services, fitted with ETS, refurbished from 47/4 fleet

Most locos have now been withdrawn, but upon privatisation a significant number passed to the private passenger and freight operators and today a number of the smaller operators and 'spot-hire' companies operate Class 47s.

Many modifications have been carried out to the design over the years; these are reflected in the sub-classes formed. Several sub-classes have now been eliminated and are not included in the technical data.

The remaining class members in 2014 are operated by several main stream passenger and freight power providers, with the class frequently seen throughout the country.

Following withdrawal, a significant number of Class 47s were preserved and several of these are now returning to the National Network on a 'spot-hire' basis. ■

Above: *The UK's most prolific diesel-electric type was the Brush Type 4, later Class 47, of which over 500 were in traffic from the mid 1960s. The Class can still be found in front line service today working for West Coast Railway, Direct Rail Services, HNR, Colas and Riviera Trains. A large number are also preserved. A member of the original Class 47/0 sub-class, No. 47245, is illustrated in West Coast colours. It is seen from the No. 2 end and this example sports three section snow ploughs and a Green spot multiple control jumper socket.* **Nathan Williamson**

Below Left and Right: *Class 47 front end layout. Several different designs exist on this large fleet; these illustrations show most of the equipment found. A: Cab radio aerial, B: Marker lights, C: Green dot multiple control socket, D: Red rear marker light, E: Headlight, F: Main reservoir pipe (yellow), G: Vacuum brake pipe, H: Coupling, I: Air brake pipe (red), J: Snow plough, K: RCH jumper cable, L: Electric train supply jumper cable, M: Electric train supply jumper receptacle.* Left: **Mark V. Pike,** Right: **CJM**

Above: *Class 47 driving cab equipment, as refurbished by Crewe Works for operation with Rail Express Systems (RES). The loco shown is No. 47767. Equipment in same positions for all sub-classes. The missing gauge on the right side of the desk is where the steam heat pressure gauge would have been located, with control buttons below.*
1: Automatic brake valve (operates train air or vacuum brakes and proportionally the air brakes on the locomotive),
2: Automatic Warning System 'sunflower' indicator, 3: Straight air brake valve (operates air brakes on loco only),
4: Headlight switch, 5: Main reservoir air pressure gauge, 6: Bogie brake cylinder pressure gauge, 7: Vacuum gauge,
8: Speedometer, 9: Brake pipe pressure gauge, 10: Traction motor overload reset button, 11: Main generator/alternator output, 12: Electric train (heat) supply 'on' and 'off' buttons, 13: Fire alarm test button, 14: Brake overcharge button,
15: Cab heat switch, 16: Driver's ash-tray, 17: Driver's safety device (DSD) pedal, 18: Automatic Warning System (AWS) reset button, 19: Light display (left to right) - engine stop light [red], wheelslip light [amber], general alarm light [blue], 20: Warning horn valve, 21: Master key socket, 22: Engine start/stop buttons, 23: Main power controller (with anti-slip button in red knob), 24: Master switch, 25: Electric train (heat) supply warning light dimmer switch, 26: Cab to shore telephone, 27: Electric train (heat) supply warning light, 28: Switches (left to right) tail light switch, demister switch, desk light switch, marker light switch, 29: Switches (left to right) compartment light switch, foot rest warmer, cab heat driver's side, cab heat secondman's side. **CJM**

Above: *Direct Rail Services (DRS) operates a fleet of Class 47s, which are used for mixed traffic operations and are frequently made available for passenger work. This includes hire-in duties to TOCs such as Greater Anglia. No. 47810 is illustrated painted in full DRS 'Compass' livery. The loco's No. 2 end is leading.* **Mark V. Pike**

Left Middle: *Two of the Direct Rail Services Class 47s are painted in Northern Belle 'Pullman' livery and used to power the Crewe-based luxury land cruise train The locos, No. 47790 and 47832, perform other duties when not required for Northern Belle traffic. The locos also sport a unique gold DRS 'Compass' branding. No. 47832 is seen at DRS Crewe Gresty Bridge depot.* **CJM**

Left Bottom: *Colas Rail Freight operates a fleet of three Class 47/7s for general freight operations and frequently use the ETS fitted machines to power rolling stock moves which require the use of translator vehicles where an ETS supply is needed. The fleet are painted in Colas green and orange livery and carry the shortened legend Colas Rail. The trio are air brake fitted only and have nose mounted Green spot multiple jumper connections. No. 47727 is illustrated at Wimbledon Park depot.* **CJM**

Above: *The private train operators are also users of Class 47s. Riviera Trains No. 47812, restored to 1960s green livery and numbered D1916, is frequently used on main line passenger services. The air braked loco is seen from its No. 2 end and displays a sealed up former route indicator panel with sealed beam marker lights.* **CJM**

Right Middle: *Vintage Trains, based at Tysele, owns and operates Class 47/7 No. 47773 for charter train work, often working with steam charter services. The loco carries green livery with a small yellow end, it is dual braked and retains front end RCH jumpers.*
John Stretton

West Coast Railway Co (WCRC) also operates a fleet of Class 47s for charter train use, and these are painted in company maroon livery with small yellow front ends. Nos. 47786 and 47854 pass Totnes. The lead loco's No. 1 end leads, while the trailing loco has its No. 2 end forward. **Nathan Williamson**

Class 56

Sub-class:	56/0	56/3
TOPS number range:	56001-56135	56301-56312 series
Former numbers:	-	From main fleet
Built by:	56001-56030 - Electroputere at Craiova in Romania 56031-56135 - BREL Doncaster/Crewe	BREL Doncaster and Crewe
Refurbished by:	-	Brush Traction/FM Rail
Years introduced:	1976-1984	1976-1984
Years refurbished:	-	2006-2010
Wheel arrangement:	Co-Co	Co-Co
Weight:	126 tonnes	126 tonnes
Height:	13ft 0in (3.96m)	13ft 0in (3.96m)
Length:	63ft 6in (19.35m)	63ft 6in (19.35m)
Width:	9ft 2in (2.79m)	9ft 2in (2.79m)
Wheelbase:	47ft 10in (14.58m)	47ft 10in (14.58m)
Bogie wheelbase:	13ft 5⅞in (4.11m)	13ft 5⅞in (4.11m)
Bogie pivot centres:	37ft 8in (11.48m)	37ft 8in (11.48m)
Wheel diameter:	3ft 9in (1.14m)	3ft 9in (1.14m)
Min curve negotiable:	4 chains (80.46m)	4 chains (80.46m)
Engine type:	Ruston Paxman 16RK3CT	Ruston Paxman 16RK3CT
Engine output:	3,250hp (2,424kW)	3,250hp (2,424kW)
Power at rail:	2,400hp (1,790kW)	2,400hp (1,790kW)
Tractive effort:	61,800lb (275kN)	61,800lb (275kN)
Cylinder bore:	10in (250mm)	10in (250mm)
Cylinder stroke:	12in (300mm)	12in (300mm)
Maximum speed:	80mph (129km/h)	80mph (129km/h)
Brake type:	Air	Air
Brake force:	60 tonnes	60 tonnes
Route availability:	7	7
Heating type:	Not fitted	Not fitted
Multiple coupling type:	Red diamond	Red diamond
Main alternator type:	Brush BA1101A	Brush BA1101A
Aux alternator type:	Brush BAA602A	Brush BAA602A
Traction motor type:	Brush TMH73-62	Brush TMH73-62
No of traction motors:	6	6
Gear ratio:	63:16	63:16
Fuel tank capacity:	1,150gal (5,228lit)	1,150gal (5,228lit)
Cooling water capacity:	308gal (1,400lit)	308gal (1,400lit)
Lub oil capacity:	120gal (546lit)	120gal (546lit)
Sanding equipment:	Pneumatic	Pneumatic
Special fittings:	OTMR	OTMR
Present operators:	Colas, UK Rail, BAR, Europhoenix Preservation	Colas, BAR
Sub-class variations:	As built	Refurbished

Left: *After a period when most thought the Class 56s were doomed, a major number have now been restored to front line use for Colas Rail Freight and the private sector. In early summer 2014, Colas was operating a fleet of seven locos with a further four stored for main line return. The fleet operate the heavier freight and infrastructure contracts and all are painted in green and orange Colas Rail Freight livery. No. 56078 is illustrated at Newton Abbot while working on the Heathfield to Chirk log flow.* **CJM**

After a gap of many years in new diesel loco construction in the UK, the BRB sought tenders for new high power freight locos in 1974, following a belief that there would be a major upturn in coal demand due to an oil crisis.

A fleet of 135 locos was eventually built, the first 30 constructed under a contract through Brush Traction with Electroputere in Romania, with the balance built by British Rail Engineering Ltd (BREL) at its plants in Doncaster and Crewe.

The design broadly followed that of the Class 47, but incorporated then state-of-the-art electronics and a 3,250hp (2,424kW) Ruston Paxman 16RK3CT power unit.

After a troublesome entry into service the fleet settled down, powering all kinds of freight services and became a very reliable locomotive design. Under the BR banner the fleet was operated by Railfreight and upon privatisation passed to shadow freight operators and most were eventually sold to EWS, now DBS.

Due to losses in traffic and standardisation EWS decided to phase the fleet out of service in favour of Class 66s and the '56' fleet was gradually run down, being finally withdrawn in 2005.

With the expanding private freight market a large number of Class 56s have returned to front line use, the largest operator in 2014 being Colas Rail Freight. Others operate for Devon & Cornwall Railway, British American Railway and UK Rail Leasing.

A small number of Class 56/3s emerged in 2006-10 after refurbishment.

A small number of Class 56s have been exported to Floyd in Hungary and in 2014-15 others are likely to return to use under the UK Rail Leasing banner, a company that has recently taken over the closed DB-S Leicester depot. ∎

Above: *Class 56 front end layout: equipment positions are the same for different sub-classes and builds. A: Radio aerial, B: Headlight, C: Red diamond multiple control jumper cable, D: Red diamond multiple control jumper socket, E: Red tail light, F: White marker light, G: Lamp iron, H: Main reservoir pipe (yellow), I: Warning horns behind grille, J: Coupling, K: Engine air control pipe (white), L: Air brake pipe (red), M: Radio aerial. Loco No. 56071 is illustrated.* **Kevin Wills**

Below: *Operator Devon & Cornwall Railway has a small fleet of Class 56s used for 'spot-hire' work mainly involving infrastructure traffic. No. 56312 is painted in the new DCR grey livery. The loco is seen with its No. 1 end nearest the camera while stabled at Taunton. The Class 56s with their outstanding tractive effort are very useful for heavy freight/engineering trains and should remain in service for many years to come. A new business UK Rail has recently taken on a number of previously stored and withdrawn Class 56s and plans to refurbish them and return the locos to front line service.* **Antony Christie**

Class 57

Sub-class:	57/0	57/3	57/6
TOPS number range:	57001-57012	57301-57316	57601
Rebuilt by:	Brush Traction	Brush Traction	Brush Traction
Originally built by:	Brush	Brush	Brush
Years introduced – as Class 47:	1962-1964	1962-1964	1962-1964
Years introduced – as Class 57:	1998-2000	2002-2005	2001
Wheel arrangement:	Co-Co	Co-Co	Co-Co
Weight:	120.6 tonnes	117 tonnes	121 tonnes
Height:	12ft 10⅜in (3.92m)	12ft 10⅜in (3.92m)	12ft 10⅜in (3.92m)
Length:	63ft 6in (19.35m)	63ft 6in (19.35m)	63ft 6in (19.35m)
Width:	9ft 2in (2.79m)	9ft 2in (2.79m)	9ft 2in (2.79m)
Wheelbase:	51ft 6in (15.70m)	51ft 6in (15.70m)	51ft 6in (15.70m)
Bogie wheelbase:	14ft 6in (4.41m)	14ft 6in (4.41m)	14ft 6in (4.41m)
Bogie pivot centres:	37ft 0in (11.28m)	37ft 0in (11.28m)	37ft 0in (11.28m)
Wheel diameter:	3ft 9in (1.14m)	3ft 9in (1.14m)	3ft 9in (1.14m)
Min curve negotiable:	4 chains (80.46m)	4 chains (80.46m)	4 chains (80.46m)
Engine type:	General Motors 645-12E3	General Motors 645-12F3B	General Motors 645-12E3
Engine output:	2,500hp (1,864kW)	2,750hp (2,051kW)	2,500hp (1,864kW)
Power at rail:	2,025hp (1,510kW)	2,200hp (1,641kW)	2,025hp (1,510kW)
Tractive effort:	55,000lb (244.6kN)	55,000lb (244.6kN)	55,000lb (244.6kN)
Cylinder bore:	9¹/₁₆in (230mm)	9¹/₁₆in (230mm)	9¹/₁₆in (230mm)
Cylinder stroke:	10in (250mm)	10in (250mm)	10in (250mm)
Maximum speed:	75mph (121km/h)	95mph (153km/h)	95mph (153km/h)
Brake type:	Air	Air	Air
Brake force:	80 tonnes	60 tonnes	60 tonnes
Route availability:	6	6	6
Heating type:	Not fitted	Electric - index- 100	Electric - index - 100
Multiple coupling type:	Not fitted	Not fitted	Not fitted
Main alternator type:	Brush BA1101A	Brush BA1101A	Brush BA1101A
Aux alternator type:	Brush BAA602A	Brush BAA602A	Brush BAA602A
ETS alternator type:	-	Brush BAA	Brush
Traction motor type:	Brush TM68-46	Brush TM68-46	Brush TM68-46
No of traction motors:	6	6	6
Gear ratio:	66:17	66:17	66:17
Fuel tank capacity:	1,221gal (5,551lit)	1,295gal (5,887lit)	720gal (3,273lit)
Cooling water capacity:	298gal (1,355lit)	298gal (1,355lit)	298gal (1,355lit)
Lub oil capacity:	190gal (864lit)	190gal (864lit)	190gal (864lit)
Sanding equipment:	Pneumatic	Pneumatic	Pneumatic
Special fittings:		Some: Hinged Dellner Some: Hinged Tightlock	
Owner:	Porterbrook, WCRC	NRL, WCRC, Porterbrook	WCRC
Operator:	DRS, WCRC	Network Rail, DRS, WCRC	WCRC
Sub-class variations:	Porterbrook sponsored rebuild of Class 47 using secondhand/rebuilt GM power units supplied by VMV	Porterbrook/Virgin funded Class 47 rebuilds for 'Thunderbird' work. Now operated by DRS, Network Rail and WCRC	Revised specification with electric train supply

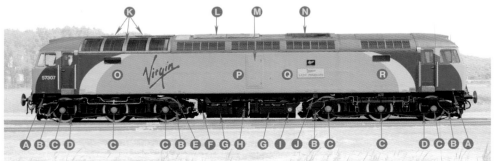

57/6
57602-57605
Brush Traction
Brush
1962-1964
2002-2003
Co-Co
117 tonnes
12ft 10⅜in (3.92m)
63ft 6in (19.35m)
9ft 2in (2.79m)
51ft 6in (15.70m)
14ft 6in (4.41m)
37ft 0in (11.28m)
3ft 9in (1.14m)
4 chains (80.46m)
General Motors 645-F3B-12
2,750hp (2,051kW)
2,200hp (1,641kW)
55,000lb (244.6kN)
9¹/₁₆in (230mm)
10in (250mm)
95mph (153km/h)
Air
60 tonnes
6
Electric - index - 100
Not fitted
Brush BA1101A
Brush BAA602A
Brush
Brush TM68-46
6
66:17
1,295gal (5,887lit)
298gal (1,355lit)
190gal (864lit)
Pneumatic
Porterbrook
FGW
Rebuilt for use on First Great Western sleeper services

Right: *The 16 Class 57/3s originally used by Virgin are now operated by Network Rail, DRS and West Coast Railway. DRS No. 57311 is illustrated, which still retains a drop-head Dellner coupling.*
Antony Christie

Fact File

The Class 57 was the brainchild of Porterbrook Leasing in conjunction with Freightliner to provide a low-cost replacement for the ageing fleet of Class 47s. The project used the bodyshell of a Class 47, which was stripped down to its main frame members and then rebuilt using refurbished/new equipment.

The original Sulzer power unit was deemed as unsuitable for the new era and a 12-cylinder General Motors 645 series engine was installed, purchased second (or even third) hand from US rebuild companies and refurbished for UK use.

Electrical equipment was provided by Brush Traction in the form of a refurbished alternator group of the same design as used on the Class 56. New cooler groups and control equipment were fitted and the cabs refurbished. Vacuum brakes were removed.

Following conversion of 12 locos for Freightliner, Porterbrook/Brush developed a version with electric train supply. A trial loco was built (57601) which was first operated by Great Western before being sold to West Coast Railway Co.

When Virgin Trains sought 'Thunderbird' traction, a fleet of 16 ETS-fitted Class 57/3s were ordered fitted with drop-head Dellner couplers.

First Great Western then invested in four Class 57/6 ETS-fitted locos for use on its Paddington-Penzance sleeper operation. These locos retain conventional drawgear, but sport three piece miniature snowploughs.

In 2007-08 Freightliner terminated its lease for the Class 57/0 fleet. Nine now operate under a lease deal with Direct Rail Services (DRS), and three have been sold to West Coast Railway Co (WCRC).

The Class 57/3s are now operated by DRS, WCRC and Network Rail. ∎

Right: *A number of Class 57 locomotives carry cast nameplates; the FGW locos in fact carry cast name and number plates. The plate Thunderbird is currently carried by DRS-operated No. 57311.* **CJM**

Thunderbird

Left: *Class 57 equipment positions, applicable to all sub-classes. No. 57601 does not have sanding equipment. A: Windscreen washer water filling point, B: Sandbox, C: Axle cover, D: Cab footsteps, E: Oil filler point, F: Sump drain tank, G: Battery box, H: Sump drain cock, I: Fuel tank and gauge, J: Fire alarm push button (behind glass screen), K: Cooler group with roof-mounted fans and radiator panels, L: Hinged covers above main power unit, M: Engine room side access door, N: Exhaust and silencer group. O: Machinery compartment including cooler group, P: Engine room, Q: Alternator compartment, R: Rectifier compartment. The locomotive illustrated is Class 57/3 No. 57307* Lady Penelope, *with its No. 1 end on the left, when the fleet were operated by Virgin Trains.* **CJM**

Left: *After Freightliner finished its hire of the 12 Class 57/0 locos, nine were taken on by Direct Rail Services to operate alongside its Class 47 fleet. The freight only locos can be seen in charge of most DRS flows, especially container services. The locos sport the DRS 'Compass' livery and have been modified to allow multiple operation. No. 57004 is seen inside DRS Crewe Gresty Bridge depot viewed from its No. 2 end.* **CJM**

Left: *When originally converted, the Class 57/3s were intended to provide traction for 'off electric route' 'Pendolino' trains or rescue failed 'Pendolino' or 'Voyager' stock fitted with Dellner couplers. To enable this the fleet were equipped with a complex 'drop-head' Dellner coupler. If used with 'Pendolino' stock, the Class 57 could provide 'hotel power' for the train's systems to allow operation away from an overhead power supply. A: Cab radio aerial, B: High-level marker light, C: Dellner coupling in stowed (raised) position, D: Lamp bracket, E: Headlight, F: Marker/tail light, G: Brake pipe supply to coupling, H: Main reservoir air supply to coupling, I: Electric train supply jumper socket, J: Electric train supply jumper cable, K: Main reservoir pipe (yellow), L: Coupling, M: Air brake pipe (red). Today, the majority of Class 57/3s have had this equipment removed, while some operated by Network Rail have had their drop-head couplers modified to allow connection to other multiple unit types, while three locos, Nos. 57301/303/306, now have a drop-head Tightlock coupling for EMU compatibility.* **CJM**

Left: *After the rebuilding of the 12 Class 57/0s for Freightliner, sponsor Porterbrook funded the conversion of a Class 57 with electric train supply, classified as 57/6 and numbered as 57601. The loco was leased to First Great Western and used on loco hauled services; after a short period a production order was placed for four similar locos to operate the First Great Western Paddington-Penzance sleeper services. No. 57601, a unique loco in many ways, was returned to Porterbrook and sold to West Coast Railway Co, which now deploys the machine on passenger charter duties. It is painted in standard WCRC maroon livery.* **Brian Garrett**

Above: *The four First Great Western Class 57/6 locos, apart from being deployed on the sleeper services between Paddington and Penzance, are available to power stock or power car moves between depots. Three of the locos are painted in FGW blue and one in Great Western Railway green. All have miniature snowploughs. No. 57605 is seen piloting a Class 43 power car past Dawlish.* **CJM**

Right Middle: *When the Virgin Trains Class 57/3s became surplus, Network Rail took on the lease of five locos for use on snow trains and recovery of failed trains due to snow and ice, as well as powering Network Rail trains in the southern area. Three locos were modified with Tightlock couplers. Tightlock No. 57306 is illustrated. In summer 2014 the Network Rail locos were transferred to DRS.* **Nathan Wiliamson**

Right Bottom: *Class 57/3 cab layout. A: Brake timing light, B: Derate warning light, C: Straight air brake valve, D: Auto train brake valve, E: Engine start/stop buttons, F: Cab radio, G: Fire alarm test button, H: AWS indicator, I: Windscreen wiper control, J: AWS reset button, K: Horn valve, L: Screenwash button, M: Main reservoir gauge, N: Bogie brake cylinder gauge, O: Brake pipe pressure gauge, P: Driver's reminder appliance, Q: Speedometer, R: Alternator output, S: Master key, T: Master switch, U: Power controller, V: DSD foot pedal.* **CJM**

Class 58

TOPS number range:	58001-58050
Design code:	58-0AA
Built by:	BREL Doncaster
Years introduced:	1983-1987
Wheel arrangement:	Co-Co
Weight:	130 tonnes
Height:	12ft 10in (3.91m)
Length:	62ft 9½in (19.14m)
Width:	9ft 1in (2.77m)
Wheelbase:	48ft 9in (14.86m)
Bogie wheelbase:	13ft 8½in (4.18m)
Bogie pivot centres:	35ft 5½in (10.81m)
Wheel diameter:	3ft 8in (1.12m)
Min curve negotiable:	4 chains (80.46m)
Engine type:	Ruston Paxman 12RK3ACT
Engine output:	3,300hp (2,460kW)
Power at rail:	2,387hp (1,780kW)
Tractive effort:	61,800lb (275kN)
Cylinder bore:	10in (250mm)
Cylinder stroke:	12in (300mm)
Maximum speed:	80mph (129km/h)
Brake type:	Air
Brake force:	60 tonnes
Route availability:	7
Heating type:	Not fitted
Multiple coupling type:	Red diamond
Main alternator type:	Brush BA1101B
Aux alternator type:	Brush BAA602B
Traction motor type:	Brush TM73-62
No of traction motors:	6
Gear ratio:	63:16
Fuel tank capacity:	927gal (4,214lit)
Cooling water capacity:	264gal (1,200lit)
Lub oil capacity:	110gal (500lit)
Sanding equipment:	Pneumatic
Special fittings:	OTMR
Owner:	DBS Finance
Present operators:	DBS (used as hire locos), TSO, ETF (France), GIF (Spain)

Below: Class 58 equipment positions. A: No. 1 end, B: No. 2 end, C: Cab module, D: Cooler group roof fans, E: Cooler group side radiator panels, F: Exhaust port, G: Power unit module, H: Electrical module, I: Battery box, J: Battery isolating switch, K: Air reservoir. No. 58040 displays Seco Rail (Colas) livery. **Kim Fullbrook**

Fact File

Following close behind the Class 56 order for UK freight motive power came orders for 50 Class 58s, a modular-designed heavy freight loco which the BRB and its international arm Transmark thought would take BREL into the European loco export business.

The design was a break from previous tradition in having full-width cabs but a narrow body section.

The 50 Class 58s emerged between 1983 and 1987 and were initially allocated to coal traffic in the Midlands and Yorkshire; later the fleet ventured into all types of freight operations.

Under privatisation the fleet passed to EWS, which was not keen on retaining a small non-standard class. The fleet was therefore withdrawn but retained as spare by EWS, later DB-Schenker (DB-S).

EWS then entered the loco hire market offering the Class 58s to European operators. ACTS in Belgium took on three locos until 2009, while GIF in Spain operate 12; 19 locos were later operated in France for Fertis, Seco Rail and TSO powering construction trains for the TGV line between Paris and Strasbourg. These later returned to the UK.

A further lease deal with TSO and ETF saw 24 locos transferred to France in 2008-09 for use on construction trains on TGV lines.

None are currently in service, one has been preserved, 24 are stored in France, 12 in Spain and a handful in the UK. They are unlikely to see further use. ∎

Sub-class:	59/0	59/1	59/2
TOPS number range:	59001-59005	59101-59104	59201-59206
GM model:	JT26CW-SS	JT26CW-SS	JT26CW-SS
Built by:	GM-EMD, La Grange, Illinois, USA	GM-DD, London, Ontario, Canada	GM-DD, London, Ontario, Canada
Years introduced:	1985-1989	1990	1994-1995
Wheel arrangement:	Co-Co	Co-Co	Co-Co
Weight:	121 tonnes	121 tonnes	121 tonnes
Height:	12ft 10in (3.91m)	12ft 10in (3.91m)	12ft 10in (3.91m)
Length:	70ft 0½in (21.34m)	70ft 0½in (21.34m)	70ft 0½in (21.34m)
Width:	8ft 8¼in (2.65m)	8ft 8¼in (2.65m)	8ft 8¼in (2.65m)
Wheelbase:	56ft 9in (17.29m)	56ft 9in (17.29m)	56ft 9in (17.29m)
Bogie wheelbase:	13ft 7in (4.14m)	13ft 7in (4.14m)	13ft 7in (4.14m)
Bogie pivot centres:	43ft 6in (13.25m)	43ft 6in (13.25m)	43ft 6in (13.25m)
Wheel diameter:	3ft 6in (1.06m)	3ft 6in (1.06m)	3ft 6in (1.06m)
Min curve negotiable:	4 chains (80.46m)	4 chains (80.46m)	4 chains (80.46m)
Engine type:	EMD 16-645E3C	EMD 16-645E3C	EMD 16-645E3C
Engine output:	3,000hp (2,237kW)	3,000hp (2,237kW)	3,000hp (2,237kW)
Power at rail:	2,533hp (1,889kW)	2,533hp (1,889kW)	2,533hp (1,889kW)
Tractive effort:	122,000lb (542kN)	122,000lb (542kN)	122,000lb (542kN)
Cylinder bore:	9$^{1}/_{16}$in (230mm)	9$^{1}/_{16}$in (230mm)	9$^{1}/_{16}$in (230mm)
Cylinder stroke:	10in (250mm)	10in (250mm)	10in (250mm)
Maximum speed:	60mph (97km/h)	60mph (97km/h)	75mph (121km/h)
Brake type:	Air	Air	Air
Brake force:	69 tonnes	69 tonnes	69 tonnes
Route availability:	7	7	7
Heating type:	Not fitted	Not fitted	Not fitted
Multiple coupling type:	AAR (59, 66, 67, 70)	AAR (59, 66, 67, 70)	AAR (59, 66, 67, 70)
Traction alternator:	EMD AR11	EMD AR11	EMD AR11
Companion alternator:	EMD D14A	EMD D14A	EMD D14A
Aux alternator:	EMD 3A8147	EMD 3A8147	EMD 3A8147
Traction motor type:	EMD D77B	EMD D77B	EMD D77B
No of traction motors:	6	6	6
Gear ratio:	62:15	62:15	62:15
Fuel tank capacity:	1,000gal (4,546lit)	1,000gal (4,546lit)	1,000gal (4,546lit)
Cooling water capacity:	212gal (964lit)	212gal (964lit)	212gal (964lit)
Lub oil capacity:	202gal (918lit)	202gal (918lit)	202gal (918lit)
Sanding equipment:	Pneumatic	Pneumatic	Pneumatic
Present operator:	Mendip Rail	Mendip Rail	DBS
Sub-class variations:	Original fleet of five locos owned and operated by Mendip Rail	Second batch of GM locos ordered for UK for use by ARC Southern. Slight modification to original design now operated by Mendip Rail	Delivered to National Power and sold to EWS. Modified design to earlier '59s'. Originally fitted with drop-head buck-eye couplers, now removed

Fact File

Nobody could ever have imagined in 1984 when the first four Class 59s were ordered from General Motors that the same structural design would still be in production some 30 years later in the form of the Class 66.

Mendip aggregate operator Foster Yeoman was the brave private company to demand higher availability from traction and wagons and entered the self-owning market, firstly with wagons and then locomotives. As no UK builder could offer the levels of reliability sought, FY went to General Motors who jointly with the BRB designed the Class 59, broadly based on the Western front end style, but incorporating proven North American technology – namely the 645E3C power unit.

The first order for four locos was followed by a single loco add-on order for Yeomans.

ARC Southern was the next operator to see the benefits of private ownership and purchased four locos.

Next on the ladder was National Power, which eventually purchased six locos. All three breeds are slightly different, with the later two batches built at the then GM/EMD plant in London, Ontario, Canada.

Today the Foster Yeoman and ARC locos operate as one pool under the Mendip Rail banner, while the National Power fleet was later sold to EWS, now DB-Schenker, and is now deployed on a variety of duties and maintained alongside the Mendip Rail fleet. ∎

Left Top: *Of the five original Foster Yeoman Class 59/0s, four remain in the UK, with one operating for HHPI in Mainland Europe. Of the UK locos, two are painted in un-branded Foster Yeoman blue and silver and two carry Aggregate Industries green, blue and silver livery. No. 59004, identifiable by four stars on the buffer beam, is seen from its exhaust end, while powering empty hoppers through Gospel Oak.* **Michael J. Collins**

Left Middle: *The first locomotive of the original Foster Yeoman build, No. 59005, has a cast brass bell mounted on its No. 1 end, but this in non-operational. This view clearly shows the original front end design with two groups or marker/tail lights and a pair of high-powered central headlights, immediately identifying the original locos from a distance. All locos, together with the Class 59/1s, are maintained by Merehead depot and operate as a common pool. The DB-S Class 59/2s are also maintained at Merehead.* **Nathan Williamson**

Below: *The four original ARC Southern Class 59/2s were the first of the design to include Group Standard head and marker light clusters, which changed the front end appearance. Viewed from its No. 2 end, No. 59101 painted in Hanson blue and silver passes Newbury with a loaded aggregate train bound for Acton. The Class 59s are common power on the Westbury to London corridor.* **Nathan Williamson**

Right: *Class 59 front end equipment (applicable to Class 59/0); similar equipment on all sub-classes. A: Warning horns behind grille, B: Radio aerial, C: Red tail light, D: White marker light, E: Twin headlight unit, F: Association of American Railroads (AAR) multiple jumper socket (cable when not in use stowed in engine compartment), G: Coupling, H: Air brake pipe (red), I: Main reservoir pipe (yellow). Loco No. 59001 illustrated.* **CJM**

Below: *When National Power entered the private train ownership and operation business, it turned to the US company General Motors to eventually purchase six Class 59s to power its coal and waste trains in the Yorkshire area based at Ferrybridge. Delivered in National Power blue livery and sporting knuckle couplers, the six were eventually sold to EWS, which later became DB-Schenker, and redeployed the fleet with the Mendip-based locos of Class 59/0 and 59/1 to group maintenance needs in one location. Repainted into EWS maroon, the six now sport DB-Schenker red and grey, as shown on No. 59206 powering an aggregate train from Burngullow to Westbury through Dawlish. This batch sports the same front end as the Class 59/1s, but has different bodyside equipment with fire bottles on one side and air cooling pipes on the other.* **CJM**

Class 60

TOPS number range:	60001-60100, 60500
Built by:	Brush Traction, Loughborough
Years introduced:	1989-1993
Wheel arrangement:	Co-Co
Weight:	129 tonnes (131 tonnes*)
Height:	12ft 11½in (3.95m)
Length:	70ft 0in (21.33m)
Width:	8ft 8in (2.64 m)
Wheelbase:	56ft 3⅛in (17.15m)
Bogie wheelbase:	13ft 6½in (4.13m)
Bogie pivot centres:	42ft 9¾in (13.04m)
Wheel diameter:	3ft 7in (1.09m)
Min curve negotiable:	4 chains (80.46m)
Engine type:	Mirrlees MB275T
Engine output:	3,100hp (2,311kW)
Power at rail:	2,415hp (1,800kW)
Tractive effort:	106,500lb (474kN)
Cylinder bore:	10¼in (275mm)
Cylinder stroke:	12¼in (305mm)
Maximum speed:	60mph (97km/h)
Brake type:	Air
Brake force:	74 tonnes (62 tonnes*)
Route availability:	7
Heating type:	Not fitted
Multiple coupling type:	Within class only
Main alternator type:	Brush BA1006
Aux alternator type:	Brush BAA702A
Traction motor type:	Brush TM2161A
No of traction motors:	6
Gear ratio:	19:97
Fuel tank capacity:	990gal (4,500lit*)
Cooling water capacity:	125gal (567lit)
Lub oil capacity:	220gal (1,000lit)
Sanding equipment:	Pneumatic
Special fittings:	SSC

Note:
* 60002-05/07/09/10/12/15/17/20-28/30/37/38/41/42/46/47/49-56/58/59/64/67/70/71/77/80/81/89-91/96-98, fitted with 1,150gal (5,228lit) fuel tanks, are heavier and have reduced brake force.

Left: *Class 60 front end equipment positions.*
1: Two-tone air warning horns, 2: Lamp bracket, 3: Multiple control jumper socket (behind hinged door), 4: Foot step, 5: Marker light, 6: Headlight, 7: Tail light, 8: Air brake pipe (red), 9: Main reservoir pipe (yellow), 10: Coupling.
CJM

Fact File

By the mid-1980s a need for new freight motive power was seen and after much deliberation an order for 100 state-of-the-art 3,100hp Co-Co locos was placed by the BRB with Brush Traction.

The locos were assembled by Brush in Loughborough with body shells produced by Procor Engineering, Wakefield.

The fleet started to enter service in 1989 but had a protracted delivery, with the final example not taking to the road until 1993 and numerous technical issues surrounding their slow introduction. However, the fleet settled down well and returned good availability.

Under privatisation, the entire fleet past to EWS, later DB-Schenker, which did not support the design after the introduction of the Class 66s, compounded by a decline in freight traffic, the '60s' fell from favour.

In 2011-13 a major refurbishing project entitled 'Super 60' was carried out at Toton seeing 20 returned to front line service.

When first introduced, the fleet was painted in Trainload triple-grey livery with 'sector' markings; under shadow privatisation Loadhaul, Transrail and Mainline Freight colours were applied. With EWS the corporate maroon and gold livery was carried by some machines. The first loco to sport DB-Schenker red and grey emerged in 2011. Apart from promotional liveries the 'Super 60s' are finished in DB-Schenker red.

In April 2014 Colas Rail Freight purchased 10 locos Nos. 60002/021/026/047/056/076/085/087/095/096 with a further 10 available if required in the future. In summer 2014 the locos were being returned to traffic following refurbishment at Toton. ∎

Above: *One of the UK's most powerful diesel-electric loco designs is the Class 60, of which 100 were built between 1989 and 1993. Sadly with privatisation the class fell from favour, but today 20 have been refurbished and DB-S currently operates a fleet of 24 locos. Refurbished 'Super 60' No. 60015 is illustrated from its silencer end.* **Lindsay Atkinson**

Right Middle: *DB-S 'Super 60' No. 60074 carries powder blue livery in support of the Teenage Cancer Trust. The loco is seen from its No. 1 or cooler end and compared with the above illustration shows the other side of the locomotive.* **Antony Christie**

Right Below: *In the summer of 2014, the first of 10 Colas Rail Freight Class 60s emerged from 'Super 60' modification at Toton depot. The Colas 60s, painted in the operators lime and orange livery will be used for heavier traffic flows both freight and infrastructure. The first loco of the Colas fleet No. 60087 is illustrated from its No. 1 end.* **John Tuffs**

Locomotives

Sub-class:	66/0	66/3 & 66/4	66/5
TOPS number range:	66001-66250	66301-66305, 66413-66434	66501-66599
Built by:	General Motors, London, Canada	General Motors, London, Canada & EMDD London, Canada	General Motors, London, Canada & EMDD London, Canada
GM model:	JT-42-CWR	JT-42-CWR	JT-42-CWR
Years introduced:	1998-2000	2003-2008	1999-2007
Wheel arrangement:	Co-Co	Co-Co	Co-Co
Weight:	126 tonnes	126 tonnes	126 tonnes
Height:	12ft 10in (3.91m)	12ft 10in (3.91m)	12ft 10in (3.91m)
Length:	70ft 0½in (21.34m)	70ft 0½in (21.34m)	70ft 0½in (21.34m)
Width:	8ft 8¼in (2.65m)	8ft 8¼in (2.65m)	8ft 8¼in (2.65m)
Wheelbase:	56ft 9in (17.29m)	56ft 9in (17.29m)	56ft 9in (17.29m)
Bogie wheelbase:	13ft 7in (4.14m)	13ft 7in (4.14m)	13ft 7in (4.14m)
Bogie pivot centres:	43ft 6in (13.26m)	43ft 6in (13.26m)	43ft 6in (13.26m)
Wheel diameter:	3ft 6in (1.06m)	3ft 6in (1.06m)	3ft 6in (1.06m)
Min curve negotiable:	4 chains (80.46m)	4 chains (80.46m)	4 chains (80.46m)
Engine type:	GM 12N-710G3B-EC	GM 12N-710G3B-EC	GM 12N-710G3B-EC
Engine output:	3,300hp (2,460kW)	3,300hp (2,460kW)	3,300hp (2,460kW)
Power at rail:	3,000hp (2,238kW)	3,000hp (2,238kW)	3,000hp (2,238kW)
Tractive effort (max):	92,000lb (409kN)	92,000lb (409kN)	92,000lb (409kN)
Tractive effort (cont):	58,390lb (260kN)	58,390lb (260kN)	58,390lb (260kN)
Cylinder bore:	9^1/$_{16}$in (230mm)	9^1/$_{16}$in (230mm)	9^1/$_{16}$in (230mm)
Cylinder stroke:	11in (279mm)	11in (279mm)	11in (279mm)
Design speed:	87.5mph (141km/h)	87.5mph (141km/h)	87.5mph (141km/h)
Maximum speed:	75mph (121km/h)	75mph (121km/h)	75mph (121km/h)
Brake type:	Air, Westinghouse PBL3	Air, Westinghouse PBL3	Air, Westinghouse PBL3
Brake force:	68 tonnes	68 tonnes	68 tonnes
Bogie type:	HTCR Radial	HTCR Radial	HTCR Radial
Route availability:	7	7	7
Heating type:	Not fitted	Not fitted	Not fitted
Multiple coupling type:	AAR	AAR	AAR
Traction alternator:	GM-EMD AR8	GM-EMD AR8	GM-EMD AR8
Companion alternator:	GM-EMD CA6	GM-EMD CA6	GM-EMD CA6
Traction motor type:	GM-EMD D43TR	GM-EMD D43TR	GM-EMD D43TR
No of traction motors:	6	6	6
Gear ratio:	81:20	81:20	81:20
Fuel tank capacity:	1,440gal (6,546lit)	1,440gal (6,546lit)	1,440gal (6,546lit)
Lub oil capacity:	202 gal (918lit)	202 gal (918lit)	202 gal (918lit)
Sanding equipment:	Pneumatic	Pneumatic	Pneumatic
Special fittings:	EM2000 Q-Tron, GPS Combination coupler+SSC	EM2000 Q-Tron, GPS low emission	EM2000 Q-Tron, GPS
Sub-class variations:	Standard EWS	DRS & Freightliner	Standard Freightliner
Note:	+ 66001/002 unable to be fitted with Combination couplers		

Fact File

With an American owner, the principal privatised UK freight operator EWS soon looked at North American builders when new locos were required.

The same general body structure as used for the Class 59s was adapted as this had operating authority in the UK. An all-new interior using the GM710 series power unit was incorporated.

The initial EWS order was for 250 locos, which was soon followed by sizeable orders for Freightliner, Direct Rail Services, GB Railfreight and Fastline Freight. In addition Mainland European and Egyptian orders have been fulfilled.

Without doubt this design has changed the face of UK railfreight.

Each operator has its own livery and only limited modifications have been made. Except the first two, all EWS locos are fitted with combination couplers. A small batch have

66/6	66/7	66/8	66/9
66601-66625	66701-66772	66846-66850	66951-66957
General Motors, London, Canada & EMDD London, Canada	General Motors, London, Canada & EMDD London, Canada Caterpiller, Muncie, IN	General Motors, London, Canada	General Motors, London, Canada
JT-42-CWR	JT-42-CWR	JT-42-CWR	JT-42-CWR
2000-2007	2001-2014	Orig: 2004, 66/8: 2011	2004
Co-Co	Co-Co	Co-Co	Co-Co
126 tonnes	126 tonnes	126 tonnes	126 tonnes
12ft 10in (3.91m)	12ft 10in (3.91m)	12ft 10in (3.91m)	12ft 10in (3.91m)
70ft 0½in (21.34m)	70ft 0½in (21.34m)	70ft 0½in (21.34m)	70ft 0½in (21.34m)
8ft 8¼in (2.65m)	8ft 8¼in (2.65m)	8ft 8¼in (2.65m)	8ft 8¼in (2.65m)
56ft 9in (17.29m)	56ft 9in (17.29m)	56ft 9in (17.29m)	56ft 9in (17.29m)
13ft 7in (4.14m)	13ft 7in (4.14m)	13ft 7in (4.14m)	13ft 7in (4.14m)
43ft 6in (13.26m)	43ft 6in (13.26m)	43ft 6in (13.26m)	43ft 6in (13.26m)
3ft 6in (1.06m)	3ft 6in (1.06m)	3ft 6in (1.06m)	3ft 6in (1.06m)
4 chains (80.46m)	4 chains (80.46m)	4 chains (80.46m)	4 chains (80.46m)
GM 12N-710G3B-EC	GM 12N-710G3B-EC	GM 12N-710G3B-EC	GM 12N-710G3B-EC
3,300hp (2,460kW)	3,300hp (2,460kW)	3,300hp (2,460kW)	3,300hp (2,460kW)
3,000hp (2,238kW)	3,000hp (2,238kW)	3,000hp (2,238kW)	3,000hp (2,238kW)
105,080lb (467kN)	92,000lb (409kN)	92,000lb (409kN)	92,000lb (409kN)
66,630lb (296kN)	58,390lb (260kN)	58,390lb (260kN)	58,390lb (260kN)
9¹/₁₆in (230mm)	9¹/₁₆in (230mm)	9¹/₁₆in (230mm)	9¹/₁₆in (230mm)
11in (279mm)	11in (279mm)	11in (279mm)	11in (279mm)
87.5mph (141km/h)	87.5mph (141km/h)	87.5mph (141km/h)	87.5mph (141km/h)
65mph (105km/h)	75mph (121km/h)	75mph (121km/h)	75mph (121km/h)
Air, Westinghouse PBL3	Air, Westinghouse PBL3	Air, Westinghouse PBL3	Air, Westinghouse PBL3
68 tonnes	68 tonnes	68 tonnes	68 tonnes
HTCR Radial	HTCR Radial	HTCR Radial	HTCR Radial
7	7	7	7
Not fitted	Not fitted	Not fitted	Not fitted
AAR	AAR	AAR	AAR
GM-EMD AR8	GM-EMD AR8	GM-EMD AR8	GM-EMD AR8
GM-EMD CA6	GM-EMD CA6	GM-EMD CA6	GM-EMD CA6
GM-EMD D43TR	GM-EMD D43TR	GM-EMD D43TR	GM-EMD D43TR
6	6	6	6
83:18	81:20	81:20	81:20
1,440gal (6,546lit)	66701-66717 – 1,440gal (6,546lit) 66718-66722 – 1,220gal (5,546lit) 66723-66727 – 1,100gal (5,000lit)	1,440gal (6,546lit)	1,220gal (5,546lit)
202 gal (918lit)	202 gal (918lit)	202 gal (918lit)	202 gal (918lit)
Pneumatic	Pneumatic	Pneumatic	Pneumatic
EM2000 Q-Tron, GPS	EM2000 Q-Tron, GPS 66718-772 - low emission	EM2000 Q-Tron, GPS	EM2000 Q-Tron, GPS
Freightliner modified gearing	GBRf Some locos from Mainland Europe	Ex-Freightliner now with Colas	Low-emission locos

automatic uncouplers for banking duties, while those of other operators use conventional hook and shackle couplers.

The most significant change has been the installation of low-emissions technology by EMD, which changed the engine/cooler group layout, with an extra external carbody door on the 'A' side of later-built locos introduced after mid-2006.

Specification changes to Group Standards have seen a number of different head, marker and tail light clusters fitted on different builds.

The original 10 DRS locos were returned to their lease owners in 2008-09 and found further work with Advenza Freight until this operator went into liquidation. Five locos were later taken over by Colas Rail Freight.

In 2013 a further 21 locos of the same design were ordered by GB Railfreight.

A considerable number of DBS and Freightliner locos now operate in France and Poland. ∎

Above and Above Right: *Class 66 body equipment positions. A: No. 1 end, B: No. 2 end, C: Exhaust and silencer group, D: Hinged inspection hatches for top of engine, E: Cooler group air outlet, F: Internal air filtration group, G: Engine/alternator group position, H: Cooler group air intakes, I: Sandboxes, J: Battery box, K: Fuel tank, L: Equipment rack position. The No. 1 cab of a Class 66 (and on a Class 59) is much larger than the No. 2 cab; this is immediately identified by the larger space between the external cab door and the cab side windows. No. 66618 above is shown at York and No. 66578 above right at Ipswich. The members of the 66/6 sub-class have a higher tractive effort than normal Class 66/5s operated by Freightliner and are thus able to shift heavier loads. Both:* **CJM**

Below: *Several different detail designs of the Class 66 front end can be found, especially involving headlight and marker lights. The two views below show all the equipment positions. A: Warning horns behind grille, B: Radio aerial, C: High-level marker light, D: Association of American Railroads (AAR) multiple control jumper socket (jumper cable kept in engine room), E: Marker light, F: Headlight, G: Red tail light, H: Main reservoir pipe (yellow), I: Combination coupler (66003-250 only), J: Lamp bracket, K: Main reservoir pipe (yellow), L: Screw coupling, M: Combination white marker/red tail LED light. Both:* **CJM**

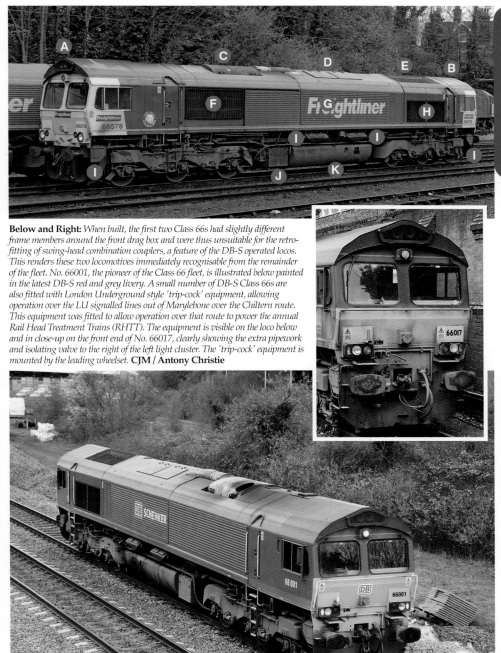

Below and Right: *When built, the first two Class 66s had slightly different frame members around the front drag box and were thus unsuitable for the retro-fitting of swing-head combination couplers, a feature of the DB-S operated locos. This renders these two locomotives immediately recognisable from the remainder of the fleet. No. 66001, the pioneer of the Class 66 fleet, is illustrated below painted in the latest DB-S red and grey livery. A small number of DB-S Class 66s are also fitted with London Underground style 'trip-cock' equipment, allowing operation over the LU signalled lines out of Marylebone over the Chiltern route. This equipment was fitted to allow operation over that route to power the annual Rail Head Treatment Trains (RHTT). The equipment is visible on the loco below and in close-up on the front end of No. 66017, clearly showing the extra pipework and isolating valve to the right of the left light cluster. The 'trip-cock' equipment is mounted by the leading wheelset.* **CJM / Antony Christie**

Above: *Class 66 cab layout. 1: Brake timing indicator - passenger, 2: Brake timing indicator - freight, 3: Parking brake 'on' button, 4: Parking brake indicator, 5: Parking brake 'off' button, 6: Brake overcharge button, 7: Engine start button, 8: Engine stop button, 9: Cab-cab radio, 10: Buzzer, 11: Dimmer switch, 12: Windscreen wiper (driver's), 13: Main reservoir pressure gauge, 14: Bogie brake cylinder pressure, 15: Air flow indicator, 16: Brake pipe pressure gauge, 17: Speedometer, 18: Alternator output, 19: AWS indicator. 20: Cab radio, 21: Power controller, 22: Master switch, 23: Control switches, 24: TPWS controls, 25: DSD foot pedal, 26: Emergency brake plunger, 27: Train length button, 28: Straight air brake valve, 29: Speed control, 30: Sand valve, 31: Horn valve, 32: Auto air brake valve, 33: Hazard warning light switch, 34: AWS reset button.* **CJM**

Left Middle and Bottom: *Two views of a standard Class 66/0, as operated by EWS, now DB-Schenker, showing both sides of the locomotive viewed from the cooler group end. Both locos sport swing-head combination couplers. No. 66046 (middle) was recorded at Ealing, and No. 66039 (bottom) is seen at Didcot.* **CJM/Norman E. Preedy**

Above: *In 2011 a start was made at repainting the DB-S fleet into corporate DB red and grey livery; this looks like being a drawn-out affair as by mid-2014 only six operating in the UK had been repainted. The new colours do suit the loco design and tend to make the loco look longer and with a deeper underframe than in their original colour. All DB-S operated Class 66s are fitted with wing or reverse mirrors. No. 66097 is seen passing Barnetby.* **CJM**

Right Middle: *The second operator to deploy Class 66s was Freightliner, with two sub-classes ordered, Class 66/5 for standard locomotives and Class 66/6 for engines with increased tractive effort. Externally the locos are the same. Some later Freightliner locos have an extra external door on one side at the cooler group end; this was due to interior changes to reduce emissions. Various front end light arrangements can be found on the fleet. No. 66542 sports large headlights and LED red/white marker/tail lights. The loco is seen at Stratford.* **CJM**

Right Bottom: *In May 2013 the first Class 66/5 emerged in the revised Freightliner 'Power Haul' livery, when No. 66504 was released from the Crewe paintshop. To many observers the grey on the upper section of the bufferbeam is too overpowering. The loco is seen with its cooler group end leading on the Felixstowe branch.* **Antony Guppy**

Left: *Freight operator GB Railfreight (GBRf) is a rapidly expanding business that is still taking delivery of new Class 66s in 2014 with a batch built at the new EMD plant in Muncie, Indiana, USA. By late 2014, GBRf will have a fleet of 72 Class 66/7s. The fleet carries a wide range of liveries and includes examples with all front end body designs. The fleet consists of standard four and modified five door designs. The locos are officially allocated to Peterborough, but in reality receive maintenance all around the country. Displaying the standard GBRf blue and orange livery, No. 66733 is seen passing Didcot.* **Norman E. Preedy**

Left and Below: *GBRf is very supportive of innovative liveries and in 2013 two of the Class 66 fleet emerged in advertising liveries to promote London Underground during its 150 year celebrations. No. 66718 was outshopped in a black livery with branding supporting the London Transport Museum in London, while No. 66721 was painted in a light grey livery onto which two different versions of the London Underground map were applied - two stunning liveries which do have to be kept clean to be fully appreciated.* **Lindsay Atkinson / Mark V. Pike**

Above and Right: *Direct Rail Services (DRS) currently operates a fleet of 19 Class 66s, five of which are Class 66/3. These locos painted in DRS 'Compass' livery are the backbone of long distance freight services. All are five door examples. Above we see Class 66/3 No. 66303 viewed from its large cab end, while right is No. 66430 viewed from its small cab end.* **CJM / Nathan Williamson**

Below: *Colas Rail Freight operates a fleet of five Class 66/8s, all are painted in Colas green/orange and used for general freight work. Nos. 66846 and 66848 are illustrated at Doncaster.* **CJM**

Above: *As GBRf required extra Class 66s , in 2012/13 five extra locos were leased from Mainland Europe where some spare capacity existed. As these locos were constructed for the Mainland European market, they were fitted with different cabs and European equipment such as draw gear and air conditioning. To enable operation in the UK these locos had to receive extensive rebuilding done under the control of Electro Motive. With European style light clusters, buffers and air pipe connections, No. 66750, painted in blue livery, works a light test run in the UK.* **Cliff Beeton**

Below: *GB Railfreight Class 66 No. 66748 passes Whitley Bridge Junction with train 6C72, the 09.45 Hull Coal Terminal to Eggborough Power Station via Goole and a run round at Sudforth Lane, on 4 March 2014. This view shows the revised livery applied to three of the imported locos, showing a grey livery with yellow GBRf number and branding.* **Robin Patrick**

Above: *Perhaps the most 'stunning' livery to adorn a GBRf Class 66 is this multi-coloured offering carried by No. 66720, a livery reflecting day and night design by a six year old as part of a staff and family competition.* **CJM**

Right: *To allow semi-automatic release on banking locos used on the Lickey incline, Nos. 66055-059 were modified in 2003 with auto release auto-couplers and fitted with extra lights to see the equipment. No. 66057 is illustrated.* **Antony Christie**

Below: *A handful of off-lease DRS Class 66s have been taken over by Freightliner, but still carry DRS livery. In this view No. 66415 is seen working for Freightliner powering a ballast train while still carrying full DRS livery.* **Antony Christie**

Class 67

TOPS number range:	67001-67030
Built by:	Alstom/General Motors, Valencia, Spain
GM model:	JT-42-HWHS
Years introduced:	1999-2000
Wheel arrangement:	Bo-Bo
Weight:	90 tonnes
Height:	12ft 9in (3.88m)
Length:	64ft 7in (19.68m)
Width:	8ft 9in (2.66m)
Wheelbase:	47ft 3 in (14.40m)
Bogie wheelbase:	9ft 2 in (2.79m)
Bogie pivot centres:	38ft 1in (11.63m)
Wheel diameter:	3ft 2in (965mm)
Min curve negotiable:	3.8 chains (75m)
Engine type:	GM 12N-710G3B-EC
Engine output:	3,200hp (2,386kW)
Power at rail:	2,493hp (1,860kW)
Maximum tractive effort:	31,750lb (141kN)
Continuous tractive effort:	20,200 (89.8kN) (with HEP active)
Cylinder bore:	$9^{1}/_{16}$in (230mm)
Cylinder stroke:	11in (279mm)
Design speed:	125mph (201km/h)*
Maximum speed:	110mph (177km/h)
Brake type:	Air, Westinghouse PBL3
Brake force:	78 tonnes*
Bogie type:	Alstom high speed
Route availability:	8
Heating type:	Electric - index 66 (in multiple each loco - 48)
Multiple coupling type:	AAR
Traction alternator:	GM-EMD AR9A
Companion alternator:	GM-EMD CA6HEX
Traction motor type:	GM-EMD D43FM
No of traction motors:	4
Gear ratio:	59:28
Fuel tank capacity:	1,201gal (5,460lit)
Cooling water capacity:	212gal (964lit)
Lub oil capacity:	202gal (918lit)
Sanding equipment:	Pneumatic
Special fittings:	GPS
Operator:	DBS, Chiltern Railways, Arriva

Note:
* 67004/007/009/011/030 fitted with cast iron brake blocks for Fort William sleeper and have a top speed of 80mph (129km/h) and a brake force of 68 tonnes

Fact File

Designed and built as part of the EWS traction modernisation plan to provide the company with a 125mph capability, the Class 67s had a specific design to operate on Royal Mail postal and parcel trains. In the event after just a few years the contract was lost and the locos have since operated as part of the general EWS, now DB-Schenker-fleet, especially on charter, passenger and 'Thunderbird' duties.

Ordered at the same time as the Class 66 locos, these 30 very expensive machines were assembled at the Alstom plant in Valencia, Spain, and classified by General Motors as JT-42-HWHS.

Of the fleet of 30 all originally painted in EWS maroon and gold, two locomotives (67005/006) are now painted in Royal Train 'claret' and used for Royal Train duties when needed; Nos. 67026/029 are painted in silver VIP livery. Three locos which operate for Arriva Trains Wales are painted in Arriva blue, and five used for Chiltern Railways London to Birmingham services are painted in two-tone grey. Locos are now in the process of being repainted into DB-S red and grey livery. ■

Right: *Class 67 front end equipment. 1: Warning horns behind grilles, 2: High-level marker light, 3: RCH jumper cables, 4: AAR multiple control jumper socket (cable stored in engine compartment), 5: White marker light, 6: Headlight, 7: Red tail light, 8: Combination coupling release handle, 9: Combination coupler, 10: Air brake pipe (red), 11: Main reservoir pipe (yellow), 12: Head end power cable (electric train supply), 13: Head end power socket (electric train supply). Loco No. 67002 is illustrated.* **CJM**

Below: *The two bodysides of the Class 67 have different ventilation grilles, with no opening on the B side at the exhaust end. Delivered painted in EWS maroon and gold livery, locos are now in the process of repainting into DB-Schenker red and grey. Several locos carry special liveries for Royal Train and line of use. No. 67023 is illustrated, stabled at Didcot.* **Norman E. Preedy**

Left: *Class 67 equipment positions. 1: Electrical equipment control cabinet, 2: Equipment air filters, 3: Traction and auxiliary alternator, 4: Main power unit, 5: Engine rack, oil filter, oil cooler, engine water tank, 6: Side maintenance doors, 7: Radiator side air intake, 8: Exhaust silencer unit, 9: Removable and opening roof hatches, 10: Roof air intake, 11: Wheel guard, 12: Sandbox filler, 13: Cab steps, 14: Lifting socket, 15: Traction motors, 16: Main air reservoirs, 17: Battery isolating switch, 18: Battery box, 19: Fuel tank, 20: Fuel tank filler, 21: Fuel tank gauge. The loco illustrated is No. 67014, now operated under contract by Chiltern Railways until Class 68s are introduced.* **CJM**

Left Top: *Five locos, Nos. 6767010/012-015 carry two-tone grey livery, first applied when the locos were hired to power Wrexham & Shropshire Railway services over the Chiltern route. When this business ceased trading the locos were transferred to Chiltern Railways operation, keeping the grey livery but with branding removed. No. 67012 is illustrated at Birmingham Moor Street. These locos operate on the northern end of push-pull Mk3 trains between London Marylebone and Birmingham. They will be replaced by DRS Class 68s in early 2015.* **Nathan Williamson**

Left Middle: *Soon after the EWS Class 67s were introduced, the company allocated a pair (Nos. 67005/006) to Royal Train use, replacing a pair of Class 47s. The 'Royal' 67s were repainted into Royal claret and used within the core fleet until Royal Train duties called. In immaculate condition, No. 67005 is seen with the Royal Train approaching Shaldon Bridge, Teignmouth.* **CJM**

Below: *In 2012, as part of the Queen's Diamond Jubilee celebrations, DB-S repainted a third loco for Royal Train use, when No. 67026 emerged in silver and given Diamond Jubilee branding. The loco was used on some Royal Train operations but is otherwise a part of the core fleet. The Class 67s see deployment as 'Thunderbird' locos on the East Coast, power the diesel legs of the Scottish sleepers, operate Chiltern and Arriva Trains Wales passenger services, and charter services as well as operating freight and engineers duties. No. 67026 is seen on the East Coast acting as a 'Thunderbird' powering an empty Mk4 formation.* **Jamie Squibbs**

Right: *Class 67 driving cab layout (as built).* 1: Marker light left side indicator, 2: Headlight night left side indicator, 3: Tail light left side indicator, 4: Top marker light indicator, 5: Tail light right side indicator, 6: Headlight day right side indicator, 7: Marker light right side indicator, 8: Brake test switch, 9: Passenger/goods changeover switch, 10: Speaker, 11: Condition warning lights, 12: Condition warning lights, 13: Parking brake apply button, 14: Parking brake release button, 15: Engine start button, 16: Engine stop button, 17: Main alternator ammeter, 18: Propelling Advisory Control System (PACS), 19: Main reservoir and Main reservoir pipe gauge, 20: Brake cylinder pressure gauge, 21: Speedometer, 22: Brake pipe control and Brake pipe gauge, 23: Air flow gauge, 24: AWS Alarm, 25: Cab-signalbox/control centre radio, 26: Driver's Safety Device (DSD) hold over button, 27: Speed control 'up' or 'down', 28: Cab computer display, 29: Status indicator lights, 30: Driver's Reminder Appliance (DRA) button, 31: Train length button, 32: Display dimmer switch, 33: Display dimmer switch, 34: AWS 'sunflower' indicator, 35: Datacord 6100 input terminal, 36: Emergency brake plunger, 37: Auto air brake controller (train), push forward to apply, pull back to release, 38: Direct brake controller (loco), push forward to apply, pull back to release, 39: Hazard warning light button, 40: Brake overcharge button, 41: Lighting switches, 42: Control switches, 43: Head/marker/tail light control switch, 44: Radio/ Telephone hand set, 45: Sander switch, 46, Horn switch, 47: Master switch socket (AAR reverser handle - key removed), 48: Power controller (8 notches), 49: Driver's Safety Devise (DSD) pedal, 50: AWS reset button, 51: Auxiliary cab heater, 52: Windscreen de-mister switch, 53: Windscreen wiper/washer control, 54: Damp start button, 55: Call button (other cab). The cab illustrated is loco No. 67003. Several small modifications were done after arrival in the UK, the most noticeable being the fitting of TPWS and the slight inclination of the switch panel (41-43 on picture). **CJM**

Below: *After a period of Arriva Trains Wales using Class 57s on Holyhead to Cardiff services, Class 67s have now been introduced with the trains using modified Mk3 DVTs at the remote ends. The locos allocated to the duty, Nos. 67001-003, are painted in Arriva Trains blue but do not carry ATW branding. No. 67002 is illustrated with a Mk3 DVT at Gloucester.* **Norman E. Preedy**

Class 68

TOPS number range:	68001-68025 (on delivery)
Built by:	Vossloh Espania, Valencia, Spain
Classification:	UK-Light
Years introduced:	2014
Wheel arrangement:	Bo-Bo
Weight:	86 tonnes
Height:	12ft 6½in (3.82m)
Length:	67ft 3in (20.50m)
Width:	8ft 10in (2.69m)
Wheel diameter:	43¼in (1,100mm)
Min curve negotiable:	4 chains (80.46m)
Engine type:	Caterpiller C175-16
Engine output:	3,750hp (2,800kW) at 1,740rpm
Starting tractive effort:	71,264lb (317kN)
Continuous tractive effort:	tba
Cylinder bore:	6.9in (175mm)
Cylinder stroke:	8.7in (220mm)
Maximum speed:	100mph (160km/h)
Brake type:	Air Disc, EP, dynamic regen
Brake force:	65.2 tonnes
Bogie type:	Vossloh Fabricated
Route availability:	7
Axle load:	21.4 tonnes per axle
Heating type:	Electric - 500kW, Index - 100
Multiple coupling:	Within class and Class 88 (two locos only)
Traction alternator:	ABB WGX560
Traction motor type:	ABB 4FRA6063
No of traction motors:	4 x ABB frame mounted
Fuel tank capacity:	1,100gal (5,000lit)
Lub oil capacity:	117gal (530lit)
Water capacity:	67gal (304lit)
Sanding equipment:	Pneumatic
Special fittings:	WSP
Operator:	Direct Rail Services
Owner:	Beacon Rail

Above: *Class 68 front end equipment.*
1: Warning horn behind grille, 2: High level marker light, 3: Multiple control jumper socket (cable stowed in engine bay), 4: Windscreen wiper, 5: Head/marker/tail light, 6: ETS jumper cable, 7: ETS jumper socket, 8: Main reservoir pipe (yellow), 9: Air brake pipe (red), 10: Coupling, 11: Obstacle deflector, 12: Lamp bracket. **CJM**

Fact File

DRS expanded its loco fleet following the placing of an order for 15 Vossloh 'EuroLight' Bo-Bo diesel-electric locos on 19 January 2012, the order was increased to 25 locos in mid-2014. Built at the same plant in Valencia, Spain, as the Class 67s, the '68s' are a stunning-looking design introduced from 2014 for mixed traffic duties.

Allocated to Crewe Gresty Bridge depot, the locos will power DRS charter services and are fitted with electric train supply; they will also operate container, freight, flask and engineers trains.

The locos are finished in a new version of the DRS livery including a map motif within the DRS 'Compass' logo. From 2015 five locos will take over Chiltern line loco-hauled services. ■

Below: *Class 68 broadside with No. 1 end on the left. Behind the full width cab and transverse walkway is the equipment compartment housing the power cabinet, dynamic brake towers, brake frame and No. 1 end traction motor blower. The external grilles on the Class 68 are the same on both sides (opposite direction). Between bogie equipment are the battery box, fuel tank and sanding equipment.* **CJM**

Above: *A total of 25 Class 68s are on order, which should be delivered by 2015. The locos are based at Crewe and will operate all types of services from freight to passenger. This view shows the loco from its No. 2 or cooler group end.* **CJM**

Right: *The state-of-the-art Class 68 driving cab. The power controller is on the right and the brake controllers on the left side. The driving position is in the middle of the cab with a non-driving fold down seat attached to the bulkhead.* **CJM**

Class 70

TOPS number range:	Freightliner: 70001-70020
	Colas Rail Freight: 70801-70810
Built by:	General Electric, Erie, Pennsylvania
GE model:	JPH37ACmi
Years introduced:	2009-2014
Wheel arrangement:	Co-Co
Weight:	129 tonnes
Height:	12ft 10in (3.91m)
Length:	71ft 2½in (21.71m)
Width:	8ft 8in (2.64m)
Wheel diameter:	42in (1,067mm)
Min curve negotiable:	4 chains (80.46m)
Engine type:	General Electric/Jenbacher V16 GEJ616
Engine output:	3,686hp (2,750kW)
Maximum tractive effort:	122,100lb (544kN)
Continuous tractive effort:	98,000lb (427kN)
Cylinder bore:	7.48in (190mm)
Cylinder stroke:	8.66in (220mm)
Maximum speed:	75mph (121km/h)
Brake type:	Air, dynamic
Brake force:	97.6 tonnes
Bogie type:	GE Fabricated
Route availability:	7
Heating type:	Not fitted
Multiple coupling type:	AAR
Traction alternator:	GE GTA
Companion alternator:	GE
Traction motor type:	GE AC 5GEB30
No of traction motors:	6
Fuel tank capacity:	1,320gal (6,000lit)
Lub oil capacity:	212gal (802lit)
Sanding equipment:	Pneumatic
Operator:	Freightliner, Colas Rail Freight

Fact File

In 2008, Freightliner announced a radical departure from recent new loco building, when the company entered into a contract with General Electric of Erie, Pennsylvania, to build a new design of twin-cab loco delivering around 3,700hp and classified under the US system as JPH37ACmi.

The first six locos were delivered to the UK at the end of 2009, with a further 13 delivered in 2010-11.

In the UK the locos were subjected to a major period of commissioning, powering both Intermodal and Heavy Haul trains.

Their performance was poor when first delivered with countless on-line failures.

In 2013 Colas Rail Freight purchased 10 of the design for new Network Rail contracts; one (70801) was built as a trials loco in Turkey and the remaining nine were built in Erie, Pennsylvania, entering traffic in 2014. It is likely that GE will be up to ten more locos of the design. ∎

Below:. *Freightliner currently has a fleet of 19 Class 70s in traffic working both Heavy Haul and Intermodal flows. The design has not been totally successful with many on-line failures and problems. No. 70010 is seen from its electrical end. Note the recessed body and rather ugly front design.* **Antony Christie**

Above: *Viewed from its cooler group end, Intermodal-operated No. 70016 passes Oxford with a container train bound for Southampton. The strongholds for this class on Intermodal traffic are Southampton and Felixstowe, while on paper the fleet are allocated to Leeds Midland Road. All locos are painted in Freightliner PowerHaul colours. This loco has received a modification of a protruding ventilation fan and grille on the bodyside above the end of the near bogie.* **CJM**

Below: *Class 70 driving cab layout. 1: Windscreen washer, 2: Windscreen wiper switch (left), 3: Windscreen wiper switch (right), 4: Computer display screen, 5: AWS display and sounder, 6: AWS/TPWS fully isolated warning light, 7: TPWS controls, 8: Computer display screen, 9: GSM-R radio, 10: GSM-R radio handset, 11: Auto engine stop/start suspend, 12: Manual sand valve, 13: AWS reset button, 14: Warning horn valve, 15: Straight air brake controller, 16: Train brake controller, 17: Power controller, 18: Master switch (reverse, engine only, forward), 19: Air brake overcharge button, 20: Drink recess, 21; Emergency brake plunger, 22: Heating and air conditioning control switches, 23: Generator field and engine run switches, 24: 74V dc power output, 25: DSD pedal, 26: Head, marker, tail light switch, 27: Gauge light dimmer switch, 28: Window heater, gauge light and foot step light switches, 29: Desk light and dimmer switch. Cab of No. 70007 is illustrated.* **CJM**

Left: *Class 70 front end layout, applicable to both Freightliner and Colas-operated locomotives. 1: High level marker light, 2: Air warning horns (behind grille), 3: White (marker) red (tail) light LED, 4: Headlight, 5: Screenwash filler port, 6: AAR multiple control jumper socket (cable stowed in cab walkway), 7: Lamp bracket, 8: Air brake pipe, 9: Main reservoir pipe (yellow), 10: Coupling, 11: Obstacle deflector. Cab of No. 70003 is illustrated when new.* **Kevin Wills**

Below: *The pioneer of the Class 70 design, No. 70001* PowerHaul, *is seen from its electrical equipment end. It is interesting to note that these are the only locos currently in traffic with visible anti-climber 'blocks' on the nose end. The ridged sections around the marker and headlights, would, during an end impact with a like-fitted vehicle, engage and restrict the amount of vertical overclimb.* **Nathan Williamson**

Above and Below: *In 2014 Colas Rail Freight took delivery of 10 Class 70s; one, No. 70801, was a demonstrator built in Turkey and shipped to the UK as No. 70099, while the remaining nine were new built in the GE plant in Erie, Pennsylvania, USA. These locos are a refinement of the Freightliner fleet and have a large number of modifications to increase reliability, the most noticeable being extra cooling systems in boxes overhanging the side walkway at the cooler group end. The 10 are painted in Colas green and orange and are used for general Network Rail infrastructure traffic. In the above view No. 70802 is seen from its electrical end at Dawlish Warren when engaged in Dawlish sea wall reconstruction work in March 2014. The view below shows the first of the Colas locos, No. 70801, which was originally No. 70099 and used as a demonstrator in mainland Europe before being imported to the UK. It has received many major modifications since arriving in this country. Both:* **CJM**

Class 73

Sub-class:	73/1	73/2
TOPS number range:	73101-73142	73201-73235
1957 BR number range:	E6007-E6049	From Class 73/1 fleet
Southern Region class code:	JB	JB
Built by:	English Electric, Vulcan Foundry	Modified by BR Stewarts Lane depot
Years introduced:	1965-1967	1984-1990
Wheel arrangement:	Bo-Bo	Bo-Bo
Weight:	77 tonnes	77 tonnes
Height:	12ft 5⁵/₁₆in (3.79m)	12ft 5⁵/₁₆in (3.79m)
Length - buffers retracted:	52ft 6in (16.00m)	52ft 6in (16.00m)
Length - buffers extended:	53ft 8in (16.35m)	53ft 8in (16.35m)
Width:	8ft 8in (2.64m)	8ft 8in (2.64m)
Wheelbase:	40ft 9in (12.42m)	40ft 9in (12.42m)
Bogie wheelbase:	8ft 9in (2.66m)	8ft 9in (2.66m)
Bogie pivot centres:	32ft 0in (9.75m)	32ft 0in (9.75m)
Wheel diameter:	3ft 4in (1.01m)	3ft 4in (1.01m)
Min curve negotiable:	4 chains (80.46m)	4 chains (80.46m)
Power supply:	660-850V dc third rail	660-850V dc third rail
Electric output (Nom):	1,600hp (1,193kW)	1,600hp (1,193kW)
Electric power at rail (Cont):	1,200hp (895kW)	1,200hp (895kW)
Electric power at rail (Max):	3,150hp (2,349kW)	3,150hp (2,349kW)
Engine type:	English Electric 4SRKT Mk2	English Electric 4SRKT Mk2
Engine output:	600hp (447kW)	600hp (447kW)
Diesel power at rail:	402hp (300kW)	402hp (300kW)
Electric tractive effort:	40,000lb (178kN)	40,000lb (178kN)
Diesel tractive effort:	36,000lb (160kN)	36,000lb (160kN)
Cylinder bore:	10in (250mm)	10in (250mm)
Cylinder stroke:	12in (300mm)	12in (300mm)
Maximum speed:	90mph (145km/h)	90mph (145km/h)
Brake type:	Dual, with high-level air pipes, some modified to air brake only	Dual, with high-level air pipes. all modified to air brake only
Brake force:	31 tonnes	31 tonnes
Route availability:	6	6
Heating type:	Electric - index (electric only)	Electric - index 66 (electric only)
Multiple coupling type:	Electric, 1951-1966 EMU jumpers Diesel - Blue star	Electric, 1951-1966 EMU jumpers Diesel - Blue star
Main generator type:	EE824-5D	EE824-5D
Aux generator type:	EE908-5C	EE908-5C
Traction motor type:	EE546-1B	EE546-1B
No of traction motors:	4	4
Gear ratio:	61:19	61:19
Fuel tank capacity:	310gal (1,409lit)	310gal (1,409lit)
Sanding equipment:	Pneumatic	Pneumatic
Special fittings:	Drop-head buck-eye, Loudaphone	Drop-head buck-eye, Loudaphone
Sub-class variations:	Production fleet, mounted on revised bogies with modified grilles	Locos originally dedicated to Gatwick Express operation

Left: *GBRf, now part of the Eurotunnel Group, is the prime user of Class 73 dual-power electro-diesel locomotives with an expanded fleet in recent months. The main equipment positions for all sub-classes are A: No. 2 end, B: No. 1 end, C: Radiator compartment, D: Engine compartment, E: Resistance frame, F: Electrical compartment, G: Fuel tank, H: Battery box, I: Motor generator set. No. 73206 displays early GBRf livery at Eastleigh.* **Nathan Williamson**

73/9	73/9
73951-73952	73961-73965
From Class 73/1 and 73/2 fleet	From Class 73/2 fleet
-	-
Modified by RVEL Derby	Modified by Brush-Wabtec
2014-2015	2014-2015
Bo-Bo	Bo-Bo
To be advised	To be advised
12ft 5⁵/₁₆in (3.79m)	12ft 5⁵/₁₆in (3.79m)
52ft 6in (16.00m)	52ft 6in (16.00m)
53ft 8in (16.35m)	53ft 8in (16.35m)
8ft 8in (2.64m)	8ft 8in (2.64m)
40ft 9in (12.42m)	40ft 9in (12.42m)
8ft 9in (2.66m)	8ft 9in (2.66m)
32ft 0in (9.75m)	32ft 0in (9.75m)
3ft 4in (1.01m)	3ft 4in (1.01m)
4 chains (80.46m)	4 chains (80.46m)
660-850V dc third rail	660-850V dc third rail
To be advised	To be advised
To be advised	To be advised
To be advised	To be advised
2 x Cummins QSK10 of 750hp	MTU V8 R43 4000
1,500hp (1,119kW)	1,500hp (1,119kW)
To be advised	To be advised
To be advised	To be advised
To be advised	To be advised
6¼in (159mm)	6.7in (170mm)
6¼in (159mm)	8.3in (210mm)
90mph (145km/h)	90mph (145km/h)
Air	Air
31 tonnes	31 tonnes
6	6
To be advised	To be advised
AAR	To be advised
AAR	To be advised
To be advised	To be advised
To be advised	To be advised
To be advised	tba
4	4
61:19	61:19
310gal (1,409lit)	310gal (1,409lit)
Pneumatic	Pneumatic
Network Rail fleet	GBRf fleet (Previously 73209/204 206/205)

Fact File

These universal electro-diesel locos were the brainchild of the Southern Region, which wanted to exploit the most from its third rail electric network, while having the ability to operate 'off the juice'.

The original prototype Class 73/0 fleet has now been withdrawn and only a handful of the original Class 73/1 and 73/2 fleet remain in use. The fleet are best remembered for powering the Gatwick Express service between 1984 and 2006. One loco, No. 73202, still remains with Southern for 'Thunderbird' duties.

In the privatised railway, operator GBRf has taken a number of locos for departmental and freight service, and the private sector has several locos available for 'spot-hire'.

Network Rail operates one loco for powering track testing trains.

Currently, two major rebuilding projects for the class are under way, with RVEL in Derby rebuilding locos for Network Rail and installing Cummins engines, and Brush Traction rebuilding locos for GB Railfreight and installing MTU prime movers.

The preservation sector has purchased a sizeable number of locos, with many now fully operational under diesel conditions. ∎

Right: *The Class 73s are without doubt the most universal locomotives ever built, being able to operate under electric conditions from the third rail power supply, or from their own on board diesel engine, together with a narrow-body profile allowing the locos to have a wide route availability. In 2014 a major rebuild operation is under way for both GBRf and Network Rail at Wabtec Loughborough and RVEL Derby. Class 73/1 No. 73136 painted in standard GBRf livery is seen at Eastleigh, a popular location to find class members stabled between work.* **CJM**

Above: *GBRf has in recent months obtained a number of Class 73s from smaller operators and returned them to the main line. One which was at one time 'preserved', No. 73201, the original No. 73142 Broadlands, is now operating for GBRf. Painted in BR rail blue the loco is seen with its electrical end on the right, stabled at Eastleigh in March 2014.* **CJM**

Left Middle: *Another loco recently obtained by GBRf is No. 73107, which is painted in double grey livery with no branding except for a Hither Green 'oast house' logo on the cab side. It is not clear yet how many of these existing Class 73/1s and 73/2s will be subject to rebuilding with new power units and electrical equipment.* **CJM**

Left: *Class 73 front end layout, applicable to all of Class 73/1 and 73/2 1: Air operated warning horns, 2: High level dual main reservoir and air brake pipe connections, 3: 27 way multiple control jumper for use with post-1951 EMU stock, 4: 27 way multiple control jumper socket for use with post-1951 EMU stock, 5: Headlight, 6: Pullman rubbing plate, 7: Electric train supply socket, 8: Electric train supply cable, 9: Drop-head buck-eye coupling 10: Air brake pipe (red), 11: Main reservoir pipe (yellow).* **CJM**

Sub-class:	86/1, 86/2 , 86/7 & 86/9	86/5	86/6
TOPS number range:	86101 86201-86261 86701-86702*	86501	86602-639
1957 BR number range:	E3101-E3200 series	86608	From 86/4 fleet
Former class code:	AL6	AL6, Class 86	AL6, Class 86
Built by:	English Electric, Vulcan Foundry and BR Doncaster Rebuilt by BREL Crewe * Rebuilt by ETL Long Marston	Modified by Adtranz Crewe	Modified by BR Crewe
Years introduced:	1965-1966	-	-
Years Modified:	86/1 - 1972 86/2 - 1972-1975 86/7 - 2009	2000	2000
Wheel arrangement:	Bo-Bo	Bo-Bo	Bo-Bo
Weight:	85 tonnes	84 tonnes	84 tonnes
Height (pan down):	13ft 0⁹/₁₆in (3.97m)	13ft 0⁹/₁₆in (3.97m)	13ft 0⁹/₁₆in (3.97m)
Length:	58ft 6in (17.83m)	58ft 6in (17.83m)	58ft 6in (17.83m)
Width:	8ft 8¼in (2.65m)	8ft 8¼in (2.65m)	8ft 8¼in (2.65m)
Wheelbase:	43ft 6in (13.25m)	43ft 6in (13.25m)	43ft 6in (13.25m)
Bogie wheelbase:	10ft 9in (3.28m)	10ft 9in (3.28m)	10ft 9in (3.28m)
Bogie pivot centres:	32ft 9in (9.98m)	32ft 9in (9.98m)	32ft 9in (9.98m)
Wheel diameter:	3ft 9¼in (1.15m)	3ft 9¼in (1.15m)	3ft 9¼in (1.15m)
Min curve negotiable:	4 chains (80.46m)	4 chains (80.46m)	4 chains (80.46m)
Power supply:	25kV ac overhead	25kV ac overhead	25kV ac overhead
Traction output (max):	6,100hp (4,549kW)	5,900hp (4,400kW)	5,900hp (4,400kW)
Traction output (cont):	4,040hp (3,017kW)	3,600hp (2,684kW)	3,600hp (2,684kW)
Tractive effort:	46,500lb (207kN)	58,000lb (258kN)	58,000lb (258kN)
Maximum speed:	100mph (161km/h)	75mph (121km/h)	75mph (121km/h)
Brake type:	Dual, or Air only	Air	Air
Brake force:	40 tonnes	40 tonnes	40 tonnes
Route availability:	6	6	6
Heating type:	Electric - index 66	Electric - isolated	Electric - isolated
Multiple coupling type:	Jumper system, then TDM	TDM	TDM
Control system:	HT tap changing	HT tap changing	HT tap changing
Traction motor type:	AEI G282BZ	AEI G282AZ	AEI G282AZ
No of traction motors:	4	4	4
Gear ratio:	22:65	18:70	22:65
Sanding equipment:	Pneumatic	Pneumatic	Pneumatic
Operator:	Network Rail, Private	Freightliner	Freightliner
Sub-class variations:	Locomotives fitted with flexicoil suspension, SAB	Class 86/6 with lower gearing and improved sanding to provide better performance on Freightliner trains	Locos operated by Freightliner, vacuum brake equipment removed and restricted to 75mph

Note:
86/2 - Presently out of service, 86/7 are 'spot-hire' locos.

Fact File

Originally introduced for use on the West Coast Main Line in 1965-66 as the second generation of ac main line power, this 100-strong fleet formed the backbone of services on the Euston main line for many years.

By the early 1970s rebuilding with revised bogies to reduce track wear saw the introduction of several sub-classes: 86/0 for original locos, 86/1 for development locos and 86/2 for flexicoil bogie fitted examples, 86/3 - 86/5 for parcels, mail and freight use.

Newer West Coast classes ousted most of the '86s' from front line use with a batch transferring to the London-Norwich main line following electrification.

After privatisation the fleet was split between Virgin Trains, Anglia and the freight operators EWS and Freightliner.

Today, only one of the original passenger locos is still in service, privately owned.

Freightliner operates the Class 86/5 and 86/6 fleets on long distance liner services.

For a period, Network Rail operated two Class 86/9s as mobile ice breakers and load banks.

Several Class 86s have been exported for use in mainland Europe. ∎

Above: *Class 86 equipment positions. A: No. 1 end, B: No. 2 end, C: Pantograph, D: Fire bottle, E: Sandbox filler, F: Flexicoil suspension, G: Air compressor, H: Battery charger, I: Main rectifier, J: Transformer, K: Control cubicle, L: Traction motor blower. No. 86609 is seen from its equipment side.* **CJM**

Left: *Owned by Electric Traction Ltd, the two Class 86/7s are now both stored at Barrow Hill. These two refurbished Class 86/2s operated for a limited period on the main line and could be the subject of an export contract.* **Antony Guppy**

Above: *Owned by Electric Traction Ltd, the pioneer member of Class 86/1 is fully certified and available for main line operation. It is usually stabled at Willesden when not in use. It is currently painted in 1970s BR rail blue and in the above view is seen powering a Network Rail test train at South Tottenham.* **Antony Guppy**

Above: *The Freightliner-operated Class 86/5 and 86/6 locos are based at Crewe and are deployed on intermodal traffic usually on the Crewe/Liverpool/Manchester to Ipswich corridor and are thus frequently seen on the West Coast Main Line and the Anglia route. Working in multiple, Nos. 86613 and 86610 pass Runcorn with a southbound liner train on 9 October 2013.* **Antony Christie**

Below: *Class 86/2 No. 86259 is privately owned by Les Ross and is mainline certified. It is frequently used for passenger charter traffic on the West Coast and when not in use is usually stabled at Oxley. In this view the loco is seen stabled at London Euston on 9 February 2014, after arriving on a Cumbrian Mountain Express charter.* **Mark Fishlock**

Class 87

Locomotives

TOPS number range:	87001-87035
Built by:	BREL Crewe
Years introduced:	1973-1975
Wheel arrangement:	Bo-Bo
Weight:	83.3 tonnes
Height (pan down):	13ft 1¼in (3.99m)
Length:	58ft 6in (17.83m)
Width:	8ft 8¼in (2.65m)
Wheelbase:	43ft 6⅛in (13.26m)
Bogie wheelbase:	10ft 9⅛in (3.28m)
Bogie pivot centres:	32ft 9in (9.98m)
Wheel diameter:	3ft 9½in (1.16m)
Min curve negotiable:	4 chains (80.47m)
Power supply:	25kV ac overhead
Traction output (max):	7,860hp (5,861kW)
Traction output (con):	5,000hp (3,728kW)
Tractive effort:	58,000lb (258kN)
Maximum speed:	110mph (177km/h)
Brake type:	Air
Brake force:	40 tonnes
Route availability:	6
Heating type:	Electric - index 95
Multiple coupling type:	Originally multi-pin jumpers, modified to TDM
Control system:	HT tap changing
Traction motor type:	GEC G412AZ
No of traction motors:	4
Gear ratio:	32:73
Sanding equipment:	Pneumatic
Owner:	Porterbrook Leasing, private owners
Operator:	Private sector, BZK Bulgaria

Fact File

Built by BREL as the 'new' power for the West Coast 'Electric Scot' services in 1973, the Class 87s were the backbone of the Euston-Glasgow, Manchester and Liverpool routes until the introduction of Class 90s and eventually 'Pendolino' stock after privatisation.

The '87s' were always used by the passenger sector, except for trials loco No. 87101 which was fitted on construction with advanced thyristor control equipment. This example eventually worked for the freight sector and was withdrawn early.

Following withdrawal from Virgin Trains' West Coast operations, the fleet owned by Porterbrook was stored, with several of the smaller operators, including DRS and Cotswold Rail, testing the locos for short periods.

Export potential was seen by the owners with some of the Eastern European countries using a similar power system being options for future use. In early 2007 locos started to be exported to BZK in Bulgaria.

The pioneer of the fleet, No. 87001, is now the property of the National Railway Museum, York, and two others are preserved. ■

Left: Considerable interest has surrounded the 21 Class 87/0s now operating in Bulgaria. The locos carry a variety of liveries and in the main retain their original Class 87 numbers. No. 87003-0 is seen painted in the standard green and yellow BZK colours at Bunovo on special train BV3691 from Sofia to Kazanlak on 21 May 2010. Front end equipment items are:
A: Pantograph, B: BZK-style warning horns,
C: Twin headlight unit, D: Wing mirrors,
E: RCH multiple jumper cables, F: Red tail light,
G: White marker light, H: Air brake pipe, I: Main reservoir pipe, J: Coupling.
Philip Wormald

Above: *Eighteen of the Class 87s in Bulgaria are operated by BZK; the remaining three, Nos. 87009/017/023, are operated by Bulmarket, a 'spot-hire' company. No. 87034-5 is seen in BZK green and yellow livery.* **A. P. Sayer**

Right: *When exported to Bulgaria, some locos retained their UK livery, such as the Cotswold grey locos, DRS blue, LNWR black and rail blue. In the remnants of Cotswold Rail grey, No. 87007-1 is illustrated. Note the roof headlights and side facing horns.* **A. P. Sayer**

Below: *In the UK two Class 87s are preserved and one, No. 87002, is maintained operational on the main line, owned by Electric Traction Ltd it is used for 'spot-hire' and charter work. Here it is seen on the East Coast Main Line.* **Lindsay Atkinson**

Class 88

Locomotives

TOPS number range:	88001-88010 (on order)
Built by:	Vossloh Espania, Valencia, Spain
Classification:	UK-Dual-Mode
Years introduced:	2015
Wheel arrangement:	Bo-Bo
Weight:	tba
Height:	12ft 6½in (3.82m)
Length:	67ft 3in (20.50m)
Width:	8ft 10in (2.69m)
Wheel diameter:	43¼in (1,100mm)
Min curve negotiable:	4 chains (80.46m)
Electric traction equipment:	ABB
Power supply:	25kV ac overhead
Electric output:	5,360hp (4,000kW)
Engine type:	Caterpillar C27
Engine output:	938hp (700kW)
Starting tractive effort:	71,264lb (317kN)
Continuous tractive effort:	tba
Cylinder bore:	5.42in (137.7mm)
Cylinder stroke:	6in (152.4mm)
Maximum speed:	100mph (160km/h)
Brake type:	Air Disc, EP, dynamic regen
Brake force:	tba
Bogie type:	Vossloh Fabricated
Route availability:	7
Axle load:	21.4 tonnes per axle
Heating type:	Electric - 500kW
Multiple coupling:	Within class and Class 68 (two locos only)
Traction package:	ABB
Traction alternator:	tba
Traction motor type:	ABB 4FRA6063 of 600kW at 4,400rpm
No of traction motors:	4 x ABB frame mounted
Fuel tank capacity:	tba
Lub oil capacity:	tba
Sanding equipment:	Pneumatic
Operator:	Direct Rail Services
Owner:	Beacon Rail

Fact File

As a further part of Direct Rail Services (DRS) upgrading its loco fleet for expanding business, the operator through Beacon Rail ordered 10 dual-mode (electro-diesel) locos from Vossloh in September 2013, to be classified in the UK as Class 88.

The locos will sport the same body, cab and brake system as the Class 68 but have a 4MW ABB electrical system as well as a 'final mile' Caterpillar 700kW diesel engine.

The 10 locos, due for delivery in 2015-16, will be based at Carlisle and operate passenger, container and freight services. ∎

Below: *Artist's impression of how the Class 88 will look. The body is based on the DRS Class 86, using many common structural items. The livery is expected to be changed before delivery.*

Fact File

The 50 third generation main line ac electric locos of Class 90 were intended for West Coast use. When built in 1987-90 they were used on both passenger and freight services. The first 15 locos were dedicated to passenger operations and the balance to freight, parcels and Royal Mail operations.

The Class 90/0s used on main West Coast passenger services were replaced by 'Pendolino' stock and are now deployed on Abellio Greater Anglia services, while the remaining locos are operated by DB Schenker and Freightliner. One loco is jointly operated by Direct Rail Services / Virgin Trains

Greater Anglia locos are in a mix of blue and white liveries, DBS locos are in maroon, DBS red, grey or First ScotRail colours for sleeper operation. Freightliner locos are in green or grey with Freightliner branding.

The sole loco operated by Virgin/DRS is painted in Direct Rail Services blue. ∎

TOPS number range:	90001-90050
Built by:	BREL Crewe
Years introduced:	1987-1990
Wheel arrangement:	Bo-Bo
Weight:	84.5 tonnes
Height (pan down):	13ft 0¼in (3.96m)
Length:	61ft 6in (18.74m)
Width:	9ft 0in (2.74m)
Wheelbase:	43ft 6in (13.25m)
Bogie wheelbase:	10ft 9in (3.27m)
Bogie pivot centres:	32ft 9in (9.98m)
Wheel diameter:	3ft 9½in (1.16m)
Min curve negotiable:	4 chains (80.43m)
Power supply:	25kV ac overhead
Traction output (max):	7,860hp (5,861kW)
Traction output (con):	5,000hp (3,728kW)
Tractive effort:	58,000lb (258kN)
Maximum speed:	90001-90040 - 110mph (177km/h)
	90041-90050 - 75mph (121km/h)
Brake type:	Air
Brake force:	40 tonnes
Route availability:	7
Heating type:	90001-90040 - Electric - index 95
	90041-90050 - Electric - isolated
Multiple coupling type:	TDM
Control system:	Thyristor
Traction motor type:	GEC G412CY
No of traction motors:	4
Gear ratio:	32:73
Sanding equipment:	Pneumatic
Special fittings:	90001-90015 - Drop-head buck-eye couplings
Operator:	Greater Anglia, DBS, Freightliner, DRS

Right: *Class 90 front end equipment. Applicable to all sub-classes, but freight locos do not have a Pullman rubbing plate or buck-eye couplers. A: Light cluster, marker, tail and headlight, B: Air horns behind grille, C: RCH control jumper cables, D: Pullman rubbing plate, E: Electric train supply socket, F: Electric train supply cable, G: Air brake pipe (red), H: Main reservoir pipe (yellow), I: Buck-eye coupling in lowered position. Loco shown is Greater Anglia No. 90014.*
Antony Christie

Above: *The Abellio Greater Anglia franchise operates 15 Class 90s based at Norwich. The locos are in a variety of liveries – No. 90005 displays the latest Greater Anglia colours.* **Antony Christie**

Left: *DB-Schenker operates 24 Class 90s, but many are stored out of use. In 2014 a start was made at repainting the fleet into DB red and grey as displayed on No. 90018 at Edinburgh.* **Bill Wilson**

Below: *Freightliner has a fleet of 10 locos. No. 90045 shows the latest Freightliner 'Powerhaul' colours.* **Antony Christie**

Above: Class 90 equipment positions, equipment compartment side (five grilles). A: No. 1 end, B: No. 2 end, C: Pantograph, D: Sandbox filler, E: Grilles for electrical equipment, F: Battery box, G: Air compressors (2). Loco No. 90016 operated by Freightliner is illustrated. **CJM**

Right: DB-Schenker is the current provider of Class 90s to operate the ScotRail sleeper services, and to promote this four locos carry First ScotRail livery. These locos are, however, not used exclusively on the sleeper duties. No. 90021 is seen at London Euston. **Antony Christie**

In March 2014 a new contract was cemented between Direct Rail Services and Virgin Trains to provide a Class 90 (hired from DB-S) to power the Virgin Mk3 passenger set. No. 90034 is the dedicated loco which is painted in full DRS livery and is usually kept at Wembley with the train for quick deployment. The loco is shown from its two grille side at Crewe Gresty Bridge. **CJM**

Class 91

TOPS number range:	91101-91132 (originally 91001-91031)
Built by:	BREL Crewe
Rebuilt:	Adtranz/Bombardier Doncaster
Years introduced:	1988-1991
Years refurbished to 91/1:	2000-2002
Wheel arrangement:	Bo-Bo
Weight:	84 tonnes
Height (pan down):	12ft 4in (3.76m)
Length:	63ft 8in (19.40m)
Width:	9ft 0in (2.74m)
Wheelbase:	45ft 4½in (13.83m)
Bogie wheelbase:	10ft 1⅞in (3.09m)
Bogie pivot centres:	34ft 5½in (10.50m)
Wheel diameter:	3ft 3½in (1.00m)
Min curve negotiable:	4 chains (80.49m)
Traction output (max):	6,300hp (4,698kW)
Traction output (con):	6,090hp (4,531kW)
Maximum design speed:	140mph (225km/h)
Maximum operating speed:	125mph (201km/h)
	110mph (177km/h) slab end leading
Brake type:	Air
Brake force:	45 tonnes
Route availability:	7
Heating type:	Electric - index 95
Multiple coupling type:	TDM
Control system:	Thyristor
Traction motor type:	GEC G426AZ
No of traction motors:	4
Gear ratio:	1.74:1
Sanding equipment:	Pneumatic
Special fittings:	Drop-head buck-eye couplings
Operator:	East Coast

Fact File

Designed and built for the proposed 140mph (225km/h) electrified railway between London King's Cross and Edinburgh, plus the route from Doncaster to Leeds, the 31 Class 91s were a new design to the UK in having a single raked-back No. 1 end and a slab cab at the No. 2 end.

The locos operate together with Mk4 stock and usually work in a fixed formation, only being split for extended maintenance.

Originally operated by BR InterCity, at privatisation the fleet was transferred to operator GNER, which refurbished and reliveried the fleet into dark blue and red.

With franchise changes National Express took over the East Coast route and reliveried a number of vehicles. Following the franchise being withdrawn from National Express in 2009 and the Government-owned East Coast Railways taking over, a new white/grey-based East Coast livery was adopted.

Originally classified as Class 91, after refurbishment the fleet became Class 91/1, renumbered in the 911xx series.

All are allocated to Bounds Green depot in North London, and receive classified attention at Wabtec, Doncaster.

In normal operation the locos are coupled to the north end of formations, with a driving van trailer (DVT) at the London or south end. ∎

Above and Below: *The 31 Class 91 East Coast locos are allocated to Bounds Green and operate at the northern end of East Coast services. The majority are painted in East Coast grey/silver, with one or two in full advertising colours, as demonstrated below with No. 91125 (and its train) carrying Sky TV blue, applied as part of a documentary promotion in 2013. No. 91109 in standard livery is shown above.* **Antony Christie / Jamie Squibbs**

Above: *The Class 91s are able to power trains with their 'slab' end leading, although at reduced speed. This is usually only done following a failure of the normal leading cab or in an emergency. The Class 91s and Mk4 formations will be replaced on the East Coast route from London to Leeds, Newcastle, Edinburgh and Glasgow by the introduction of Class 800 and 801 stock. No. 91017 is seen passing Harringay with a northbound express.* **CJM**

Right : *Class 91 nose end layout. The same equipment can be found on the slab or inner No. 2 end. A: Forward facing camera (inside cab), B: Light cluster (marker, head, tail). C: Warning horns behind grille, D: Pullman rubbing plate, E: Electric train supply jumper, F: Electric train supply jumper cable, G: Main reservoir pipe (yellow), H: Air brake pipe (red), I: Drop-head buck-eye coupling (in lowered position).*
Jamie Squibbs

Class 92

Locomotives

TOPS number range:	92001-92046
Built by:	Brush Traction
Years introduced:	1993-1995
Wheel arrangement:	Co-Co
Power supply:	Overhead at 25kV ac or
	Third rail at 750V dc
Weight:	126 tonnes
Height (pan down):	13ft 0in (3.96m)
Length:	70ft 1in (21.34m)
Width:	8ft 8in (2.67m)
Wheelbase:	56ft 6in (17.22m)
Bogie wheelbase:	14ft 1in (4.29m)
Bogie pivot centres:	41ft 10$\frac{1}{2}$in (12.75m)
Wheel diameter:	3ft 9in (1.16m)
Min curve negotiable:	6 chains (120.7m)
Traction output (max):	6,700hp (5,000kW) - overhead ac power supply
	5,360hp (4,000kW) - third rail dc power supply
Tractive effort:	Normal - 81,000lb (360kN)
	Boost - 90,000lb (400kN)
Maximum speed:	87mph (140km/h)
Brake type:	Air, rheostatic and regenerative
Brake force:	63 tonnes
Route availability:	8
Heating type:	Electric – ac supply - index 108,
	dc supply - index 70
Multiple coupling type:	TDM
Control system:	Asynchronous 3-phase
Traction motor type:	Brush
No of traction motors:	6
Special fittings:	TVM430, CTO
Present operator:	DBS, GBRf (some exported)
Notes:	Some locos stored

Fact File

Designed by BR Railfreight Distribution, with a major input from French operator SNCF and the Channel Tunnel authority, the 46-strong Class 92 fleet was built for cross-Channel services using the Channel Tunnel.

The locos are basically two locomotives in one bodyshell, meaning that in all but the most serious failures a loco would be able to continue its journey through and clear of the Channel Tunnel.

The locos were ordered and funded by Railfreight Distribution (30 locos), SNCF (nine locos) and Eurostar UK (seven locos). During the course of delivery, the Eurostar overnight operation was abandoned and these locos were redundant; shortly afterwards the SNCF-owned locos were stored in the UK.

The Railfreight Distribution locos were taken over by EWS, later DB-Schenker, upon privatisation.

In February 2007, five of the Eurostar UK locos, Nos. 92028/032/038/043 and 044, were sold to Eurotunnel, and more recently GB Railfreight (GBRf) has purchased all non DB-S locos and is returning many to active service. DRS also hire Class 92s from DB-S.

All locos are fitted for dual 25kV ac and 750V dc operation and have TVM430 cab signalling. Some locos are modified to allow operation over HS1 between the Channel Tunnel and London. Some locos owned by DB-S have been exported to Bulgaria and Romania. ∎

Below: Built for use through the Channel Tunnel, the fleet of Class 92s have never been fully utilised, far too many were built for the projected business, compounded by the failure of the rail industry to operate an overnight passenger service through the Channel Tunnel. DB-S who officially operate a fleet of 30 always have a number stored out of use, and in 2013-14 commenced modifying locos for export to Romania and Bulgaria. In the UK the locos mainly operate through services from the Channel Tunnel UK terminal at Dollands Moor to the Midlands. No. 92037 is illustrated in double-grey livery with EWS branding. **CJM**

Above: *A handful of DB-S Class 92s have emerged in the latest DB red and grey livery. Those exported to either Bulgaria or Romania have received repairs and major modifications to meet local Group Standards. No. 92031 is seen operating on third rail passing Kensington Olympia.* **CJM**

Right: *GBRf and its parent EuroPorte now have a fleet of 16 Class 92s which are progressively being returned to service. No. 92032 shows GBRf blue and orange livery.* **Nathan Williamson**

Below: *With Channel Tunnel roundels, GBRf-operated No. 92010 passes Stafford; this loco, like many others, has spent long periods stored.* **Antony Christie**

Vehicle type:	DMBS
Number range:	55020, 55032, 55034
Set numbers:	121020, 121032, 121034
TOPS classification:	121
Introduced:	1960
Built by:	Pressed Steel
Vehicle length (over body):	64ft 6in (19.65m)
Height:	12ft 8½in (3.87m)
Width:	9ft 3in (2.81m)
Seating:	65S
Internal layout:	2+3
Gangway:	No
Toilets:	Not fitted
Weight:	38 tonnes
Brake type:	Vacuum
Power unit:	2 x Leyland 1595 of 150hp (112kW) per vehicle
Horsepower (total):	300hp (224kW)
Transmission:	Mechanical
Max speed:	70mph (113km/h)
Coupling type:	Screw
Multiple restriction:	Blue square
Door type:	Slam
Bogie type:	DD10
Special features:	Central Door Locking (passenger)
Body structure:	Steel
Owner/operator:	Chiltern Railways
Certified for main line use:	Chiltern Railways

Fact File

Built to the BR Derby high-density design for general branch line use, these Pressed Steel railcars, which operated originally with unpowered single-ended trailers, were the equivalent of the original Great Western AEC diesel railcars.

Sufficient power existed to haul one or two vacuum braked vehicles. A total of 16 powered twin-ended cars were built in 1960.

Allocated to BR Western Region, the cars worked in the London, Bristol and Plymouth areas.

After withdrawal the fleet became popular for departmental use, being of a twin-cabbed design.

In privatisation, three returned to main line use, fitted with central door locking and upgraded to modern Group Standards.

Originally two operated with Chiltern based at Aylesbury and one for Arriva Trains Wales in Cardiff; in 2013 the Arriva vehicle was sold to Chiltern Railways. ■

Left: *The only first generation 'heritage' DMMU stock still in operation are three Class 121 'Bubble cars', used by Chiltern Railways. Vehicle No. 55032 retains exterior body-mounted exhaust stacks on the front end at the guard's equipment end. Front end equipment positions are, A: Roof mounted train-land radio aerial, B: Former four-character route display box, C: Exhaust stack, D: Marker light, able to show white for frontal identification and red for rear identification, E: Headlight, F: Vacuum brake pipe, G: Multiple working jumpers, H: Screw coupling, I: Air control air pipe, J: Multiple control jumper socket. Exhaust stacks on the other two vehicles have been repositioned through the bodywork.* **CJM**

Above: *With its exhaust stacks poking through the roof, just behind the cab area, Chiltern Railways-liveried No. 55020 (121020) is illustrated from its guard's van end. To conform with the latest regulations these vehicles have been fitted with a basic central door locking system. The sets based at Aylesbury operate on the Aylesbury to Princes Risborough route.* **Kim Fullbrook**

Below: *Chiltern Class 121 'Bubble car' No. 55034 has been restored to 1960s BR green livery with a small yellow warning end, but to meet latest Group Standards has central door locking and a central headlight. The original four character headcode box is not restored and shows a black panel. No. W55034 is seen on display at Didcot Railway Centre.* **Darren Ford**

Diesel Multiple Units

Vehicle type:	DMS
Number range:	39001-39002
Set numbers:	139001-139002
TOPS classification:	139
Introduced:	2007-2008
Built by:	Main Road Sheet Metal, Leyland, for Parry People Movers
Vehicle length (over body):	28ft 6in (8.7m)
Height:	12ft 3in (3.77m)
Width:	7ft 10in (2.81m)
Seating:	20S
Internal layout:	1+1
Gangway:	Not fitted
Toilets:	Not fitted
Weight:	12.5 tonnes
Brake type:	Regen using flywheel & air
Primary power:	Ford MVH-420 engine
Horsepower (total):	86hp (64kW)
Flywheel (stored power):	500kg/1m dia 1,000-1,500rpm wheel
Transmission:	Tandler bevel box with Linde hydrostatic transmission and spiral bevel gearbox
Max speed:	45mph (72km/h)
Coupling type:	Emergency
Multiple restriction:	Not fitted
Door type:	Double-leaf folding
Body structure:	Steel
Owner/operator:	London Midland
Certified for main line use:	Stourbridge Junction to Stourbridge Town only

Fact File

In 2005-06 Parry People Movers refined its light-weight flywheel hydrostatic controlled small railcar and offered two vehicles to London Midland for use on the very short line between Stourbridge Junction and Stourbridge Town.

When first introduced in 2009 performance was poor with frequent substitution by Class 153 units. However, performance is now much improved.

Two single vehicles are based in a small shed at Stourbridge Junction, with one vehicle usually operating the service for several days.

It was hoped that further lightly used branch lines would be able to be operated using Parry People Mover products in the future, but this did not happen.

In 2011 trials were undertaken with another design of PPM on the Mid-Hants Railway. ∎

Below: *Operated by Pre-Metro Operations for London Midland are two Class 139 Parry People Movers, used on the Stourbridge Junction to Stourbridge Town 'shuttle' service. The two vehicles introduced in 2007-08 released a main line set off the branch for other use and with such low patronage the 20 seat Class 139 is adequate for the service. The vehicles are twin ended and have one pair of double leaf folding doors. No drawgear is provided, only an emergency 'loop'. The vehicles have headlights, marker lights and tail lights. Set No. 139001 is illustrated.* **Antony Christie**

Above: *The 20 passenger seats in a Class 139 are set out as a single row on one side facing one direction and a row of inward seats on the other. On both sides fold-down seats are provided thus providing room for buggies, trolleys and luggage. The seating is in London Midland green moquette with yellow grab poles. No luggage racks are provided.* **Antony Christie**

Below: *Class 139 driving cab; this is located on the right side of the front end and is of a very basic layout.* **Antony Christie**

Class 142 'Pacer'

Diesel Multiple Units

Number range:	142001-142096
Introduced:	1985-1987
Built by:	Leyland bus body on BREL underframe, assembled at BREL Derby
Formation:	DMS+DMSL
Vehicle numbers:	DMS - 55542-55591, 55701-55746
	DMSL - 55592-55641, 55747-55792
Vehicle length:	51ft 0½in (15.55m)
Height:	12ft 8in (3.86m)
Width:	9ft 2¼in (2.80m)
Seating:	Total - 96-122S
	DMS - 46-62S (depending on layout)
	DMSL - 50-60S (depending on layout)
Internal layout:	2+3 or 2+2 (depending on operator)
Gangway:	Within set only
Toilets:	DMSL - 1
Weight:	Total - 49.5 tonnes
	DMS - 24.5 tonnes
	DMSL - 25 tonnes
Brake type:	Air EP
Bogie type:	4-wheel chassis
Power unit:	1 x Cummins LTA10-R of 225hp (165kW) per vehicle
Transmission:	Hydraulic
Transmission type:	Voith T211r
Horsepower (total):	450hp (330kW)
Max speed:	75mph (121km/h)
Coupling type:	Outer - BSI, Between cars - Bar
Multiple restriction:	Class 14x, 15x units
Door type:	Twin-leaf inward pivot
Body structure:	Aluminium alloy (bus body sections) on steel frame
Owner:	Angel Trains
Operator:	Northern Rail, Arriva Trains Wales

Fact File

The largest fleet of 'Railbus'- type vehicles, introduced by the BRB as a low cost replacement for branch line services are the BREL/Leyland Class 142s, introduced in several batches between 1985 and 1987 for use on London Midland, Eastern and Western Regions.

The trains were not welcomed by staff or passengers, with a basic bus interior not entirely suitable for rail transport.

Today, the sets are all owned by Angel Trains and are operated on the Northern Rail and Arriva Trains Wales franchises.

Many refinements have been made to the interiors, which has improved perception of the trains. To meet the Disabilities Discrimination Act regulations, which require all public transport to be accessible by disabled passengers, the '142s' will need to be withdrawn by 2019.

Sets 142001-050 are officially 142/0 and 142051-096 are 142/1 but this is not reflected in numbering or equipment. ■

Left: *Class 142 front end equipment (also applicable to Class 143 and 144 stock). A: Destination/route display, B: Group Standard light cluster (from outer edge - white marker light, headlight, red tail light), C: Ventilation grille, D: Lamp bracket, E: BSI auto coupler with pneumatic connections, electrical connections below in roll-covered box, F: Warning horns (behind grille). Set No. 142069 from the Arriva Trains Wales allocation is illustrated at Cardiff.* **CJM**

Right: *Inner end Class 142 vehicle connections. A: Exhaust pipe, B: Bar coupler, C: Air connection socket, D: Battery box, E: Between vehicle electrical jumper box.* **CJM**

Right Top: *Northern Rail is the largest user of Class 142 'Pacer' stock with, during 2014, 79 two-car sets in traffic from Newton Heath (Manchester) and Heaton (Newcastle) depots. All sets are painted in Northern blue, mauve and grey livery with full yellow warning ends. Slight differences exist in the style of route indicator, with some sets having a small dot-matrix display and others having a near full width assembly. Some minor detail differences exist with nose end ventilation grilles. With its DMSL vehicle nearest the camera (identified by the opaque window at the inner end), set No. 142087 is seen at departing from Doncaster coupled to a Class 144.* **CJM**

Right Middle: *Viewed from its DMS end, which also has a small disabled seating area, set No. 142067 is seen at Selby, displaying a small roller-blind destination indicator showing York. This is one of the later phase 2 sets.* **CJM**

Right Lower: *Arriva Trains Wales operates a fleet of 15 Class 142s, based at Cardiff Canton. These sets are fully refurbished and sport 2+2 low-density seating. They are used on the Cardiff Valley branch lines alongside Class 143 and 150 stock. Sets are painted in Arriva Trains Wales livery, with a start made in 2014 to apply the new dark and light turquoise colours. Set No. 142085 is seen at Taffs Well.* **CJM**

Right Bottom: *The Northern Rail operated Class 142s have 2+3 high-density seating, using low-back seats, giving a maximum number of seats per vehicle as 62.* **Antony Christie**

Class 143 'Pacer'

Number range:	143601-143625
Introduced:	1985-1986
Built by:	Walter Alexander body mounted on Andrew Barclay underframe, assembled by Hunslet of Kilmarnock
Formation:	DMS+DMSL
Vehicle numbers:	DMS - 55642-55666
	DMSL - 55667-55691
Vehicle length:	51ft 0½in (15.55m)
Height:	12ft 2¾in (3.73m)
Width:	8ft 10½in (2.70m)
Seating:	Total - 92S + 12 tip up
	DMS - 48S + 6 tip up
	DMSL - 44S + 6 tip up
Internal layout:	2+2
Gangway:	Within set only
Toilets:	DMSL - 1
Weight:	Total - 48.5 tonnes
	DMS - 24 tonnes
	DMSL - 24.5 tonnes
Brake type:	Air EP
Bogie type:	4-wheel chassis
Power unit:	1 x Cummins LTA10-R of 225hp (165kW) per vehicle
Transmission:	Hydraulic
Transmission type:	Voith T211r
Horsepower (total):	450hp (330kW)
Max speed:	75mph (121km/h)
Coupling type:	Outer - BSI, Between cars - Bar
Multiple restriction:	Class 14x, 15x
Door type:	Twin-leaf inward pivot
Body structure:	Aluminium alloy (bus body sections) on steel frame
Owner:	Porterbrook, Rail Assets Investments, Bridgend Council, Cardiff City Council
Operator:	Arriva Trains Wales, First Great Western

Fact File

Built concurrently with the Class 142 fleet, these 'Pacer' sets were assembled at the Kilmarnock plant of Andrew Barclay, with bodies supplied by Walter Alexander and mounted on frames supplied by Andrew Barclay of Kilmarnock.

These sets were originally allocated to the North East, based at Heaton. However, after a short period they were transferred south and allocated to Cardiff in South Wales and today are operated by Arriva Trains Wales and First Great Western.

When originally built, sets were numbered in the 1430xx series; this changed to the 1433xx series and then to the 1436xx range.

Sets are owned by Porterbrook Leasing, but two are owned by Rail Assets Investments Ltd and three by South Wales councils.

Today the interiors are refurbished and have 2+2 'Chapman' seats. The livery is either FGW 'local lines' or Arriva Trains Wales colours. Front end equipment is the same style as the Class 142. ■

Right: *The largest user of Class 143s is Arriva Trains Wales, with 15 sets allocated to Cardiff Canton to operate alongside Class 142s on Cardiff Valley and West Wales services. ATW sets all carry corporate livery and all have been refurbished with 2+2 high back seating. Set No. 143622 is seen at Swansea while operating a Pembroke Dock service.* **CJM**

Left: *Class 143 front end layout. A: Destination/route indicator, B: Group Standard light cluster (from the outside, marker, head and tail light), C: Lamp bracket, D: BSI coupling incorporating pneumatic connection, electrical connection box below (protected by rolling drum cover), E: Emergency air connection, F: Warning horns (behind grille). Arriva Trains Wales allocated No. 143625 is illustrated.* **CJM**

Below: *View of a Class 143 driving car from the inner end, showing that on the non-driving side two pairs of folding doors are provided, while on the driver's side only one set of doors exists, directly to the rear of the cab. This view also shows the position of the vertical exhaust stack fitted to the non-driving inner end of all vehicles.* **CJM**

Left: *A fleet of eight Class 143s is allocated to First Great Western. Based at Exeter these sets operate on the Barnstaple, Paignton and Exmouth lines, frequently operating in pairs providing seating for 184 passengers. The sets are painted in FGW 'local lines' names livery and are scheduled to remain in traffic for the foreseeable future. The sets can operate in multiple with Class 150, 153 and 158 stock. A pair of units emerge from Kennaway Tunnel, Dawlish, led by set No. 143620.* **CJM**

Traction Recognition

Number range:	144001-144013 – 2-car
	144014-144023 – 3-car
Introduced:	1986-1987
Built by:	Walter Alexander body on BREL underframe
	Assembled at BREL Derby Litchurch Lane
Formation:	144001-144013 - DMS+DMSL
	144014-144023 - DMS+MS+DMSL
Vehicle numbers:	DMS - 55801-55823
	MS - 55850-55859
	DMSL - 55824-55846
Vehicle length:	50ft 2in (15.29m)
Height:	12ft 2¾in (3.73m)
Width:	8ft 10½in (2.70m)
Seating:	144001-144013 - Total 87S + 6 tip up
	144014-144023 - Total 145S + 6 tip up
	DMS - 45S + 3 tip up
	MS - 58S
	DMSL - 42S + 3 tip up
Internal layout:	2+2
Gangway:	Within set only
Toilets:	DMSL - 1
Weight:	Total - 72 tonnes
	DMS - 24 tonnes
	MS - 23.5 tonnes
	DMSL - 24.5 tonnes
Brake type:	Air EP
Bogie type:	4-wheel chassis
Power unit:	1 x Cummins LTA10-R of 225hp per vehicle
Transmission:	Hydraulic
Transmission type:	Voith T211r
Horsepower (total):	144001-144013 - 450hp (330kW)
	144014-144023 - 675hp (495kW)
Max speed:	75mph (121km/h)
Coupling type:	Outer - BSI, Between cars - Bar
Multiple restriction:	Class 14x, 15x
Door type:	Twin-leaf inward pivot
Body structure:	Aluminium alloy (bus body sections)
	on steel frame
Owner:	Porterbrook
Operator:	Northern Rail

Fact File

The 23 members of Class 144 form the final 'Pacer' breed using Walter Alexander bus body sections mounted on a BREL produced underframe. Assembly was undertaken at BREL Derby.

The first 13 sets are two-car, with the remaining 10 having an intermediate Motor Second (MS), added later and funded by West Yorkshire PTE to strengthen services.

Originally seating was in the 2+3 bus style, but refurbishment has seen a more pleasing 2+2 interior using Richmond seats.

All sets are painted in Northern Rail livery and are allocated to Leeds Neville Hill. ■

Below: *After the Walter Alexander/ BREL Class 144 two-car sets were in traffic, growth in the West Yorkshire PTE area saw the need for extra vehicles; this came with an order for 10 intermediate Motor Standard (MS) vehicles, the only non-driving 'Pacer' vehicles built. The vehicles were inserted into the final 10 sets, Nos. 144014-023. The intermediate coaches seat 58 in the 2+2 style. Car No. 55851 from set 144015 is illustrated.*
Antony Christie

Above: *Allocated to Leeds Neville Hill depot, the Class 144s can be seen throughout the Yorkshire operating area. The sets are painted in Northern Rail blue, mauve and grey livery. The intermediate MS vehicles are painted in all over blue. Two-car set No. 144006 departs from Doncaster with a service to Sheffield.* **CJM**

Right: *The 10 three-car Class 144s tend to be used on the busy routes radiating from Leeds on PTE services, with each three-car set having seating for 145 standard class passengers. Three-car set No. 144022 is seen near Bingley with a Keighley to Leeds service.*
Keith Dungate

Traction Recognition

Class 150 'Sprinter'

Sub-class:	150/0	150/1	150/2
Number range:	150001-150002	150101-150150	150201-150285
Introduced:	1984	1985-1986	1986-1987
Built by:	BREL York	BREL York	BREL York
Formation:	DMSL+MS+DMS	DMSL+DMS	DMSL+DMS
Vehicle numbers:	DMSL - 55200-55201	DMSL - 52101-52150	DMSL - 52201-52285
	MS - 55400-55401	DMS - 57101-57150	DMS - 57201-57285
	DMS - 55300-55301	-	-
Vehicle lengths:	DMSL - 65ft 9¾in (20.06m)	DMSL - 65ft 9¾in (20.06m)	DMSL - 65ft 9¾in (20.06m)
	MS - 66ft 2½in (20.18m)	DMS - 65ft 9¾in (20.06m)	DMSL - 65ft 9¾in (20.06m)
	DMS - 65ft 9¾in (20.06m)		
Height:	12ft 4½in (3.77m)	12ft 4½in (3.77m)	12ft 4½in (3.77m)
Width:	9ft 3⅛in (2.82m)	9ft 3⅛in (2.82m)	9ft 3⅛in (2.82m)
Seating:	Total - 240S	Total - 124-144S	Total - 116-149S
	DMSL - 72S	DMSL - 59-71S	DMSL - 60-73S
	MS - 92S	DMS - 65-73S	DMS - 56-76S
	DMS - 76S	-	-
Internal layout:	2+3	2+3	2+3 or 2+2
Gangway:	Within set	Within set	Throughout
Toilets:	DMSL - 1	DMSL - 1	DMSL - 1
Weight:	Total - 99.3 tonnes	Total - 76.4 tonnes	Total - 74 tonnes
	DMSL - 35.4 tonnes	DMSL - 38.3 tonnes	DMSL - 37.5 tonnes
	MS - 34.1 tonnes	DMS - 38.1 tonnes	DMS - 36.5 tonnes
	DMS - 29.8 tonnes		
Brake type:	Air EP	Air EP	Air EP
Bogie type:	Powered - BX8P	Powered - BP38	Powered - BP38
	Trailer - BX8T	Trailer - BT38	Trailer - BT38
Power unit:	1 x NT855R4 of	1 x NT855R5 of	1 x NT855R5 of
	285hp (213kW) per vehicle	285hp (213kW) per vehicle	285hp (213kW) per vehicle
Transmission:	Hydraulic	Hydraulic	Hydraulic
Transmission type:	Voith T211r	Voith T211r	Voith T211r
Horsepower:	855hp (639kW)	570hp (426kW)	570hp (426kW)
Max speed:	75mph (121km/h)	75mph (121km/h)	75mph (121km/h)
Coupling type:	Outer - BSI	BSI	BSI
	Between cars - Bar		
Multiple restriction:	Class 14x, 15x, 170, 172	Class 14x, 15x, 170, 172	Class 14x, 15x, 170, 172
Door type:	Bi-parting sliding	Bi-parting sliding	Bi-parting sliding
	(cab door slam)	(cab door slam)	(cab door slide)
Body structure:	Steel	Steel	Steel
Owner:	Angel Trains	Angel, Porterbrook	Angel Trains
Operator:	FGW	London Midland, FGW,	FGW, Arriva Trains Wales
		Northern	Northern
Notes:	Original prototype sets		

150/9
150921 & 150927
Orig: 1985-86, 150/9: 2012
BREL York
DMSL+DMS+DMS
DMSL - 52121, 52127
DMS - 57209, 57212
DMS - 57121, 57127
DMSL - 65ft 9¾in (20.06m)
DMS - 65ft 9¾in (20.06m)
DMS - 65ft 9¾in (20.06m)
12ft 4½in (3.77m)
9ft 3⅛in (2.82m)
Total - 222S
DMSL - 73S
DMS - 73S
DMS - 76S
2+3
Within set
DMSL - 1
Total - 112.9 tonnes
DMSL - 38.3 tonnes
DMS - 36.5 tonnes
DMS - 38.1 tonnes
Air EP
Powered - BP38
Trailer - BT38
1 x NT855R5 of
285hp (213kW) per vehicle
Hydraulic
Voith T211r
855hp (639kW)
75mph (121km/h)
BSI
Class 14x, 15x, 170, 172
Bi-parting sliding
(cab door slam, middle slide)
Steel
Porterbrook
FGW
150/1 with 150/2 DMS between

By the early 1980s the BRB had to act quickly to procure new generation suburban and mid-distance DMU stock, as the 1950s-built first generation units were quickly becoming life-expired.

Prototypes from two builders, BREL and Metro-Cammell, were ordered and tested on the main line. The BREL train was classified as 150/0 and the Met-Cam product as 151.

The BREL product was selected as the squadron replacement and two production designs of '150' were ordered from BREL York. The Class 150/1 sets were two-car sets without end gangways, while the later 150/2s were gangway fitted throughout.

Although basic in design these sets revolutionised rail travel and over the years much refurbishing has been done, resulting in a substantial number now sporting 2+2 seating.

For a period, a number of 150/1 sets were reformed with a 150/2 car marshalled between, providing three-car units for busy London Midland routes.

Currently two Class 150/1 sets are reformed with Class 150/2 DMSs formed in the middle to provide three-car sets for FGW local operations.

Class 150s can be found operating throughout England and Wales. ■

Above: *FGW operates 15 two-car and two three-car Class 150/1 sets, and these are allocated to Bristol and Exeter depots for local services. These sets are painted in the FGW all-over blue colour with FGW bodyside branding. Set No. 150102 is illustrated at Gloucester.* **CJM**

Below: *Northern Rail is the largest user of Class 150/1s with 30 two-car sets on its books, operating from Newton Heath depot. All sets carry the Northern-style blue, mauve and grey livery, with some sets sporting local pictogram images. Set No. 150116 is seen at Manchester Victoria.* **Antony Christie**

Left: *Members of the Class 150/1 production two-car sets are operated by London Midland, First Great Western and Northern Rail. London Midland has three sets allocated to Tyseley. These operate on the Bedford to Bletchley line and on limited services from Birmingham towards Worcester and Hereford. The three sets have been refurbished and sport the latest London Midland livery. Set No. 150107 is seen at Hereford from its DMSL vehicle, recognisable by having an opaque window at the inner end adjacent to the toilet compartment.* **CJM**

Diesel Multiple Units

Left Top: *When the follow-on order for Class 150 stock was placed, it was decided to order two-car sets with end gangways, thus allowing sets to operate together with full passenger and staff access. The modification only allowed a one-third-width driving cab but did increase flexibility. Also sliding staff doors were provided rather than the slam type. The sets are operated by Arriva Trains Wales, First Great Western and Northern Rail. ATW set No. 150283 is shown from its DMSL vehicle at Newport.* **CJM**

Left Middle: *Arriva Trains Wales sets are currently passing through works for overhaul and repainting into a revised Arriva Welsh Railways livery of two-tone turquoise, which suits the body profile well. Set No. 150236 is illustrated. Note the roof mounted aerial for on-board communications.* **CJM**

Left Below: *A total of 19 Class 150/2 sets are allocated to First Great Western, five to Bristol and the balance to Exeter. The sets are used on Avon, Devon and Cornish main line and branch line services and seat 116 standard class passengers in each set. All but two sets are painted in FGW local lines colours, as shown on set No. 150261 at Bristol Temple Meads.* **CJM**

Below: *The two Class 150/2s operated by FGW which are not in local lines colours are Nos. 150202/216 which sport FGW blue. These received this colour scheme as they arrived in the west after the remainder of the fleet had been painted and branded. Set No. 150216 is illustrated.* **CJM**

Right: *A fleet of 29 Class 150/2s is operated by the Northern Rail franchise, allocated to Manchester Newton Heath. Sets are painted in standard Northern Rail livery, but a considerable number sport line of route advertising, carefully designed and placed towards the centre of the vehicles. Set No. 150228 is seen at Knottingley sporting Yorkshire livery.* **CJM**

Right Middle: *FGW operates two three-car Class 150/9 sets, formed of Class 150/1 driving cars, with a Class 150/2 DMS marshalled between. The two Class 150/2 cars could not operate together as neither had a toilet. FGW also saw a need to operate some three-car sets in the Bristol/Exeter area. Set No. 150927 is illustrated.* **Antony Christie**

Below: *Two different designs of front end exist on the Class 150 fleet. The Class 150/0s and 150/1s have a full-width cab, while the Class 150/2s have a one-third-width cab layout. Equipment postions are: A: Radio aerial, B: Route display, C: Lamp bracket, D: Light cluster housing one headlight and one dual marker/tail light, E: BSI coupling, F: Electrical/pneumatic connection box, G: Obstacle deflector, H: Warning horns.* **Both: CJM**

Diesel Multiple Units

Left Top: *A large number of different interior layouts exist within the Class 150 fleet, with all sets having seen major refurbishment and upgrade since original construction. Some sets retain 2+3 high-density seating, while others, suitable for longer distance work, have 2+2 seating with some seats grouped around tables. This view shows the interior of FGW Class 150/2 No. 150216 which retains 2+3 seating.* **CJM**

Left Middle: *Most of the First Great Western Class 150/2 sets now have refurbished 2+2 interiors as shown in this view of set No. 150248. If this and the above view are compared this is the same area of the vehicle, directly behind the driving cab transverse walkway.* **CJM**

Below: *The driving cab of a Class 150/2 set, showing refurbished condition with a driver's reminder appliance and sander fitted.* **CJM**

Fact File

The 70 single-car Class 153s were rebuilt from 35 two-car Class 155 Leyland sets for secondary and branch line use, where on grounds of economy two-car trains could not be justified.

The rebuilding work was undertaken by Hunslet-Barclay of Kilmarnock and included the fitting of a very small cab in the original vestibule end of each '155' car, and building a new cab end.

The vehicles, usually referred to as 'bubble cars', are operated by five TOCs on branch line work. Interiors are refurbished in the 2+2 style with a bicycle and luggage space as well as a toilet at one end. ∎

Number range:	153301-153385
Introduced:	As 153 - 1991-1992
	Originally as Class 155 2-car sets - 1987-1988
Original build:	Leyland Bus, Workington
Rebuilt (single car) by:	Hunslet-Barclay, Kilmarnock
Formation:	DMSL
Vehicle numbers:	52301-52335, 57351-57387
Vehicle length:	76ft 5 in (23.29m)
Height:	12ft 3⅜in (3.75m)
Width:	8ft 10in (2.69m)
Seating:	66 or 72S depending on operator
Internal layout:	2+2
Gangway:	Throughout
Toilets:	1
Weight:	41.2 tonnes
Brake type:	Air EP
Bogie type:	Powered - BREL P3-10
	Trailer - BREL BT38
Power unit:	1 x Cummins NT855R5
Transmission:	Hydraulic
Transmission type:	Voith T211r
Horsepower (total):	285hp (213kW)
Max speed:	75mph (121km/h)
Coupling type:	BSI
Multiple restriction:	Class 14x, 15x, 170, 172 series
Door type:	Single-leaf sliding plug
Body structure:	Aluminium alloy on steel frame
Owner:	Angel Trains, Porterbrook
Operator:	Northern Rail, East Midlands Trains, Arriva Trains Wales, Greater Anglia, First Great Western
Notes:	Rebuilt from 35 Class 155 twin sets

Below: *First Great Western operates a fleet of 14 single-car Class 153 'Bubble' vehicles, allocated to Exeter for use on branch line services, as well as some longer distance duties. A few years ago all the FGW vehicles were repainted into FGW local lines livery with location, attraction and people's names on the lower body section; in recent times these have been removed due to corrosion of the bodyside, and the vehicles repainted into FGW blue, as displayed by set No. 153369 viewed from its small cab end.* **CJM**

Above: *Class 153 bodyside equipment positions. No. 1 (original cab) on right. A: Toilet water filler port, B: Roof aerial, C: Radiator, D: Door open warning light, E: Cummins NT855R5 engine, F: Battery box, G: Cooler water filler port, H: Fuel tank. Vehicle No. 52306 forming set No. 153306 is illustrated.* **CJM**

Left: *Front end arrangement for Class 153 set No. 153372 showing the No. 1 or original cab. A: Roof aerial, B: Destination indicator, C: Front gangway door, D: Group Standard light cluster with one headlight and one dual white marker/red tail light on each side, E: BSI coupling with pneumatic connection, electrical connections below behind roll cover panel, F: Emergency jumper connection socket, G: Warning horns, H: Obstacle deflector plate.* **CJM**

Below: *A total of 18 Class 153s are operated by the Northern Rail franchise, allocated to Leeds Neville Hill depot and found throughout the BR system. The vehicles carry standard Northern Rail blue, mauve and grey livery with the operator's website address prominent on the bodyside. Set No. 153330 is seen departing from Doncaster on a Sheffield service. This vehicle is one of seven of the Northern fleet owned by Porterbrook Leasing; the remainder are owned by Angel Trains.* **CJM**

Diesel Multiple Units

Traction Recognition

Above: *Eight of the Class 153s are operated by Arriva Trains Wales, mainly deployed on West Wales routes as well as on the Cardiff Queen Street to Cardiff Bay 'shuttle'. Seen from its original 'large' cab, set No. 153303 heads towards Cardiff Bay from Cardiff Queen Street in summer 2013. Three of the Arriva Trains Wales '153s' are owned by Porterbrook and the remainder by Angel Trains.* **CJM**

Right Middle: *Nottingham Eastcroft is the home to 17 Class 153s owned by Angel Trains and Porterbrook and operated by East Midlands Trains. These vehicles carry the Stagecoach-based blue (outer suburban) livery. Set No. 153384 is seen at Doncaster from its small cab end.* **CJM**

Right Bottom: *The rural lines of the Greater Anglia franchise have a fleet of five Class 153s based at Norwich Crown point depot, operating on the branch routes radiating from Norwich. All now carry the Greater Anglia off-white body colour offset by orange passenger doors. The sets have all recently been refurbished. Set No. 153306 is illustrated at Norwich.* **Nathan Williamson**

Traction Recognition

Class 155 'Super Sprinter'

Number range:	155341-155347
Introduced:	1988
Built by:	Leyland Bus, Workington
Formation:	DMSL+DMS
Vehicle numbers:	DMSL - 52341-52347
	DMS - 57341-57347
Vehicle length:	76ft 5 in (23.29m)
Height:	12ft 3⅜in (3.75m)
Width:	8ft 10in (2.69m)
Seating:	Total - 156S
	DMSL - 76S
	DMS - 80S
Internal layout:	2+2
Gangway:	Throughout
Toilets:	DMSL - 1
Weight:	Total - 77.8 tonnes
	DMSL - 39.2 tonnes
	DMS - 38.6 tonnes
Brake type:	Air EP
Bogie type:	Powered - BREL P3-10
	Trailer - BREL BT38
Power unit:	1 x Cummins NT855R5 of 285hp
	(213 kW) per vehicle
Transmission:	Hydraulic
Transmission type:	Voith T211r
Horsepower (total):	570hp (426kW)
Max speed:	75mph (121 km/h)
Coupling type:	BSI
Multiple restriction:	Class 14x, 15x, 170, 172 series
Door type:	Single-leaf sliding plug
Body structure:	Aluminium alloy on steel frame
Owner:	Porterbrook Leasing
Operator:	Northern

Fact File

These seven Class 155s are all that is left of the original order of 42 sets, the other 35 having been rebuilt into single-car Class 153s (see previous section).

Built by Leyland and using bus technology and original fittings, these sets are now refurbished with 2+2 facing and uni-directional seats; one toilet is provided per set. The fleet is maintained at Leeds Neville Hill depot and can usually be found operating in and around the Leeds area under the Northern Rail franchise. ■

Below: *The Leeds Neville Hill-allocated Class 155s, used for West Yorkshire services, are now all painted in Northern Rail livery with pictogram line of route advertising pictures applied as part of the livery colour sweep. Viewed from its 80-seat DMS coach, set No. 155343 is seen at Harrogate on 30 March 2014.* **John Binch**

Above: *Viewed from its DMSL coach, set No. 155345 is seen in the north-facing bay at York station on 17 October 2013. Owned by Porterbrook Leasing and fitted with a BSI auto coupling, these sets can operate in multiple with 'Pacer', 'Sprinter' and 'Turbostar' sets, but usually operate on their own.*
Brian Garrett

Right: *Class 155 front end equipment positions. A: Roof-mounted radio aerial, B: Destination indicator, C: Lamp bracket, D: Front gangway door (covered by plastic outer door), E: Group Standard light cluster (from outer edge white marker light, headlight, red tail light), F: Warning horn, G: BSI coupling with pneumatic connection, electrical connections below behind roll cover panel, H: Emergency jumper socket, I: Obstacle deflector plate.* **CJM**

Diesel Multiple Units

Class 156 'Super Sprinter'

Number range:	156401-156514
Introduced:	1987-1989
Built by:	Metro-Cammell, Birmingham
Formation:	DMSL+DMS
Vehicle numbers:	DMSL - 52401-52514
	DMS - 57401-57514
Vehicle length:	75ft 6in (23.03m)
Height:	12ft 6in (3.81m)
Width:	8ft 11in (2.73m)
Seating:	Total - 140-152S
	DMSL - 68-74S
	DMS - 72-78S
Internal layout:	2+2
Gangway:	Throughout
Toilets:	DMSL - 1
Weight:	Total - 74.7 tonnes
	DMSL - 38.6 tonnes
	DMS - 36.1 tonnes
Brake type:	Air EP
Bogie type:	Powered - BREL P3-10
	Trailer - BREL BT38
Power unit:	1 x Cummins NT855R5 of 285hp (213kW) per vehicle
Transmission:	Hydraulic
Transmission type:	Voith T211r
Horsepower (total):	570hp (426kW)
Max speed:	75mph (121km/h)
Coupling type:	BSI
Multiple restriction:	Class 14x, 15x, 170, 172 series
Door type:	Single-leaf sliding
Body structure:	Steel
Owner:	Porterbrook, Angel Trains
Operator:	East Midlands Trains, Greater Anglia, Northern, First ScotRail

Fact File

The largest batch of 'Super Sprinter' DMUs ordered by the then BRB Provincial Sector came from Birmingham-based Metro-Cammell and were delivered between 1987 and 1989.

Although destined for outer suburban use, the sets have a top speed of 75mph (121km/h).

Seating is in the 2+2 low-density style with a mix of airline and group seats. Today configurations depend on the operator, with a mix of original, Chapman and Richmond seats.

External equipment follows the design of the Class 153 and 155.

In 2014, four national operators use the fleet.

Few major modifications have been made since this fleet was delivered, which is among of the most reliable in the UK.

Some sets operated by Northern carry location and route promotional liveries under sponsorship deals. ■

Above: *The largest operator of Class 156 'Super Sprinter' sets is First ScotRail, which in summer 2014 operated a fleet 48 units based at Corkerhill depot in Glasgow. The 2+2 seated units operate longer distance diesel services and provide seated accommodation for 142 passengers. No first class area is provided. Fitted with standard BSI couplers, the sets can operate with Class 158 and 170 stock also operated by First ScotRail. Set No. 156500 painted in Saltire blue and white is seen at Springburn.* **Murdoch Currie**

Right: *Northern Rail operates a fleet of 42 long-distance Class 156s, allocated to Heaton depot in Newcastle and Allerton depot near Liverpool. With the exception of one set in pictogram colours, the fleet carries standard Northern Rail blue, mauve and grey. Seating is for 146 standard class passengers. Set No. 156428 is illustrated at Manchester Victoria.* **Antony Christie**

Above: *Nottingham Eastcroft depot has an allocation of 15 Class 156s operated by East Midland Trains; painted in outer-suburban blue livery the sets operate longer distance duties. Set No. 156473 is illustrated.* **Brian Garrett**

Right: *Greater Anglia has a small fleet of nine Class 156s allocated to Norwich Crown Point for Anglia branch line duties. The sets are all refurbished and sport Anglia white livery, and the interiors have 2+2 seating in a mix of airline and group seats around tables. The interior of set No. 156422 is shown.* **Nathan Williamson**

Traction Recognition

Sub-class:	158/0 (2-car)	158/0 (3-car)
Number range:	158701-158741 / 158763-158797 / 158799-158872	158752-158759 / 158798
Introduced:	1990-1992	1990-1992 (3-car) 2000
Built by:	BREL Derby	BREL Derby
Formation:	DMSL(A) + DMSL(B) or	DMSL(A)+MS+DMSL(B)
	DMSL(A) + DMCL	
Vehicle numbers:	DMSL(A) - 57701-57745 / 57763-57797 / 57799-57872	DMSL(A) - 52752-52759 / 52798
	DMSL(B) or DMCL - 52701-52745 / 763-797 / 799-872	MSL - 58702-58716
		DMSB(B) - 57752-57759 / 57798
Vehicle length:	76ft 1¾in (23.20m)	76ft 1¾in (23.20m)
Height:	12ft 6in (3.81m)	12ft 6in (3.81m)
Width:	9ft 3¼in (2.82m)	9ft 3¼in (2.82m)
Seating:	Total - 128-146S - 15-32F / 96-127S*	Total - 204S
	DMSL - 64-72S	DMSL(A) - 68S
	DMCL - 13-32F / 32-53S	MS - 66S + 3 tip up
		DMSL(B) - 70S
Internal layout:	2+2S 2+2F	2+2
Gangway:	Throughout	Throughout
Toilets:	DMSL, DMCL, MSL - 1	DMSL - 1
Weight:	Total - 77 tonnes	Total - 115.5 tonnes
	DMSL - 38.5 tonnes	DMSL - 38.5 tonnes
	DMCL - 38.5 tonnes	MS - 38.5 tonnes
		DMSL - 38.5 tonnes
Brake type:	Air EP	Air EP
Bogie type:	Powered - BREL P4	Powered - BREL P4
	Trailer - BREL T4	Trailer - BREL T4
Power unit:	158701-814 1 × NT855R of 350hp (260kW) per vehicle	1 × NT855R of 350hp per vehicle
	158815-862 1 × Perkins 2006-TWH of 350hp	
	(260kW) per vehicle	
	158863-872 1 × NT855R of 400hp (300kW) per vehicle	
Transmission:	Hydraulic	Hydraulic
Transmission type:	Voith T211r	Voith T211r
Horsepower (total):	158701-158862 - 700hp (522kW)	1050hp (780kW)
	158863-158872 - 800hp (597kW)	
Max speed:	90mph (145km/h)	90mph (145km/h)
Coupling type:	BSI	BSI
Multiple restriction:	Class 14x, 15x, 170, 172	Class 14x, 15x, 170, 172
Door type:	Bi-parting sliding plug	Bi-parting sliding plug
Special features:	RETB ready	RETB ready
Body structure:	Aluminium	Aluminium
Owner:	Porterbrook, Angel Trains	Porterbrook
Operator:	FSR, Northern, FGW, East Midlands Trains, Arriva	Northern, FGW
Notes:	* Depending on layout	
	Northern 3-car sets fitted with chemical retention toilets	

Diesel Multiple Units

Fact File

In the late 1980s the British Railways Board, then Provincial Sector, was in need of main line capability stock to operate long distance services. A new design of multiple unit was put forward and a sizeable fleet ordered from the then BREL Works in Derby, using aluminium body technology and including a high-quality passenger environment, good seating, carpeted throughout and fitted with air conditioning. Classified as '158', the first 'Express' vehicles emerged in 1990.

With various follow-on orders, a fleet of over 200 two- and three-car sets was built.

The Class 158s soon became commonplace in all areas of the UK, operating short distance domestic services as well as long distance cross-country trains.

Today a large number of different interiors can be found, as operators tailor trains to suit their local needs. Some sets have first class seating in differing qualities.

All seating in standard class is 2+2, while first class is a mix of 2+2 and 2+1. A wide diversity of external liveries is carried.

Few modifications have been carried out externally since construction.

The fleet has now been refurbished with, in the main, the quality interior retained.

Several extra three-car sets have been formed to operate on First Great Western; these are formed of three driving cars. Extra two-car sets were also modified for South West Trains.

ETRMS equipment is fitted to the Arriva Trains Wales fleet. ∎

158/8	158/9	158/0
158880-158890	158901-158910	158950-158961
1991, as 158/8 - 2007	1991	1992 (as 3-car 2008)
BREL Derby, Wabtec Doncaster	BREL Derby	BREL Derby
DMCL+DMSL	DMSL(A)+DMSL(B)	DMSL+DMSL+DMSL
DMCL - 52737-52814 series	DMSL(A) - 52901-52910	DMSL - 527xx and 577xx series
DMSL - 57737-57814 series	DMSL(B) - 57901-57910	DMSL - 527xx and 577xx series
		DMSL - 527xx and 577xx series
76ft 1¾in (23.20m)	76ft 1¾in (23.20m)	76ft 1¾in (23.20m)
12ft 6in (3.81m)	12ft 6in (3.81m)	12ft 6in (3.81m)
9ft 3¼in (2.82m)	9ft 3¼in (2.82m)	9ft 3¼in (2.82m)
Total - 13F/114S	Total - 142S	Total - 200S - 202S
DMCL - 13F/44S	DMSL(A) - 70S	DMSL - 66S
DMSL - 70S	DMSL(B) - 72S	DMSL - 68S
		DMSL - 66S or 68S
2+2S, 2+1F	2+2	2+2
Throughout	Throughout	Throughout
DMCL, DMSL - 1	DMSL - 1	DMSL - 1
Total - 77 tonnes	Total - 77 tonnes	Total - 115.5 tonnes
DMCL - 38.5 tonnes	DMSL(A) - 38.5 tonnes	DMSL - 38.5 tonnes
DMSL - 38.5 tonnes	DMSL(B) - 38.5 tonnes	DMSL - 38.5 tonnes
		DMSL - 38.5 tonnes
Air EP	Air EP	Air EP
Powered - BREL P4	Powered - BREL P4	Powered - BREL P4
Trailer - BREL T4	Trailer - BREL T4	Trailer - BREL T4
1 x NT855R of 350hp per vehicle	1 x NT855R of 350hp per vehicle	1 x NT855R of 350hp per vehicle
Hydraulic	Hydraulic	Hydraulic
Voith T211r	Voith T211r	Voith T211r
700hp (522kW)	700hp (522kW)	1050hp (780kW)
90mph (145km/h)	90mph (145km/h)	90mph (145km/h)
BSI	BSI	BSI
Class 14x, 15x, 170, 172	Class 14x, 15x, 170, 172	Class 14x, 15x, 170, 172
Bi-parting sliding plug	Bi-parting sliding plug	Bi-parting sliding plug
RETB ready	RETB ready	RETB ready
Aluminium	Aluminium	Aluminium
Porterbrook	Eversholt	Porterbrook
South West Trains	West Yorkshire PTE	First Great Western

Diesel Multiple Units

Right: *The Regional Railways 'Express' units introduced from 1990 and classified as 158 were a turning point in high-quality DMU design in the UK. Originally built by BREL the design used state-of-the-art aluminium technology with a quality 2+2 interior. Over the past 20-plus years in service some major refurbishment and upgrades have taken place. Now painted in Scottish Railways Saltire livery No. 158867 is illustrated, showing a Scottish light cluster modification and revised obstacle deflector plate.* **Bill Wilson**

Diesel Multiple Units

Above: *Class 158 main equipment positions. A: Emergency door controls, B: Passenger door controls, C: Air conditioning intake, D: Emergency opening hopper window, E: Air ventilation grille, F: Door release warning light, G: GPS pick up, H: Radiator, I: Engine, J: Local controls, K: Battery isolating switch, L: Battery box, M: Fuel tank will filler port to left. Equipment positions also apply to Class 159s.* **CJM**

Left Middle: *Class 158 front end equipment. A: Air conditioning roof vent, B: Destination indicator, C: Front gangway door (solid type), D: Light cluster with a headlight and combined white marker and red tail LED light on each side (this is a modification to the original design which had three lights each side, white marker, head and red tail light), E: BSI coupling with pneumatic connection, electrical connections below behind roll cover panel, F: Emergency air socket (behind flap), G: Warning horns, H: Obstacle deflector.* **CJM**

Left Bottom: *For longer distance East Midlands Trains services, Nottingham Eastcroft has a fleet of 25 two-car Class 158s. These are painted in the main line white livery and have a raised swirl in the bottom blue line just behind the leading passenger doors. Three of the East Midlands Trains batch, Nos. 158863-865, are fitted with the more powerful 400hp engines. Set No. 158812 is illustrated, which is owned by Porterbrook Leasing.* **Antony Christie**

Above: *The Arriva Trains Wales depots of Cardiff and Machynlleth operate 24 refurbished Class 158s for longer distance 'main line duties'. The fleet carries the latest Welsh Trains two-tone turquoise livery. Set No. 158839 is illustrated. All these sets are fitted with ERTMS signalling and control equipment.* **CJM**

Right and Below: *South West Trains have 11 two-car Class 158s painted in SWT white livery allocated to Salisbury for operation on non-Class 159 services. The sets are refurbished and have a first class area of 13 seats in the DMCL vehicle. Below is set No. 158885 from its DMCL coach. On the right is the standard class seating area. These sets are furnished as the Class 159s.* **CJM**

Above and Left: *First Great Western operates two two-car and 13 three-car Class 158s; these are allocated to Bristol and work long distance services such as the Cardiff-Portsmouth route. All but one of the three-car sets are formed of three driving cars. These sets are standard class only. All are finished by FGW local lines colours. In the above view, three-car set No. 158958 arrives at Southampton with a Portsmouth to Cardiff service. On the left is two-car set No. 158763 at Bristol Temple Meads. Both:* **CJM**

Below: *Northern Rail is the operator of the ten Eversholt-owned Class 158/9 sets operated on West Yorkshire services. Allocated to Leeds Neville Hill, these sets carry Yorkshire pictogram liveries and were the sets originally finished in West Yorkshire PTE maroon and cream. Set No. 158901 is illustrated at Doncaster.* **CJM**

15

Above: *Due to passenger levels, Northern has eight three-car Class 158s allocated to Neville Hill for longer distance work. These sets have the blue, mauve and grey livery on the driving cars, while the central Motor Standard is in all-over dark blue. Set No. 158753 is seen at Preston.*
Robin Ralston

Right: *Twenty-seven standard Class 158s are on Norther Rail books, allocated to Neville Hill and Newton Heath depots. These are finished in a mix of standard and pictogram liveries. Set No. 158872 is seen at Doncaster.* **CJM**

The interior of a Northern Rail Class 158, showing the 2+2 seating, high back seats, hinged arm-rests and above seat luggage racks. Seating is in both airline and group layouts.
Nathan Williamson

Sub-class:	159/0	159/1
Number range:	159001-159022	159101-159108
Former number range:	-	158800-158814 range
Introduced:	1992-1993	As 158 - Originally 1991
		As 159 - 2006 (Rebuilt from Class 158)
Built by:	BREL Derby,	Rebuilt: Wabtec, Doncaster
	fitted out by Rosyth Dockyard	
Formation:	DMCL+MSL+DMSL	DMCL+MSL+DMSL
Vehicle numbers:	DMCL - 52873-52894	DMCL - 52800-52811 range
	MSL - 58718-58739	MSL - 58701-58717 range
	DMSL - 57873-57894	DMSL - 57800-57811 range
Vehicle length:	76ft 1¾in (23.20m)	76ft 1¾in (23.20m)
Height:	12ft 6in (3.81m)	12ft 6in (3.81m)
Width:	9ft 3¼in (2.82m)	9ft 3¼in (2.82m)
Seating:	Total - 23F/170S	Total - 24F/170S
	DMCL - 23F/28S	DMCL - 24F/28S
	MSL - 70S	MSL - 70S
	DMSL - 72S	DMSL - 72S
Internal layout:	2+1F/2+2S	2+1F/2+2S
Gangway:	Throughout	Throughout
Toilets:	DMCL, DMSL, MSL - 1	DMCL, DMSL, MSL - 1
Weight:	Total - 114.3 tonnes	Total - 114.3 tonnes
	DMCL - 38.5 tonnes	DMCL - 38.5 tonnes
	MSL - 38 tonnes	MSL - 38 tonnes
	DMSL - 37.8 tonnes	DMSL - 37.8 tonnes
Brake type:	Air EP	Air EP
Bogie type:	Powered - BREL P4-4	Powered - BREL P4-4
	Trailer - BREL T4-4	Trailer - BREL T4-4
Power unit:	1 x Cummins NTA855R of 400hp (300kW)	1 x Cummins NTA855R of 350hp (260kW)
	per vehicle	per vehicle
Transmission:	Hydraulic	Hydraulic
Transmission type:	Voith T211r	Voith T211r
Horsepower (total):	1,200hp (900kW)	1,050hp (780kW)
Max speed:	90mph (145km/h)	90mph (145km/h)
Coupling type:	BSI	BSI
Multiple restriction:	14x, 15x, 170, 172	14x, 15x, 170, 172
Door type:	Bi-parting swing plug	Bi-parting swing plug
Body structure:	Aluminium	Aluminium
Owner:	Porterbrook	Porterbrook
Operator:	South West Trains	South West Trains

Fact File

Built as Class 158s and upgraded before entry to service by Babcock Rail, the original 22 Class 159s were the 'Rolls-Royce' of the 'Express' build and modified especially for Network SouthEast.

Replacing loco-hauled services on the Waterloo to West of England route, these sets have proved to be most popular.

Seating is in 2+2 for standard and 2+1 for first class.

The sets are allocated to Salisbury and always maintained to a high standard.

In 2006-07 an additional eight three-car Class 158s were converted to Class 159 standards by Wabtec at Doncaster to supplement SWT services and replace Class 170s.

All units are painted in SWT 'white' express livery and operate on the Waterloo to Exeter route. ■

Above: *The Class 159/0s are recognisable from the 159/1s by having four opening hopper windows on each side of each coach. These are for emergency use as the sets are fully air conditioned. Set No. 159017 is seen at Salisbury led by the DMCL vehicle.* **CJM**

Below: *The intermediate vehicle of the Class 159 is a MS, seating 70 in the 2+2 layout in a mix of airline and group seats. In terms of equipment, these are the same as driving cars, just lacking the cab compartment. Vehicle No. 58734 is illustrated.* **CJM**

Bottom: *First class seating on Class 159/0s is in the 2+1 layout with 23 seats per three-car train provided. On 159/0s each seat has a power supply and down lighting.* **CJM**

Left: *The 22 original Class 159/0s, now operated in common with the Class 159/1s, are allocated to Salisbury depot for the Waterloo to Exeter route. The sets usually operate with their DMCL vehicle at the London end. Set No. 159016 passes Vauxhall coupled to a Class 158 with its DMSL nearest the camera. On the right a Class 455/9 heads south on a Woking service.* **CJM**

Above: *In 2006 an extra eight Class 159s were introduced, by converting existing Class 158 stock. The 'new' 159s were slightly lower powered as the vehicles had 350hp engines rather than the 400hp units of the 159/1. The vehicles are also recognisable from the outside with only two opening hopper windows per side of each vehicle. Set No. 159108 is seen at Reading. Seating is slightly different in the DMCL vehicle with one less first class seat.* **Darren Ford**

Left: *Class 159 cab layout. Equipment positions also apply to Class 158 stock. A: Door release light, B: Automatic warning system 'sunflower' indicator and buzzer, C: Driver's reminder appliance (DRA), D: Cab ventilator, E: One shot sander button, F: Cab fan, G: Headlight, marker light and tail light switch with display below, H: Main reservoir and brake cylinder pressure gauge, I: Speedometer, J: Couple button, K: Uncouple button (below cover), L: Signal button, M: Transmission fault unit, N: Transmission fault train, P: Wheel slip protection (WSP) fault, Q: Engine stop button, R: Engine start button, S: Fault lamp test button, T: Safety systems isolated indicator, U: Brake controller, V: Windscreen wiper control, W: Warning horn valve, X: Automatic warning system (AWS) reset button, Y: Power controller, Z: Master key switch. The cab illustrated is from Class 159/1 No. 159102.* **CJM**

Above: *A Class 159/1 intermediate Motor Standard vehicle. These are the same as the Class 159/0 vehicles except they are fitted with the slightly lower powered engine and have only two emergency opening hopper windows on each side. Car No. 58701 from set No. 159108 is illustrated. These MS cars were the original vehicles built for the Trans-Pennine three-car units but are now married with different driving cars.*
Antony Christie

Right: *Class 159 front end equipment positions. A: Route indicator display, B: Front gangway door (solid design), C: Light cluster, with headlight and dual white marker/red tail light on each side, D: Lamp bracket, E: BSI coupling with pneumatic connection, electrical connections below behind roll cover panel, F: Air warning horns, G: Emergency air connection (behind flap - open).* **CJM**

Class 165 'Network Turbo'

Sub-class:	165/0	165/1
Number range:	165001-165039	165101-165137
Introduced:	1990-1992	1992-1993
Built by:	BREL/ABB York	BREL/ABB York
Formation:	165001-165028 - DMSL+DMS	165101-165117 - DMCL+MS+DMS
	165029-165039 - DMSL+MS+DMS	165118-165137 - DMCL+DMS
Vehicle numbers:	165001-165028:	165101-165117:
	DMSL - 58801-58822, 58873-58878	DMCL - 58953-58969
	DMS - 58834-58855, 58867-58872	MS - 55415-55431
	165029-165039:	DMS - 58916-58932
	DMSL - 58823-58833	165118-165137:
	MS - 55404-55414	DMCL - 58879-58898
	DMS - 58856-58866	DMS - 58933-58952
Vehicle length:	DMSL - 75ft 2½in (22.92m)	DMCL - 75ft 2½in (22.92m)
	MS - 74ft 6½in (22.72m)	MS - 74ft 6½in (22.72m)
	DMS - 75ft 2½in (22.92m)	DMS - 75ft 2½in (22.92m)
Height:	12ft 5¼in (3.79m)	12ft 5¼in (3.79m)
Width:	9ft 2½in (2.81m)	9ft 2½in (2.81m)
Seating:	165001-165028 - Total - 176S + 7 tip up	165101-165117 - Total - 16F/270S
	DMSL - 82S + 7 tip up	DMCL - 16F/66S
	DMS - 94S	MS - 106S
	165029-165039 - Total - 282S + 7 tip up	DMS - 98S
	DMSL - 82S + 7 tip up	165118-165137 - Total - 16F/170S
	MS - 106S	DMCL - 16F/72S
	DMS - 94S	DMS - 98S
Internal layout:	2+2/2+3	2+2F/2+3S
Gangway:	Within set	Within set
Toilets:	DMSL - 1	DMCL - 1
Weight:	165001-165028 - Total - 79.5 tonnes	165101-165117 - Total - 112 tonnes
	DMSL - 40.1 tonnes	DMCL - 38 tonnes
	DMS - 39.4 tonnes	MS - 37 tonnes
	165029-165039 - Total - 116.5 tonnes	DMS - 37 tonnes
	DMSL - 40.1 tonnes	165118-165137 - Total - 75 tonnes
	MS - 37 tonnes	DMCL - 38 tonnes
	DMS - 39.4 tonnes	DMS - 37 tonnes
Brake type:	Air EP	Air EP
Bogie type:	Powered - BREL P3-17	Powered - BREL P3-17
	Trailer - BREL T3-17	Trailer - BREL T3-17
Power unit:	1 x Perkins 2006TWH of 350hp (260kW)	1 x Perkins 2006TWH of 350hp (260kW)
	per vehicle	per vehicle
Transmission:	Hydraulic	Hydraulic
Transmission type:	Voith T211r	Voith T211r
Horsepower (total):	165001-165028 - 700hp (520kW)	165101-165117 - 1,050hp (780kW)
	165029-165039 - 1,050hp (780kW)	165118-165137 - 700hp (520kW)
Max speed:	75mph (121km/h)	75mph (121km/h)
Coupling type:	BSI	BSI
Multiple restriction:	Class 165, 166, 168, 172 only	Class 165, 166, 168, 172 only
Door type:	Bi-parting swing plug	Bi-parting swing plug
Special features:	Chiltern ATP/trip-cocks, air conditioning	
Body structure:	Welded aluminium	Welded aluminium
Owner:	Angel Trains	Angel Trains
Operator:	Chiltern	First Great Western

Designed and introduced by Network SouthEast to modernise the Chiltern Lines from Marylebone and the Paddington suburban network, these two- and three-car trains brought new levels of comfort to these routes.

On privatisation Chiltern Railways acquired all the Class 165/0 sets, while Thames, the then Paddington local operator, took all the 165/1s.

Chiltern later undertook refurbishment with new interiors, eliminating first class seats

and increasing the number of passengers per coach. To permit operation over the London Underground-equipped line between Harrow-on-the-Hill and Amersham 'trip-cock' apparatus is fitted.

The Thames sets now operated by First Great Western were refurbished in 2010-11 and still retain first and standard class seating. All are painted in the First Group 'dynamic lines' livery. ∎

Above: *Both Chiltern Railways and FGW operate Class 165s in two- and three-car formation. The 165/0s are operated by Chiltern and now sport some detail differences from the once common design. These sets have a modified front end light cluster and now have air conditioning thus seeing the removal of the original hopper windows. Painted in Chiltern Railways blue and white, three-car set No. 165039 is illustrated.* **Nathan Williamson**

Right Middle: *Chiltern Railways operates 28 two-car Class 165/0s, all are allocated to Aylesbury. All two- and three-car sets are one class, the original first class having been removed several years ago. The seating is in the 2+2 and 2+3 style. All Chiltern operated Class 165s are fitted with what looks like a third rail shoe beam on the leading bogie. This is the support for the trip-cock apparatus used on the LT signalled sections of the line. Set No. 165022 is illustrated.* **John Binch**

Right Below: *An elevated view of a Chiltern Railways Class 165 intermediate Motor Standard, showing the revised roof layout with air conditioning equipment. The end of vehicle exhaust stack is also clearly visible, as is the slight livery change of the doors to meet the needs of the Disabilities Discrimination Act which requires doors to be visually identifiable for sight impaired passengers. Car No. 56414 from set No. 165039 is shown.* **Antony Christie**

Above and Left: *The Class 165s operated by First Great Western on Thames line services and based at Reading come in both two- and three-car formations. They are not air conditioned and retain hopper windows. First class seating is retained in the DMCL vehicles. Above is three-car set No. 165108, and left is two-car set No. 165137. Both are seen at West Ealing and have their DMCL coach leading. Both:* **CJM**

Below: *The intermediate MS vehicles of the three-car Class 165/1s for FGW seat 106 in the 2+3 style. These sets will remain on the Thames Valley routes until the CrossRail and Great Western electrification is fully introduced; they will then cascade to other FGW lines. Car No. 55431 illustrated.* **CJM**

Right: *Class 165 front end layout. Equipment positions are the same on Chiltern Class 165/0 sets but a revised more streamlined light cluster has been installed. A: Destination indicator, B: Forward facing camera, C: Group Standard light cluster with, from the outside, white marker, head and red tail lights, D: Emergency air supply socket, E: BSI coupling with pneumatic connection, electrical connections below behind roll cover panel.* **CJM**

Below: *First Great Western Class 165 standard class interior, showing 2+3 seats in a mix of airline and group, above seat luggage racks and a passenger information system at roof height by the door positions.* **Antony Christie**

Diesel Multiple Units

Number range:	166201-166221
Introduced:	1992-1993
Built by:	BREL/ABB York
Formation:	DMSL+MS+DMCL
Vehicle numbers:	DMSL - 58101-58121
	MS - 58601-58621
	DMCL - 58122-58142
Vehicle length:	DMSL, DMCL - 75ft 2½in (22.92m)
	MS - 74ft 6½in (22.72m)
Height:	12ft 5¼in (3.79m)
Width:	9ft 2½in (2.81m)
Seating:	Total - 16F/243S
	DMSL - 84S, MS - 91S
	DMCL - 16F/68S
Internal layout:	2+2/2+3S, 2+1F
Gangway:	Within set
Toilets:	DMSL, DMCL - 1
Weight:	Total - 117.2 tonnes
	DMSL - 39.6 tonnes, MS - 38 tonnes
	DMCL - 39.6 tonnes
Brake type:	Air EP
Bogie type:	Powered - BREL P3-17, Trailer - BREL T3-17
Power unit:	1 x Perkins 2006TWH of 350hp (260kW) per vehicle
Transmission:	Hydraulic
Transmission type:	Voith T211r
Horsepower (total):	1,050hp (780kW)
Max speed:	90mph (145km/h)
Coupling type:	BSI
Multiple restriction:	Class 165, 166 and 168 only
Door type:	Bi-parting swing plug
Special features:	Air conditioning
Body structure:	Welded aluminium
Owner:	Angel Trains
Operator:	First Great Western

Fact File

Introduced as the long distance or main line version of the Class 165, the 'Network Express Turbo' was designed for use on the 'Express' network from Paddington to Oxford and Newbury, taking over from loco-hauled operations.

These sets were air conditioned from new and therefore have only emergency hopper windows.

First class seating is now only provided in one driving car behind the cab position. Seating is a mix of 2+2 and 2+3. Luggage stacks are provided.

All Class 166s carry the First Great Western 'dynamic lines' livery and are allocated to the new Reading depot. ■

Left: *Class 166 front end equipment. A: Destination indicator, B: Forward facing CCTV camera, C: White marker light, D: Headlight, E: Red tail light, F: Emergency air connection, G: BSI coupling with pneumatic connection, H: Air warning horns, I: Electrical connections for coupling behind roll cover panel. Set No. 166209 is illustrated.* **CJM**

Right Above: *The 21 longer distance or 'Express' NSE-built 'Turbo' units operate the main line services as well as the Reading-Gatwick Airport corridor, they have air conditioning and a slightly improved travelling environment. Owned by Angel Trains and allocated to the new Reading depot, the units originally had first class seating in both driving cars, but this has now been removed from one vehicle to increase the number of standard class seats. Set No. 166201 is illustrated from its DMCL end at Oxford.* **CJM**

Right Middle: *The Class 166 intermediate vehicles are recognisable from the like carriages formed in three-car Class 165 sets by having only four opening hopper windows and the presence of air-conditioning equipment on the roof. MS No. 58614 from set No. 166214 is illustrated.* **CJM**

Below: *First class seating area in Class 166, located behind the driving compartment in the DMCL vehicle; 16 seats are provided mainly at tables. Reading lights are provided but no power sockets for passenger use.* **CJM**

Diesel Multiple Units

Diesel Multiple Units

Sub-class:	168/0	168/1	168/2
Design:	'Networker' outline	'Turbostar' outline	'Turbostar' outline
Number range:	168001-168005	168106-168113	168214-168219
Introduced:	1997-1998	2000-2002	2003-2006
Built by:	Adtranz Derby	Adtranz/Bombardier Derby	Bombardier Derby
Formation:	DMSL(A)+MSL+MS+DMSL(B)	168106 - 168107: DMSL(A)+MSL+MS+DMSL(B) 168108 - 168113: DMSL(A)+MS+DMSL(B)	168214, 168218-168219: DMSL(A)+MS+DMSL(B) 168215 - 168217: DMSL(A)+MS+MS+DMSL(B)
Vehicle numbers:	DMSL(A) - 58151-58155 MSL - 58651-58655 MS - 58451-58455 DMSL(B) - 58251-58255	DMSL(A) - 58156-58163 MSL - 58756-58757 MS - 58456-58463 DMSL(B) - 58256-58263	DMSL(A) - 58164 - 58169 MS - 58365-58367 MS - 58464-58469 DMSL(B) - 58264 - 58269
Vehicle length:	77ft 6in (23.62m)	77ft 6in (23.62m)	77ft 6in (23.62m)
Height:	12ft 4½in (3.77m)	12ft 4½in (3.77m)	12ft 4½in (3.77m)
Width:	8ft 10in (2.69m)	8ft 10in (2.69m)	8ft 10in (2.69m)
Seating:	Total - 275S DMSL(A) - 57S MSL - 73S MS - 77S DMSL(B) - 68S	168106-168107 - Total - 275S 168108-168113 - Total - 202S DMSL(A) - 57S MSL - 73S MS - 76S DMSL(B) - 69S	168214/218/219 - Total 202S 168215-168217 - Total 278S DMSL(A) - 57S MS - 76S MS - 76S DMSL(B) - 69S
Internal layout:	2+2	2+2	2+2
Gangway:	Within set	Within set	Within set
Toilets:	DMSL, MSL - 1	DMSL, MSL - 1	DMSL, MSL - 1
Weight:	168.8 tonnes DMSL(A) - 43.7 tonnes MSL - 41 tonnes MS - 40.5 tonnes DMSL(B) - 43.6 tonnes	168106-107 - 175.1 tonnes 168108-113 - 132.2 tonnes DMSL(A) - 45.2 tonnes MSL - 42.9 tonnes MS - 41.8 tonnes DMSL(B) - 45.2 tonnes	168214/218/219 - 134.9 tonnes 168215-168217 - 178.2 tonnes DMSL(A) - 45.4 tonnes MSL - 43.3 tonnes MS - 44 tonnes DMSL(B) - 45.5 tonnes
Brake type:	Air EP	Air EP	Air EP
Bogie type:	Powered - P3-23 Trailer - T3-23	Powered - P3-23 Trailer - T3-23	Powered - P3-23 Trailer - T3-23
Power unit:	1 x MTU 6R183TD13H of 422hp (315kW) per car	1 x MTU 6R183TD13H of 422hp (315kW) per car	1 x MTU 6R183TD13H of 422hp (315kW) per car
Transmission:	Hydraulic	Hydraulic	Hydraulic
Transmission type:	Voith T211r	Voith T211r	Voith T211r
Horsepower (total):	1,688hp (1,260kW)	168106-107 - 1,688hp (1,260kW) 168108-113 - 1,266hp (945kW)	168214/18/19 - 1,266hp (945kW) 168215-217 - 1,688hp (1,260kW)
Max speed:	100mph (160km/h)	100mph (160km/h)	100mph (160km/h)
Coupling type:	Outer - BSI Inner - Bar	Outer - BSI Inner - Bar	Outer - BSI Inner - Bar
Multiple restriction:	Class 165, 166, 168, 172	Class 165, 166, 168, 172	Class 165, 166, 168, 172
Door type:	Bi-parting swing plug	Bi-parting swing plug	Bi-parting swing plug
Special features:	Chiltern ATP, trip-cocks	Chiltern ATP, trip-cocks	Chiltern ATP, trip-cocks
Body structure:	Welded aluminium, bolt-on steel ends	Welded aluminium, bolt-on steel ends	Welded aluminium, bolt-on steel ends
Owner:	Porterbrook	Porterbrook, Eversholt	Porterbrook
Operator:	Chiltern Railways	Chiltern Railways	Chiltern Railways

Fact File

The first of the 'new generation' diesel units to be ordered were these Class 168 'Clubman' sets for Chiltern Railways. The design was the forerunner of the Class 170 'Turbostar' fleet which is now in use throughout the UK.

The first five 'Clubman' units, set out for one-class accommodation, were built to a different body profile and front end design from the remainder of the fleet. These were built as three-car sets and later augmented to four-car status.

As passenger growth expanded on the Chiltern route, especially the London-Birmingham corridor, extra vehicles were ordered, but by this time Adtranz had standardised on the Class 170 design; therefore all subsequent ordered trains were of this style.

Interiors are set out in the 2+2 style, with above seat luggage stacks. Toilets are provided in both driving cars and one MS vehicle in four-car sets.

Units are equipped with 'trip-cock' equipment to allow operation over the London Underground-signalled Harrow-on-the-Hill to Amersham section. Livery is Chiltern Railways blue and white or two-tone grey. ■

Above: *Five Class 168/0 sets are in traffic with Chiltern; these four-car sets were the forerunner to the 'Turbostar' and have a slightly different body profile. Painted in the new Chiltern silver, grey and white livery set No. 168003 is illustrated. Note the 'trip-cock' equipment on the leading bogie.* **Antony Christie**

Right Middle: *Class 168/0 front end design. A: High-level marker light, B: Group Standard light cluster with headlight and combined white marker/red tail light, C: BSI coupling with pneumatic connection, electrical connections below behind roll cover panel, D: Warning horns. Set No. 168005 is seen at Marylebone.* **Antony Christie**

Below: *The intermediate vehicles of Class 168 sets are Motor Standards, and some have toilet compartments. All have 2+2 seating and seat between 73 and 77 depending on design. Painted in the new Chiltern Railways livery with 'Mainline' branding, vehicle 58453 is illustrated, from set No. 168003.* **Antony Christie**

Above and Below: *By the time the second batch of Class 168s had been ordered the standard 'Turbostar' body profile had been established and Class 168/1s and 168/2s follow this design. Eight Class 168/1s are allocated to Aylesbury. Two sets are four-car formations and the remainder three. In the above view, set No. 168112 is shown at Banbury, alongside a later-built Class 168/2 set with revised front end light clusters. The set is painted in the older Chiltern white and blue livery. In the view below we see a Class 168/1 intermediate vehicle, of which 10 are in traffic. These coaches are fully air conditioned and have seating in the 'Clubman' 2+2 style. Vehicle No. 58462 is illustrated from set No. 168112.* **CJM / John Binch**

Above: *The final batch of Class 168s, classified as 168/2, emerged between 2003 and 2006, with today the sub-class consisting of six units, three two-car and three three-car. These follow the bodylines of the then current 'Turbostar' fleet with one large headlight and one small joint marker/tail light. In 2013-14 the sets were in the process of being overhauled and repainted into the latest silver, grey and white livery with 'Mainline' branding. Set No. 168219 is illustrated at Birmingham Moor Street.* **John Binch**

Below: *Nine intermediate Motor Standard vehicles exist within the Class 168/2 sub-class, and these seat either 73 or 76 passengers based on the 2+2 low-density style. Vehicle No. 58467 from set No. 168217 shown the latest two-tone grey livery. Note the roof mounted air conditioning modules, end exhaust stack and destination indicator in the central bodyside window.* **Antony Christie**

Diesel Multiple Units

Sub-class:	170/1	170/2	170/3
Number range:	170101-170117	170201-170208 and 170270-170273	170301-170309
Introduced:	1998-1999 (2001 MC)	170201-170208 - 1999 170270-170273 - 2002	2000-2001
Built by:	Adtranz Derby	170201-170208: Adtranz Derby 170270-170208: Bombardier Derby	Adtranz Derby
Formation:	170101-170110: DMSL+MS+DMCL 170111-170117: DMSL+DMCL	170201-170208: DMCL+MSL+DMSL 170270-170273: DMSL+DMCL	DMCL+DMSL
Vehicle Nos.:	170101-170110: DMSL - 50101-110 MS - 55101-55110 DMCL - 79101-110 170111-170117: DMSL - 50111-50117 DMCL - 79111-79117	170201-170208: DMCL - 50201-50208 MSL - 56201-56208 DMSL - 79201-79208 170270-170273: DMSL - 50270-50273 DMCL - 79270-79273	DMCL - 50301-50308/399 DMSL - 79301-79308/399
Vehicle length:	77ft 6in (23.62m)	77ft 6in (23.62m)	77ft 6in (23.62m)
Height:	12ft 4½in (3.77m)	12ft 4½in (3.77m)	12ft 4½in (3.77m)
Width:	8ft 10in (2.69m)	8ft 10in (2.69m)	8ft 10in (2.69m)
Seating:	170101-170110: Total - 9F/191S 170111-170117: Total - 9F/111S 170102-170110: DMSL - 59S MS - 80S DMCL - 9F/52S 170111-170117: DMSL - 59S DMCL - 9F/52S	170201-170208: Total - 7F/173S 170270-170273: Total - 9F/110S 170201-170208: DMCL - 7F/39S MSL - 68S DMSL - 66S 170270-170273: DMSL - 57S DMCL - 9F/53S	Total - 8F/108S DMCL - 8F/43S DMSL - 65S
Internal layout:	2+2F, 2+2S	2+1F, 2+2S	2+1F/2+2
Gangway:	Within set	Within set	Within set
Toilets:	DMSL - 1, DMCL - 1	One per vehicle	One per vehicle
Weight:	170101-170110: Total - 132.8 tonnes 170111-170116: Total - 89.8 tonnes DMSL - 45 tonnes MS - 43.0 tonnes DMCL - 44.8 tonnes	170201-170208: Total - 133.7 tonnes 170270-170273: Total - 88.4 tonnes DMCL- 45 tonnes MSL - 45.3 tonnes DMSL – 43.4 tonnes	Total - 91.6 tonnes DMCL - 45.8 tonnes DMSL - 45.8 tonnes
Brake type:	Air	Air	Air
Bogie type:	One P3-23c and one T3-23c per car	One P3-23c and one T3-23c per car	One P3-23c and one T3-23c per car

170/3	170/4	170/5	170/6
170393-170398,	170401-170434 170450-170478	170501-170523	170630-170639
2002-2004	1999-2005	1999-2000	2000
Bombardier Derby	Adtranz Derby/ Bombardier Derby	Adtranz Derby	Adtranz Derby
170393-170396: DMCL+MSLRB+DMSL 170397-170398: DMSL+MS+DMCL	170401-170424: DMCL(A)+MS+DMCL(B) 170425-170434: DMCL(A)+MS+DMSL(B) 170450-170461: DMSL(A)+MS+DMSL(B) 170470-170478: DMSL(A)+MS+DMSL(B)	170501-170517: DMSL(A)+DMSL(B) 170518-170523: DMSL+DMCL	170630-170635: DMSL(A)+MS+DMSL(B) 170636-170639: DMSL+MS+DMCL
170393 - 170396: DMCL - 50393-50396 MSLRB - 56393-56396 DMSL - 79393-79396 170397-170398: DMSL - 50397-50398 MS - 56397-56398 DMCL - 79397-79398	170401-170424: DMCL(A) - 50401-50424 MS - 56401-56424 DMCL(B) - 79401-79424 170425-170434: DMCL(A) - 50425-50434 MS - 56425-56434 DMCL(B) - 79425-79434 170450-170478: DMSL(A) - 50450-50478 MS - 56450-56478 DMSL(B) - 79450-79478	170501-170517: DMSL(A) 50501-50517 DMSL(B) 79501-79517 170518-170523: DMSL 50518-50523 DMCL 79518-79523	170630-170635: DMSL(A) - 50630-50635 MS - 56630-56635 DMSL(B) - 79630-79635 170636-170639: DMSL - 50636-50639 MS - 56636-56639 DMCL - 79636-79639
77ft 6in (23.62m) 12ft 4½in (3.77m) 8ft 10in (2.69m) 170393-170396: Total: 7F/161S DMCL - 7F/41S MSLRB - 53S DMSL - 67S 170397-170398: Total: 9F/191S DMSL - 59S MS - 80S DMCL - 9F/52S	77ft 6in (23.62m) 12ft 4½in (3.77m) 8ft 10in (2.69m) 170401-170434: 18F/168S 170450-170461: Total - 198S 170470-170478: Total - 200S 170401-170434: DMC(A) - 9F/43S MS - 76S DMC(B) - 9F/49S 170450-170461: DMSL(A) - 55S MS - 76S DMSL(B) - 67S 170470-170478: DMS(A) - 57S MS - 76S DMSL(B) - 67S	77ft 6in (23.62m) 12ft 4½in (3.77m) 8ft 10in (2.69m) 170501-170517: Total - 122S DMSL(A) - 55S DMSL(B) - 67S 170518-170523: Total - 9F/111S DMSL - 59S DMCL - 9F/52S	77ft 6in (23.62m) 12ft 4½in (3.77m) 8ft 10in (2.69m) 170630-170635: Total - 196S DMSL(A) - 55S MS - 74S DMSL(B) - 67S 170636 - 170639: Total - 9F/191S DMSL - 55S MS - 80S DMCL - 9F/52S
2+1F, 2+2S Within set One per vehicle Total - 137.5 tonnes DMCL - 46.5 tonnes MSLRB/MS - 44.7 tonnes DMSL - 46.3 tonnes	2+1F, 2+2S Within set One per vehicle Total - 133.2 tonnes DMCL(A) - 45.8 tonnes DMSL - 46.3 tonnes MS - 41.4 tonnes	2+1F/2+2S Within set One per vehicle Total - 91.7 tonnes DMSL(A) - 45.8 tonnes DMSL(B) - 45.9 tonnes DMCL - 45.9 tonnes	2+1F/2+2S Within set One per vehicle Total - 134.1 tonnes DMSL(A) - 45.8 tonnes MS - 42.4 tonnes DMSL(B) - 45.9 tonnes DMCL - 45.9 tonnes
Air One P3-23c and one T3-23c per car	Air One P3-23c and one T3-23c per car	Air One P3-23c and one T3-23c per car	Air One P3-23c and one T3-23c per car

Diesel Multiple Units

Class 170 'Turbostar'

Sub-class:	170/1	170/2	170/3
Power unit:	1 x MTU 6R 183TD 13H of 422hp (315kW) per car	1 x MTU 6R 183TD 13H of 422hp (315kW) per car	1 x MTU 6R 183TD 13H of 422hp (315kW) per car
Transmission:	Hydraulic Voith T211r	Hydraulic Voith T211r	Hydraulic Voith T211r
Horsepower:	3-car - 1,266hp (945kW) 2-car - 844hp (630kW)	3-car - 1,266hp (945kW) 2-car - 844hp (630kW)	844hp (630kW)
Max speed:	100mph (161km/h)	100mph (161km/h)	100mph (161km/h)
Coupling type:	BSI	BSI	BSI
Multiple working:	Class 15x, 170-172	Class 15x, 170-172	Class 15x, 170-172
Door type:	Bi-parting slide plug	Bi-parting slide plug	Bi-parting slide plug
Special features:	Air conditioned	Air conditioned RETB	Air conditioned
Body structure:	Welded aluminium	Welded aluminium	Welded aluminium
Owner:	Porterbrook	Porterbrook	Porterbrook
Operator:	CrossCountry	Greater Anglia	First TransPennine (for Chiltern Railways in 2015)

Left: *The pioneer Class 170s, originally operated by Midland Main Line, came in both a two- and three-car formation and were used to supplement HST stock on St Pancras to Nottingham/Sheffield services. Displaced by Class 222s, these sets now operate for CrossCountry Trains and have been fully refurbished with revised interiors. The sets are all painted in XC silver and maroon livery and operate with other XC Class 170 sub-classes as one pool. Two-car set No. 170115 is illustrated.*
Antony Christie

Fact File

The most popular of the 'new generation' of DMUs is the Adtranz/Bombardier-built 'Turbostar' of which around 140 sets are in operation. The aluminium-built vehicles, assembled in Derby, are owned by Porterbrook with a handful funded by Eversholt Leasing.

Sets come in two- or three-car formations and by nature of their design can have virtually any interior configuration to suit an operator.

All exteriors are of the same basic design, with some minor revision on later sets in the style of front end light clusters.

Sets are fully air conditioned and are relatively low-noise considering each vehicle has a 422hp underfloor engine. The top speed is 100mph and the sets can be seen throughout the UK rail network. In 2014 units were still officially in the Bombardier product portfolio. ■

170/3	170/4	170/5	170/6
1 x MTU 6R 183TD 13H of 422hp (315kW) per car Hydraulic Voith T211r 1,266hp (945kW)	1 x MTU 6R 183TD 13H of 422hp (315kW) per car Hydraulic Voith T211r 1,266hp (945kW)	1 x MTU 6R 183TD 13H of 422hp (315kW) per car Hydraulic Voith T211r 844hp (630kW)	1 x MTU 6R 183TD 13H of 422hp (315kW) per car Hydraulic Voith T211r 1,266hp (945kW)
100mph (161km/h)	100mph (161km/h)	100mph (161km/h)	100mph (161km/h)
BSI	BSI	BSI	BSI
Class 15x, 170-172	Class 15x, 170-172	Class 15x, 170-172	
Bi-parting slide plug	Bi-parting slide plug	Bi-parting slide plug	Bi-parting slide plug
Air conditioned	Air conditioned	Air conditioned	Air conditioned
Some RETB	RETB	Some RETB	Some RETB
Welded aluminium	Welded aluminium	Welded aluminium	Welded aluminium
Porterbrook	Porterbrook, Eversholt	Porterbrook	Porterbrook
First ScotRail, CrossCountry	First ScotRail	London Midland/ CrossCountry	London Midland/ CrossCountry

Above: *Class 170 equipment positions. 1: Screen wash filler port, 2: Mechanical cab door release, 3: Cab door, 4: Vehicle lifting point, 5: Passenger bi-parting doors, 6: Air conditioning unit, 7: Fuel tank and filler, 8: Battery box, 9: Electrical connections, 10: Equipment box, 11: Fire system activation handle, 12: Local engine controls, 13: Engine and transmission unit, 14: Emergency passenger door release handle, 15: Toilet tank, 16: Exhaust system, 17: Door release and warning light. Class 170/1 illustrated.* **CJM**

Right: *First ScotRail operates a fleet of 59 Class 170s, allocated to Haymarket depot in Edinburgh. These are members of Class 170/3 and 170/4. Several different interior designs exist, with the main batch (170401-434) having limited first class seating in the driving cars. Painted in Saltire livery, set No. 170474, an all standard class set, is illustrated.* **Murdoch Currie**

Above: *The Class 170/2 sub-class is allocated to the Greater Anglia franchise, having eight three-car and four two-car sets. These units operate the local and medium distance services from Norwich. Set No. 170207 is illustrated at March.* **Antony Christie**

Left: *When originally introduced the Class 170/3s were allocated to South West Trains; they were then transferred to First TransPennine Express and in 2015 will move to Chiltern Railways. At present sets are operated on the Manchester to East Coast corridor. The nine sets each seat eight first and 108 standard class passengers in the 2+2 seating style. Set No. 170304 is illustrated at Selby.* **CJM**

Above: *Class 170 intermediate vehicles exist within sub-classes 170/1, 170/2, 170/3, 170/4 and 170/6. These are basically a driving car without a cab. A CrossCountry Class 170/1 vehicle is illustrated, but all are of the same design.* **CJM**

Right Top: *The Class 170/5 two-car sets are now split between operators London Midland and CrossCountry Trains, with all sets allocated to Tyseley depot. The 17 London Midland sets are painted in LM green, grey and black livery and operate longer distance services. All are refurbished with quality 2+2 standard class seating for 122.* **CJM**

Right Middle: *The six CrossCountry Class 170/5 two-car sets have standard CrossCountry interiors and retain first class accommodation in one driving car, giving a seating figure of nine first and 111 standard class passengers per two-car set. All sets are painted in advertising branded XC silver and maroon with pink doors and a standard yellow band over the first class area. Set No. 170523 is illustrated.* **Antony Christie**

Below: *It is quite amazing how a livery can completely change the appearance and perception of a vehicle. If viewed against the CrossCountry MS on the opposite page, this London Midland City-liveried Class 170/6 intermediate MS looks a totally different product. London Midland operates a fleet of six three-car Class 170/6 sets, based at Tyseley. These vehicles have 2+2 seating for 74 standard class passengers. Vehicle 56633 is illustrated at Worcester.* **CJM**

Diesel Multiple Units

Sub-class:	171/7	171/8
Number range:	171721-171730	171801-171806
Introduced:	2003-2005	2004
Built by:	Bombardier Derby	Bombardier Derby
Formation:	DMCL+DMSL	DMCL(A)+MS+MS+DMCL(B)
Vehicle numbers:	DMCL - 50721-729/392	DMCL(A) - 50801 - 50806
	DMSL - 79721-729/392	MS - 54801 - 54806
		MS - 56801 - 56806
		DMCL(B) - 79801 - 79806
Vehicle length:	77ft 6in (23.62m)	77ft 6in (23.62m)
Height:	12ft 4½in (3.77m)	12ft 4½in (3.77m)
Width:	8ft 10in (2.69m)	8ft 10in (2.69m)
Seating:	Total - 9F/107S	Total - 18F/241S
	DMCL 9F/43S	DMCL(A) 9F/43S
	DMSL 64S	MS 74S
		MS 74S
		DMCL(B) 9F/50S
Internal layout:	2+1F, 2+2S	2+1F, 2+2S
Gangway:	Within set	Within set
Toilets:	DMCL, DMSL - 1	DMCL - 1
Weight:	Total - 95.4 tonnes	Total - 180.4 tonnes
	DMCL - 47.6 tonnes	DMCL(A) - 46.5 tonnes
	DMSL - 47.8 tonnes	MS - 43.7 tonnes
		MS - 43.7 tonnes
		DMCL(B) - 46.5 tonnes
Brake type:	Air	Air
Bogie type:	One P3-23c and one	One P3-23c and one
	T3-23c per car	T3-23c per car
Power unit:	1 x MTU 6R 183TD of	1 x MTU 6R 183TD of
	422hp (315kW) per car	422hp (315kW) per car
Transmission:	Hydraulic	Hydraulic
Transmission type:	Voith T211r to	Voith T211r to
	ZF final drive	ZF final drive
Horsepower:	844hp (630kW)	Total 1,688hp (1,260kW)
Max speed:	100mph (161km/h)	100mph (161km/h)
Coupling type:	Dellner 12	Dellner 12
Multiple restriction:	Class 171	Class 171
Door type:	Bi-parting slide plug	Bi-parting slide plug
Special features:	Air conditioned	Air conditioned
Body structure:	Aluminium	Aluminium
Owner:	Porterbrook	Porterbrook
Operator:	Southern	Southern

Fact File

When operator South Central (later Southern) re-equipped its diesel multiple unit fleet for non-electrified lines from London to Sussex and Kent, it chose the Bombardier 'Turbostar' Class 170 product.

Soon after delivery of the first two-car sets to Selhurst depot, the operator decided to change the end couplers from the BSI to Dellner 12 type, in keeping with its 'Electrostar' EMU fleet, thus aiding 'on line' assistance if needed. The refitting saw the fleet identity change to '171'.

Two sub-classes exist: two-car sets are Class 171/7 and four-car sets are Class 171/8. Two-car units are usually used on the non-electrified Ashford-Hastings route, while a mix of two- and four-car sets are to be found on the London Bridge-Oxted-Uckfield line.

Units are finished in Southern green and white livery; the fleet has good quality interiors with seating in the 2+2 low-density style for standard and 2+1 seating in first. ∎

Left: *Allocated to Southern's Selhurst depot are the 44 Class 171 'Turbostar' vehicles. These are formed as 10 two-car and six four-car sets and used for Southern non-electrified services on the London Bridge-Oxted-Uckfield and Ashford-Hastings lines. The sets were built as Class 170s, but reclassified as 171 by Southern after the fitting of Dellner 12 couplers in place of the usual 'Turbostar' BSI couplings. Two-car set No. 171722 is seen from its DMSL end, identified by the omission of first class branding above the seating bay directly behind the driving cab.* **CJM**

Above: *On the six four-car Class 171/8 sets both driving cars have first class accommodation for nine directly to the rear of the driving cab. All sets are painted in Southern green and white livery. Set No. 171801 is illustrated at Honor Oak Park passing a TfL Class 378 unit.* **CJM**

Right Middle: *The intermediate Class 171 Motor Standard vehicles seat 74 passengers in the 2+2 style. Each vehicle has two pairs of sliding plug doors on each side. Technically the vehicles are the same as driving cars with a full traction package mounted below, thus giving a four- car set a total of 1,688hp (1,259kW). MS 54802 from set No. 171802 is illustrated.* **Antony Christie**

Right Below: *The first class Class 171 seating is in the 2+1 low-density style, giving a pleasing travelling environment. The design uses high-back reclining seats with either fixed or fold down tables. Above seat lighting is provided as are hinged armrests to the seats. The first class seating area of set No. 171802 is shown.* **Antony Christie**

Class 172 'Turbostar'

Sub-class:	172/0	172/1	172/2
Number range:	172001-172008	172101-172104	172211-172222
Introduced:	2010	2011	2011
Built by:	Bombardier Derby	Bombardier Derby	Bombardier Derby
Formation:	DMS+DMS	DMSL+DMS	DMSL+DMS
Vehicle numbers:	DMS - 59311-59318	DMSL - 59111-59114	DMSL - 50211-50222
	DMS - 59411-59418	DMS - 59211-59214	DMS - 79211-79222
	-	-	-
Vehicle lengths:	DMS - 76ft 3in (23.27m)	DMSL - 76ft 3in (23.27m)	DMSL - 76ft 3in (23.27m)
	DMS - 76ft 3in (23.27m)	DMS - 76ft 3in (23.27m)	DMS - 76ft 3in (23.27m)
Height:	12ft 4½in (3.77m)	12ft 4½in (3.77m)	12ft 4½in (3.77m)
Width:	8ft 8in (2.69m)	8ft 8in (2.69m)	8ft 8in (2.69m)
Seating:	Total - 124S	Total - 145S	Total - 121S + 7 tip up
	DMS - 60S	DMSL - 65S	DMSL - 53S + 4 tip up
	DMS - 64S	DMS - 80S	DMS - 68S + 3 tip up
	-	-	-
Internal layout:	2+2	2+2	2+2
Gangway:	Within set	Within set	Throughout
Toilets:	None	DMSL - 1	DMSL - 1
Weight:	Total - 83.1 tonnes	Total - 82.2 tonnes	Total - 83.2 tonnes
	DMS - 36.5 tonnes	DMSL - 41.4 tonnes	DMSL - 41.9 tonnes
	DMS - 41.6 tonnes	DMS - 40.8 tonnes	DMS - 41.3 tonnes
Brake type:	Air EP	Air EP	Air EP
Bogie type:	B5006	B5006	B5006
Power unit:	1 x MTU 6H1800R83 of	1 x MTU 6H1800R83 of	1 x MTU 6H1800R83 of
	484hp (360kW) per vehicle	484hp (360kW) per vehicle	484hp (360kW) per vehicle
Transmission:	Mechanical	Mechanical	Mechanical
Transmission type:	ZG	ZG	ZG
Horsepower:	968hp (720kW)	968hp (720kW)	968hp (720kW)
Max speed:	75mph (121km/h)	75mph (121km/h)	100mph (161km/h)
Coupling type:	BSI	BSI	BSI
Multiple restriction:	Class 14x, 15x, 170, 172	Class 14x, 15x, 170, 172	Class 14x, 15x, 170, 172
Door type:	Twin-leaf swing plug	Twin-leaf swing plug	Twin-leaf swing plug
Body structure:	Aluminium	Aluminium	Aluminium
Owner:	Angel Trains	Angel Trains	Porterbrook
Operator:	London Overground	Chiltern Railways	London Midland

Below: *London Overground, a part of Transport for London, operates a fleet of eight two-car Class 172/0 sets on its Gospel Oak-Barking route. These sets seat 124 standard class passengers with a large amount of standing room. The sets are based on the body design of the Class 170. The sets are finished in Transport for London blue and white, offset by orange passenger doors. Set No. 172006 is seen at Crouch Hill. These sets will be displaced following electrification of the Gospel Oak-Barking route and are likely to transfer to Chiltern Railways.* **CJM**

Fact File

In 2007-08, orders were placed with Bombardier by two rolling stock lease companies to purchase Class 172 'Turbostar' trains. In December 2007, Porterbrook ordered 15 three-car and 12 two-car trains for London Midland. In January 2008, Angel Trains, on behalf of London Overground and Chiltern Railways, ordered 12 two-car trains. The first of these were delivered in 2010 for London Overground.

The first London Midland three-car set emerged in early 2011 and the Chiltern sets were delivered from summer 2011.

The sets are a derivative of the Class 170 design but have a diesel-mechanical transmission and more austere design. ∎

172/3

172331-172345	
2011	
Bombardier Derby	
DMSL+MS+DMS	
DMSL - 50331-50345	
MS - 56331-56345	
DMS - 79331-79345	
DMSL - 76ft 3in (23.27m)	
MS - 76ft 6in (23.36m)	
DMS - 76ft 3in (23.27m)	
12ft 4½in (3.77m)	
8ft 8in (2.69m)	
Total - 193S + 7 tip up	
DMSL - 53S + 4 tip up	
MS - 72S	
DMS - 68S + 3 tip up	
2+2	
Throughout	
DMSL - 1	
Total - 121.3 tonnes	
DMSL - 41.9 tonnes	
MS - 38.1 tonnes	
DML - 41.3 tonnes	
Air EP	
B5006	
1 x MTU 6H1800R83 of	
484hp (360kW) per vehicle	
Mechanical	
ZG	
1,449hp (1,080kW)	
100mph (161km/h)	
BSI	
Class 14x, 15x, 170, 172	
Twin-leaf swing plug	
Aluminium	
Porterbrook	
London Midland	

Above: *Chiltern Railways operates a fleet of four Class 172/1 sets allocated to Aylesbury. These are finished in blue/white livery. Set No. 172104 is shown. Note the different design bogies compared to a Class 170.* **Antony Christie**

Right Middle & Inset: *London Midland is the largest user of Class 172s, with 12 two-car and 15 three-car sets. Finished in London Midland green, grey and black livery they are the only 172s to sport an end gangway connection, using a front end similar to an 'Electrostar' set. The intermediate vehicles have a full traction package and seat 72 in the 2+2 layout. Set No. 172337 is illustrated at Worcester. The MS vehicle is No. 56341 from set 172341.* **CJM**

Right: *Class 172 front end layout. A: High-level marker light, B: Destination indicator, C: Light cluster, with headlight and joint marker/tail light, D: Forward facing camera, E: Hinged lamp bracket (in stowed position), F: BSI coupling with pneumatic connection, electrical connections below behind roll cover panel, G: Warning horns. This front end layout applies to all non-corridor '172s'.* **CJM**

Class 175 'Coradia 1000'

Sub class:	175/0	175/1
Number range:	175001-175011	175101-175116
Introduced:	1999-2001	1999-2001
Built by:	Alstom, Birmingham	Alstom, Birmingham
Formation:	DMSL(A)+DMSL(B)	DMSL(A)+MSL+DMSL(B)
Vehicle numbers:	DMSL(A) - 50701-50711	DMSL(A) - 50751-50766
	DMSL(B) - 79701-79711	MSL - 56751-56766
		DMSL(B) - 79751-79766
Vehicle length:	75ft 7in (23.03m)	DMSL - 75ft 7in (23.03m)
		MSL - 75ft 5in (22.98m)
Height:	12ft 4in (3.75m)	12ft 4in (3.75m)
Width:	9ft 2in (2.79m)	9ft 2in (2.79m)
Seating:	Total - 118S	Total - 186S
	DMSL(A) - 54S	DMSL(A) - 54S
	DMSL(B) - 64S	MSL - 68S
		DMSL(B) - 64S
Internal layout:	2+2	2+2
Gangway:	Within set	Within set
Toilets:	DMSL(A), DMSL(B) - 1	DMSL(A), MSL, DMSL(B) - 1
Weight:	Total - 99.5 tonnes	Total - 147.7 tonnes
	DMSL(A) - 48.8 tonnes	DMSL(A) - 50.7 tonnes
	DMSL(B) - 50.7 tonnes	MSL - 47.5 tonnes
		DMSL(B) - 49.5 tonnes
Brake type:	Air	Air
Bogie type:	Alstom FBO	Alstom FBO
	LTB-MBS1, TB-MB1, MBS1-LTB	LTB-MBS1, TB-MB1, MBS1-LTB
Power unit:	One Cummins N14 of	One Cummins N14 of
	450hp (335kW) per car	450hp (335kW) per car
Transmission:	Hydraulic	Hydraulic
Transmission type:	Voith T211rzze to ZF final drive	Voith T211rzze to ZF final drive
Horsepower (total):	900hp (670kW)	1,350hp (1,005kW)
Max speed:	100mph (161km/h)	100mph (161km/h)
Coupling type:	Outer - Scharfenberg, Inner - Bar	Outer - Scharfenberg, Inner - Bar
Multiple restriction:	Within type and Class 180	Within type and Class 180
Door type:	Single-leaf sliding plug	Single-leaf sliding plug
Special features:	Air conditioned	Air conditioned
Body structure:	Steel	Steel
Owner:	Angel Trains	Angel Trains
Operator:	Arriva Trains Wales	Arriva Trains Wales

Below: *Class 175 side equipment positions. 1: Windscreen washer filler port, 2: Cab door, 3: Manual release for cab door, 4: Passenger door open button, including lock, 5: Single leaf sliding plug passenger door, 6: Manual release for passenger door, 7: Lifting socket, 8: Fuel tank and filler, 9: Local electrical equipment, 10: saloon ventilator, 11: Air conditioning module, 12: Door release and warning light, 13: radiator water filler and water gauge, 14: Removable doors covering engine and transmission and control equipment.* **CJM**

Above: *Introduced by First Group when it held the North West franchise, the Class 175s are now operated by Arriva Trains Wales and operate the long distance services. A fleet of 11 two-car sets of Class 175/0 are in traffic, seating 118 in the 2+2 style. Set No. 175002 is seen at Newport.* **CJM**

Right: *To provide greater capacity and flexibility in train formations, a fleet of 16 three-car Class 175/1s was introduced; these seat 186 standard class passengers. No first class is provided and these sets are designed with the longer distance passenger in mind. Passenger doors feed a transverse walkway at either end with doors leading to the air conditioned passenger saloons. Three-car set No. 175108 is shown at Cardiff.* **CJM**

Fact File

When longer distance new generation DMUs were sought in the late 1990s, Alstom put forward its 'Coradia 1000' product range. This design platform was taken by First Group for deployment on its then North Western and Great Western franchises.

The North Western sets are now operated by Arriva Trains Wales and based at purpose-built maintenance facilities at Chester.

The Class 175 comes in both two- and three-car formations; all have 2+2 seating in a mix of airline and group layouts. All seating is of one class.

The fleet can be found forming the main line services operated by Arriva Trains Wales.

Originally sets were painted in First Group 'Barbie' livery, but all sets now sport Arriva Trains Wales turquoise and white livery offset by powder blue passenger doors. ■

Left Top: *The intermediate MS vehicles in the Class 175s have a full traction package and are basically a driving car without a cab; as with all Class 175 carriages seating is in the 2+2 style. The single leaf sliding plug doors again feed a cross vestibule from which sliding doors give access to the saloon area. All vehicles carry Arriva Trains Wales turquoise livery.* **CJM**

Left Middle: *Class 175 interior, showing the high-quality 2+2 seating with high back seats with hinged armrests in both the aircraft and group layouts. Above seat and end of vehicle luggage racks are provided, as is a passenger information system.* **CJM**

Left Bottom: *Class 175 front end layout. A: Roof mounted high-level marker light, B: Destination indicator, C: Dual white marker and red tail light, D: Headlight, E: Roll cover electric connection box, F: BSI coupling including pneumatic connections, G: Warning horns behind grilles.* **CJM**

Fact File

The second, main line Alstom 'Coradia 1000' order was for the First Great Western franchise, with 14 five-car 125mph 'Adelante' sets ordered for use on main lines.

Unlike the Class 175s, these sets were built with a streamlined front end and looked very impressive.

Passenger accommodation is of a high standard with a mix of 2+2 in airline and group layouts in standard class and 2+1 in airline and group style in first class.

A small buffet is provided in one MS vehicle which reduces seating by 12, while a serving bay is provided at one end of the first class vehicle to provide an 'at seat' service.

Sets have end Scharfenberg couplings, originally housed behind a hinged front panel.

Operations on First Great Western were problematic and, following full refurbishment of the FGW HST fleet and securing of additional HSTs, the Class 180s were phased out of service, being returned to owners Angel Trains.

Soon new operators came forward. First Group's Hull Trains operation took four sets, while Open Access operator Grand Central leased five sets classified as 'Zephyrs' for its Sunderland/Bradford to London King's Cross service. The remaining sets did 'spot-hire' for a period with Northern before being stored.

As passenger growth expanded on First Great Western the off-lease sets were returned to their original operator, which refurbished them and applied the latest First 'dynamic lines' livery. In 2014 the sets can be found operating on the Paddington to Worcester corridor.

Sadly all the original front coupling cover doors have now been removed. ∎

Number range:	180101-180114
Introduced:	2000-2001
Built by:	Alstom, Birmingham
Formation:	DMSL(A)+MFL+MSL+MSLRB+DMSL(B)
Vehicle numbers:	DMSL(A) - 50901-50914
	MFL - 54901-54914
	MSL - 55901-55914
	MSLRB - 56901-56914
	DMSL(B) - 59901-59914
Vehicle length:	DMSL(A), DMSL(B) - 77ft 7in (23.71m)
	MFL, MSL, MSLRB - 75ft 5in (23.03m)
Height:	12ft 4in (3.75m)
Width:	9ft 2in (2.79m)
Seating:	Total - 42F/226S
	DMSL(A) - 46S
	MFL - 42F
	MSL - 68S
	MSLRB - 56S
	DMSL(B) - 56S
Internal layout:	2+1F, 2+2S
Gangway:	Within set
Toilets:	DMSL(A), MFL, MSL, MSLRB, DMSL(B) - 1
Weight:	Total - 252.5 tonnes
	DMSL(A) - 51.7 tonnes
	MFL - 49.6 tonnes
	MSL - 49.5 tonnes
	MSLRB - 50.3 tonnes
	DMSL(B) - 51.4 tonnes
Brake type:	Air
Bogie type:	Alstom MB2
Power unit:	One Cummins QSK19 of 750hp (560kW) per car
Transmission:	Hydraulic
Transmission type:	Voith T312br to ZF final drive
Horsepower (total):	3,750hp (2,800kW)
Max speed:	125mph (201km/h)
Coupling type:	Outer - Scharfenberg, Inner - Bar
Multiple restriction:	Within type and Class 175
Door type:	Single-leaf swing plug
Body structure:	Steel
Special features:	Air conditioned
Owner:	Angel Trains
Operator:	First Great Western, First Hull Trains, Grand Central Railway

Below: *First Great Western currently operates a fleet of five Class 180 'Adelante' five-car main line DMUs. These are deployed on the Paddington-Worcester route. All are painted in FGW 'dynamic lines' livery, are based at Old Oak Common and seat 42 first and 226 standard class passengers. Set No. 180108 is shown.* **Nathan Williamson**

Left Top: *All three intermediate vehicles of the Class 180 are different. There is one Motor Standard, one Motor First with buffet position and one Motor Standard with a buffet counter/serving area. The structural design of the vehicles is the same, it is only the interior fitting which is different. Coach No. 56903, a Motor Standard with a buffet counter/serving area, is illustrated.* **Antony Christie**

Left Middle: *After the Class 180s were withdrawn by First Great Western for the first time, other operators were keen to take on these main line trains, one was fledgling Open Access operator Grand Central, which took on the lease of five sets to operate its Sunderland / Bradford to London service. The sets were repainted into company black livery offset by a orange band at the base of the body. Standard class carriages have silver doors while the first class vehicle has gold doors. The interior, fully refurbished, seats 42 first and 226 standard class passengers in the 2+1 and 2+2 styles. The MF vehicle from set 180105 is illustrated.* **CJM**

Below: *The five-car Grand Central sets do look very smart in their black and orange livery, with the sets referred to by the operators as 'Zephyrs', a name derived by the company from the US railroad industry. Set No. 180105 is seen approaching Doncaster. It is a pity that the original hinged coupling cover doors have been removed, spoiling the otherwise streamlined front end. On sets which are named, these are applied below the Grand Central branding behind the cab.* **CJM**

Right Top: *First Hull Trains, which operates an Open Access service between London King's Cross and Hull, deploys a fleet of four Class 180s. These have been refurbished to First Group standards and carry 'dynamic lines' livery, with some minor variation to branding and label positions compared to the FGW sets. Set No. 180113 is seen at Selby with a service bound for Hull.* **CJM**

Right Middle: *Class 180 driving cab layout, with a joint power and brake controller on the left side. Note the fitting of Western Region-style Automatic Train Protection (ATP) equipment. This has been removed from First Hull Trains and Grand Central sets.* **CJM**

Below: *First Class interior of a refurbished First Great Western Class 180, showing the high quality leather seats, all grouped around tables in the 2+1 style. The revised seating on these sets is based on the seating of the operator's HST fleet, but tend to be more comfortable. Above seat luggage racks, downward lighting and power points are provided by each seat.* **CJM**

Class 185 'Desiro'

Number range:	185101-185151
Introduced:	2005-2007
Built by:	Siemens Transportation, Germany
Formation:	DMCL+MSL+DMS
Vehicle numbers:	DMCL - 51101-51151
	MSL - 53101-53151
	DMS - 54101-54151
Vehicle length:	DMCL, DMS - (77ft 11in) (23.76m)
	MSL - 77ft 10in (23.75m)
Height:	12ft 4in (3.75m)
Width:	9ft 3in (2.84m)
Seating:	Total - 15F/154S + 12 tip up
	DMCL - 15F/18S + 8 tip up
	MSL - 72S
	DMS - 64S + 4 tip up
Internal layout:	2+2S, 2+1F
Gangway:	Within set
Toilets:	MSL - 1, DMCL - 1
Weight:	Total - 163.1 tonnes
	DMCL - 55.4 tonnes
	MSL - 52.7 tonnes
	DMS - 55 tonnes
Brake type:	Air
Bogie type:	Siemens
Power unit:	One Cummins QSK19 of 750hp (560kW) per car
Transmission:	Hydraulic
Transmission type:	Voith Turbopack T312 and SK-485 final drive
Horsepower (total):	2,250hp (1,680kW)
Max speed:	100mph (161km/h)
Coupling type:	Dellner 12
Multiple restriction:	Within class only
Door type:	Bi-parting sliding plug
Body structure:	Aluminium
Special features:	Air conditioned, power points, CCTV
Owner:	Eversholt
Operator:	First TransPennine

Fact File

The first Siemens Transportation diesel-powered 'Desiro' stock for the UK is this fleet of 51 three-car Class 185s, introduced for First TransPennine Express services.

The high-quality units were constructed and tested in Germany before being shipped as complete trains to the UK via the Channel Tunnel.

The fleet is allocated to a purpose-built Siemens-operated depot at Ardwick, Manchester.

The Class 185 is a low-density train with 2+2 standard and 2+1 first class seating; trains are fully air conditioned, have passenger information displays and are very quiet even though each vehicle has a 750hp underfloor power unit. Sets are gangwayed within each unit. Units are finished in First Group's 'dynamic lines' livery. ■

Left: Class 185 front end equipment positions. A: Cab air conditioning unit, B: High-level marker light, C: Destination/route indicator, D: Front light cluster with headlight and joint white marker/red tail light on each side, E: Lamp bracket, F: Anti-climber plates, G: Warning horns, H: Dellner 12 auto coupling.
Brian Morrison

Above: *Based in Manchester, the 51 TransPennine Class 185 'Desiro' sets have different design driving cars at either end. This view shows the DMCL vehicle with 15 first and 18 standard class seats and a solid side wall between the cab and first door position. Set No. 185113 is seen at Doncaster.* **CJM**

Right: *The DMS vehicle leads set No. 185151 and shows that two windows are located on this design behind the driving cab. These vehicles seat 64 standard class passengers. All Class 185s are painted in First Group 'dynamic lines' livery and are the only Siemens 'Desiro' diesel stock operating in the UK.* **CJM**

Below: *Class 185 intermediate Motor Standard Lavatory vehicle; seating in these vehicles is for 72 in the 2+2 mode.* **CJM**

Number range:	220001-220034
Introduced:	2000-2001
Built by:	Bombardier Transportation*
Formation:	DMSL+MS+MSL+DMFL
Vehicle numbers:	DMSL - 60301-60334
	MS - 60701-60734
	MSL - 60201-60234
	DMFL - 60401-60434
Vehicle length:	77ft 6in (23.62m)
Height:	12ft 4in (3.76m)
Width:	8ft 11in (2.72m)
Seating:	Total - 26F/174S
	DMSL - 42S
	MS - 66S
	MSL - 66S
	DMFL - 26F
Internal layout:	2+1F, 2+2S
Gangway:	Within set
Toilets:	DMSL, MSL, DMFL - 1
Weight:	Total - 194.7 tonnes
	DMSL - 51.2 tonnes
	MS - 45.9 tonnes
	MSL - 46.7 tonnes
	DMFL - 50.9 tonnes
Brake type:	Air, EP rheostatic
Bogie type:	Bombardier B5005
Power unit:	1 x Cummins of 750hp (560kW) per car
Transmission:	Electric
Transmission package:	Onix
Traction motor type:	8 x Alstom Onix 800 per train
Horsepower:	3,000hp (2,240kW)
Max speed:	125mph (201km/h)
Operating range:	1,350 miles (2,173km)
Route availability:	2
Coupling type:	Outer: Dellner 12, Inner: Bar
Multiple restriction:	Class 220, 221 and Class 57/3
Door type:	Single-leaf swing plug
Body construction:	Steel
Special fittings:	Air conditioning, non tilt
Owner:	Halifax/Bank of Scotland
Operator:	Arriva CrossCountry

* Body shells assembled in Belgium, fitted out at Bombardier plants in Wakefield, UK, and Brugge, Belgium.

Above: *CrossCountry Trains operates all 34 of the four-car 'Voyager' sets, originally introduced by Virgin Trains in 2000. Based at Central Rivers depot near Burton, each set seats 26 first and 174 standard class passengers. All sets are painted in XC silver and maroon. Set No. 220018 is seen near Powderham in Devon led by its DMF vehicle.* **CJM**

Fact File

After privatisation in the mid-1990s and Virgin Group taking over two of the most important franchises, CrossCountry and West Coast, new train orders followed.

For CrossCountry a diesel train was needed as the majority of services operated for all or part of their journey away from overhead power supplies. A number of options were studied and eventually a significant number of four- and five-car DMUs were ordered from Bombardier.

To facilitate tilting on selected routes two distinct fleets of trains, which became known as 'Voyager', were ordered, 34 sets with conventional running gear (Class 220) and 44 sets with full body tilt (Class 221).

The sets are high-powered with 3,000hp available for just four cars, using underfloor-mounted power units.

Passenger accommodation is limited with a single four-car train seating just 160 standard class passengers; this has subsequently been increased to 174 standard and 26 first class passengers, compared to around 400 in an HST they replaced.

One driving car in each set is set out for first class, identified by a yellow cant-rail band.

Following franchise changes in 2007, Virgin lost the CrossCountry operation to Arriva Trains, which took over the entire Class 220 fleet and many Class 221s. Arriva reliveried its fleet in a two-tone silver/grey, offset by pink passenger doors and maroon driving car ends, with a large stylised XC on the cab sides.

Originally under the Virgin franchise all sets were named, but these were removed following the franchise change. All sets have now lost their buffet car/shop thus increasing seating. All sets are allocated to Central Rivers depot near Burton. ■

Above: *'Voyager' front end equipment positions, also applicable to Class 221 sets. A: High-level marker light, B: Destination indicator, C: Light clusters each housing one white marker, red tail and headlight, D: Lamp bracket, E: Roller cover to electrical connections - on DMFL cars these are painted yellow to identify the first class end, F: Dellner coupling, G: Warning horns, H: Power jumper socket. DMFL from set No. 220032 illustrated.* **CJM**

Right Middle and Below: *On Class 220 stock there are two intermediate MS vehicles; originally one of was a buffet/shop, but under XC this has been removed. In the view right is car 60218, one of the original shop cars viewed from its toilet end. The view below shows No. 60724, an original MS shown from its vestibule end.* **CJM**

Diesel Multiple Units

Class:	221 (5-car)	221 (5-car)	(4-car)
Number range:	221101-221118, 221142-221143	221119-221140	221141
Introduced:	2001-2002	2001-2002	
Built by:	Bombardier Transportation*	Bombardier Transportation*	
Formation:	DMSL+MSL(A)+MSL(B)+MSRMB+DMFL	DMSL+MS+MSL(A)+MSL(B)+DMFL	
Vehicle numbers:	DMSL - 60351-60368 , 60392-60393	DMSL - 60369-60390, 60391	
	MSL(A) - 60951-60968, 60992-60993	MS - 60769-60790, 60791	
	MSL(B) - 60851-60868 , 60994, 60794	MSL(A) - 60969-60990, 60991	
	MSRMB - 60751-60768, 60792-60793	MSL(B) - 60869-60890, -	
	DMFL - 60451-60468, 60492-60493	DMFL - 60469-60490, 60491	
Vehicle length:	77ft 6in (23.67m)	77ft 6in (23.67m)	
Height:	12ft 4in (3.75m)	12ft 4in (3.75m)	
Width:	8ft 11in (2.73m)	8ft 11in (2.73m)	
Seating:	5-car Total - 26F/224S,	5-car Total - 26F/238S,	
		4-car Total - 26F/176S	
	DMSL - 42S	DMSL - 42S	
	MSL(A) - 68S	MS - 66S	
	MSL(B) - 62S	MSL(A) - 68S	
	MSRMB - 52S	MSL(B) - 62S	
	DMFL - 26F	DMFL - 26F	
Internal layout:	2+1F, 2+2S	2+1F, 2+2S	
Gangway:	Within set	Within set	
Toilets:	DMSL, MSL, DMFL - 1	DMSL, MSL, DMFL - 1	
Weight:	Total - 278.3 tonnes	Total - 5-car - 280.7 tonnes, 4-car - 226.3 tonnes	
	DMSL - 58.9 tonnes	DMSL - 58.5 tonnes	
	MSRMB - 53.1 tonnes	MS - 54.1 tonnes	
	MSL(A) - 56.6 tonnes	MSL(A) - 54.8 tonnes	
	MSL(B) - 53.1 tonnes	MSL(B) - 54.4 tonnes	
	DMFL - 56.6 tonnes	DMFL - 58.9 tonnes	
Brake type:	Air, EP rheostatic	Air, EP rheostatic	
Bogie type:	Bombardier HVT	Bombardier HVT	
Power unit:	1 x Cummins of 560kW (750hp)	1 x Cummins of 560kW (750hp)	
	at 1800rpm per car	at 1800rpm per car	
Transmission:	Electric Onix	Electric Onix	
Traction motor:	10 or 8 x Alstom Onix 800 per train	10 or 8 x Alstom Onix 800 per train	
Horsepower:	3,750hp (2,796kW)	5-car - 3,750hp (2,796kW)	
		4-car - 3,000hp (2,237kW)	
Max speed:	125mph (201km/h)	125mph (201km/h)	
Operating range:	1,200 miles (1,931km)	1,200 miles (1,931km)	
Route availability:	4	4	
Coupling type:	Outer: Dellner 12, Inner: Bar	Outer: Dellner 12, Inner: Bar	
Multiple restriction:	Class 220/221 only	Class 220/221 only	
Door type:	Single-leaf swing plug	Single-leaf swing plug	
Body construction:	Steel	Steel	
Special fittings:	Air conditioning, tilt fitted	Air conditioning, tilt (isolated)	
Owner:	Halifax/Bank of Scotland	Halifax/Bank of Scotland	
Operator:	Virgin Trains	Arriva CrossCountry	

* Body shells assembled in Belgium, fitted out at Bombardier plants in Wakefield, UK, and Brugge, Belgium.

Left: *Today, Virgin Trains operates a fleet of just 20 'Super Voyager' Class 221 sets on West Coast and North Wales services, allocated to Central Rivers depot. These sets sport Virgin silver and red livery with black/white 'zebra' doors. With its DMF nearest the camera, identifiable by the yellow roller cover to the front end electrical box, set No. 221114 passes South Kenton heading for Euston. These Virgin sets retain a shop and seat 26 first and 222 standard class passengers.* **CJM**

Diesel Multiple Units

To enable higher speeds to be accomplished in selected areas on the West Coast Main Line and on the Didcot-Birmingham route, a tilt system was introduced by Virgin Trains, where trackside beacons supplied 'authority' for trains to activate the tilt system on selected sections and travel around 10 per cent faster without discomfort to passengers and with total safety.

These 'tilt' sets were considerably modified from conventional 'Voyager' stock and have different bogies and control equipment.

After testing in France, the system was activated in the UK on Virgin 'Super Voyager' and 'Pendolino' stock.

Originally the Class 221s came in both five- and four-car formations. The five-car sets were designed for general use, and the four-car sets for use on the Euston-Holyhead route. Following franchise changes and Virgin losing the CrossCountry operation to Arriva, the '221' fleet was split between the two operators; the VT sets retain tilting capability, while tilt has been isolated on the CrossCountry sets. All but one of the original four-car Class 221s were reformed in 2010 to five-car formation.

The Class 221s are basically the same train as the '220'; the interiors are identical. Buffet/shops have been removed from CrossCountry sets. All sets are allocated to Central Rivers. ∎

Above: *A fleet of 23 'Super Voyager' Class 221 sets is operated by CrossCountry and works alongside the Class 220 sets. These '221s' have had their original tilt system isolated. These five-car sets for XC seat 26 first and 238 second class passengers. All sets carry standard XC livery and are maintained at Central Rivers depot, Burton. Set No. 221128 is shown arriving at Basingstoke with a Bournemouth to Manchester Piccadilly service.* **CJM**

Above: *The intermediate vehicles of the XC Class 221s are all classified as MS and seat 62-66 passengers depending on configuration. All vehicles are externally the same. Middle MS No. 60978 from set No. 221128 is shown viewed from its vestibule end.* **CJM**

Below: *In 2013 a start was made on replacing the nose end valance of the 'Voyager' fleet with a more aerodynamic unit, slightly changing the shape of the unit front ends. In this view, a new front end is seen on set No. 221130 on the left coupled to set No. 221126 still sporting the original front end design. The design change has also seen the repositioning of the running number* **Nathan Williamson**

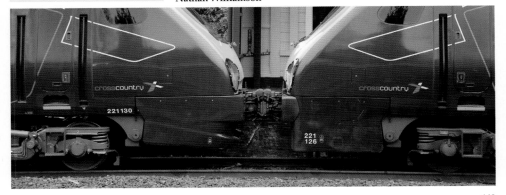

Class 222 'Meridian'

Sub-class:	222/0 'Meridian' (7-car)	222/4 'Meridian' (5-car)	222/1 (4-car)
Number range:	222001 - 222006	222007 - 222023	222101 - 222104
Introduced:	2004-2005	Built 2004-05	2005
Built by:	Bombardier Brugge	Bombardier Brugge	Bombardier Brugge
Formation:	DMF+MF+MF+ MSRMB MS+MS+DMS	DMF+MC+MSRMB+ MS+DMS	DMF+MC+MSRMB+DMS
Vehicle numbers:	DMF - 60241-60246 MF - 60345-47/60445-47 MF - 60341-44/60441-43 MSRMB - 60621-60626 MS - 60561-60566 MS - 60544-60556 DMS - 60161-60166	DMF - 60247-60263 MC - 60442/60918-60933 MSRMB - 60627-60643 MS - 60531-60567 DMS - 60167-60183	DMF - 60271-60274 MC - 60571-60574 MSRMB - 60681-60684 DMS - 60191-60194
Vehicle length:	Driving - 78ft 2in (23.85m) Int - 78ft 2in (23.00m)	Driving - 78ft 2in (23.85m) Int - 78ft 2in (23.00m)	Driving - 78ft 2in (23.85m) Int - 75ft 4in (23.00m)
Height:	12ft 4in (3.75m)	12ft 4in (3.75m)	12ft 4in (3.75m)
Width:	8ft 11in (2.73m)	8ft 11in (2.73m)	8ft 11in (2.73m)
Seating:	Total - 106F/236S DMF - 22F MF - 42F MF - 42F MSRMB - 62S MS - 68S DMS - 38S	Total - 50F/192S DMF - 22F MC - 28F/22S MSRMB - 62S MS - 68S DMS - 40S	Total - 33F/148S DMF - 22F MC - 11F/46S MSRMB - 62S DMSO - 40S
Internal layout:	2+1F, 2+2S	2+1F, 2+2S	2+1F, 2+2S
Gangway:	Within set	Within set	Within set
Toilets:	DMF, MF, MS, DMS - 1	DMF, MC, MS, DMS - 1	DMF, MC, DMS - 1
Weight:	Total - 337.8 tonnes DMS - 52.8 tonnes MF - 46.8 tonnes MF - 46.8 tonnes MSRMB - 48 tonnes MS - 47 tonnes DMSO - 49.4 tonnes	Total - 249 tonnes DMF - 52.8 tonnes MC - 48.6 tonnes MSRMB - 49.6 tonnes MS - 47 tonnes DMS - 51 tonnes	Total - 197.3 tonnes DMF - 52.8 tonnes MC - 47.1 tonnes MSRMB - 48 tonnes DMSO - 49.4 tonnes
Brake type:	Air, EP regenerative	Air, EP regenerative	Air, EP regenerative
Bogie type:	Bombardier B5005	Bombardier B5005	Bombardier B5005
Power unit:	1 x Cummins QSK9R of 560kW (750hp) per car	1 x Cummins QSK9R of 560kW (750hp) per car	1 x Cummins QSK9R of 560kW (750hp) per car
Transmission:	Electric 16 x Alstom Onix 800 per train	Electric 10 x Alstom Onix 800 per train	Electric 8 x Alstom Onix 800 per train
Horsepower:	5,250hp (3,920kW)	3,750hp (2,800kW)	3,000hp (2,240kW)
Max speed:	125mph (201km/h)	125mph (201km/h)	125mph (201km/h)
Operating range:	1,350 miles (2,173km)	1,350 miles (2,173km)	1,350 miles (2,173km)
Route availability:	4	2	2
Coupling type:	Dellner 12	Dellner 12	Dellner 12
Multiple restriction:	Class 222	Class 222	Class 222 only
Door type:	Single-leaf swing plug	Single-leaf swing plug	Single-leaf swing plug
Body construction:	Steel	Steel	Steel
Owner:	Eversholt	Eversholt	Eversholt
Operator:	East Midlands Trains	East Midlands Trains	East Midlands Trains
Notes:			Previously 'Pioneer' sets Operated by Hull Trains

Fact File

When Midland Mainline and Hull Trains required new stock, the Bombardier 'Voyager' product was ordered. This time a more luxurious product with improved seating was supplied, and all were built at the Brugge plant.

Hull Trains operated four four-car sets and MML three batches, seven eight-car, seven five-car and eight four-car sets. The body structure of these sets differs slightly from the Virgin product.

Following franchise changes, the Hull Trains sets are now operated East Midlands Trains.

Various reformations have taken place and the fleet is now formed as six seven-car sets, 17 five-car sets and four four-car units.

All sets carry Stagecoach white livery. Sets are allocated to purpose-built maintenance facilities at Derby, with the '222s' mainly operating on the core London to Sheffield route. ∎

Above and Below: *Although built in different formations for operator Midland Mainline, the original Class 222 sets are formed as six seven-car and 17 five-car trains, allocated to Derby Etches Park and used on East Midlands Trains main line services. The DMF vehicles sport a sizeable food preparation area directly behind the driving cab which feeds the first class area, while standard class catering is supplied from a MSRMB vehicle. The sets are all painted in Stagecoach/EMT main line white livery with a seven-car set providing seating for 106 first and 236 standard class passengers. The five-car formations seat 50 first and 192 standard. In the upper view seven-car set No. 222005 approaches Clay Cross Junction with a Sheffield to London service, while the illustration below shows a five-car set also approaching Clay Cross Junction with a Sheffield bound service. Both:* **CJM**

Left: *The Class 222 sets, based on the previously-built Class 220/221 'Voyager' stock, have passenger doors at either end of vehicles which give access to transverse walkways, from which saloon sliding doors give access to the seating area. Seats in standard class are in the 2+2 style, while those in first class are in the 2+1 layout. The Class 222 sets were not designed for tilt operation. The five-car sets have a Motor Composite vehicle with 28 first and 22 standard class seating; this is coupled with the first class end attached to the DMRFO vehicle. First class seating is identified by a row of red spots above the passenger windows. Car 60919 is illustrated.* **Antony Christie**

Right: *The Motor Standard (MS) vehicles of Class 222/0 and 222/4 sets each seat 68 with a toilet compartment and a luggage stack at one end. Viewed from its toilet end, MS No. 60542 from set No. 222022 is seen at St Pancras.* **Antony Christie**

Below: *Four Class 222/1 sets were originally built for Hull Trains, but when this route received other longer trains, the four-car Class 222s were transferred to East Midlands Trains to supplement their expanding operation. The sets were refurbished and now sport EMT livery. Some minor interior detail differences exist. Set No. 222102 passes southbound through Loughborough with its DMF vehicle leading.* **John Stretton**

Right: *Based on the original Virgin Trains 'Voyager' front end, the body profile adopted for the original Midland Mainline and Hull Trains (now East Midlands Trains) sets was slightly revised. Main equipment positions are - A: High-level marker light, B: Destination indicator, C: Screen wash jets, D: Light cluster, with one main headlight and a joint white marker/red tail light on each side, E: Emergency lamp bracket, F: Dellner coupling with electrical connection box above, which if painted yellow indicates first class accommodation is at that end of the train.* **CJM**

Diesel Multiple Units

Below: *Class 222/0 interior showing one of the first class vehicles from set No. 222007. In first class seating is in the 2+1 style, using individual seats with hinged arm rests. Each seat is by a table. Above seat and end of coach luggage racks are provided. An above seat electronic seat reservation system is provided and a passenger information system is located at coach ends.* **Alexis Hulme**

Sub-class:	313/0 & 313/1	313/2
Number range:	313018-313064, 313121-313134	313201-313220
Former number range:	-	313101-313120 (ex 313001-313020)
Introduced:	1976-1977	As 313/2 - 2010
Built/rebuilt by:	BREL York	As 313/2 - Wolverton
Formation:	DMSO+PTSO+BDMSO	DMSO+PTSO+BDMSO
Vehicle numbers:	DMSO - 62546-62592	DMSO - 62529-62548
	PTSO - 71230-71276	PTSO - 71213-71232
	BDMSO - 62610-62656	BDMSO - 62593-61612
Set length:	199ft 6in (60.83m)	199ft 6in (60.83m)
Vehicle length:	DMSO/BDMSO - 64ft 11½in (19.80m)	DMSO/BDMSO - 64ft 11½in (19.80m)
	PTSO - 65ft 4¼in (19.92m)	PTSO - 65ft 4¼in (19.92m)
Height:	11ft 9in (3.58m)	11ft 9in (3.58m)
Width:	9ft 3in (2.82m)	9ft 3in (2.82m)
Seating:	Total - 231S	Total - 202S
	DMSO - 74S	DMSO - 66S
	PTSO - 83S	PTSO - 70S
	BDMSO - 74S	BDMSO - 66S
Internal layout:	2+2/2+3 high density	2+2/2+3 high density
Gangway:	Within set, emergency end doors	Within set, emergency end doors
Toilets:	Not fitted	Not fitted
Weight:	Total - 104.5 tonnes	Total - 104.5 tonnes
	DMSO - 36 tonnes	DMSO - 36 tonnes
	PTSO - 31 tonnes	PTSO - 31 tonnes
	BDMSO - 37.5 tonnes	BDMSO - 37.5 tonnes
Brake type:	Air (Westcode), rheostatic	Air (Westcode), rheostatic
Bogie type:	BX1	BX1
Power collection:	25kV ac overhead &	750V dc third rail
	750V dc third rail	
Traction motor type:	8 x GEC G310AZ	8 x GEC G310AZ
Horsepower:	880hp (657kW)	880hp (657kW)
Max speed:	75mph (121km/h)	75mph (121km/h)
Coupling type:	Outer - Tightlock	Outer - Tightlock
	Inner - Bar	Inner - Bar
Multiple restriction:	Within class only	Within class only
Door type:	Bi-parting sliding	Bi-parting sliding
Special features:	CCTV	CCTV
Total sets in traffic:	44 sets	20 sets
Construction:	Steel frame, aluminium alloy body	Steel frame, aluminium alloy body
Owner:	Eversholt (313121 = Beacon Rail)	Beacon Rail
Operator:	First Capital Connect, Network Rail	Southern
Sub-class differences:	As-built units (refurbished), originally	Fitted with extra shoegear
	for Great Northern electrification	Pantographs removed

Electric Multiple Units

These sets were the first production order for 1972-design high-density stock, devised from the prototype PEP unit used on the Southern Region.

Originally all sets were used on the Great Northern suburban electrification system (now operated by First Capital Connect), but later a number of units were transferred to the North London Line and operated between London Euston and Watford as well as on the West London Line. The sets were later taken under the umbrella of London Overground and phased out with the introduction of Class 378s.

The displaced sets from London Overground were taken over by Southern and FCC.

The Southern Class 313/2 sets are allocated to Brighton for 'Coastway' use, and carry Southern white and green livery.

The main Class 313/0 fleet still remains on the Great Northern, and operates on First Capital Connect suburban services from Moorgate/London King's Cross; the units are painted in FCC colours.

Dual voltage operation is retained on FCC sets; Southern sets are DC only. ∎

Right: *Class 313 front end equipment positions. A: Air warning horns, B: Destination indicator, C: Front end emergency door (for tunnel working), D: White marker light, E: Red tail light, F: Headlight, G: Lamp bracket, H: Emergency air connection. I: Tightlock coupling with roller-cover pneumatic and electric connections below, J: Drum switch box, K: Emergency coupling release handle, L: Forward facing CCTV camera. Set No. 313050 is illustrated from the FCC fleet. Equipment is the same on 313/2 sets.* **CJM**

Below Left: *The largest operator of Class 313 stock is First Capital Connect, which in 2014 had a fleet of 44 dual voltage sets allocated to Hornsey depot in north London for Great Northern route services radiating from London King's Cross and Moorgate. The first derivative of the 1972 prototype high-density PEP stock, these sets were introduced for the Great Northern electrification. Now painted in First Group 'Urban' livery, set No. 313036 is seen passing Harringay.* **CJM**

Below Right: *The high-density Class 313/0 and 313/1 interiors use the 2+3 seating layout, with two double-leaf sliding doors on each side of each vehicle feeding directly into the passenger saloon. Opening hopper windows are provided in each window as no air conditioning is provided. Local passenger operation of doors is by buttons at chest height.* **CJM**

Above: *The intermediate trailer standard on the Class 313s houses the roof mounted pantograph and underslung transformer, which changes the window positioning at that end of the vehicle. Seating in these intermediate coaches is for 83. Vehicle No. 71251 from set No. 313039 is illustrated.* **CJM**

Below: *Network Rail is currently leasing set No. 313121 from Beacon Rail, as a test facility for European Rail Traffic Management System (ERTMS) for use on the Hertford Loop. This pioneering project involved resignalling a 5½-mile section of the double-track route to allow passenger services to use one line, freeing the other for Network Rail ERTMS test running. The unit was overhauled at Alstom Wembley and repainted into Network Rail yellow livery. Internally its was refurbished to include a revised driving desk, engineering equipment, a kitchen and toilet. Full ERTMS equipment is fitted. It was completed in June 2013 and commenced testing in July 2013 and in 2014 was frequently seen operating over the Hertford Loop line. In this view the set is seen at Willesden depot.* **Antony Christie**

Traction Recognition

Above: *In 2010 operator Southern took over a fleet of 19 Class 313s for deployment on its Coastway operation radiating from Brighton, and they were reclassified as 313/2. The sets were fully refurbished and now sport low-density 2+2 seating and a pictogram version of Southern green and white livery. Based at Brighton these sets are now deemed as dc only. Units are owned by Beacon Rail. Set No. 313202 is seen arriving at Fratton with a Portsmouth to Brighton duty.* **CJM**

Right Middle: *Intermediate vehicle showing the Southern Coastway branding. These vehicles now seat 70 in the 2+2 style.* **CJM**

Right Bottom: *The spacious 2+2 style interior of the 313/2 sets, a vast contrast to the original high-density low-back seat style when first introduced.* **CJM**

Below: *Bodyside applied route specific pictogram branding.* **CJM**

Class 314

Number range:	314201-314216
Introduced:	1979-1980
Built by:	BREL York
Formation:	DMSO+PTSO+DMSO
Vehicle numbers:	DMSO - 64583-64614
	PTSO - 71450-71465
Set length:	199ft 6in (60.83m)
Vehicle length:	DMSO - 64ft 11½in (19.80m)
	PTSO - 65ft 4¼in (19.92m)
Height:	11ft 6½in (3.58m)
Width:	9ft 3in (2.82m)
Seating:	Total - 212S
	DMSO - 68S
	PTSO - 76S
	DMSO - 68S*
Internal layout:	2+3 high density *
Gangway:	Within set (emergency end doors)
Toilets:	Not fitted
Weight:	Total - 102 tonnes
	DMSO - 34.5 tonnes
	PTSO - 33 tonnes
	DMSO - 34.5 tonnes
Brake type:	Air (Westcode), rheostatic
Bogie type:	BX1
Power collection:	25kV ac overhead
Traction motor type:	314201-314206 - 8 x Brush TM61-53
	314207-314216 - 8 x GEC G310AZ
Horsepower:	880hp (657kW)
Max speed:	75mph (121km/h)
Coupling type:	Outer - Tightlock, Inner - Bar
Multiple restriction:	Within class only
Door type:	Bi-parting sliding
Total sets in traffic:	16
Construction:	Steel frame, aluminium alloy body
Owner:	Angel Trains
Operator:	First ScotRail

Note: * Set 314203 has an ex-Class 507 DMSO (64426) seating 74S.

Fact File

Built as inner-suburban stock for the Glasgow area, these are similar to the previously covered Class 313s but take power only from the ac overhead.

Sets were built at BREL York and delivered between May and July 1979, entering service in October the same year.

As with the Class 313s, these sets were required to operate through tunnel sections in the central Glasgow area, and to provide an emergency egress end doors were provided.

Seating is in the 2+2/2+3 high-density style with two pairs of double-leaf sliding doors on each vehicle, allowing rapid entry/exit of passengers at peak times.

To meet the then BRB dual supply of traction equipment policy the first six units were equipped with Brush equipment, and the remainder GEC.

Originally the sets were painted in BR blue/grey 'Trans-Clyde' livery; this changed to Strathclyde orange, then carmine and cream; currently Scottish Railways blue Saltire livery is applied.

All sets are allocated to Glasgow Shields Road. ■

Electric Multiple Units

Traction Recognition

Above: *The fleet of 16 First ScotRail-operated, Angel Trains-owned Class 314 sets is allocated to Glasgow Shields Road depot and used on the Glasgow suburban system. Recently overhauled, most now sport the latest blue and white Saltire livery. DMSO No. 64605 from set No. 314212 is illustrated at Glasgow Works.*
Bill Wilson

Right Middle: *The intermediate Class 314 vehicle is a Pantograph Trailer Standard Open, seating 76 in the high-density 2+3 style. This view shows the coach from its pantograph end with the slightly revised bodyside window arrangement.* **Bill Wilson**

Left: *Front end equipment positions for the Class 314 fleet are the same as the previously detailed Class 313s. The sets mainly operate on the Cathcart Circle Line services to Cathcart, Neilston and Newton. Some sets also work Inverclyde Line services to Gourock and Wemyss Bay, during peak hours. In more recent times the class has been operating the Paisley Canal Line during off-peak times following electrification of the branch.* **Murdoch Currie**

Right Bottom: *The Class 314 interiors have changed little in design since first introduced, still retaining the low back sets of the 1970s favoured in all the 1972-design stock when introduced. However today it is covered in ScotRail moquette. Passenger saloons are fed by two pairs of sliding doors on each side.*
Bill Wilson

Traction Recognition

Class 315

Number range:	315801-315861
Introduced:	1980-1981
Built/rebuilt by:	BREL York
Formation:	DMSO+TSO+PTSO+DMSO
Vehicle numbers:	DMSO - 64461-64582
	TSO - 71281-71341
	PTSO - 71389-71449
Set length:	264ft 10in (80.72m)
Vehicle length:	DMSO - 64ft 11½in (19.80m)
	TSO, PTSO - 65ft 4¼in (19.92m)
Height:	11ft 9in (3.58m)
Width:	9ft 3in (2.82m)
Seating:	Total - 318S
	DMSO - 74S
	TSO - 86S
	PTSO - 84S
	DMSO - 74S
Internal layout:	2+2/2+3 high density
Gangway:	Within set, end emergency door
Toilets:	Not fitted
Weight:	Total - 127.5 tonnes
	DMSO - 35 tonnes
	TSO - 25.5 tonnes
	PTSO - 32 tonnes
	DMSO - 35 tonnes
Brake type:	Air (Westcode), rheostatic
Bogie type:	BX1
Power collection:	25kV ac overhead
Traction motor type:	315801-315841 - 8 x Brush TM61-53
	315842-315861 - 8 x GEC G310AZ
Horsepower:	880hp (657kW)
Max speed:	75mph (121km/h)
Coupling type:	Outer - Tightlock, Inner - Bar
Multiple restriction:	Within class
Door type:	Bi-parting sliding
Total sets in traffic:	61
Construction:	Steel frame, aluminium alloy body
Owner:	Eversholt
Operator	Greater Anglia

Fact File

The modernisation of the Liverpool Street 'Great Eastern' suburban lines from 1980 saw a fleet of 61 four-car high-density sets built to the 1972 design by BREL York Works.

The sets, with accommodation for 318, plus an equal number standing, replaced the Class 306 sliding door sets firstly on the Shenfield route and then other inner-suburban lines.

Designed for ac only operation, the sets were delivered in BR blue/grey livery. This later gave way to Network SouthEast colours and following privatisation the colours of Great Eastern then 'one' Railway, National Express East Anglia and recently Abellio Greater Anglia liveries have been applied.

All sets are allocated to Ilford depot. The sets will be replaced following the opening of the CrossRail project. ∎

Below: *The 61 Great Eastern route Class 315s, introduced in 1980 to replace Class 306 stock will be replaced when CrossRail opens in a few years time. At present the sets are based at Ilford and progressively are being repainted in Greater Anglia white livery with orange doors. Modified front end fitted No. 315804 is seen arriving at Stratford. This derivative of the 1972-design 'standard' EMU is for ac operation only.* **CJM**

Above Left and Right: *Class 315 front end design: on the left is the original layout, still carried by the majority of sets; on the right is a refurbished front end. Equipment positions are - A: Air warning horns, B: Emergency front door, C: Forward facing camera, D: White marker light, E: Red tail light, F: Headlight, G: Lamp bracket, H: Tightlock coupling, I: Emergency air connector, J: Drum switch, K: Combined white marker/ red tail light. L: High intensity headlights, M: High-level marker light. Both:* **CJM**

Right Middle: *Class 315 Pantograph Trailer Standard viewed from the pantograph end showing the revised window positions and the transformer below the nearest pair of passenger doors. The vehicle, No. 71443, is from set No. 315855 and shows the latest Greater Anglia white and orange colours.* **CJM**

Right Bottom: *Class 315 Trailer Standard Open, viewed from the DMSO end. With high-density seating these vehicles seat 86 in the 2+3 mode. Opening hopper windows are provided as the sets do not have air conditioning. Passenger doors have local controls located on either side of the bi-parting doors. Vehicle No. 71335 from set No. 315855 is illustrated at Stratford.* **CJM**

Sub-class:	317/3	317/5	317/6
Number range:	317337-317348	317501-317515	317649-317672
Previous numbers:	-	317301-317320	317349-317372
Introduced:	1981-1982	1981-1982	1985-1986
Refurbished:	-	from 2005	1999-2000
Built by:	DTSO, MSO - BREL York TCO - BREL Derby	DTSO, MSO - BREL York TCO - BREL Derby	BREL York
Refurbished by:	-	Ilford	Railcare Wolverton
Formation:	DTSO(A)+MSO+ TCO+DTSO(B)	DTSO(A)+MSO+ TCO+DTSO(B)	DTS+MSO+ TSO+DTCO
Vehicle numbers:	DTSO(A) - 77036-77047 MSO - 62671-62708 TCO - 71613-71624 DTSO(B) - 77084-77095	DTSO(A) - 77001-77024 MSO - 62661-62680 TCO - 71577-71596 DTO - 77048-77067	DTSO - 77200-19, 280-283 MSO - 62846-65, 886-889 TSO - 71734-53, 762-765 DTCO- 77220-39, 285-287
Set length:	265ft 6in (80.94m)	265ft 6in (80.94m)	265ft 6in (80.94m)
Vehicle length:	DTSO(A)- 65ft ¾in (19.83m) MSO - 65ft 4¼in (19.92m) TCO - 65ft 4¼in (19.92m) DTSO(B) 65ft ¾in (19.83m)	DTSO(A)- 65ft ¾in (19.83m) MSO - 65ft 4¼in (19.92m) TCO - 65ft 4¼in (19.92m) DTSO(B) 65ft ¾in (19.83m)	DTSO(A)- 65ft ¾in (19.83m) MSO - 65ft 4¼in (19.92m) TCO - 65ft 4¼in (19.92m) DTCO 65ft ¾in (19.83m)
Height:	12ft 1½in (3.70m)	12ft 1½in (3.70m)	12ft 1½in (3.70m)
Width:	9ft 3in (2.82m)	9ft 3in (2.82m)	9ft 3in (2.82m)
Seating:	Total - 22F/270S DTSO(A) - 74S MSO - 79S TCO - 22F/46S DTSO(B) - 71S	Total - 22F/269S DTSO(A) - 74S MSO - 79S TCO - 22F/46S DTSO(B) - 70S	Total - 24F/244S DTSO - 64S MSO - 70S TSO - 62S DTCO - 24F/48S
Internal layout:	2+2F/2+3S	2+2F/2+3S	2+2F/2+2S
Gangway:	Throughout	Throughout	Throughout
Toilets:	TCO - 2	TCO - 2	TSO - 2
Weight:	Total - 137 tonnes DTSO(A) - 29.5 tonnes MSO - 49 tonnes TCO - 29 tonnes DTSO(B) - 29.5 tonnes	Total - 137 tonnes DTSO(A) - 29.5 tonnes MSO - 49 tonnes TCO - 29 tonnes DTSO(B) - 29.5 tonnes	Total - 137 tonnes DTSO - 29.5 tonnes MSO - 49 tonnes TSO - 29 tonnes DTCO - 29.5 tonnes
Brake type:	Air	Air	Air
Bogie type:	Powered - BREL BP20 Trailer - BREL BT13	Powered - BREL BP20 Trailer - BREL BT13	Powered - BREL BP20 Trailer - BREL BT13
Power collection:	25kV ac overhead	25kV ac overhead	25kV ac overhead
Traction motor type:	4 x GEC G315BZ	4 x GEC G315BZ	4 x GEC G315BZ
Horsepower:	1,328hp (990kW)	1,328hp (990kW)	1,328hp (990kW)
Max speed:	100mph (161km/h)	100mph (161km/h)	100mph (161km/h)
Coupling type:	Outer - Tightlock Inner – Bar	Outer - Tightlock Inner – Bar	Outer - Tightlock Inner – Bar
Multiple restriction:	Within class	Within class	Within class
Door type:	Bi-parting sliding	Bi-parting sliding	Bi-parting sliding
Special fittings:	Pressure ventilated	Pressure ventilated	Convection heating
Total sets in traffic:	12	15	24
Construction:	Steel	Steel	Steel
Owner:	Angel Trains	Angel Trains	Angel Trains
Operator:	First Capital Connect	Abellio Greater Anglia	Abellio Greater Anglia
Sub-class detail:	Phase 1 sets	Phase 1 sets	Phase 2 refurbished

Electric Multiple Units

Left: *First Capital Connect has a fleet of 12 Class 317/2 sets allocated to Hornsey for outer-suburban use. These are members of the original 1981-introduced 'Bed-Pan' stock with the original roof mounted horn front end design. Seating 22 first and 270 standard class passengers these 100mph sets are popular with passengers. Set No. 317341 is seen approaching Harringay.* **CJM**

317/7	317/8
317708-317732 (nine units)	317881-317892
317308-317332 (random)	317321-317336
1981-1982	1981-1982
2000	2006-2007
BREL York	DTSO, MSO - BREL York
	TCO - BREL Derby
Railcare Wolverton	Ilford
DTSO+MSO+TSO+DTCO	DTSO+MSO+TCO+DTSO
DTSO - 77007-77031 series	DTSO - 77020-77035
MSO - 62668-62692 series	MSO - 62681-62696
TSO - 71584-71608 series	TCO - 71597-71612
DTCO - 77055-77079 series	DTSO - 77068-77083
265ft 6in (80.94m)	265ft 6in (80.94m)
DTSO(A)- 65ft ¾in (19.83m)	DTSO(A)- 65ft ¾in (19.83m)
MSO - 65ft 4¼in (19.92m)	MSO - 65ft 4¼in (19.92m)
TSO - 65ft 4¼in (19.92m)	TCO - 65ft 4¼in (19.92m)
DTCO 65ft ¾in (19.83m)	DTSO(B) 65ft ¾in (19.83m)
12ft 1½in (3.70m)	12ft 1 ½in (3.70m)
9ft 3in (2.82m)	9ft 3in (2.82m)
Total - 22F/172S	Total - 20F/245S
DTS0(A) - 52S	DTSO(A) - 66S
MSO - 62S	MSO - 71S
TSO - 42S	TCO - 20F/42S
DTCO - 22F/16S	DTSO(B) - 66S
2+1F/2+2S	2+2F/2+3S
Throughout	Throughout
TSO- 2	TCO - 2
Total - 144.5 tonnes	Total - 137 tonnes
DTS - 31.4 tonnes	DTSO(A) - 29.5 tonnes
MSO - 51.3 tonnes	MSO - 49 tonnes
TSO - 30.2 tonnes	TCO - 29 tonnes
DTC - 31.6 tonnes	DTSO(B) - 29.5 tonnes
Air	Air
Powered - BREL BP20	Powered - BREL BP20
Trailer - BREL BT13	Trailer - BREL BT13
25kV ac overhead	25kV ac overhead
4 x GEC G315BZ	4 x GEC G315BZ
1,328hp (990kW)	1,328hp (990kW)
100mph (161km/h)	100mph (161km/h)
Outer - Tightlock	Outer - Tightlock
Inner – Bar	Inner – Bar
Within class	Within class
Bi-parting sliding	Bi-parting sliding
Pressure ventilated	Pressure ventilated
9	12
Steel	Steel
Angel Trains	Angel Trains
Currently off-lease	Abellio Greater Anglia

Fact File

Originally introduced for the 'Bed-Pan' electrification between Bedford and St Pancras/Moorgate, a total of 48 sets were built. The class saw a protracted entry into service as they were the first sets to be worked under driver-only operation.

Soon, a follow-on order for 24 'phase 2' units for use on the Great Northern route was placed; these were slightly different in exterior appearance.

After Class 319s were introduced on 'Thameslink' services, the '317s' were transferred to the Euston-Birmingham route; after a short time the sets were replaced here by '321s', and the '317s' moved again to West Anglia, some operating for a short time on LTS services.

The sets today operate for Abellio Greater Anglia and on First Capital Connect routes.

Nine units were rebuilt in 2000 with new front ends and revised seating to provide an improved service on the then developing Stansted Express Liverpool Street-Stansted Airport service. These sets are currently off-lease.

In 2014 five sub-classes of Class 317s exist.

In 2013 set No. 317722 was given a trial refurbishment as a demonstrator for future overhauls. The work was undertaken by Bombardier at Ilford. ∎

Right: *A fleet of 15 of the original 'Bed-Pan' Class 317s, now classified as 317/5, is operated by Greater Anglia on West Anglia services, based at Ilford depot. Seating 22 first and 269 standard class passengers, these sets sport a mix of former National Express grey and white livery with Greater Anglia branding, or the latest Greater Anglia white livery. Set No. 317501 is illustrated.* **Antony Christie**

Left: *Class 317/3 and 317/5 front end equipment positions. A: Air warning horns, B: Destination/route indicator, C: Front end gangway door, D: White marker light, E: Red tail light, F: Headlight, G: Lamp bracket, H: Cab vent grille, I: Pneumatic and electric coupling connections behind roll door, J: Tightlock coupling, K: Emergency coupling release handle. L: Drum switch.* **CJM**

Below: *By the time the follow-on order for Class 317s was placed, the new standard EMU front end had been introduced, eliminating the ugly roof line of the original design. A fleet of 24 units was built which are now classified as 317/6; they were originally numbered in the 317349-317372 series. These sets are allocated to Greater Anglia at Ilford for outer suburban duties. Seating is for 24 first and 244 standard class passengers in the 2+2/2+3 style. Set No. 317649 is illustrated from its DTCO end.* **CJM**

Right Top: *A Class 317/6 intermediate TSO vehicle, showing the two passenger operated bi-parting sliding doors on each side. The smaller window at the near end is adjacent to the small toilet compartment; apart from brake and lighting equipment no other underslung equipment is carried on these vehicles.* **CJM**

Right Middle Upper: *Greater Anglia also operates a fleet of 12 Class 317/8s which are modified phase 1 units. These were upgraded for Stansted Airport use and seat 20 first and 245 standard class passengers. Sets are painted in a mix of Greater Anglia white and Greater Anglia branded former National Express grey and white colours. Set No. 317890 stands next to phase 2 set No. 317672 at Tottenham Hale, clearly showing the different front end designs.* **Antony Christie**

Right Middle Lower and Right Bottom: *In 2014 Bombardier Transportation was using off-lease Class 317/7 unit No. 317722 as a testbed. It has been rebuilt with a new traction equipment. Its original DC traction motors and thyristors have been removed and four new AC motors and two 3-phase converters fitted while the original transformer remains. Regenerative braking has also be fitted. New interiors have been installed to Driving Trailer Standard Open No. 77021 and Motor Standard Open No. 62682. If accepted by the owner/operators, this refurbishing could extend the Class 317 life expectancy by 20 years. The interior refurbishment gives a Metro style layout. On the right No. 317722 with its already modified Stansted front end is seen inside the main shop at Bombardier Ilford, while below is one of the revised interior designs. Both:* **Antony Christie**

Traction Recognition

Number range:	318250-318270
Introduced:	1985-1986
Built/rebuilt by:	BREL York
Formation:	DTSOL+MSOP+DTSO
Vehicle numbers:	DTSOL - 77240-77259/77288
	MSO - 62866-62885/62890
	DTSO - 77260-77279/77289
Vehicle length:	DTSOL/DTSO - 65ft 0¾in (19.83m)
	MSO - 65ft 4¼in (19.92m)
Height:	12ft 1½in (3.70m)
Width:	9ft 3in (2.82m)
Seating:	Total: 213S
	DTSOL - 64S, MSO - 77S, DTSO - 72S
Internal layout:	2+2/2+3 high density
Gangway:	Within set
Toilets:	DTSOL - 1
Weight:	Total - 107.5 tonnes
	DTSOL - 30 tonnes
	MSO - 50.9 tonnes
	DTSO - 26.6 tonnes
Brake type:	Air (Westcode)
Bogie type:	DTSOL/DTSO - BREL BT13
	MSO - BREL BP20
Power collection:	25kV ac overhead
Traction motor type:	4 x Brush TM2141
Horsepower:	1,438hp (1,072kW)
Max speed:	90mph (145km/h)
Coupling type:	Outer - Tightlock
	Within set - Bar
Multiple restriction:	Within type only
Door type:	Bi-parting sliding
Special features:	PA, CCTV, PIS
Total sets in traffic:	21
Construction:	Steel
Owner:	Eversholt
Operator:	First ScotRail

Fact File

With authorisation for the electrification of the route from Paisley to Ayr in 1982 came the need in the early 1980s for extra electric stock to operate through services between Glasgow and Ayr.

A batch of 21 trains of similar appearance to the already delivered Class 317s was ordered from BREL, being three-car outer-suburban sets with high-density interiors and end gangways.

The first train of the build was handed over in June 1986, more than a year before electric passenger workings commenced.

The sets have remained in the Glasgow area, and in recent years have been fully refurbished by Hunslet-Barclay, Kilmarnock, which has included removing the original front gangway connection, changing the appearance of these sets completely. ■

Electric Multiple Units

Right: *Modified Class 318 front end layout and equipment positions. A: Route indicator, B: Lamp bracket, C: Light cluster, with one headlight and one dual white marker/red tail light, D: Air warning horns, E: Tightlock coupling, F: drum switch. The front end of set No. 318258 is illustrated.* **Bill Wilson**

Below: *Allocated to Glasgow Shields Road depot, the Class 318s currently operate on the Argyle and North Clyde Line. In 2013-14 a major upgrade programme commenced with sets visiting Wabtec Rail at Doncaster; this light refurbishment work will see the latest Scottish blue and white livery applied. Set No. 318263 is seen at Milngavie.* **Murdoch Currie**

Below: *The intermediate vehicle of the Class 318 is an MSO, housing all the traction equipment, as well as the roof mounted pantograph. Internally the vehicles seat 77 in the 3+2 style. Passenger access is by two pairs of bi-parting doors feeding direct into the passenger saloon. As these sets are not fitted with air conditioning, opening hopper windows are provided. Car No. 62876 from set No. 318260 is illustrated.* **Bill Wilson**

Left: *Originally built with the same front end style as the previously described Class 317 phase 2 sets, the 21 Scottish allocated Class 318s have been rebuilt to eliminate the front gangway door and install a middle forward facing window New deeper cab side windows have also been fitted. Set No. 318251 shows the latest Scottish Railways livery applied to refurbished sets from 2014 on release from Wabtec Doncaster.* **Bill Wilson**

Sub-class:	319/0	319/2	319/3
Number range:	319001-319013	319214-319220	319361-319386
Former number range:	-	319014-319020	319161-319186
Introduced:	1987	1987-1988	1990
Rebuilt:	-	1996-1997	1997-1999
Built by:	BREL York	-	-
Rebuilt by:	-	Railcare Wolverton	Alstom Eastleigh
Formation:	DTSO(A)+MSO+ TSOL+DTSO(B)	DTSO+MSO+ TSOL+DTCO	DTSO(A)+MSO+ TSOL+DTSO(B)
Vehicle numbers:	DTSO(A) - 77291-77315 (odd) MSO - 62891-62903 TSOL - 71772-71784 DTSO(B) - 77290-77314 (even)	DTSO - 77317-77329 (odd) MSOL - 62904-62910 TSOL - 71785-71791 DTCO - 77316-77328 (even)	DTSO - 77459-77497, 77973-77983 (odd) MSO - 63043-63062, 63094-63098 TSOL - 71929-71948, 71979-71984 DTSO(B) - 77458-77496, 77974-77984 (even)
Vehicle length:	DTSO(A) - 65ft ¾in (19.83m) DTSO(B) - 65ft ¾in (19.83m) MSO - 65ft 4¼in (19.93m) TSOL - 65ft 4¼in (19.93m)	DTSO - 65ft ¾in (19.83m) DTCO - 65ft ¾in (19.83m) MSOL - 65ft 4¼in (19.93m) TSOL - 65ft 4¼in (19.93m)	DTSO(A) - 65ft ¾in (19.83m) DTSO(B) - 65ft ¾in (19.83m) MSO - 65ft 4¼in (19.93m) TSOL - 65ft 4¼in (19.93m)
Height:	11ft 9in (3.58m)	11ft 9in (3.58m)	11ft 9in (3.58m)
Width:	9ft 3in (2.82m)	9ft 3in (2.82m)	9ft 3in (2.82m)
Seating:	Total - 319S DTSO(A) - 82S MSO - 82S TSOL - 77S DTSO(B) - 78S	Total - 18F/212S DTSO - 64S MSOL - 60S TSOL - 52S DTCO - 18F/36S	Total - 297S DTSO(A) - 70S MSO - 78S TSOL - 74S DTSO(B) - 75S
Internal layout:	2+2, 2+3	2+1F, 2+2S	2+2, 2+3
Gangway:	Within set, emergency end doors	Within set, emergency end doors	Within set, emergency end doors
Toilets:	TSOL - 2	MSOL - 2, TSOL - 1	TSOL - 2
Weight:	Total - 136.5 tonnes DTSO(A) - 28.2 tonnes MSO - 49.2 tonnes TSOL - 31 tonnes DTSO(B) - 28.1 tonnes	Total - 136.5 tonnes DTSO - 28.2 tonnes MSOL - 49.2 tonnes TSOL - 31 tonnes DTCO - 28.1 tonnes	Total - 140.3 tonnes DTSO(A) - 29 tonnes MSO - 50.6 tonnes TSOL - 31 tonnes DTSO(B) - 29.7 tonnes
Brake type:	Air (Westcode)	Air (Westcode)	Air (Westcode)
Bogie type:	DTSO, TSOL - BREL T3-7 MSO - BREL P7-4	DTSO, DTCO, TSOL - T3-7 MSO - BREL P7-4	DTSO, TSOL - BREL T3-7 MSO - BREL P7-4
Power collection:	25kV ac overhead and 750V dc third rail	25kV ac overhead and 750V dc third rail	25kV ac overhead and 750V dc third rail
Traction motor type:	4 x GEC G315BZ	4 x GEC G315BZ	4 x GEC G315BZ
Horsepower:	1,438hp (1,072kW)	1,438hp (1,072kW)	1,438hp (1,072kW)
Max speed:	100 mph (161km/h)	100 mph (161km/h)	100 mph (161km/h)
Coupling type:	Outer - Tightlock Inner - Bar	Outer - Tightlock Inner - Bar	Outer - Tightlock Inner - Bar
Multiple restriction:	Within Class 319 series	Within Class 319 series	Within Class 319 series
Door type:	Bi-parting sliding	Bi-parting sliding	Bi-parting sliding
Total sets in traffic:	13	7	26
Owner:	Porterbrook	Porterbrook	Porterbrook
Operator:	First Capital Connect	First Capital Connect	First Capital Connect
Sub-class differences:	Original phase 1 units		'Metro' units Original phase 2 units

Fact File

Designed especially for the 'Thameslink' operation linking north and south London via Clerkenwell Tunnels and fitted for dual 25kV ac overhead and 750V dc third rail operation, the Class 319s have remained on this route since introduction. Now operated by First Capital Connect, four sub-classes exist.

Class 319/0 and 319/2 are the former Southern-operated sets, but now working for First Capital Connect.

Sets have 2+2 and 2+3 seating, sliding doors and end emergency doors for tunnel working.

Two batches of units were built: phase 1 sets emerged between September 1987 and October 1988, with phase 2 units entering service between October 1990 and March 1991.

Electric Multiple Units

319/4

319421-319460
319021-319060
1988-1989
1997-1999
-
Railcare Wolverton
DTCO+MSO+
TSOL+DTSO
DTCO - 77331-77381,
77431-77457 (odd)
MSO - 62911-62974
TSOL - 71792-71879
DTSO - 77330-77380,
77470-77456 (even)

DTCO - 65ft ¾in (19.83m)
DTSO - 65ft ¾in (19.83m)
MSO - 65ft 4¼in (19.93m)
TSOL - 65ft 4¼in (19.93m)
11ft 9in (3.58m)
9ft 3in (2.82m)
Total: 12F/263S
DTCO - 12F/51S
MSO - 74S
TSOL - 67S
DTSO - 71S
2+1F, 2+2, 2+3S
Within set,
emergency end doors
TSOL - 2
Total - 136.5 tonnes
DTSO(A) - 28.2 tonnes
MSO - 49.2 tonnes
TSOL - 31 tonnes
DTSO(B) - 28.1 tonnes
Air (Westcode)
DTSO, DTCO, TSOL - BREL T3-7
MSO - BREL P7-4
25kV ac overhead and
750V dc third rail
4 x GEC G315BZ
1,438hp (1,072kW)
100 mph (161km/h)
Outer - Tightlock
Inner - Bar
Within Class 319 series
Bi-parting sliding
40
Porterbrook
First Capital Connect
'CityFlier' units

Above: *Designed and introduced to operate on the Thameslink electrified route the Class 319s are still used on the route but will soon be replaced by Class 700 stock. Thirteen members of the Class 31/0 sub-class are in service with First Capital Connect, allocated to Selhurst. These all standard class sets seat 319. Set No. 319010 is seen passing West Hampstead.* **Antony Christie**

Above: *Specifically designed to operate through the tunnel below London, the Class 319s are fitted with end emergency doors, which could if needed be used to evacuate a train in the tunnel section. Set No. 319002 is seen operating on the south Thames dc system.* **Antony Christie**

In early 2014, the majority of sets were painted First Capital Connect 'urban lights' colours, while some of the former Southern-operated sets still carried Southern white and green with FCC branding.

Sets are allocated to Bedford Cauldwell Walk and Selhurst depots. These units will soon be displaced by Siemens Class 700 stock. '319s' will then be transferred to other areas. Numbers 319 361-367/369/371/374-378 are going in 2015 to the Northern Rail franchise at Allerton. ∎

Above: *Once used for 'express' London-Brighton services, the seven Class 319/2 sets are now part of the core '319' fleet for Thameslink work. Sporting First Capital Connect branded Southern livery, set No. 319217 is recorded heading south at West Hampstead, led by its DTSO vehicle.* **Antony Christie**

Electric Multiple Units

Above: *A fleet of 26 Class 319/3 sets is allocated to Bedford and has all standard class seating, with accommodation for 297 passengers. These were the original phase 2 sets fitted with a slightly revised fairing around the drawgear. Set No. 319364 is shown operating under third rail conditions at Wimbledon.*
Antony Christie

Left Middle: *Clearly showing the earlier draw gear area design, Class 319/4 No. 319440 is seen passing a TfL Class 378 unit. Forty Class 319/4s are in traffic, and tend to operate the through Bedford-Brighton services as they include first class accommodation for 12 in one of the driving cars. Standard class seating is for 263.*
CJM

Left Bottom: *The Class 319 Motor Standard Open vehicles contain all the power and traction equipment, including the roof mounted 25kV pantograph. Depending on the sub-class, the MSO seats between 60 and 82 The vehicle shown from its non-pantograph and is No. 62900 from a Class 319/0 set. The bogies used below the power car are the BREL P7-4.*
Antony Christie

Right: *Class 319 front end equipment. A: Light cluster with from the outer edge white marker light, headlight and red tail light. B: Front emergency door, C: Route and destination indicator, D: Air warning horn, E: Tightlock coupler, F: Emergency air connection. Equipment is in the same position on all sub-classes.* **CJM**

Below: *The interior layout of the Class 319s is largely based on the 2+3 for standard class areas (the Class 319/2s have 2+2). Most sets have been internally facelifted and now sport modern wall and ceiling panels, updated floor coverings and First Group seat moquette.*
Antony Christie

Number range:	320301-320322
Introduced:	1990
Built/rebuilt by:	BREL York
Formation:	DTSO+MSO+DTSOL
Vehicle numbers:	DTSO - 77899-77920
	MSO - 63021-63042
	DTSOL -77921-77942
Vehicle length:	DTSO - 65ft 0¾in (19.83m)
	MSO - 65ft 4¼in (19.92m)
	DTSOL - 65ft 0¾in (19.83m)
Height:	12ft 4¾in (3.78m)
Width:	9ft 3in (2.82m)
Seating:	Total - 227S
	DTSO - 76S
	MSO - 76S
	DTSOL - 75S
Internal layout:	2+3
Gangway:	Within set
Toilets:	1 - DTSOL
Weight:	Total - 111 tonnes
	DTSO - 29.1 tonnes
	MSO - 51.9 tonnes
	DTSOL - 30.0 tonnes
Brake type:	Air (Westcode)
Bogie type:	DTSO, DTSOL - BREL T3-7
	MSO - BREL P7-4
Power collection:	25kV ac overhead
Traction motor type:	4 x Brush TM2141B
Horsepower:	1,438hp (1,072kW)
Max speed:	90mph (145km/h)
Coupling type:	Outer - Tightlock, Inner - Bar
Multiple restriction:	Within class
Door type:	Bi-parting sliding
Total sets in traffic:	22
Construction:	Steel
Owner:	Eversholt
Operator:	First ScotRail

Fact File

At the time the Class 321 units emerged from BREL York, the BRB placed an order for 22 standard class only three-car sets for ScotRail, with similar exterior design. The sets were for use on the North Clyde routes.

Assembly followed the phase 1 Class 321s through York works, with the first sets being tested on the East Coast Main Line in the York area in May 1990. Units were allocated to Yoker depot, entering service from August.

The sets were formed with two near identical DTSOs (one, the 'A' vehicle, having wheelchair space and identified by a yellow band on the front end). With an MSO with pantograph in the middle, all seating is in 2+3.

When delivered, sets were painted in Strathclyde orange; this later gave way to carmine and cream and now standard Scottish Railways blue/white Saltire colours are applied.

In 2011 a major refurbishment saw a toilet installed in one DTSO coach, making it a DTSOL, and extra yaw dampers fitted to power bogies, allowing a speed increase to 90mph. ■

Electric Multiple Units

Above: *Based on the Class 321 body profile, the 22 Scottish Class 320s are standard class only units allocated to Glasgow Shields. The sets are refurbished and sport Scottish Railways blue and white livery. No. 320318 is seen at Dalmuir.* **Nathan Williamson**

Right Middle: *The intermediate Motor Standard Open (MSO) vehicles from the '320s' seat 76 in the 2+3 style. All traction equipment, including the pantograph, is carried on this vehicle. Both bogies are powered. Vehicle No. 63023 from set No. 320303 is illustrated.* **Robin Ralston**

Left Bottom: *The Class 320 fleet is to be found operating on the North Clyde Line between Helensburgh and Airdrie via Glasgow Queen Street and the Argyle Line between Lanark and Dalmuir. Each three-car set provides seats for 227 passengers. Set No. 320313 is seen awaiting departure from Springburn.* **Murdoch Currie**

Right: *Class 320 interior, showing the 3+2 seating in the area directly behind the driving cab. Note that small tables are provided by the near set of seats - not suitable for work, but satisfactory for resting a coffee cup.* **Nathan Williamson**

Traction Recognition

Electric Multiple Units

Sub-class:	321/3	321/4	321/9
Number range:	321301-321366	321401-321448	321901-321903
Introduced:	1988-1990	1989-1990	1991
Built by:	BREL York	BREL York	BREL York
Facelifted by:	Ilford	Ilford	Ilford
Formation:	DTCO+MSO+TSOL+DTSO	DTCO+MSO+TSOL+DTSO	DTSO(A)+MSO+TSOL+DTSO(B)
Vehicle numbers:	DTCO - 78049-78094, 78131-78150 MSO - 62975-63020, 63105-63124 TSOL - 71880-71925, 71991-72010 DTSO - 77853-77898, 78280-78299	DTCO - 78095-78130, 78151-78162 MSO - 63063-63092, 62099-63104, 63125-63136 TSOL - 71949-71978, 71985-71990, 72011-72022 DTSO - 77943-77972, 78274-78279, 78300-78310	DTSO(A) - 77990-77992 MSO - 63153-63155 TSOL - 72128-72130 DTSO(B) - 77993-77995
Vehicle length:	DTCO - 65ft 0¾in (19.83m) MSO - 65ft 4¼in (19.92m) TSOL - 65ft 4¼in (19.92m) DTSO - 65ft 0¾in (19.83m)	DTCO - 65ft 0¾in (19.83m) MSO - 65ft 4¼in (19.92m) TSOL - 65ft 4¼in (19.92m) DTSO - 65ft 0¾in (19.83m)	DTSO(A) - 65ft 0¾in (19.83m) MSO - 65ft 4¼in (19.92m) TSOL - 65ft 4¼in (19.92m) DTSO(B) 65ft 0¾in (19.83m)
Height:	12ft 4¾in (3.78m)	12ft 4¾in (3.78m)	12ft 4¾in (3.78m)
Width:	9ft 3in (2.82m)	9ft 3in (2.82m)	9ft 3in (2.82m)
Seating:	Total - 16F/292S DTCO - 16F/57S MSO - 82S TSOL - 75S DTSO - 78S	321401-321420: Total - 28F/271S DTCO - 28F/40S MSO - 79S TSOL - 74S DTSO - 78S 321421-321448: Total - 16F/283S DTCO - 16F/52S MSO - 79S TSOL - 74S DTSO - 78S	Total - 293S + 15 tip up DTSO(A) - 70S + 8 tip up MSO - 79S TSOL - 74S DTSO(B)- 70S + 7 tip up
Internal layout:	2+2F/2+3S	2+2F/2+3S	2+3S
Gangway:	Within unit only	Within unit only	Within unit only
Toilets:	TSOL - 2	TSOL - 2	TSOL - 2
Weight:	Total - 140 tonnes DTCO - 29.7 tonnes MSO - 51.5 tonnes TSOL - 29.1 tonnes DTSO - 29.7 tonnes	Total - 140.4 tonnes DTCO - 29.8 tonnes MSO - 51.6 tonnes TSOL - 29.2 tonnes DTSO - 29.8 tonnes	Total - 138.5 tonnes DTCO - 29.2 tonnes MSO - 51.1 tonnes TSOL - 29.0 tonnes DTSO - 29.2 tonnes
Brake type:	Air (Westcode)	Air (Westcode)	Air (Westcode)
Bogie type:	MSO - BREL P7-4 DTCO, DTSO, TSOL - BREL T3-7	MSO - BREL P7-4 DTCO, DTSO, TSOL - BREL T3-7	MSO - BREL P7-4 DTSO, TSOL - BREL T3-7
Power collection:	25kV ac overhead	25kV ac overhead	25kV ac overhead
Traction motor:	4 x Brush TM2141C	4 x Brush TM2141C	4 x Brush TM2141C
Horsepower:	1,438hp (1,072kW)	1,438hp (1,072kW)	1,438hp (1,072kW)
Max speed:	100mph (161km/h)	100mph (161km/h)	100mph (161km/h)
Coupling type:	Outer - Tightlock Inner - Bar	Outer - Tightlock Inner – Bar	Outer - Tightlock Inner - Bar
Multiple working:	Classes 317-323	Classes 317-323	Classes 317-323
Door type:	Bi-parting sliding	Bi-parting sliding	Bi-parting sliding
Total sets in traffic:	66	48	3
Construction:	Steel	Steel	Steel
Owner:	Eversholt	Eversholt	Eversholt
Operator:	Greater Anglia	London Midland Greater Anglia, FCC	Northern Rail

Above: *The original fleet of 66 four-car Class 321 main line EMUs built by BREL York was a replacement for ageing Great Eastern route stock. Introduced from 1988 these sets are still in service today. Painted in white Greater Anglia livery with blue passenger doors, set No. 321355 departs from Stratford bound for Liverpool Street with its DTCO vehicle leading.* **CJM**

Right: *Originally built for the Euston-Birmingham LMR route in 1989, 28 members of Class 321/4 are now operated on Greater Anglia along with the Class 321/3 sets. Some slight variation to seating exists on these sets. Painted in Greater Anglia white with orange passenger doors, set No. 321439 passes eastbound through Pudding Mill Lane with its DTSO coach leading.* **Antony Christie**

Three batches of Class 321 four-car outer-suburban EMU were built by BREL York.

The first 66 units were designated to replace ageing stock on the Great Eastern routes from Liverpool Street; these emerged from 1988 under a Network SouthEast modernisation plan.

A second batch of 48 nearly identical sets with slightly more first class accommodation appeared from 1989 for use on the Euston-Northampton/Birmingham route, displacing Class 317s. All these sets emerged in NSE livery.

In 1991, West Yorkshire PTE funded three units for its Metro service between Doncaster and Leeds, replacing aged ex-NSE sets which were used on the rapidly expanding commuter service.

The NSE sets were set out with 2+2 and 2+3 standard class and 2+2 first class seating; the WYPTE sets, classified 321/9, were standard class only.

After Class 350 'Desiro' stock was launched on the London Midland operation, most Euston area sets have been transferred to the Greater Anglia franchise, with a handful remaining with London Midland for peak hour use. A small number also operate for First Capital Connect for peak hour services. ∎

Above and Left: *London Midland operates a fleet of seven Class 321/4s for peak hour operations. These are painted in LM green, grey and black livery and are allocated to Northampton depot. These sets have received little internal attention since NSE days and seat 28 first and 271 standard class passengers. Set No. 321416 is seen above approaching Watford, and TS No. 71965 from set 321417 is seen left.* **Ron Cover / Antony Christie**

Below: *First Capital Connect has a fleet of 13 Class 321/4s allocated to Hornsey for peak hour operation. Led by its DMCO set No. 321403 passes Harringay.* **CJM**

Above: *Class 321 driving car equipment positions. 1: Radio aerial, 2: Ventilator, 3: Cab door, 4: Local door control, 5: Lifting lug, 6: Suspension air tank, 7: Door open / alarm light, 8: Passenger bi-parting doors, 9: Passenger door controls. This equipment is applied to all sub-classes of the fleet.* **CJM**

Right Upper: *West Yorkshire PTE ordered just three Class 321 sets for its Doncaster to Leeds line to replace ageing stock. Classified as 321/9 these sets emerged from York Works in 1991 and are based at Leeds Neville Hill depot. These are standard class only sets with accommodation for 293 passengers. The sets seldom stray from the Doncaster to Leeds route. Set No. 321902 is seen in the bay platform at Doncaster.* **CJM**

Right Middle: *Class 321/3 interior showing the 3+2 seating layout, with cross vestibules feeding direct into the passenger saloons. Luggage racks are provided above seats and as the stock is not air conditioned opening hopper windows are provided.* **Michael J. Collins**

Right Bottom: *Class 321 driving cab. The master switch and power controller are operated by the driver's right hand, while a five position electronic brake controller is operated by his left hand.* **CJM**

Traction Recognition

Class 322

Number range:	322481-332485
Introduced:	1990
Refurbished:	2006
Built by:	BREL York
Refurbished by:	Hunslet-Barclay, Kilmarnock
Formation:	DTSO(A)+MSO+TSOL+DTSO(B)
Vehicle numbers:	DTSO(A) - 78163-78167
	MSO - 63137-63141
	TSOL - 72023-72027
	DTSO(B) - 77985-77989
Vehicle length:	DTSO - 65ft 0¾in (19.83m)
	MSO/TSOL - 65ft 4¼in (19.92m)
Height:	12ft 4¾in (3.78m)
Width:	9ft 3in (2.82m)
Seating:	Total - 291S + 2 tip up
	DTSO(A) - 58S
	MSO - 83S
	TSOL - 76S
	DTSO(B) - 74S + 2 tip up
Internal layout:	2+3
Gangway:	Within unit
Toilets:	TSOL - 2
Weight:	Total - 138.7 tonnes
	DTSO(A) - 29.3 tonnes
	MSO - 51.5 tonnes
	TSOL - 28.8 tonnes
	DTSO(B) - 29.1 tonnes
Brake type:	Air (Westcode)
Bogie type:	MSO - BREL P7-4
	DTSO, TSOL - BREL T3-7
Power collection:	25kV ac overhead
Traction motor type:	4 x Brush TM2141C
Horsepower:	1,438hp (1,072kW)
Max speed:	100mph (161km/h)
Coupling type:	Outer - Tightlock, Inner - Bar
Multiple restriction:	Within class, Class 317-323
Door type:	Bi-parting, sliding
Total sets in traffic:	5
Construction:	Steel
Owner:	Eversholt
Operator:	Northern Rail

Fact File

Built under a Network SouthEast order to an identical body design to the Class 321s, these five units designated Class 322 were intended for use on the then new London Liverpool Street to Stansted Airport route. They were built with 2+2 seating and extra luggage space, finished in a grey and green livery and allocated to Ilford depot.

By 1998 the sets were taken off this service and under the privatised railway commenced work for First North Western, working Euston-Manchester 'domestic' services. After a short time the sets were taken off lease to FNW and re-leased to Anglia Railways to provide extra capacity on the Ipswich-London Liverpool Street route. Later, after a brief period working in Scotland the sets were again returned to Ilford for West Anglia duties.

In 2005 in a major about-turn, the sets again returned to ScotRail for use on the Edinburgh-North Berwick line and were subsequently refurbished by Hunslet-Barclay of Kilmarnock, fitted out with 3+2 high-density seating.

Following introduction of new Class 380 'Desiro' stock in Scotland, the Class 322s were again on the move and are currently operated by Northern Rail on the Doncaster-Leeds-Bradford suburban routes. ∎

Left: *Based on the Class 321 stock, the Class 322s were built for the Stansted Airport route and later operated for Northern, ScotRail and Anglia, before settling down based at Leeds Neville Hill for Leeds area local services, frequently being used on the Doncaster to Leeds route. Painted in all over blue livery with Northern branding, set No. 322481 is seen in the Leeds bay platform at Doncaster.*
Antony Christie

Above: *The Class 322 fleet is laid out for standard class occupancy, with a total of 291 seats provided, a considerable increase from when the sets were first built for Stansted Airport services when 2+2 low-density seating and lots of luggage space was provided. The DTSO(B) vehicle seen nearest the camera in this view seats 74 standard class passengers, while the DTSO(A) at the other end only seats 58. Set No. 322483 is seen on the outskirts of Doncaster.* **Antony Christie**

Below: *The interior of a Class 322 MSO vehicle showing where the main cables pass through the saloon from the roof mounted pantograph to the underfloor equipment boxes. This section also has a lower ceiling.* **Michael J. Collins**

Number range:	323201-323243
Introduced:	1992-1993
Built/rebuilt by:	Hunslet TPL Leeds
Formation:	DMSO(A)+PTSOL+DMSO(B)
Vehicle numbers:	DMSO(A) - 64001-64043
	PTSOL - 72201-72243
	DMSO(B) - 65001-65043
Vehicle length:	DMSO - 76ft 8¾in (23.37m)
	PTSOL - 76ft 10¾in (23.44m)
Height:	12ft 4¾in (3.78m)
Width:	9ft 2¼in (2.80m)
Seating:	All except 323223-323225 - Total - 284S
	DMSO(A) - 98S
	PTSOL - 88S + 5 tip up
	DMSO(B) - 98S
	Sets 323223-323225 - Total - 244S
	DMSO(A) - 82S
	PTSOL - 80S
	DMSO(B) - 82S
Internal layout:	2+3 high density
	323223-225 - 2+2
Gangway:	Within unit only
Toilets:	PTSOL - 1
Weight:	Total - 121.4 tonnes
	DMSO(A) - 41 tonnes
	PTSOL - 39.4 tonnes
	DMSO(B) - 41.0 tonnes
Brake type:	Air (Westcode)
Bogie type:	Powered - RFS BP62
	Trailer - RFS BT52
Power collection:	25kV ac overhead
Traction motor type:	4 x Holec DMKT 52/24
Horsepower:	1,566hp (1,168kW)
Max speed:	90mph (145km/h)
Coupling type:	Outer - Tightlock, Inner - Bar
Multiple restriction:	Class 317-323
Door type:	Bi-parting sliding plug
Total sets in traffic:	43
Construction:	Welded aluminium alloy
Owner:	Porterbrook
Operator:	London Midland, Northern Rail

Fact File

Among the more problematic EMU classes during delivery and commissioning were these Class 323s, ordered by the BR Regional Sector for Birmingham CrossCity and Manchester area use. The sets were built by Hunslet TPL in 1992-93, but it was not until 1996 that the trains entered full service.

These are true high-density inner-suburban trains and feature 2+3 seating with a three-car set accommodating up to 284 passengers.

Three sets were built with a modified 2+2 interior and extra luggage space for the Manchester Piccadilly to Manchester Airport service.

Sets are allocated to London Midland at Soho, Birmingham, and Northern Rail in Longsight, Manchester.

When built, these units sported bodyside digital destination displays but these have now been plated over.

The majority of '323s' have now been internally refurbished. Sets all carry operator livery, either London Midland green, grey and black or Northern Rail blue/purple. ■

Above: *A fleet of 17 Class 323s is operated by the Northern Rail franchise, based at Longsight and used in the Manchester area. Painted in standard Northern Rail blue, mauve and grey livery, set No. 323229 is illustrated. Three of the Northern sets (323223-225) have reduced seating for forming Manchester Airport services.* **Antony Christie**

Right Middle: *The normal intermediate PTSOL vehicle in a Northern Rail '323' seats 88 in the 2+3 mode, with a small toilet compartment at the opposite end of the vehicle to the pantograph. These are chemical retention toilets and the tank can be seen at the near end in this illustration of vehicle No. 72229.* **Antony Christie**

Left: *Soho depot in Birmingham has an allocation of 26 Class 323s for the Birmingham CrossCity route. Painted in full London Midland livery the sets each seat 284 standard class passengers. Set No. 323206 is seen arriving at Birmingham New Street.* **John Stretton**

Right Bottom: *The Class 323 seating uses the high-density 2+3 style layout, with a basic interior as most journeys are short. Luggage racks are provided above seats and some space exists between seat backs. Seating is a mix of group and airline.* **Antony Christie**

Traction Recognition

Number range:	325001-325016
Introduced:	1995-1996
Built by:	Adtranz Derby
Formation:	DTPMV(A)+MPMV+TPMV+DTPMV(B)
Vehicle numbers:	DTPMV(A) - 68300-68330 (even numbers)
	MPMV - 68340-68355
	TPMV - 68360-68375
	DTPMV(B) - 68301-68331 (odd numbers)
Vehicle length:	DTPMV - 65ft 0¾in (19.83m)
	MPMV/TPMV - 65ft 4¼in (19.92m)
Height:	12ft 4¼in (3.77m)
Width:	9ft 3in (2.82m)
Seating:	None - Parcel/Mail space
Internal layout:	Open
Gangway:	Not fitted
Toilets:	Not fitted
Weight:	Total - 138.4 tonnes
	DTPMV(A) - 29.1 tonnes
	MPMV - 49.5 tonnes
	TPMV - 30.7 tonnes
	DTPMV(B) - 29.1 tonnes
Brake type:	Air (EP/auto)
Bogie type:	Powered - Adtranz P7-4
	Trailer - Adtranz T3-7
Power collection:	25kV ac overhead and 750V dc third rail
Traction motor type:	4 x GEC G315BZ
Horsepower:	1,438hp (1,072kW)
Max speed:	100mph (161km/h)
Coupling type:	Drop-head buck-eye/screw
Multiple restriction:	Within type, TDM wired
Door type:	Roller shutter
Total sets in traffic:	15 (not all operational)
Construction:	Steel
Special features:	Retractable buffers, intruder alarm
Owner:	Royal Mail
Operator:	Royal Mail/DBS

Fact File

In the mid-1990s Royal Mail made a considerable investment in new post and parcel-carrying trains with the funding for 16 four-car EMUs, built by Adtranz Derby, the fleet able to operate from 25kV ac overhead power supply or 750V dc third rail supply as well as operating with locos fitted with TDM style jumpers.

Painted in classic Royal Mail red livery the coaches have no end access, with all external entry being through two roller shutter doors on each side. The cabs are a separate module and have sliding access doors.

Following Royal Mail's decision to end the Mail by Rail contract with operator EWS in 2004, the Class 325s were stored. However, after a couple of years GB Railfreight (GBRf) took over the operation of the sets and jointly with Royal Mail worked a daily service between London and Scotland. This contract expired in early 2010 and DB-Schenker is again the operator of the sets, working a very limited Royal Mail service on a north-south daily route. ∎

Electric Multiple Units

Below: *Of the 15 remaining Class 325 Royal Mail 'Railnet' Class 325s, only a handful are operational and these work a limited DB-S staffed duty over the West Coast Main Line, working as a single, double or triple unit formation depending of load forecast. The sets only operate between Royal Mail rail connected terminals such as Shieldmuir, Warrington and the Princess Royal Distribution Centre in London. A three-set formation let by No. 325005 is seen on the WCML.* **John Tuffs**

Above: *Each vehicle within the Class 325 sets is an individual stand alone mail van with no gangway connections between coaches. Access is by two roller shutter doors on each side of each vehicle which are locked and under the control of terminal based Royal Mail staff. The train crew have no requirement to enter these vehicles, except in the driving cabs. TPMV No. 68364 is illustrated.* **CJM**

Right: *Class 325 front end equipment positions. A: Group Standard light cluster (from the outside, white marker, head and red tail light), B: Drop-head buck-eye coupling, C: Retractable buffer, D: Main reservoir pipe (yellow), brake pipe (red), E: Electric train supply jumper socket, F: Electric train supply jumper cable, G: Time Division Multiplex (TDM) jumper cables, H: Air warning horns. Unit illustrated is No. 325007.* **CJM**

Below: *Running as a single four-car unit, No. 325016 nears Lamington on the WCML with train 1M03, the 17.49 Shieldmuir to Warrington, on 19 April 2013.* **Robin Ralston**

Number range:	332001-332004, 332010-332014	332005-332009
Introduced:	1997-1998, 2002	1997-1998, 2002
Built by:	Siemens Germany, CAF Spain	Siemens Germany, CAF Spain
Formation:	332001-332004: DMFO+TSO+PTSOL+DMSO 332010-332014: DMSO+TSO+PTSOL+DMFLO	332005-333007: DMFO+TSO+PTSOL+TSO+DMSO 332008-333009: DMSO+TSO+PTSOL+TSO+DMFLO
Vehicle numbers:	332001-332004: DMFO - 78400-78406 (even numbers) TSO - 72405-72412 (random) PTSO - 63400-63403 DMSO - 78401-78407 (odd numbers) 332010-332014: DMSO - 78418-78426 (even numbers) TSO - 72402-72408 (random) PTSO - 63409-63413 DMFLO - 78419-78427 (odd numbers)	DMFO - 78408-78417 (even numbers) TSO - 72400-72413 (random) PTSO - 63404-63408 TSO - 72414-72418 DMFLO - 78409-78417 (odd numbers)
Vehicle length:	Driving cars - 77ft 10¾in (23.74m) Intermediate cars - 75ft 11in (23.14m)	Driving cars - 77ft 10¾in (23.74m) Intermediate cars - 75ft 11in (23.14m)
Height:	12ft 1½in (3.70m)	12ft 1½in (3.70m)
Width:	9ft 1in (2.75m)	9ft 1in (2.75m)
Seating:	332001-332004 - Total - 26F/148S DMFO - 26F, TSO - 56S PTSOL - 44S, DMSO - 48S 332010-332014 - Total - 14F/148S DMSO - 48S, TSO - 56S PTSOL - 44S, DMFLO - 14F	332005-332007 - Total - 26F/204S DMFO - 26F, TSO - 56S PTSOL - 44S, TSO - 56S DMSO - 48S 332008-332009 - Total - 14F/204S DMSO - 48S, TSO - 56S PTSOL - 44S, TSO - 56S DMFLO - 14F
Internal layout:	2+1F/2+2S	2+1F/2+2S
Gangway:	Within set	Within set
Toilets:	PTSOL + DMFLO - 1	PTSOL + DMFLO- 1
Weight:	Total - 179 tonnes (all types) DMFO - 48.8 tonnes TSO - 35.8 tonnes PTSO - 45.6 tonnes DMSO - 48.8 tonnes DMFLO - 48.8 tonnes	Total - 214.8 tonnes DMSO - 48.8 tonnes TSO - 35.8 tonnes PTSO - 45.6 tonnes TSO - 35.8 tonnes DMFLO - 48.8 tonnes
Brake type:	Air (regenerative)	Air (regenerative)
Bogie type:	CAF	CAF
Power collection:	25kV ac overhead	25kV ac overhead
Traction motor type:	4 x Siemens	4 x Siemens
Horsepower:	1,877hp (1,400kW)	1,877hp (1,400kW)
Max speed:	100mph (161km/h)	100mph (161km/h)
Coupling type:	Outer - Scharfenberg, Inner - Semi-auto	Outer - Scharfenberg, Inner - Semi-auto
Multiple restriction:	Within class and 333	Within class and 333
Door type:	Bi-parting sliding plug	Bi-parting sliding plug
Owner:	BAA	BAA
Operator:	Heathrow Express	Heathrow Express

Fact File

Designed and purchased by British Airports Authority for use on the new London Paddington-Heathrow Airport 'Heathrow Express' service, these 14 sets were ordered from and equipped by Siemens in Germany with bodyshells assembled by CAF in Spain.

Originally sets were delivered as three-car units; later reformations saw nine four-car and five five-car sets marshalled.

Both standard and first class seating is provided and originally aircraft hold luggage could be checked in at Paddington and taken 'bonded' in modified DMFLO vehicles to the airport. After various terrorist threats the Paddington check-in was abolished.

Sets are finished in 'Heathrow Express' silver with sponsored major advertising campaigns which sees complete trains branded inside and out. Currently the advertising contract is with mobile communications supplier Vodafone.

Sets are allocated to Old Oak Common depot and operate four trains per hour between Paddington and all terminals at Heathrow. ■

Right: *Allocated to the Heathrow Express depot at Old Oak Common, the Class 332s operate exclusively on the Paddington to Heathrow Airport 'Heathrow Express' service, operating as a four-, five- or nine-car formation. The service receives considerable funding from on train advertising, currently with phone operator Vodafone with the company branding on all vehicles. Set No. 332010 is seen at Paddington.* **CJM**

Right Middle: *Two different types of intermediate vehicles exist, a TSO or a PTSO. On five-car sets the pantograph-fitted TSO is in the middle of the formation. The PTSO vehicles seat 44 in the 2+2 layout. The first class seating is in the 2+1 style. Throughout the trains luggage racks are provided by exit doors and level access is provided from train to platform at all stations. Vehicle No. 63411 is illustrated from set No. 332012.* **CJM**

Below: *The 'Heathrow Express' operates between dedicated platforms at London Paddington and two stations at Heathrow Airport, one serving Terminals 1-3 and the other Terminal 5. A shuttle service operates between Terminals 1-3 station and Terminal 4. The Class 332s were originally delivered as three-car sets and have been progressively increased in length to satisfy passenger demand. Set No. 332012 is seen at Paddington.* **CJM**

Electric Multiple Units

Class 333

Number range:	333001-333016
Introduced:	2000, TSO added 2002-03
Built by:	Siemens Germany and CAF Spain
Formation:	DMSO(A)+PTSO+TSO+DMSO(B)
Vehicle numbers:	DMSO(A) - 78451-78481 (odd numbers)
	PTSO - 74461-74476
	TSO - 74477-74492
	DMSO(B) - 78452-78482 (even numbers)
Vehicle length:	DMSO - 77ft 10¾in (23.74m)
	PTSO/TSO - 75ft 11in (23.14m)
Height:	12ft 1½in (3.70m)
Width:	9ft 0¼in (2.75m)
Seating:	Total - 353S + 6 tip up
	DMSO(A) - 90S
	PTSO - 73S + 6 tip up
	TSO - 100S
	DMSO(B) - 90S
Internal layout:	2+3
Gangway:	Within set
Toilets:	PTSO - 1
Weight:	Total - 182.2 tonnes
	DMS(A) - 50.0 tonnes
	PTS - 46.7 tonnes
	TS - 38.5 tonnes
	DMS(B) - 50.0 tonnes
Brake type:	Air
Bogie type:	CAF
Power collection:	25kV ac overhead
Traction motor type:	4 x Siemens
Horsepower:	1,877hp (1,400kW)
Max speed:	100mph (161km/h)
Coupling type:	Outer - Scharfenberg, Inner - Bar
Multiple restriction:	Within class and 332
Door type:	Bi-parting sliding plug
Total sets in traffic:	16
Construction:	Steel
Owner:	Angel Trains
Operator:	Northern Rail (WYPTE)

Fact File

When authorisation was given for new EMUs to operate in the West Yorkshire PTE area, the Siemens suburban EMU was selected, being an almost identical product to the 'Heathrow Express' Class 332 fleet, except these were set out for high-density standard class only occupancy.

Originally 16 three-car sets were ordered, but due to growth on the Aire Valley routes a fourth car was subsequently added to all sets.

Livery when delivered was a mix of Northern Spirit (the then franchise operator) and WYPTE. In recent times refurbishment has been undertaken and sets are now in standard joint WYPTE/Northern Rail livery.

Passenger information displays are fitted both inside and outside vehicles. All sets are based at Leeds Neville Hill depot. ■

Right: *Class 333 front end layout, also applicable to the 'Heathrow Express' Class 332 fleet. A: High-level marker light, B: Destination indicator, C: Light cluster (from outer edge - white marker light, headlight and red tail light), D: Scharfenberg coupling incorporating physical, pneumatic and electrical connections.* **Brian Morrison**

Below Left: *The 16 Class 333 sets, based on the structural design of the Class 332 stock, are allocated to Leeds Neville Hill and operate the Aire Valley electric services radiating from Leeds. They are operated by Northern Rail and are all painted in Northern Rail deep red with mauve and grey on the driving car sides. Set No. 333010 is seen at Crossflats with its DMSO(A) vehicle nearest the camera. These sets are fitted with Scharfenberg couplers and are not compatible with any other stock.* **Antony Christie**

Right Middle: *Class 333s are set out for high-density loadings with a train accommodation for 353 standard class passengers; standing room, especially around the door vestibules, would be a crush loading figure of around 450 per four-car train. The urban style layout is basic, but most journeys are only short. One toilet is provided per four-car set located in the PTSO vehicle. Interior and exterior passenger information screens are provided.* **Antony Christie**

Right Bottom: *Just one member of the fleet, No. 333007 carries a nameplate, a stick-on 'plate' located above the side windows, just below cant rail height. The name Alderman J Arthur Godwin First Lord Mayor of Bradford 1907 was applied in 2007 to mark the centenary of the event.* **Antony Christie**

Electric Multiple Units

Class 334 'Juniper'

Number range:	334001-334040
Introduced:	1999-2002
Built by:	Alstom, Washwood Heath
Formation:	DMSO(A)+PTSO+DMSO(B)
Vehicle numbers:	DMSO(A) - 64101-64140
	PTSO - 74301-74340
	DMSO(B) - 65101-65140
Vehicle length:	DMSO(A) - 69ft 0¾in (21.05m)
	PTSO - 65ft 4¼in (19.92m)
	DMSO(B) - 69ft 0¾in (21.05m)
Height:	12ft 3in (3.73m)
Width:	9ft 2¾in (2.81m)
Seating:	Total - 183S
	DMSO(A) - 64S
	PTSO - 55S
	DMSO(B) - 64S
Internal layout:	DMSO 2+2, PTSO 2+3
Gangway:	Within set
Toilets:	PTSO - 1
Weight:	Total - 124.6 tonnes
	DMSO(A) - 42.6 tonnes
	PTSO - 39.4 tonnes
	DMSO(B) - 42.6 tonnes
Brake type:	Air (regenerative)
Bogie type:	Alstom DMSO - LTB3, PTSO - TBP3
Power collection:	25kV ac overhead
Traction motor type:	4 x Alstom Onix
Horsepower:	1,448hp (1,080kW)
Max speed:	90mph (145km/h)
Coupling type:	Outer - Tightlock, Inner - Bar
Multiple restriction:	Within class only
Door type:	Bi-parting sliding plug
Total sets in traffic:	40
Construction:	Steel
Owner:	Eversholt
Operator:	First ScotRail

Fact File

When Scotland's privatised railway invested in the network in the late 1990s, it opted for the then popular Alstom 'Juniper' product range, ordering a three-car medium-density standard class only train with seating for 183.

A protracted introduction took place between 1999 and 2002 due to numerous technical issues. The 'Juniper' or Class 334 fleet is allocated to Glasgow Shields Road depot and operates principally on the Ayrshire routes.

To save construction costs, these sets were fitted with the older-style pressure ventilation equipment, rather than full air conditioning, and thus have opening hopper windows.

All sets were delivered in Strathclyde Passenger Transport (SPT) carmine and cream livery; they are non-gangwayed and fitted with Tightlock couplers.

In recent times, as workshop overhauls have taken place, the latest blue/white Saltire livery has been applied. ■

Electric Multiple Units

Right: *Based on the Alstom 'Juniper' platform, 40 Class 334 three-car outer suburban sets were delivered for Glasgow area use between 1999 and 2002. Allocated to Shields Road depot they operate North Clyde services. When delivered the sets were in the then current 'carmine and cream' livery, but recent overhauls has seen the Scottish Railways blue and white colours applied. Set No. 334028 is illustrated at Partick.* **Bill Wilson**

Right Middle: *The intermediate vehicle is a Pantograph Trailer Standard Open (PTSO) and seats 55 in the 2+3 style. These vehicles use a common body shell and thus at the pantograph end, by the toilet compartment, the windows between the vestibule doors and the end of the coach on one side are blanked out. Vehicle No. 74316 in carmine and cream livery is shown.* **Bill Wilson**

Left Below: *Set No. 334031 painted in the latest Saltire livery is shown at Helensburgh Central. These sets are fitted with Tightlock couplers and have a standard light cluster of headlight, white marker and red tail light on each side. A roof level marker light is also fitted.* **Murdoch Currie**

Below: *The Class 334s have low-density 2+2 seating with a three-car set accommodating 183 passengers.* **Bill Wilson**

Number range:	345001-345065
	Plus option for further 18
Introduced:	2017-2018
Built by:	Bombardier Derby
Formation:	Nine-car sets
Vehicle numbers:	To be advised
Vehicle length:	Total - 660ft (200m)
	Each vehicle - 73ft 9in (22.5m)
Height:	To be advised
Width:	To be advised
Seating:	Total - 400S (seats) Capacity for 1,500
Internal layout:	2+2
Gangway:	Within set
Toilets:	To be advised
Weight:	Total - 300 tonnes (approx)
Brake type:	Air (regenerative)
Bogie type:	Bombardier
Power collection:	25kV ac overhead
Traction motor type:	To be advised
Horsepower:	To be advised
Max speed:	90mph (145km/h)
Coupling type:	Outer - Dellner, Inner - Bar
Multiple restriction:	Within class only
Door type:	Bi-parting sliding plug (3 pairs per coach side)
Total sets in traffic:	On delivery (65)
Construction:	Aluminium
Owner:	Transport for London (funded by European Investment Bank)
Operator:	TfL - CrossRail

Fact File

The Class 345 electric multiple units are currently on order from Bombardier Transportation for the London CrossRail project, which will see a new electric high-intensity service operate from Reading and Heathrow through central London to Shenfield and Abbey Wood.

The contract worth £1 billion covers 65 nine-car 'Aventra' train sets measuring around 200m in length and carrying up to 1,500 passengers.

The trains will be based at a new depot at Old Oak Common, and should be delivered between 2015 and 2018. ∎

Below: *Artist's impression of how the CrossRail Class 345 should look. Note the three pairs of double leaf sliding doors on each side of each vehicle.* **TfL**

Above: *London Midland has concentrated its modern outer suburban and long distance EMU stock on the Siemens 'Desiro' product line, with three batches now in traffic, all with slightly different detail changes. The first tranche of 30 emerged in 2004/05 and operated for Silverlink and Central Trains before the new London Midland franchise was formed. The sets are based at Northampton depot with Siemens holding a lifelong maintenance contract. These sets sport London Midland livery with a full height yellow end gangway door. Set No. 350104 is illustrated from its DMSO(A) coach.* **CJM**

Below: *A follow-on order for 37 Class 350s for London Midland was fulfilled in 2008-09, when a fleet of near identical sets was delivered to the UK with revised seating to increase capacity. The second tranche, identified as Class 350/2 has its front end gangway door painted with a black top section. Set No. 350247 is illustrated from its DMSO(B) coach.* **CJM**

Electric Multiple Units

Sub-class	350/1	350/2
Number range:	350101-350130	350231-350267
Introduced:	2004-2005	2008-2009
Built by:	Siemens - Vienna, Austria, and Duewag, Germany	Siemens - Duewag, Germany
Formation:	DMSO(A)+TCO+PTSO+DMSO(B)	DMSO(A)+TCO+PTSO+DMSO(B)
Vehicle numbers:	DMSO(A) - 63761-63790	DMSO(A) - 61431-61467
	TCO - 66811-66840	TCO - 65231-65267
	PTSO - 66861-66890	PTSO - 67531-67567
	DMSO(B) - 63711-63740	DMSO(B) - 61531-61567
Vehicle length:	66ft 9in (20.34m)	66ft 9in (20.34m)
Height:	12ft 1½in (3.69m)	12ft 1½in (3.69m)
Width:	9ft 2in (2.79m)	9ft 2in (2.79m)
Seating:	Total - 24F/200S + 9 tip up	Total - 24F/243S + 9 tip up
	DMSO(A) - 60S	DMSO(A) - 70S
	TCO - 24F/32S	TCO - 24F/42S
	PTSO - 48S + 9 tip up	PTSO - 61S + 9 tip up
	DMSO(B) - 60S	DMSO(B) - 70S
Internal layout:	2+2	2+2, 2+3
Gangway:	Throughout	Throughout
Toilets:	TCO, PTSO - 1	TCO, PTSO - 1
Weight:	Total - 179.3 tonnes	Total - 166.1 tonnes
	DMSO(A) - 48.7 tonnes	DMSO(A) - 43.7 tonnes
	TCO - 36.2 tonnes	TCO - 35.3 tonnes
	PTSO - 45.2 tonnes	PTSO - 42.9 tonnes
	DMSO(B) - 49.2 tonnes	DMSO(B) - 44.2 tonnes
Brake type:	Air (regenerative)	Air (regenerative)
Bogie type:	SGP SF5000	SGB SF5000
Power collection:	25kV ac overhead	25kV ac overhead
Traction motor type:	4 x Siemens 1TB2016-0GB02	4 x Siemens 1TB2016-0GB02
Horsepower:	1,341hp (1,000kW)	1,341hp (1,000kW)
Max speed:	110mph (177km/h)	100mph (161km/h)
Coupling type:	Outer - Dellner 12, Inner - Bar	Outer - Dellner 12, Inner - Bar
Multiple restriction:	Within class	Within class
Door type:	Bi-parting sliding plug	Bi-parting sliding plug
Total number in fleet:	30	37
Construction:	Aluminium	Aluminium
Owner:	Angel Trains	Porterbrook
Operator:	London Midland	London Midland
Special features:	Air conditioned, CCTV, PIS	Air conditioned, CCTV, PIS
Notes:	Wired for 750V dc operation	

Above: *The intermediate Pantograph Trailer Standard Open on Class 350/1 sets seats 48, while on the later Class 350/2 sets this increases to 61 with more 2+3 seating and reduced space. A PTSO is viewed from its non-pantograph end showing the two pairs of sliding plug doors and the high level of equipment carried below a trailer vehicle.* **CJM**

Right: *Class 350 front end layout. A: High-level marker light, B: White marker light, C: Red tail light, D: Headlight, E: Route indicator, F: Front gangway folding door, G: Dellner 12 coupler incorporating physical, electrical and pneumatic connections, H: Anti-climber grooves, I: Air warning horn, J: Obstacle deflector plate.* **CJM**

350/3	350/4
350368-350377	350401-350410
2014	2014
Siemens - Duewag, Germany	Siemens - Duewag, Germany
DMSO(A)+TCO+PTSO+DMSO(B)	DMSO(A)+TCO+PTSO+DMSO(B)
DMSO(A) - 60141-60150	DMSO(A) - 60691-60700
TCO - 60511-60520	TCO - 60901-60910
PTSO - 60651-60660	PTSO - 60941-60950
DMSO(B) - 60151-60160	DMSO(B) - 60671-60680
66ft 9in (20.34m)	66ft 9in (20.34m)
12ft 1½in (3.69m)	12ft 1½in (3.69m)
9ft 2in (2.79m)	9ft 2in (2.79m)
Total - 19F/191S	Total - 19F/178S
DMSO(A) - tba	DMSO(A) - 56S
TCO - 19F/tba	TCO - 19F/24S
PTSO - tba	PTSO - 42S
DMSO(B) - tba	DMSO(B) - 56S
2+1F /2+2S	2+1F / 2+2S
Throughout	Throughout
TCO, PTSO - 1	TCO, PTSO - 1
Total - 170 tonnes	Total - 170 tonnes
DMSO(A) - 44.2 tonnes	DMSO(A) - 44.2 tonnes
TCO - 36.2 tonnes	TCO - 36.2 tonnes
PTSO - 44.6 tonnes	PTSO - 44.6 tonnes
DMSO(B) - 45 tonnes	DMSO(B) - 45 tonnes
Air (regenerative)	Air (regenerative)
SGB SF5000	SGB SF5000
25kV ac overhead	25kV ac overhead
4 x Siemens 1TB2016-0GB02	4 x Siemens 1TB2016-0GB02
1,341hp (1,000kW)	1,341hp (1,000kW)
110mph (177km/h)	100mph (161km/h)
Outer - Dellner 12, Inner - Bar	Outer - Dellner 12, Inner - Bar
Within class	Within class
Bi-parting sliding plug	Bi-parting sliding plug
10	10
Aluminium	Aluminium
Angel Trains	Angel Trains
London Midland	First TransPennine
Air conditioned, CCTV, PIS	Air conditioned, CCTV, PIS

The original 30-strong fleet of Class 350/1 'Desiro' sets was formed of the vehicles ordered by Angel Trains for Class 450/2 sets for SWT and subsequently cancelled.

The four-car sets, built in Germany, were operated under the West Coast name, incorporating Silverlink Railways and Central Trains, and deployed on the Euston-Birmingham and North West services.

Until the franchise changes at the end of 2007 and the formation of London Midland the units were painted in mid-grey with blue doors.

After the 2007 franchise alterations and the formation of London Midland, 37 additional four-car sets classified as 350/2 were ordered from Siemens. These looked the same as their earlier counterparts but incorporated a more high-density passenger layout. All sets were delivered in London Midland green, grey and black livery.

Sets are allocated to a purpose-built depot at Northampton and maintained under contract by Siemens.

Interiors on Class 350/1 sets are laid out in the 2+2 low-density style in a mix of facing and airline; tables are provided at the facing positions in standard and first class. On the later Class 350/2 sets a mix of 2+2 and 2+3 seating is used with a more cramped layout; seat-back tables have also been omitted.

The design was furthered in 2012 with two orders for 10 four-car sets, 10 for London Midland (Class 350/3) and 10 for First TransPennine Express (Class 350/4) to operate new electrified services between Manchester and Scotland via the West Coast Main Line. The Class 350/4 sets for FTPE, built in Germany, were shipped to the UK in 2013-14 and entered service at the end of 2013. The sets are painted in a First Group swirl livery and are allocated to Ardwick depot.

The Class 350/3s are due to enter traffic in mid-2014. ■

Above: *The Class 350/4 sets, operated by First TransPennine Express on electrified services between Manchester and Scotland, were delivered in base grey livery but First Group 'dynamic lines' style colours have now been applied. These sets seat 19 first and 178 standard class passengers in the 2+2 low-density style. The sets are allocated to the Siemens-operated Ardwick depot, Manchester. Set No. 350402 is seen at Preston on 16 July 2014 with a Manchester to Edinburgh service.* **CJM**

Class 357 'Electrostar'

Sub-class:	357/0	357/2
Number range:	357001-357046	357201-357228
Introduced:	1999-2001	2001-2002
Built by:	Adtranz Derby	Adtranz/Bombardier Derby
Formation:	DMSO(A)+MSO+PTSO+DMSO(B)	DMSO(A)+MSO+PTSO+DMSO(B)
Vehicle numbers:	DMSO(A) - 67651-67696	DMSO(A) - 68601-68628
	MSO - 74151-74196	MSO - 74701-74728
	PTSO - 74051-74096	PTSO - 74601-74628
	DMSO(B) - 67751-67796	DMSO(B) - 68701-68728
Vehicle length:	DMSO(A), DMSO(B) - 68ft 1in (20.75m)	DMSO(A), DMSO(B) - 68ft 1in (20.75m)
	PTSO, MSO - 65ft 11½in (20.10m)	PTSO, MSO - 65ft 11½in (20.10m)
Height:	12ft 4½in (3.77m)	12ft 4½in (3.78m)
Width:	9ft 2¼in (2.80m)	9ft 2¼in (2.80m)
Seating:	Total - 278S + 4 tip up	Total - 278S + 4 tip up
	DMSO(A) - 71S	DMSO(A) - 71S
	MSO - 78S	MSO - 78S
	PTSO - 58S + 4 tip up	PTSO - 58S + 4 tip up
	DMSO(B) - 71S	DMSO(B) - 71S
Internal layout:	2+2, 2+3	2+2, 2+3
Gangway:	Within set	Within set
Toilets:	PTSOL - 1	PTSOL - 1
Weight:	Total - 157.6 tonnes	Total - 157.6 tonnes
	DMSO(A) - 40.7 tonnes	DMSO(A) - 40.7 tonnes
	MSO - 36.7 tonnes	MSO - 36.7 tonnes
	PTSO - 39.5 tonnes	PTSO - 39.5 tonnes
	DMSO(B) - 40.7 tonnes	DMSO(B) - 40.7 tonnes
Brake type:	Air (rheostatic/regen)	Air (rheostatic/regen)
Bogie type:	Power - Adtranz P3-25	Power - Adtranz P3-25
	Trailer - Adtranz T3-25	Trailer - Adtranz T3-25
Power collection:	25kV ac overhead (750v dc equipped)	25kV ac overhead (750v dc equipped)
Traction motor type:	6 x Adtranz (250kW)	6 x Adtranz (250kW)
Output:	2,010hp (1,500kW)	2,010hp (1,500kW)
Max speed:	100mph (161km/h)	100mph (161km/h)
Coupling type:	Outer - Tightlock, Inner - Bar	Outer - Tightlock, Inner - Bar
Total sets in service:	46	28
Multiple restriction:	Within class only	Within class only
Door type:	Bi-parting sliding plug	Bi-parting sliding plug
Owner:	Porterbrook	Angel Trains
Operator:	c2c	c2c
Special features:	Air conditioning	Air conditioning

Under the terms of the original franchise to operate the London, Tilbury & Southend route, new trains were stipulated. These were ordered from Adtranz (later Bombardier), which supplied its 'Electrostar' product in its non-gangway form.

Originally 46 units funded by Porterbrook were introduced from 1999; these were supplemented by 28 identical sets owned by Angel Trains introduced between 2001 and 2002.

All sets are now painted in the National Express c2c white livery, offset by blue doors; all sets are allocated to East Ham depot.

Seating is provided in the 2+3 high-density style and no provision is made for first class.

Power is collected by an intermediate PTSO feeding traction power to the two outer DMSO vehicles. Provision is also made for 750V dc operation if required for conversion at a later date. ∎

Right Top: *As a follow-on to the first order for c2c Class 357 'Electrostar' sets, Angel Trains funded a further 28 units, classified as 357/2; these were introduced in 2001-02 and are identical in every way to the original Class 357/0 sets. With its DMSO(B) leading, set No. 357221 approaches London Fenchurch Street. All sets carry National Express white livery offset by blue passenger doors.* **CJM**

Right Middle: *The intermediate Motor Standard Open, which houses two of the train's six traction motors, has seating for 78 standard class passengers in a mix of 2+2 and 2+3 modes. Total seating for a four-car train is 278 and no provision is made for first class travel. MSO No. 74703 is shown from set No. 357203.* **CJM**

Right Bottom: *The Pantograph Trailer Standard Open coach seats 58 and has a toilet compartment at one end (near end in illustration). These vehicles also have the disabled seating area with a fixing point for a wheelchair and a bicycle stowage area; these are identified on the outside of the coach by a blue surround and door branding. Vehicle No. 74079 from Class 357/0 set No. 357029 is seen at London Fenchurch Street.* **CJM**

Left: *Allocated to East Ham depot, the Class 357s are some of the most reliable train sets in the UK and form a part of the Bombardier 'Electrostar' family; they are non-gangwayed sets with full corridor connection within each train. The first 46 sets introduced in 1999-2001 are funded by Porterbrook and classified as Class 357/0. All are currently painted in National Express white offset by blue passenger doors. The sets have both National Express and c2c branding. Set No. 357029 is seen arriving at London Fenchurch Street.* **CJM**

Class 360 'Desiro'

Sub-class:	360/0	360/2
Number range:	360101-360121	360201-360205
Introduced:	2002-2003	2004-2006
Built by:	Siemens Transportation - Vienna, Austria, and Duewag, Germany	Siemens Transportation - Duewag, Germany
Formation:	DMCO(A)+PTSO+TSO+DMCO(B)	DMSO(A)+PTSO+TSO(A)+TSO(B)+DMSO(B)
Vehicle numbers:	DMCO(A) - 65551-65571	DMSO(A) - 78431-78435
	PTSO - 72551-72571	PTSO - 63421-63425
	TSO - 74551-74571	TSO(A) - 72431-72435
	DMCO(B) - 68551-68571	TSO(B) - 72421-72425
		DMSO(B) - 78441-78445
Vehicle length:	66ft 9in (20.34m)	66ft 9in (20.34m)
Height:	12ft 1½in (3.95m)	12ft 1½in (3.95m)
Width:	9ft 2in (2.79m)	9ft 2in (2.79m)
Seating:	Total - 16F/256S + 9 tip up	Total - 333S + 9 tip up
	DMCO(A) - 8F/59S	DMSO(A) - 63S
	PTSO - 60S + 9 tip up	PTSO - 59S + 9 tip up
	TSO - 78S	TSO(A) - 74S
	DMCO(A) 8F/59S	TSO(B) - 74S
		DMSO(B) 63S
Internal layout:	2+2F/2+2 & 2+3S	2+3
Gangway:	Within set only	Within set only
Toilets:	PTOS - 1	PTOS - 1
Weight:	Total - 168 tonnes	Total - 202.9 tonnes
	DMCO(A) - 45.0 tonnes	DMSO(A) - 44.8 tonnes
	PTSO - 43 tonnes	PTSO - 44.2 tonnes
	TSO - 35 tonnes	TSO(A) - 35.4 tonnes
	DMCO(B) - 45 tonnes	TSO(B) - 34.1 tonnes
		DMSO(B) - 44.4 tonnes
Brake type:	Air (regenerative)	Air (regenerative)
Bogie type:	SGP SF5000	SGP SF5000
Power collection:	25kV ac overhead	25kV ac overhead
Traction motor type:	1TB2016 - 0GB02 three phase	1TB2016 - 0GB02 three phase
Output:	1,341hp (1,000kW)	1,341hp (1,000kW)
Max speed:	100mph (161km/h)	100mph (161km/h)
Coupling type:	Outer - Dellner 12, Inner - Semi-auto	Outer - Dellner 12, Inner - Semi-auto
Multiple restriction:	Within sub-class	Within sub-class
Door type:	Bi-parting sliding plug	Bi-parting sliding plug
Number in traffic:	21	5
Construction:	Aluminium	Aluminium
Owner:	Angel Trains	British Airports Authority
Operator:	Greater Anglia	Heathrow Connect/FGW
Special features:	Air conditioning, PIS	Air conditioning, PIS, Great Western ATP
Notes:		360201-204 were original demonstrator 'Desiro' sets. Rebuilt without end gangways for 'Heathrow Connect'. Additional TSO(B) cars added in 2006-07, 360205 delivered as five-car

Below: *Heading over the River Stour at Manningtree, Class 360/0 set No. 360110 forms an Ipswich to London Liverpool Street service led by its DMCO(A) vehicle which provides seating for 8 first and 59 standard class passengers.* **Antony Christie**

Electric Multiple Units

Above: *The Class 360 non-gangwayed 'Desiro' EMU was first ordered by First Great Eastern with 21 sets delivered in 2002-03 for outer suburban use to assist the removal of the final slam-door stock. The four-car medium-density sets with a mix of 2+2 and 2+3 seating are allocated to Ilford and operate on longer distance outer suburban routes. Painted in original blue livery with Greater Anglia branding, set No. 360107 passes Pudding Mill station with its DMCO(B) nearest the camera.* **CJM**

Right: *The two intermediate Class 360/1 vehicles are both trailers; one is mounted with a pantograph and has a large amount of electrical equipment including the transformer mounted below. The car fitted with the pantograph seats 60 as it also houses the toilet compartment. The TSO seats 78. TSO No. 74567 from set 360117 is illustrated carrying original First Group blue with Greater Anglia branding.* **Michael J. Collins**

A s part of the First Great Eastern franchise, new stock was sought for outer suburban services. A contract was awarded to Siemens for 21 four-car sets, using an aluminium body structure. This was the first UK order for the 'Desiro' product and also saw four demonstration sets produced.

The sets, now classified as 360/0, were built at the Duewag plant in Germany (driving cars) and the plant in Vienna, Austria (intermediate vehicles). All cars were then brought together and tested on the Siemens test track at Wildenrath, Germany, before delivery to the UK.

The 21 original sets, now operated by Abellio Greater Anglia, have a small first class area in each driving car set out in the 2+2 style, with standard class seating in the 2+3 mode.

British Airports Authority and First Group sought new trains in 2006 for the stopping service linking London Paddington and Heathrow Airport marketed as 'Heathrow Connect'.

The 'Desiro' train was selected and the four pre-delivery prototype sets were rebuilt for this role; an additional TSO was built for each and one totally new five-car set was built to provide a fleet of five five-car sets.

The BAA/FGW sets are laid out for all standard class in the 2+3 mode; the sets are fitted with FGW-style Automatic Train Protection. Livery is all-over grey with a blue window band and orange doors. One set, No. 360205, was dedicated to the Heathrow Central-Heathrow Terminal 4 shuttle and has revised seating. ■

Above: *Class 360 'Desiro' driving cab. These sets are designed for full driver-only operation, with the driver being responsible for traction and door control. Power and braking is operated from a small control switch on the left side, being pushed forward to apply power and pulled rearwards of a central position to apply the brake. The train's on-board diagnostic computer screen is seen on the driver's right side. Note the crude 'slider' positioned on the top edge of the driving desk showing a number '4'; this can have the cover moved to reveal either '4', '8' or '12' to remind the driver how many coaches he has on the train.* **CJM**

Left: *Class 360 'Desiro' front end layout, applicable to both the Greater Anglia Class 360/1 fleet and the Class 360/2 'Heathrow Connect' stock. A: High-level marker light, B: White marker light, C: Red tail light, D: Headlight, E: Route indicator, F: Air warning horn, G: Air supply, H: Dellner 12 coupling, including physical, electrical and pneumatic connections, I: Obstacle deflector plate.* **CJM**

Above: *When the joint First Group/BAA 'Heathrow Connect' local service between London Paddington and Heathrow Airport was announced, a fleet of five 'Desiro' Class 360 sets were ordered. Four of these used the vehicles of the original 'Desiro' prototype trains, which were heavily rebuilt, and one new five-car set was built. The original four four-car sets were strengthened to five vehicles. The Class 360/2s are allocated to Old Oak Common 'Heathrow Express' depot and operate slow services between Paddington and Heathrow Terminals 1-3, with a 'shuttle' service between Terminals 1-3 and Terminal 4. Set No. 360204 is seen from its DMSO(A) end at West Ealing.* **CJM**

Right Middle: *The two driving cars are the motor vehicles, with three trailers between, one of which houses the pantograph and transformer equipment. Seating on these vehicles is for 59 and a toilet compartment is also installed.* **CJM**

Right Below: *The two standard TSO vehicles both seat 74 in the 2+3 high-density mode. Two pairs of double leaf sliding plug doors are provided on each vehicle. TSO No. 72422 is shown from the DMSO(B) end. Set No. 360205 (the purpose-built set) has revised 2+2 seating and extra luggage stacks.* **CJM**

Class 365 'Networker Express'

Number range:	365501-365541
Introduced:	1994-1995
Built by:	ABB/Adtranz York
Formation:	DMCO(A)+TSO+PTSO+DMSO(B)
Vehicle numbers:	DMCO(A) - 65894-65934
	TSOL - 72241-72321 (odd numbers)
	PTSOL - 72240-72320 (even numbers)
	DMCO(B) - 65935-65975
Vehicle length:	DMCO - 68ft 6½in (20.89m)
	TSO/PTSO - 65ft 9¾in (20.06m)
Height:	12ft 4½in (3.77m)
Width:	9ft 2½in (2.81m)
Seating:	Total - 24F/244S (245S on sets 365517-365541)
	DMCO(A) - 12F/56S
	TSO - 64S (65S on sets 365517-365541)
	PTSO - 68S
	DMCO(B) - 12F/56S
Internal layout:	2+2F, 2+2 & 2+3S
Gangway:	Within unit only
Toilets:	TSO, PTSO - 1
Weight:	Total - 150.9 tonnes
	DMCO(A) - 41.7 tonnes
	TSOL - 32.9 tonnes
	PTSOL - 34.6 tonnes
	DMCO(B) - 41.7 tonnes
Brake type:	Air (rheostatic/regenerative)
Bogie type:	Powered: Adtranz P3-16
	Trailer: Adtranz T3-16
Power collection:	25Kv ac overhead*
Traction motor type:	4 x GEC G354CX of 210hp (157kW)
Horsepower:	1,680hp (1,256kW)
Max speed:	100mph (161km/h)
Coupling type:	Outer - Tightlock, Inner - Semi-auto
Multiple restriction:	Within class only
Door type:	Bi-parting sliding plug
Total sets in traffic:	40 (one set withdrawn)
Construction:	Aluminium alloy
Owner:	Eversholt
Operator:	First Capital Connect
Note:	* Wired for 750V dc operation

Fact File

Dubbed as 'Networker Express' units, these four-car outer-suburban sets were introduced by Network SouthEast and originally used on the South Eastern Division (16 sets) and the remainder on West Anglia Great Northern.

Following privatisation and new rolling stock deliveries, the entire fleet was allocated to West Anglia duties and now all are operated by First Capital Connect based at Hornsey depot and mainly painted in FCC livery.

In the early years of the decade, the traditional 'Networker' front end was revised following installation of a new cab ventilation system.

Internally sets are laid out in 2+2 and 2+3 mode with carpeted floors and good quality seats.

These sets could be modified for dc or dual voltage operation if required. ∎

Right: *The 40 Class 365 'Networker Express' sets introduced between 1994 and 1995 and the final development of the NSE 'Networker' product are now all allocated to First Capital Connect; originally some were allocated to South Eastern. Since introduction revised front ends have been applied. The sets operate the outer suburban and long distance Great Northern line services and have a mix of 2+2 and 2+3 seating. First class seating is provided in both driving cars. In Peterborough advertising livery, set No. 365519 passes Harringay, led by its DMCO(A) vehicle.* **CJM**

Right: *Class 365 front end equipment positions. A: Destination and route indicator, B: Light cluster group with, from the outer edge, a red tail light, white marker light and a headlight, C: Lamp bracket, D: Air warning horns, E: Tightlock coupling with pneumatic and electrical connections below in a roll-covered box.* **Brian Morrison**

Left Below: *The Class 365 sets have total accommodation for 24 first and either 244 or 245 standard class passengers (the original sets operated on South Eastern had an additional seat). These sets are currently in the process of passing through works and will emerge in a new Thameslink livery. Set No. 365509 is shown from its DMCO(B) vehicle at Harringay.* **CJM**

Below: *The intermediate Pantograph Trailer Standard Open (PTSO) seats 68 standard class passengers and also has one standard design toilet compartment, identified by a single opaque window, seen at the near end in this view of vehicle No. 72280.* **CJM**

Electric Multiple Units

Class 373 'Eurostar'

Sub-class:	373/0	373/2
Number range:	373001-022 / 373101-108 / 373201-232	373301-373314
	3999 (spare PC)	
Introduced:	1992-1996	1996
Built by:	GEC Alsthom	GEC Alsthom
Formation:	DM+MS+TS+TS+TS+TS+TBK+TF+TF+TBF	DM+MS+TS+TS+TS+TBK+TF+TBF
Set length:	1,291ft 8in (393.72m)	1,046ft 4in (318.92m)
Vehicle length:	DM - 72ft 8in (22.15m)	DM - 72ft 8in (22.15m)
	MS - 71ft 8in (21.84m)	MS - 71ft 8in (21.84m)
	TS, TBK, TF, TBF - 61ft 4in (18.69m)	TS, TBK, TF, TBF - 61ft 4in (18.69m)
Height:	12ft 4½in (3.77m)	12ft 4½in (3.77m)
Width:	9ft 3in (2.82m)	9ft 3in (2.82m)
Seating:	Total - 103F/280S (half train)	Total - 57F/222S
	DM - 0	DM - 0
	MS - 48S	MS - 48S
	TS - 58S	TS - 58S
	TS - 58S	TS - 58S
	TS - 58S	TS - 58S
	TS - 58S	TBK - 0
	TBK - 0	TF - 39F
	TF - 39F	TBF - 18F
	TF - 39F	
	TBF - 25F	
Internal layout:	2+1F, 2+2S	2+1F, 2+2S
Gangway:	Within set and at half set end	Within set and at half set end
Toilets:	MS - 2, TBF - 1, TF - 1, TS - 1 or 2	MS - 1, TBF - 1, TF - 1, TS - 1 or 2
Weight:	Total - 816.1 tonnes	Total - 682.2 tonnes
	DM - 68.5 tonnes	DM - 68.5 tonnes
	MS - 44.6 tonnes	MS - 44.6 tonnes
	TS - 28.1-29.7 tonnes	TS - 28.1-29.7 tonnes
	TBK - 31.1 tonnes	TBK - 31.1 tonnes
	TF - 29.6 tonnes	TF - 29.6 tonnes
	TBF - 39.4 tonnes	TBF - 39.4 tonnes
Brake type:	Air	Air
Power collection:	25kV ac overhead, 3kV dc overhead¤ *	25kV ac overhead
Horsepower:	25kV ac operation - 16,400hp (12,240kW)	25kV ac operation - 16,400hp (12,240kW)
	3kV dc operation - 7,368hp (5,000kW)	
Max speed:	25kV ac operation 186mph (300km/h)	25kV ac operation 186mph (300km/h)
Coupling type:	Outer - Scharfenberg, Inner - Bar	Outer - Scharfenberg, Inner - Bar
Multiple restriction:	Not permitted	Not permitted
Door type:	Single-leaf sliding plug	Single-leaf sliding plug
Special features:	TVM430, CT equipment	TVM430, CT equipment
Total sets in traffic:	24 half sets	14 half sets used in mainland Europe
Construction:	Steel	Steel
Owner:	Eurostar UK, SNCF, SNCB	Eurostar UK
Operator:	Eurostar UK, SNCF, SNCB	SNCF
Notes:	¤ isolated	

* Sets 3201-04/07-10/15/16/23-30 are fitted with French 1,500V overhead equipment to allow South of France running.

+ Sets 373203/04/25/26/27/28 modified for domestic French operation only and not part of Eurostar fleet.

Fact File

To operate through the Channel Tunnel, on services from the UK to France and Belgium, this most impressive fleet of scaled-down French-style TGV sets was built in the early 1990s.

Thirty-two half train 'three-capitals' sets were originally built, owned by the UK (Eurostar UK), SNCB (Belgian Railways) and SNCF (French Railways). Since original introduction some scaling down of the fleet has taken place with some sets stored and others transferred to French domestic services on the Paris-Lille and South of France routes.

Originally it was planned to operate North of London to Europe services and for this 14 short-length half sets were built. However, this service was abandoned and the sets stored, being used for testing and hire to GNER, the UK East Coast operator on the London-York/Leeds route for a few years.

All operational 'three-capitals' sets are now refurbished, and the 'short' sets operate on domestic French services. ∎

Above: *Now devoid of their original ability to operate from the third rail supply, the 'Eurostar' Class 373 fleet operates entirely from the 25kV ac supply in the UK. Showing the latest 'Eurostar' livery, half train No. (37)3015 leads a train bound for London at Ashford (Kent).* **Antony Christie**

Right: *The Class 373 sets from the UK, France and Belgium operate as one pool, receiving maintenance in any country. Sets 373008/009 pass Tutt Hill on HS1 bound for the Channel Tunnel.* **Brian Stevenson**

Electric Multiple Units

Above: *Travelling at the line speed of 300km/h (186mph) a 'Eurostar' set storms towards London crossing the iconic Medway Bridge. This view gives a good impression of the length of a 20 vehicle set. The refreshment vehicles from both half sets are easily recognisable by having deeper blue bands around the window positions. This view shows one of the Belgian sets numbered in the 3731xx series.* **Antony Christie**

Above: *The 'Eurostar' driving cab is one of the most complex in the world, with the ability to operate from multi-voltages and in different countries and deal with many different signal systems. The power controllers are located either side of the central panel, with the TVM430 cab signalling on the facing display above. The system voltage changeover switchgear is on the right hand side.* **CJM**

Left Middle: *The 'Eurostar' passenger coaches used on the three-capitals services are finished in white, yellow and blue, but a new colour scheme is likely to be launched soon. The first and standard class saloons as well as the buffet are articulated with a bogie supporting one end of two vehicles. Here we see a standard class vehicle seating 58 is the 2+2 style in a mix of airline and group seats. The first class vehicles of the same structural design seat 39 in the 2+1 layout, again in a mix of airline and group layout.* **Antony Christie**

Left Bottom: *The buffet vehicles, which divide the standard and first class seating, have a much deeper blue upper band and are thus recognisable. These vehicles also have service doors to load trolleys and supplies. No seats are provided in these vehicles, with a large standing bar area.* **Antony Christie**

Above: *The first and last vehicle of each half train has end bogies, allowing the two half trains to couple conventionally and the power cars to attach to the train. The vehicle attached to the power car is a Motor Standard (MS) and has a power block and traction bogie at the power car end, as illustrated above.* **Antony Christie**

Class 374 'e320'

Fact File

The Class 374 or 'Eurostar e320' high speed trains are for use by Eurostar on its multi-national services from London through the Channel Tunnel. A fleet of 10 400-metre-long trainsets of the Siemens 'Velaro' family, formed of 16 carriages is on order.

The fleet will expand Eurostar operations beyond the core routes to Paris and Brussels. These trains carry full international numbers with the 93 (high-speed EMU), and 70 (UK) prefix.

In 2009, Eurostar announced a £700m project to update its fleet, with £550m to buy new trains to augment its existing fleet, and having the ability to operate away from the London-Paris/Brussels network.

In October 2010 Siemens was selected to provide the stock given the title 'Velaro e320', based on Eurostar's plan to operate the trains at 320 km/h (200 mph).

The 'e320' features distributed traction, located along the length of the train.

Extensive testing is currently in process, with six trains built by early 2014. One set is in the UK at Temple Mills depot. ■

Number range:	374001-374020 (half sets) (see below)
Introduced:	2015-2016*
Built by:	Siemens, Krefeld
Formation:	DM, T, M, T, T, M, T, M
Set length:	To be advised
Vehicle length:	Driving - tba, Intermediate - tba
Height:	To be advised
Width:	To be advised
Seating:	Total - 450
Internal layout:	2+1F, 2+2S
Gangway:	Within set and at half set end
Toilets:	To be advised
Weight:	To be advised
Brake type:	Air, regenerative
Power collection:	25kV ac overhead, 15kV ac overhead
	3,000V dc overhead, 1500V dc overhead
Horsepower:	25kV ac operation - 21,000hp (16,000kW)
	15kV, 3,000V dc, 1,500V dc - tba
Max speed:	200mph (320km/h)
Coupling type:	Outer - Scharfenberg, Inner - Bar
Multiple restriction:	Two half sets only
Door type:	Single-leaf sliding plug
Special features:	TVM430, CT equipment
Construction:	Aluminium
Train family:	Siemens 'Velaro'
Owner:	Eurostar
Operator:	Eurostar
Notes:	* Sets 374001-002 built 2011 for testing

The vehicles of these sets carry their full 12 digit international numbers, the 11th of which is the set's vehicle number.
Number range: 93 70 3740-011 9 GB-EIL – 93 70 3740-201 9 GB-EIL

Class 375 'Electrostar'

Sub-class:	375/3	375/6	375/7
Number range:	375301-375310	375601-375630	375701-375715
Introduced:	2001-2002	1999-2001	2001-2002
Built by:	Bombardier Derby	Adtranz/Bombardier Derby	Bombardier Derby
Formation:	DMCO (A)+TSO+DMCO(B)	DMCO(A)+MSO+ PTSO+DMCO(B)	DMCO(A)+MSO+ TSO+DMCO(B)
Vehicle numbers:	DMCO(A) - 67921-67930 TSO - 74351-74360 DMCO(B) - 67931-67940	DMCO(A) - 67801-67830 MSO - 74251-74280 PTSO - 74201-74230 DMCO(B) - 67851-67880	DMCO(A) - 67831-67845 MSO - 74281-74295 TSO - 74231-74245 DMCO(B) - 67881-67895
Vehicle length:	DMCO - 66ft 11in (20.40m) TSO - 65ft 6in (19.99m)	DMCO - 66ft 11in (20.40m) MSO, PTSO - 65ft 6in (19.99m)	DMCO - 66ft 11in (20.40m) MSO, TSO - 65ft 6in (19.99m)
Height:	12ft 4in (3.78m)	12ft 4in (3.78m)	12ft 4in (3.78m)
Width:	9ft 2in (2.80m)	9ft 2in (2.80m)	9ft 2in (2.80m)
Seating:	Total - 24F/152S DMCO(A) - 12F/48S TSO - 56S DMCO(B) - 12F/48S	Total - 24F/218S DMCO(A) - 12F/48S MSO - 66S PTSO - 56S DMCO(B) - 12F/48S	Total - 24F/218S DMCO(A) - 12F/48S MSO - 66S TSO - 56S DMCO(B) - 12F/48S
Internal layout:	2+2	2+2	2+2
Gangway:	Throughout	Throughout	Throughout
Toilets:	TSO - 1	PTSO, MSO - 1	TSO, MSO - 1
Weight:	Total - 124.1 tonnes DMCO(A) - 43.8 tonnes TSO - 36.5 tonnes DMCO(B) - 43.8 tonnes	Total - 173.6 tonnes DMCO(A) - 46.2 tonnes MSO - 40.5 tonnes PTSO - 40.7 tonnes DMCO(B) - 46.2 tonnes	Total - 158.1 tonnes DMCO(A) - 43.8 tonnes MSO - 36.4 tonnes TSO - 34.1 tonnes DMCO(B) - 43.8 tonnes
Brake type:	Air (regenerative)	Air (regenerative)	Air (regenerative)
Bogie type:	Power - Adtranz P3-25 Trailer - Adtranz T3-25	Power - Adtranz P3-25 Trailer - Adtranz T3-25	Power - Adtranz P3-25 Trailer - Adtranz T3-25
Power collection:	750V dc third rail	750V dc third rail, and 25kV ac overhead	750V dc third rail
Traction motor type:	4 x Adtranz	6 x Adtranz	6 x Adtranz
Output:	1,341hp (1,000kW)	2,012hp (1,500kW)	2,012hp (1,500kW)
Max speed:	100mph (161km/h)	100mph (161km/h)	100mph (161km/h)
Coupling type:	Outer - Dellner 12, Inner - Bar	Outer - Dellner 12, Inner - Bar	Outer - Dellner 12, Inner - Bar
Multiple restriction:	Class 375-377	Class 375-377	Class 375-377
Door type:	Bi-parting sliding plug	Bi-parting sliding plug	Bi-parting sliding plug
Total sets in traffic:	10	30	15
Construction:	Aluminium, steel cabs	Aluminium, steel cabs	Aluminium, steel cabs
Owner:	Eversholt	Eversholt	Eversholt
Operator:	SouthEastern	SouthEastern	SouthEastern
Type:	Express	Express	Express

Left: *The Class 375 'Electrostar' sets are operated exclusively by train operator SouthEastern, allocated to Ramsgate depot. Five different sub-classes currently exist. Ten three-car Class 375/3s are in service; these are dc only sets and operated on lightly used and branch line services. Seating is for 24 first and 152 standard in the 2+2 layout. Set No. 375306 is seen at Cuxton on the Maidstone to Strood line.*
Antony Christie

375/8	375/9
375801-375830	375901-375927
2003-2004	2003-2004
Bombardier Derby	Bombardier Derby
DMCO(A)+MSO+	DMCO(A)+MSO+
TSO+DMCO(B)	TSO+DMCO(B)
DMCO(A) - 73301-73330	DMCO(A) - 73331-73357
MSO - 79001-79030	MSO - 79031-79057
TSO - 78201-78230	TSO - 79061-79087
DMCO(B) - 73701-73730	DMCO(B) - 73731-73757
DMCO - 66ft 11in (20.40m)	DMCO - 66ft 11in (20.40m)
MSO, TSO - 65ft 6in (19.99m)	MSO, TSO - 65ft 6in (19.99m)
12ft 4in (3.78m)	12ft 4in (3.78m)
9ft 2in (2.80m)	9ft 2in (2.80m)
Total - 24F/218S	Total - 24F/250S
DMCO(A) - 12F/48S	DMCO(A) - 12F/59S
MSO - 66S	MSO - 73S
TSO - 52S	TSO - 59S
DMCO(B) - 12F/52S	DMCO(B) - 12F/59S
2+2	2+2, 2+3
Throughout	Throughout
TSO, MSO - 1	TSO, MSO - 1
Total - 162.3 tonnes	Total - 161.9 tonnes
DMCO(A) - 43.3 tonnes	DMCO(A) - 43.4 tonnes
MSO - 39.8 tonnes	MSO - 39.3 tonnes
TSO - 35.9 tonnes	TSO - 35.8 tonnes
DMCO(B) - 43.3 tonnes	DMCO(B) - 43.4 tonnes
Air (regenerative)	Air (regenerative)
Power - Bombardier P3-25	Power - Bombardier P3-25
Trailer - Bombardier T3-25	Trailer - Bombardier T3-25
750V dc third rail	750V dc third rail
6 x Adtranz	6 x Adtranz
2,012hp (1,500kW)	2,012hp (1,500kW)
100mph (161km/h)	100mph (161km/h)
Outer - Dellner 12,	Outer - Dellner 12,
Inner - Bar	Inner - Bar
Class 375-377	Class 375-377
Bi-parting sliding plug	Bi-parting sliding plug
30	27
Aluminium, steel cabs	Aluminium, steel cabs
Eversholt	Eversholt
SouthEastern	SouthEastern
Express	Outer suburban

The huge 1990s replacement stock orders for the former Southern Region Central and South Eastern sections under privatisation were awarded to Adtranz/Bombardier for its 'Electrostar' product.

Sets were constructed from 1999 at the rate of more than one new train per week, with 'add-on' orders increasing the Class 375 fleet to 112 sets in various sub-class configurations.

The 375/3s are three-car sets, the 375/6s four-car dual voltage sets, while 375/7 and 375/8 are four-car dc only sets and 375/9s are high-density units. Class 375/2-375/8 are officially 'express' stock while the 375/9 is 'outer-suburban'.

Interior layouts are of a high standard with quality seats with armrests and carpeted floors. All sets are fully air conditioned.

When delivered units were in unbranded white; this gave way to Connex colours, and now SouthEastern Trains livery is applied in various styles.

All sets are allocated to Ramsgate and maintained under a SouthEastern Trains/Bombardier contract. ∎

Right: *A total of 30 four-car Class 375/6 sets are in traffic; these were introduced between 1999 and 2001 and accommodate 24 first and 218 standard class passengers. While these 30 sets tend to operate in a common pool with members of Class 375/7 and 375/8, they are unique within the SouthEastern 'Electrostar' fleet in being wired for dual voltage operation, able to take power from the 25kV ac overhead or the 750V dc third rail. Set No. 375625 is seen approaching Wandsworth Road station soon after departing from London Victoria.* **Antony Christie**

Left: *Class 375 'Electrostar' front end equipment. Positions also apply to members of Class 377. Some Class 375 and 377 sub-classes have slightly different light cluster arrangements with separate marker and tail lights and a smaller headlight. A: High-level marker light, B: Route/destination indicator, C: Light cluster - one headlight and one dual white marker and red tail light on each side, D: Lamp bracket, E: Front folding gangway door, F: Dellner 12 coupling with electrical and pneumatic connections below. G: Air warning horns.* **CJM**

Below: *Class 375 interior showing the 2+2 layout in the behind cab area set out for first class occupancy. Twelve first class seats are located in each DMCO vehicle, each with either a fixed or fold down table. Note the passenger information screen and the CCTV camera. The door leads into the driving cab area.* **Antony Christie**

Above: *Showing the smaller headlight and separate marker/tail lights, Class 375/7 No. 375701 poses at London Bridge. A fleet of 15 members of the Class 375/7 sub-class was introduced in 2001-02, and seating is as usual provided for 24 first and 218 standard class passengers.* **Antony Christie**

Below: *When the final tranche of Class 375s were introduced in 2003-04 it was decided to build 27 outer suburban sets with a mix of 2+2 and 2+3 seating in the standard class areas, increasing the standard class occupancy to 250 per four car train. These sets were classified as 375/9 and numbered 375901-927. Set No. 375919 is seen at New Cross.* **Antony Guppy**

Class 376 'Electrostar'

Number range:	376001-376036
Introduced:	2004-2005
Built by:	Bombardier Derby
Formation:	DMSO(A)+MSO+TSO+MSO+DMSO(B)
Vehicle numbers:	DMSO(A) - 61101-61136
	MSO - 63301-63336
	TSO - 64301-64336
	MSO - 63501-63536
	DMS)(B) - 61601-61636
Vehicle length:	DMSO - 66ft 11in (20.40m)
	TSO, MSO - 65ft 6in (19.99m)
Height:	12ft 4in (3.78m)
Width:	9ft 2in (2.80m)
Seating:	Total - 344S (216 seat, 12 tip up, 116 perch)
	DMSO(A) - 36S, 6 tip up, 22 perch
	MSO - 48S, 24 perch
	TSO - 48S, 24 perch
	MSO - 48S, 24 perch
	DMSO(B) - 36S, 6 tip up, 22 perch
Internal layout:	2+2 low density with standing room
Gangway:	Within set
Toilets:	Not fitted
Weight:	Total - 192.9 tonnes
	DMSO(A) - 42.1 tonnes
	MSO - 36.2 tonnes
	TSO - 36.3 tonnes
	MSO - 36.2 tonnes
	DMSO(B) - 42.1 tonnes
Brake type:	Air (regenerative)
Bogie type:	Power - Bombardier P3-25
	Trailer - Bombardier T3-25
Power collection:	750V dc third rail
Traction motor type:	8 x Bombardier
Output:	2,682hp (2,000kW)
Max speed:	75mph (121km/h)
Coupling type:	Outer - Dellner 12, Inner - Bar
Multiple restriction:	Class 375-377
Door type:	Bi-parting sliding
Total sets in traffic:	36
Construction:	Aluminium with steel cabs
Owner:	Eversholt
Operator:	SouthEastern

Fact File

To cater for inner-suburban needs on SouthEastern Trains, this fleet of five-car tram-like trains was introduced in 2004-05.

The layout is very basic, with 2+2 seating supplemented by a large number of 'perch' seats in each carriage, answering an alleged need to provide more standing room for short distance passengers in peak periods.

Externally the sets were also very basic, with traditional bi-parting sliding doors and no gangway connection on unit ends, thus the cab end is unusual in having three front windows; apart from no gangway, front end equipment is standard 'Electrostar'.

These sets are finished in SouthEastern Trains white with contrasting yellow passenger doors. The fleet of 36 sets is allocated to Slade Green and operates on the high-density routes in South East London and Kent, especially the routes between London and Dartford. ■

Below: *Each five-car Class 376 seats just 216 with perch and standing room for a further 350. Painted in SouthEastern white and beige with yellow doors, set No. 376029 is seen at Lewisham.* **CJM**

Left: The Class 376 was a 'one-off' design for Bombardier, with a somewhat unusual front end as three front windows were incorporated following the stipulation by the train operator that no through gangways were needed. This did however increase the vision for the driver. Main front end equipment items are - A: High-level marker light, B: Destination/route indicator, C: Light cluster, with from the edge a headlight and a joint white marker/red tail light, D: Lamp bracket, E: Air warning horn, F: Dellner 12 coupling. **Brian Morrison**

Below: The basic design of the '376' includes non-recessed folding doors, which run down tracks and are enclosed inside the vehicle. No air conditioning is installed and opening hopper windows provide most ventilation. Each set has four motor cars, with only the middle vehicle being a Trailer Standard Open (TSO). The three intermediate vehicles each have 48 proper seats based on the 2+2 style. Motor Standard Open (MSO) No. 63331 is illustrated. The middle TSO vehicle has a lower roof section if the retro fitting of a pantograph was ever called for. When built it was announced that the slab cab ends could be modified to take a central gangway if required in the future. **CJM**

Right: Allocated to Slade Green, the main South Eastern suburban depot, the Class 376s are mainly deployed on the busy suburban routes from Cannon Street and Charing Cross to Dartford. Sets are deployed all day but their main work period is during the morning and evening peak periods. Showing a comparison with a earlier generation 'Networker', Class 376 No. 376030 approaches London Bridge, passing an Alstom 'Networker' heading towards Kent. **Antony Christie**

Sub-class:	377/1	377/2	377/3
Number range:	377101-377164	377201-377215	377301-377328
Original numbers:	-	-	375311-375338
Introduced:	2002-2004	2002-2003	2001-2002
Built by:	Bombardier Derby	Bombardier Derby	Bombardier Derby
Formation:	DMCO(A)+MSO+ TSO+DMCO(B)	DMCO(A)+MSO+ TSO+DMCO(B)	DMCO(A)+TSO+ DMCO(B)
Vehicle numbers:	DMCO(A) - 78501-78564 MSO - 77101-77164 TSO - 78901-78964 DMCO(B) - 78701-78764	DMCO(A) - 78571-78585 MSO - 77171-77185 PTSO - 78971-78985 DMCO(B) - 78771-78785	DMCO(A) - 68201-68228 TSO - 74801-74828 DMCO(B) - 68401-68428
Vehicle length:	DMCO(A) - 66ft 11in (20.40m) MSO, TSO - 65ft 6in (19.99m)	DMCO(A) - 66ft 11in (20.40m) MSO, TSO - 65ft 6in (19.99m)	DMCO - 66ft 11in (20.40m) TSO - 65ft 6in (19.99m)
Height:	12ft 4in (3.78m)	12ft 4in (3.78m)	12ft 4in (3.78m)
Width:	9ft 2in (2.80m)	9ft 2in (2.80m)	9ft 2in (2.80m)
Seating:	Total - 24F/244S DMCO(A) - 12F/48-56S MSO - 62S - 70S TSO - 52S - 62S DMCO(B) - 12F/48-56S	Total - 24F/222S DMCO(A) - 12F/48S MSO - 69S PTSO - 57S DMCO(B) - 12F/48S	Total - 24F/152S DMCO(A) - 12F/48S TSO - 56S DMCO(B) - 12F/48S
Internal layout:	2+2F, and 2+2 & 2+3S	2+2F, and 2+2 & 2+3S	2+2F, and 2+2 & 2+3S
Gangway:	Throughout	Throughout	Throughout
Toilets:	MSO, TSO - 1	MSO, PTSO - 1	TSO - 1
Weight:	Total - 162.6 tonnes DMCO(A) - 44.8 tonnes MSO - 39 tonnes TSO - 35.4 tonnes DMCO(B) - 43.4 tonnes	Total - 168.3 tonnes DMCO(A) - 44.2 tonnes MSO - 39.8 tonnes PTSO - 40.1 tonnes DMCO(B) - 44.2 tonnes	Total - 122.4 tonnes DMCO(A) - 43.5 tonnes TSO - 35.4 tonnes DMCO(B) - 43.5 tonnes
Brake type:	Air (regenerative)	Air (regenerative)	Air (regenerative)
Bogie type:	Power - Bombardier P3-25 Trailer - Bombardier T3-25	Power - Bombardier P3-25 Trailer - Bombardier T3-25	Power - Bombardier P3-25 Trailer - Bombardier T3-25
Power collection:	750V dc third rail	750V dc third rail, and 25kV ac overhead	750V dc third rail
Traction motor type:	6 x Bombardier	6 x Bombardier	4 x Bombardier
Output:	2,012hp (1,500kW)	2,012hp (1,500kW)	1,341hp (1,000kW)
Max speed:	100mph (161km/h)	100mph (161km/h)	100mph (161km/h)
Coupling type:	Outer - Dellner 12, Inner - Bar	Outer - Dellner 12, Inner - Bar	Outer - Dellner 12, Inner - Bar
Multiple restriction:	Class 375-377	Class 375-377	Class 375-377
Door type:	Bi-parting sliding plug	Bi-parting sliding plug	Bi-parting sliding plug
Total number of sets:	64	15	28
Body structure:	Aluminium, steel ends	Aluminium, steel ends	Aluminium, steel ends
Special features:	PIS Provision for ac fitting	PIS Dual voltage sets	PIS Provision for ac fitting
Owner:	Porterbrook	Porterbrook	Porterbrook
Operator:	Southern	Southern, First Cap'l Connect	Southern
Note:	When delivered, sets were classified as Class 375 and fitted with Tightlock couplers		

Left: *One of the most numerous EMU classes is the Class 377 'Electrostar' operated by Southern and found over the entire electrified network. Eight sub-classes exist. A fleet of 64 Class 377/1s introduced between 2002 and 2004 have seating for 24 first (12 in each driving car) and 244 standard class passengers in a mix of 2+2 and 2+3. Set No. 377109 passes a Class 456 at Honor Oak Park, showing the two contrasting front end designs* **CJM**

377/4	377/5	377/6
377401-377475	377501-377523	377601-377626
-	-	-
2004-2005	2008-2009	2013-2014
Bombardier Derby	Bombardier Derby	Bombardier Derby
DMCO(A)+MSO+	DMCO(A)+MSO+	DMSO(A)+MSO+TSO+
TSO+DMCO(B)	TSO+DMCO(B)	MSO+DMSO(B)
DMCO(A) - 73401-73475	DMCO(A) - 73501-73523	DMSO(A) - 70101-70126
MSO - 78801-78875	MSO - 75901-75923	MSO - 70201-70226
TSO - 78601-78675	TSO - 74901-74923	TSO - 70301-70326
DMCO(B) - 73801-73875	DMCO(B) - 73601-73623	MSO - 70401-70426
		DMSO(B) - 70510-70526
DMCO(A) - 66ft 11in (20.40m)	DMCO(A) - 66ft 11in (20.40m)	DMCO(A) - 66ft 11in (20.40m)
MSO, TSO - 65ft 6in (19.99m)	MSO, TSO - 65ft 6in (19.99m)	MSO, TSO - 65ft 6in (19.99m)
12ft 4in (3.78m)	12ft 4in (3.78m)	12ft 4in (3.78m)
9ft 2in (2.80m)	9ft 2in (2.80m)	9ft 2in (2.80m)
Total - 20F/221S	Total - 20F/218S	Total - 296S
DMCO(A) - 10F/48S	DMCO(A) - 10F/48S	DMSO(A) - 58S
MSO - 69S	MSO - 69S	MSOL - 64S
TSO - 56S	TSO - 53S	PTSOL - 46S, MOS - 66S
DMCO(B) - 10F/48S	DMSO(B) - 10F/48S	DMSO(B) - 62S
2+2F, and 2+2 & 2+3S	2+2F, and 2+2 & 2+3S	2+2F, 2+2S
Throughout	Throughout	Throughout
MSO, TSO - 1	MSO, TSO - 1	MSO, TSO - 1
Total - 160.8 tonnes	Total - 160.8 tonnes	Total - 200.1 tonnes
DMCO(A) - 43.1 tonnes	DMCO(A) - 43.1 tonnes	DMCO(A) - 43.1 tonnes
MSO - 39.3 tonnes	MSO - 39.3 tonnes	MSO - 39.3 tonnes
TSO - 35.3 tonnes	TSO - 35.3 tonnes	TSO - 35.3 tonnes
DMCO(B) - 43.1 tonnes	DMCO(B) - 43.1 tonnes	DMCO(B) - 43.1 tonnes
Air (regenerative)	Air (regenerative)	Air (regenerative)
Power - Bombardier P3-25	Power - Bombardier P3-25	Power - Bombardier P3-25
Trailer - Bombardier T3-25	Trailer - Bombardier T3-25	Trailer - Bombardier T3-25
750V dc third rail	750V dc third rail	750V dc third rail
	25kV ac overhead	
6 x Bombardier	6 x Bombardier	8 x Bombardier
2,012hp (1,500kW)	2,012hp (1,500kW)	2,680hp (2,000kW)
100mph (161km/h)	100mph (161km/h)	100mph (161km/h)
Outer - Dellner 12,	Outer - Dellner 12,	Outer - Dellner 12,
Inner - Bar	Inner - Bar	Inner - Bar
Class 375-377	Class 375-377	Class 375-377
Bi-parting sliding plug	Bi-parting sliding plug	Bi-parting sliding plug
75	23	26
Aluminium, steel ends	Aluminium, steel ends	Aluminium, steel ends
PIS	PIS	PIS
Provision for ac fitting	Dual voltage sets	Provision for ac fitting
Porterbrook	Porterbrook	Porterbrook
Southern	First Capital Connect	Southern

Right: *The Class 377/2 fleet of 15 units is wired for dual voltage operation, able to work from the 750V dc third rail supply as well as the 25kV ac overhead. Until 2014 these sets dominated the West London link service between Croydon and Milton Keynes, but soon Class 377/7s will operate this route and the 377/2s will be transferred to Thameslink. These sets seat 24 first and 222 standard class passengers. Set No. 377208 is seen at West Brompton operating on the dc system.* **CJM**

Sub-class:	377/7	387/1
Number range:	377701-377708	387101-387129
Original numbers:	-	-
Introduced:	2014	2014-2015
Built by:	Bombardier Derby	Bombardier Derby
Formation:	DMCO(A)+MSO+ TSO+MSO+DMCO(B)	DMSO(A)+MSO+ PTSO+DMSO(B)
Vehicle numbers:	DMCO(A) - 65201-65208 MSO - 70601-70608 TSO - 65601-65608 MSO -70701-70708 DMCO(B) - 65401-65408	DMSO(A) - 421101-421129 MSO - 422101-422129 PTSO - 423101-423129 DMSO(B) - 424101-424129
Vehicle length:	DMCO(A) - 66ft 11in (20.40m) MSO, TSO - 65ft 6in (19.99m)	DMCO(A) - 66ft 11in (20.40m) MSO, TSO - 65ft 6in (19.99m)
Height:	12ft 4in (3.78m)	12ft 4in (3.78m)
Width:	9ft 2in (2.80m)	9ft 2in (2.80m)
Seating:	Total - tba DMCO(A) - tba MSO - tba TSO - tba DMCO(B) - tba	Total - tba DMSO(A) - tba MSO - tba PTSO - tba DMSO(B) - tba
Internal layout:	2+2, and 2+3	2+2
Gangway:	Throughout	Throughout
Toilets:	MSO, TSO - 1	MSO, PTSO - 1
Weight:	Total - 201.6 tonnes DMCO(A) - 44.8 tonnes MSO - 39 tonnes TSO - 35.4 tonnes DMCO(B) - 43.4 tonnes	Total - 168.3 tonnes DMSO(A) - 44.2 tonnes MSO - 39.8 tonnes PTSO - 40.1 tonnes DMSO(B) - 44.2 tonnes
Brake type:	Air (regenerative)	Air (regenerative)
Bogie type:	Power - Bombardier P3-25 Trailer - Bombardier T3-25	Power - Bombardier P3-25 Trailer - Bombardier T3-25
Power collection:	750V dc third rail, and 25kV ac overhead	750V dc third rail, and 25kV ac overhead
Traction motor type:	8 x Bombardier	6 x Bombardier
Output:	2,680hp (2,000kW)	2,012hp (1,500kW)
Max speed:	100mph (161km/h)	110mph (177km/h)
Coupling type:	Outer - Dellner 12, Inner - Bar	Outer - Dellner 12, Inner - Bar
Multiple restriction:	Class 375-377	Class 375-377
Door type:	Bi-parting sliding plug	Bi-parting sliding plug
Total number of sets:	8	29 (on delivery)
Body structure:	Aluminium, steel ends	Aluminium, steel ends
Special features:	PIS Dual voltage sets	PIS Dual voltage sets
Owner:	Porterbrook	Porterbrook
Operator:	Southern	Southern
Note:	Five-car sets	For Thameslink

Fact File

A total of 268 Class 377 'Electrostar' sets of various sub-classes are either in traffic or on order being originally introduced to replace slam door stock on South Central, later Southern.

Sets have been built in either three-, four- or five-car form, and the 52 Class 377/2s, 377/7s and 377/8s and are dual voltage ac/dc sets.

The '377s' are structurally the same as the Class 375s, and have a high quality 2+2/2+3 interior with some sub-classes having a small first class area behind the driving cab.

All except the Class 377/5s are finished in Southern green and white livery; the Class 377/5s are finished in FCC colours. Stock is allocated to either Brighton, Selhurst or Bedford depots. The sets are the mainstay of all Southern operations.

At the time of going to press, the five-car dual-voltage Class 377/7s has just been delivered and the next generation of Class 387 were due for delivery from late 2014 through to spring 2015 for use on the new Thameslink, Southern, Great Northern franchise. ∎

Left: *The first members of the Southern 'Electrostar' class to be delivered, then classified as Class 375, were 28 three-car sets fitted for dc only operation. These units were later reclassified as Class 377/2 after Dellner couplers were installed. Seating is for 24 first and 152 standard. These sets sport the three light front end design, as displayed on set No. 377328 at Clapham Junction. When first delivered this set was numbered 375338.* **Antony Christie**

Right Top: *Between 2004 and 2005 a fleet of 75 Class 377/4 sets was delivered to Southern; these sets had slightly revised seating for 20 first class and 221 standard class passengers. Sporting the later design large headlight and combined marker/tail light, set No. 377448 approaches Clapham Junction. Note the yellow band above the first class area directly behind the cab.* **CJM**

Right Middle Upper: *Irrespective if fitted with a pantograph or not, all Class 377 'Electrostar' sets have a pantograph well on the roof of the TSO vehicle, making it a PTSO. With its pantograph well at the far end, PTSO No. 78648 is seen and clearly shows the red bands on the side of the near door pair and two blue pictograms on the bodyside indicating the disabled seating area and bicycle stowage area. PTSO cars have one disabled access toilet compartment.* **CJM**

Right Middle Lower: *The Class 377 Motor Standard Open (MSO) vehicles have a considerable amount of traction equipment housed in underslung boxes, seeing these vehicles weigh in at around 39 tonnes. Seating ranges from 62 to 69 depending on layout. In the main 69 seats are provided in the 2+3 style, but some of the earlier 377/1s have 2+2 seating throughout and thus have a reduced number of seats. Class 377/2 MSO No. 77174 is shown.* **CJM**

Right Bottom: *Class 377 interior showing the Southern seat style with two-tone turquoise moquette. On this class seats do not have hinged armrests in standard class, but fold down tables are provided on airline seats. Above seat luggage racks are provided and group seats have a small table attached to the bodyside. The vehicle shown is a Class 377/1.* **CJM**

Traction Recognition

Above: *Introduced in 2008-09 a fleet of 23 Class 377/5 dual voltage ac/dc sets was delivered to Southern and then sub-leased to First Capital Connect for Thameslink services. Today the fleet is deemed as FCC stock and all are painted in FCC 'urban lights' livery. The sets seat 20 first and 218 standard class and are allocated to Bedford Cauldwell Walk. Set No. 377521 is seen operating on the dc at Honor Oak Park heading for Brighton.* **CJM**

Below and Bottom Right: *In 2013-14, a fleet of 26 Class 377/6 five-car sets was delivered to Southern for suburban services to allow 10-car metro route operation. Each Class 377/6 seats 296 standard class passengers in the 2+2 mode, with ample room for more than 200 standing. These sets do not have the time honoured 'Electrostar' ribbon glazing, but have window frames set into the bodyside, giving an immediate recognition factor. These sets also have a track camera mounted in the front valance. Set No. 377605 is illustrated at London Bridge.* **Antony Christie**

Right Above: *Class 377 'Electrostar' cab layout, also applicable to Class 375 stock. A single power/brake controller is located on the left side of the cab, which is pushed for traction power and pulled back beyond the central position to apply the brakes. All other controls including TPWS, AWS and the Driver's Reminder Appliance are built into the pleasing and functional desk layout. Some detail differences exist on later builds.* **CJM**

Right Middle: *The eight members of Class 377/7 are five-car dual-voltage sets which will operate on the through Croydon to Milton Keynes/Rugby service via the West London Line, a route which has seen considerable growth and now requires longer trains. These sets will replace the Class 377/2s which were previously used on the service. In summer 2014 the eight dual-voltage sets were undergoing test running for a service introduction towards the middle-end of the year. Set No. 377707 is seen inside Bombardier Derby during final testing in May 2014.* **CJM**

Sub-class:	378/1	378/2
Number range:	378135-378154	378201-378234, 378255-378257
Original number range:	-	378001-378024
Introduced:	2009-2010	2009-2011
Built by:	Bombardier Derby	Bombardier Derby
Formation:	DMSO(A)+MSO+TSO+DMSO(B)	DMSO(A)+MSO+TSO+DMSO(B)
Vehicle numbers:	DMSO(A) - 38035-38054	DMSO(A) - 38001-38034
	MSO - 38235-38254	MSO - 38201-38234
	TSO - 38335-38354	TSO - 38301-38334
	DMSO(B) - 38135-38154	DMSO(B) - 38101-38134
Vehicle length:	DMSO - 67ft 2in (20.46m)	DMSO - 67ft 2in (20.46m)
	MSO/TSO - 66ft 1in (20.14m)	MSO/TSO - 66ft 1in (20.14m)
Height:	12ft 4½in (3.77m)	12ft 4½in (3.77m)
Width:	9ft 2in (2.80m)	9ft 2in (2.80m)
Seating:	Total - 146S + 6 tip up	Total - 146S + 6 tip up
	DMSO(A) - 36S, MSO - 40S	DMSO(A) - 36S, MSO - 40S
	TSO - 34S + 6 tip up, DMSO(B) - 36S	TSO - 34S + 6 tip up, DMSO(B) - 36S
Internal layout:	Longitudinal	Longitudinal
Gangway:	Within set, emergency end door	Within set, emergency end door
Toilets:	None	None
Weight:	Total - 160.3 tonnes	Total - 160.3 tonnes
	DMSO(A) - 43.5 tonnes, MSO - 39.4 tonnes	DMSO(A) - 43.5 tonnes, MSO - 39.4 tonnes
	TSO - 34.3 tonnes, DMSO(B) - 43.1 tonnes	TSO - 34.3 tonnes, DMSO(B) - 43.1 tonnes
Brake type:	Air	Air
Power collection:	750V dc third rail	25kV ac overhead, 750V dc third rail
Traction motor type:	6 x Bombardier	6 x Bombardier
Output:	2,012hp (1,500kW)	2,012hp (1,500kW)
Max speed:	75mph (121km/h)	75mph (121km/h)
Coupling type:	Outer - Dellner 12, Inner - Bar	Outer - Dellner 12, Inner - Bar
Multiple restriction:	Class 375-378	Class 375-378
Door type:	Bi-parting sliding	Bi-parting sliding
Total sets in traffic:	20	37
Construction:	Aluminium	Aluminium
Owner:	QW Rail Leasing	QW Rail Leasing
Operator:	London Overground (TfL)	London Overground (TfL)

Notes: All sets to be strengthened to five cars in 2014-2015

Electric Multiple Units

Fact File

A fleet of 57 four-car Class 378 'Capitalstar' EMUs was built by Bombardier for London Overground, to replace Class 313 stock and form new services from north to south through London and provide a London orbital route.

The sets come in two types: a dc only version for third rail operation and dual voltage sets having 25kV ac overhead power collection. Sets are all based at new depot facilities at New Cross, with an extra depot and stabling at Willesden.

These trains are very similar to London Underground stock on the inside with longitudinal seats and lots of standing space.

Sets Nos. 378201-234 were built as three-car units having an additional TSO added in 2010-11 when they were renumbered.

Each four-car set will be strengthened to five-car formation in 2014-2015. ■

Left: *Front end equipment positions for Class 378 stock. A: High-level marker light, B: Destination indicator, C: Tunnel light, D: Light cluster, housing headlight and joint white marker and red tail light, E: Emergency front door, F: Emergency door release handle, G: Air warning horns, H: Dellner 12 coupling, I: Front facing camera, J: Emergency light bracket.* **CJM**

Right Top: *London Overground operates the Class 378 fleet of which two types exist: those designed for dc third rail operation (Class 378/1) and those designed for dual voltage dc/dc running (Class 378/2). These that are at present four-car sets are identical in their interior layout and style. Dc only set No. 378148 is seen at Highbury & Islington. These sets usually operate on the Highbury & Islington to Clapham Junction, Crystal Palace, West Croydon and New Cross route.* **CJM**

Right Middle Upper: *A fleet of 37 dual voltage sets is in traffic and these are usually deployed on the Euston-Watford, Richmond to Stratford and Clapham Junction to Willesden Junction routes. The first 24 of these sets were built as three-car units and later augmented with an extra MSO vehicle. A four-car Class 378 seats 146 using longitudinal seating, but space exists for up to five times that number to stand. Set No. 378217 is seen at West Brompton on a Stratford to Clapham Junction service.* **CJM**

Right Middle Lower: *The Trailer Standard Open, recorded from the pantograph end, with the device in the lowered position during dc operation. Although these are trailer vehicles an amount of technical equipment is carried including the transformer in between bogie boxes. Seating in the TSO vehicles is for 34.* **CJM**

Right Bottom: *Interior seating on the Class 378 is all longitudinal, very much in keeping with an underground train. A large number of grab poles and ceiling mounted rigid straps are provided to help those standing. In door areas 'perch' seats are provided. As these sets are not air conditioned opening hopper windows are provided throughout. Class 378s operate with a guard who together with the driver has overall control of the doors; however, passenger activation is possible to open or reopen doors as a time delay auto shutting system is incorporated to retain on-board heat.* **CJM**

Electric Multiple Units

Class 379 'Electrostar'

Number range:	379001-379030
Introduced:	2011
Built by:	Bombardier Derby
Formation:	DMOS+MOSL+PTOSL+DMOC
Vehicle numbers:	DMOS - 61201-61230
	MOSL - 61701-61730
	PTOSL - 61901-61930
	DMOC - 62101-62130
Vehicle length:	DMOS/DMOC - 66ft 9in (20.4m)
	PTOSL, MOSL - 65ft 6in (19.99m)
Height:	12ft 4in (3.78m)
Width:	9ft 2in (2.80m)
Seating:	Total - 20F/189S
	DMOS - 60S
	MOSL - 62S
	PTOSL - 43S
	DMOC - 20F/24S
Internal layout:	2+1F, 2+2S
Gangway:	Throughout
Toilets:	MOSL, PTOSL - 1
Weight:	Total - 161.97 tonnes
	DMOS - 42.1 tonnes
	MOSL - 36.65 tonnes
	PTOSL - 40.92 tonnes
	DMOC - 42.3 tonnes
Brake type:	Air (regenerative)
Bogie type:	Power - Bombardier FlexxP3-25
	Trailer - Bombardier Flexx T3-25
Power collection:	25kV ac overhead
Traction motor type:	6 x Bombardier 200kW
Output:	1,609hp (1,200kW)
Max speed:	100mph (161km/h)
Coupling type:	Outer - Dellner 12, Inner - Bar
Multiple restriction:	Class 375-379
Door type:	Bi-parting sliding plug
Total sets in traffic:	30
Construction:	Aluminium with steel cabs
Owner:	Lloyds Group
Operator:	Greater Anglia

Fact File

Ordered in April 2009, this fleet of 30 'Electrostar' trains was introduced in 2011 for use on the then National Express East Anglia route between London Liverpool Street and Stansted Airport and Cambridge.

The four-car sets seat 20 first and 189 standard class passengers in the 2+1 and 2+2 mode. The first set, No. 379001, was delivered in late 2010 and shipped to the Czech Republic for testing on the Velim test track before returning to the UK at the end of the year and commencing testing on the Great Eastern main line. The sets are structurally very similar to the Class 375 and 377s.

The '379s' are fitted with wi-fi equipment and brought a new level of comfort to the route.

All 30 sets are allocated to Ilford depot and are maintained under a contract by Bombardier staff.

These were the first of the 'Electrostar' units in the UK to have a front end light in the obstacle deflector, illuminating the path for recording of the CCTV system.

Soon after introduction, franchise changes saw the route taken over by Abellio Greater Anglia which applied its branding to the as-built white livery.

In 2014 a trial fitting of set No. 379013 with battery power, to enable the set to operate for short distances away from the overhead power system, was made. ∎

Left: *The Greater Anglia franchise operates a fleet of 30 high-specification 'Electrostar' sets based at Ilford on its Liverpool Street to Stansted and West Anglia routes. Introduced right at the time of the National Express-Abellio transfer of the franchise, these low-density sets are some of the most comfortable sets operated by the company. They sport the larger headlight and joint marker/tail front end, framed windows rather than ribbon glazing and a track light in the front fairing. Set No. 379015 is seen at Tottenham Hale.*
Antony Christie

Above: *Class 379 cab layout. 1: AC system control panel, 2: Pantograph down button, 3: Cab heating and air conditioning controls, 4: Onboard computer screen, 5: Signal button, 6: Noticeboard light, 7: Cab light button, 8: Depot whistle, 9: Overhead circuit breaker, 10: Couple button, 11: Doors open left side indicator, 12/13: Left doors open button, 14: AWS indicator, 15: Door close left side interlock, 16: Line light, 17: AWS buzzer, 18: Hill start button, 19: Driver's Reminder Appliance (DRA), 20: Traction sand button, 21: Speedometer, 22: Train fault acknowledge button, 23: TPWS brake demand, 24: TPWS temporary isolation/fault, 25: TPWS train stop override, 26: Main reservoir/brake cylinder gauge, 27: Speed set adjust switch, 28: Speed set control, 29: Safety systems isolated warning, 30: AWS reset button, 31: Doors open right side indicator, 32/33: Right doors open button, 34: Door close right side interlock, 35: Hazard light button, 36: Screen wash button, 37: Uncouple button, 38: Horn switch, 39: Screen wiper control, 40: Brake plunger, 41: Master key, 42: Master switch, 43: Power/brake controller, 44: DSD pedal, 45/46: Train camera displays, 47: Telephone handset, 48: Cab radio, 49: GSM radio, 50: Radio select button, 51: Public address, 52: Cab to cab, 53: Passenger communication, 54: Radio handset, 55: Pass-com override foot button.* **CJM**

Right: *Class 379 front end equipment. A: High-level marker light, B: Destination indicator, C: Train side camera, D: Front gangway door, E: Headlight, F: White marker/red tail light, G: Lamp bracket, H: Track light for forward facing camera, I: Dellner coupling, J: Air warning horn, K: Forward facing camera.* **CJM**

Sub-class	380/0	380/1
Number range:	380001-380022	380101-380116
Introduced:	2010-2011	2010-2011
Built by:	Siemens Transportation	Siemens Transportation
	Duewag, Germany	Duewag, Germany
Formation:	DMSO(A)+PTSO+DMSO(B)	DMSO(A)+PTSO+TSO+DMSO(B)
Vehicle numbers:	DMSO(A) - 38501-38522	DMSO(A) - 38551-38566
	PTSO - 38601-38622	PTSO - 38651-38666
	DMSO(B) - 38701-38722	TSO - 38551-38866
		DMSO(B) - 38751-38766
Vehicle length:	75ft 5in (23.00m)	75ft 5in (23.00m)
Height:	12ft 4in (3.78m)	12ft 4in (3.78m)
Width:	9ft 2in (2.80m)	9ft 2in (2.80m)
Seating:	Total - 191S + 17 tip up	Total - 265S + 17 tip up
	DMSO(A) - 70S + 12 tip up	DMSO(A) - 70S + 12 tip up
	PTSO - 57S	PTSO - 57S
	DMSO(B) - 64S + 5 tip up	TSO - 74S
		DMSO(B) - 64S + 5 tip up
Internal layout:	2+2	2+2
Gangway:	Throughout	Throughout
Toilets:	PTSO - 1	PTSO - 1, TSO - 1
Weight:	Total - 132.8 tonnes	Total - 167.5 tonnes
	DMSO(A) - 45.1 tonnes	DMSO(A) - 45.1 tonnes
	PTSO - 42.4 tonnes	PTSO - 42.4 tonnes
	DMSO(B) - 45.3 tonnes	TSO - 34.7 tonnes
		DMSO(B) - 45.3 tonnes
Brake type:	Air (regenerative)	Air (regenerative)
Bogie type:	SGB5000	SGB5000
Power collection:	25kV ac overhead	25kV ac overhead
Traction motor type:	4 x Siemens 1TB2016-0GB02	4 x Siemens 1TB2016-0GB02
Output:	1,341hp (1,000kW)	1,341hp (1,000kW)
Max speed:	100mph (161km/h)	100mph (161km/h)
Coupling type:	Outer - Dellner 12, Inner - Bar	Outer - Dellner 12, Inner - Bar
Multiple restriction:	Within class only	Within class only
Door type:	Bi-parting sliding plug	Bi-parting sliding plug
Total sets in traffic:	22	16
Construction:	Aluminium with steel ends	Aluminium with steel ends
Owner:	Eversholt	Eversholt
Operator:	First ScotRail	First ScotRail

Above: *When ScotRail ordered 'Desiro' EMU stock with front corridors it opted for a different design from those already in use by South West Trains, choosing an angled front when the doors were not in use. A fleet of 22 three-car and 16 three-car sets were built, all painted from new in Scottish Railways blue and white. Three-car Class 380/0 No. 380005 is shown at Greenock Central. These sets seat 191 standard class passengers in the 2+2 style.* **Murdoch Currie**

Fact File

Ordered in July 2008, the Class 380 'Desiro' build was for use in Scotland on the Ayrshire and Inverclyde routes.

Built in Germany by Siemens, the first sets entered service on 9 December 2010. Major problems surrounded their introduction.

Twenty-two three-car Class 380/0 and 16 four-car Class 380/1 sets entered full service in mid-2011. All sets are allocated to Shields Road depot in Glasgow.

The stock is painted in the latest Scottish Railways Saltire blue and white livery.

These sets incorporate an angular front end gangway, which was designed to be folded away when not in use. ■

Right: *Class 380 front end layout. A: High-level marker light, B: Route/ destination indicator, C: Front gangway folding door, D: Light cluster, with from the outer edge headlight and combined white marker/red tail light, E: Lamp bracket, F: Obstacle deflector plate, G: Dellner coupling.* **CJM**

Below: *The 16 Class 380/1 four-car sets have an additional Trailer Standard Open (TSO) in their formation which increases the total train seating to 265 standard class. The Class 380 fleet is deployed on the Ayrshire Coast, Inverclyde, North Berwick, Edinburgh-Glasgow and Paisley Canal routes. Four-car set No. 380101 passes Craigenhill on 18 February 2013 forming the 13.51 Edinburgh to Glasgow Central via Carstairs service.* **Robin Ralston**

Number range:	9-car sets - 390001/002/005/006/008-011/013/016/020/023/035/038-040/042-047/049-050
	11-car sets - 390103/104/107/112/114/114/117-119/121/122/124-134/136/137/141/148/151-157
Introduced:	390001-390053 - 2001-2005, 390154-157 - 2010-2011§
Built by:	Alstom, Washwood Heath, body shells from Italy
	Alstom, Savigliano, Italy§
Formation:	9-car sets DMRF+MF+PTF+MF+TS+MS+PTSRMB+MS+DMSO
	11-car sets DMRF+MF+PTF+MF+TS+MS+PTSRMB+MS+MS+DMSO§

	DMRF - 69101-69157		MF - 69401-69457
	PTF - 69501-69557		MF - 69601-69657
	TS - 65303-65357 (11-car sets only)		MS - 68903-69957 (11-car sets only)
	TS - 68801-68857		MS - 69701-69757
	PTSRMB - 69801-69853		MS - 69901-69957
	DMSO - 69201-69257		

Vehicle length:	DMRF, DMSO - 81ft 3in (24.80m)
	MF, PTF, TS, MS, PTSRMB - 78ft 4in (23.90m)
Height:	11ft 6in (3.56m)
Width:	8ft 9in (2.73m)
Seating:	Total - 9-car - 145F/294S, 11-car - 145F/418S
	DMRF - 18F, MF - 37F, PTF - 44F, MF - 46F, TS - 76S, MS - 62S,
	TS - 76S, MS - 62S, PTSRMB - 48S, MS - 62S, DMSO - 46S
Internal layout:	2+1F/2+2S
Gangway:	Within set
Toilets:	MF, PTF, TS, MF, MSO, TS, MF(D) - 1
Weight:	Total - 9-car - 459.7 tonnes, 11-car 556.9 tonnes

	DMRF - 55.6 tonnes		MF - 52 tonnes
	PTF - 50.1 tonnes		MF - 51.8 tonnes
	TS - 45.5 tonnes		MS - 50 tonnes
	TS - 45.5 tonnes		MS - 51.7 tonnes§
	PTSRMB - 52 tonnes		MS - 51.7 tonnes
	DMSO - 51 tonnes		

Brake type:	Air (regenerative)
Bogie type:	Fiat/SIG tilting
Power collection:	25kV ac overhead
Traction motor type:	12 x Alstom Onix 800
Output:	9-car - 6,839hp (5,100 kW) 11-car 9,120hp (6,803kW)
Max speed:	140mph (225km/h) (Restricted to 125mph 200km/h)
Coupling type:	Outer - Dellner, Inner - Bar
Multiple restriction:	No multiple facility, operable with selected Class 57/3s for rescue
Door type:	Single-leaf sliding plug
Total sets in traffic:	56
Construction:	Aluminium
Special features:	Tilt
Owner:	Angel Trains
Operator:	Virgin Trains

Electric Multiple Units

Fact File

After privatisation of the UK railway network in the mid-1990s and the take-over of the West Coast route by Virgin Trains, new stock was quickly ordered.

A total change from previous policy followed with fixed formation unit-type trains ordered.

No suitable UK type was on offer and Alstom came up with the winning design, based on the Mainland European 'Pendolino' trains built by Fiat/Alstom. A fleet of 53 originally eight-car, later nine-car, sets was ordered and built.

Body shells were produced in Italy and then transported to the UK for fitting out and testing at Alstom, Washwood Heath. The sets entered traffic between 2001 and 2005, taking over total WCML operations from 2006.

The streamlined sets fitted with a full tilt system

are based at Manchester but receive maintenance at Wembley, Oxley and Polmadie, Glasgow.

First class seating is provided in the 2+1 mode and standard in the 2+2 style; full refreshment facilities are provided.

Growth on the West Coast route since modernisation has seen a need for extra and longer trains. Firstly an additional vehicle was installed in each train and then in 2008, 106 additional vehicles including four new 11-car Pendolino sets were ordered. The loose vehicles were introduced to strengthen 31 sets to 11-car formation.

The first of the four new sets, completely built in mainland Europe, was delivered to the UK in December 2010, with all four in service within two years. ■

Above: *The 'Pendolino' sets used by Virgin Trains on the West Coast route come in two types, 390/0 being nine-car sets and 390/1 being 11-car formations. Nine-car set No. 390002 is seen from its standard class end at Preston on 16 July 2014. These sets seat 145 first and 294 standard class passengers.* **CJM**

Right Upper: *Each Class 390 has two pantograph mounted vehicles, but only one is used at a time. Here we see PTSRMB No. 69822 with its pantograph at the far end. This type of vehicle has a cafe/shop and seating for 48 standard class passengers.* **Antony Christie**

Right Lower: *Each 'Pendolino' has four first class vehicles, including the driving car with a kitchen. In this view we see Motor First (MF) No. 69604 a vehicle from the four-set follow-on order (390154-390157) which has a deeper black band over some windows.* **Antony Christie**

Below: *Eleven-car 'Pendolino' set No. 390157, the final set of the follow on order for four trains. These longer sets seat 145 first and 418 standard.* **CJM**

Electric Multiple Units

Number range:	395001-395029
Introduced:	2007-2009
Built by:	Hitachi Industries, Kasado, Japan
Formation:	PDTSO1+MS1+MS2+MS3+MS4+PDTSO2
Vehicle numbers:	PDTSO1 - 39011-39291
	MS1 - 39012-39292
	MS2 - 39013-39293
	MS3 - 39014-39294
	MS4 - 39015-39295
	PDTSO2 - 39016-39296
Vehicle length:	PDTSO - 68ft 5in (20.88m)
	MS - 65ft 6in (20m)
Height:	12ft 6in (3.81m)
Width:	9ft 2in (2.81m)
Seating:	Total - 340S + 12 tip up
	PDTSO1 - 28S + 12 tip up
	MS1 - 66S
	MS2 - 66S
	MS3 - 66S
	MS4 - 66S
	PDTSO2 - 48S
Internal layout:	2+2
Gangway:	Within unit only
Toilets:	PDTSO - 1
Weight:	Total - 276.2 tonnes
	PDTSO - 46.7 tonnes
	MS - 45.7 tonnes
Brake type:	Air (regenerative)
Bogie type:	Hitachi
Power collection:	25kV ac overhead & 750V dc third rail
Traction motor type:	IGBT Converter, three-phase
Output:	2,253hp (1,680 kW)
Max speed:	HS1 - 140mph (225km/h)
	Normal - 100mph (161km/h)
Coupling type:	Outer: Scharfenburg, Inner - Bar
Multiple restriction:	Within class only (2-unit max)
Door type:	Single-leaf sliding
Total number in traffic:	29
Construction:	Aluminium
Owner:	Eversholt
Operator:	SouthEastern Trains
Special features:	PIS, CCTV, TVM430/KVB, GPS
	Air conditioned, SDO

Fact File

With the building of High Speed 1 (HS1) linking London with the Channel Tunnel came the option to operate a high speed domestic service between Kent and London St Pancras International using spare capacity on the route.

A fleet of 29 six-car 140mph electric multiple units were therefore ordered from Hitachi Industries in Japan and delivered via Southampton Docks from 2007. The sets were introduced into public service from late 2009.

The sets, the first Japanese trains to operate in the UK, were assembled at the Kasado and Mito factories and shipped to the UK as complete vehicles ready for testing.

The sets are laid out for all one class of seating in the 2+2 style, using an outer-suburban seat design, but with the longest journey being only just over 1 hour in duration this was deemed appropriate. The sets can operate from 750V dc third rail or 25kV ac overhead and are equipped with conventional signalling as well as TVM430 for operation over HS1.

Sets are allocated to a purpose-built depot at Ashford, Kent, as well as using modified depot facilities at Ramsgate.

In addition to operating domestic services over HS1, the sets, named 'Javelin', were used to transport participants and spectators to the 2012 Olympic Games held in Stratford (East London), operating a 7min duration link service from St Pancras International to Stratford International. ∎

Left: *The Class 395 'Javelin' train sets used for domestic services over HS1 from London St Pancras use the low-density 2+2 seating, with a mix of airline and group styles. A six-car Class 395 set seats 340 passengers, no first class is provided.* **CJM**

Above: *The streamlined Class 395 sets, based on the Japanese 'bullet' design, are allocated to Hitachi's depot at Ashford, Kent, and can operate over classic or HS1 tracks. Set No. 395029 is seen at St Pancras International.* **Antony Christie**

Right: *Class 395 'Javelin' front end layout. These streamlined sets have their Dellner couplings hidden behind hinged nose doors. Equipment shown is A: Destination indicator, B: Light cluster including a headlight and a white marker and red tail light, C: Hinged two section nose cone, protecting the Dellner coupling, D: High-level marker light.* **CJM**

Left Middle: *The Class 395 driving cab which is fitted with equipment to allow operation over conventional tracks fitted with AWS and HS1 installed with TVM430 cab signalling.* **CJM**

Left: *The four intermediate Class 395 vehicles are all classified Motor Standard and numbered MS1 - MS4. Each vehicle seats 66 in the 2+2 layout. No toilets are provided in these vehicles; these are located one in each driving car. An MS vehicle is shown.* **Antony Christie**

Number range:	442401-442424
Alpha code:	Original - 5-WES (WESsex electric)
Introduced:	1988-1989
Refurbished	2009-2010 at Wolverton
Built by:	BREL Derby
Formation:	DTSO(A)+TSO+MBC+TSOW+DTSO(B)
Vehicle numbers:	DTSO(A) - 77382-77405, TSO - 71818-71841
	MBC - 62937-62960, TSOW - 71842-71865
	DTSO(B) - 77406-77429
Vehicle length:	DTSOL - 75ft 11½in (23.15m)
	TSO, MBC, TSOW - 75ft 5½in (23m)
Height:	12ft 6in (3.81m)
Width:	8ft 11¾in (2.74m)
Seating:	Total - 24F/318S
	DTSO(A) - 74S, TSO - 76S
	MBC - 24F/28S, TSOW - 66S
	DTSL - 74S
Internal layout:	2+1F, 2+2S
Gangway:	Throughout
Toilets:	TSO-2, TSOW-1
Weight:	Total - 206.1 tonnes
	DTSO(A) - 38.5 tonnes, TSO - 37.5 tonnes
	MBC - 55.0 tonnes, TSOW - 37.8 tonnes
	DTSO(B) - 37.3 tonnes
Brake type:	Air (EP/auto)
Bogie type:	Power - BR Mk6
	Trailer - BREL T4
Power collection:	750V dc third rail
Traction motor type:	4 x EE546 of 402hp (300kW)
Horsepower:	1,608hp (1,200kW)
Max speed:	100mph (161km/h)
Coupling type:	Outer - Buck-eye
	Inner - Bar
Multiple restriction:	Within type
Number in traffic:	24
Door type:	Single-leaf sliding plug
Owner:	Angel Trains
Operator:	Southern

In the mid-1980s the need arose to replace the REP/TC stock used on the Waterloo-Bournemouth/Weymouth line, and at the same time investment was made to electrify the line between Bournemouth and Weymouth. To cover this need a fleet of 24 high-specification five-car EMUs, based on Mk3 stock, was ordered from BREL.

In many ways these were the pinnacle of electric multiple unit design and incorporated sliding-plug passenger doors.

The sets, formed with a central power car, emerged from May 1988, with the final set commissioned in February 1989.

The first 13 sets were built with luggage 'cages' either side of the guard's office; the remaining sets were built with a seating 'snug' adjacent to the buffet and earlier sets were retro-fitted.

Allocated to Bournemouth, the sets worked on the Waterloo-Weymouth route and later took over some services on the Waterloo-Portsmouth line.

With the mass replacement of slam door stock and the introduction of 'Desiro' units from 2001, the Class 442s fell from favour as non-standard and from early 2007 all 24 sets were stored.

Owner Angel Trains sought a new operator and this was found in Southern which deployed the sets on its Gatwick Express and London to Brighton route from early 2008.

Sets were fully refurbished with first class seating moving from a driving car to the central power car. Buffet facilities were removed and the sets repainted in a Gatwick Express colour scheme. From early 2011, when the Gatwick Express Class 460s were withdrawn, the '442s' were deployed on a revised London Victoria to Gatwick Airport and Brighton service.

The Class 442s are allocated to Stewarts Lane, Battersea, London. ∎

Left: *Class 442 front end equipment. 1: Radio aerial, 2: Destination indicator, 3: Front gangway door, 4: Light cluster, from outside edge white marker light, headlight, red tail light, 5: Multiple control jumper cable, 6: Multiple control jumper receptacle, 7: Main reservoir (yellow) and Air brake pipe (red), 8: Electric train supply jumper socket, 9: Air brake pipe (red), 10: Main reservoir pipe (yellow), 11: Drop-head buck-eye coupling, 12: Electric train supply jumper. Front end of set No. 442418 illustrated.* **CJM**

Above: *The five-car Class 442 Southern 'Express' units are based at Stewarts Lane and operate the prime Victoria to Gatwick Airport service with many trains continuing to Brighton. With its DTSO(B) No. 77421 leading, set No. 442416 passes Clapham Junction.* **CJM**

Right Middle Upper: *Each of the Class 442 DTSO vehicles seats 74 standard class passengers in the 2+2 configuration, with access from a transverse vestibule at each end served by a single leaf sliding plug door. Vehicle No. 77399 from set No. 442418 is seen at Gatwick Airport.* **CJM**

Right Middle: *The middle vehicle of the '442' formation is the power/brake vehicle, which also has the first class accommodation towards the 'A' end for 24 passengers. At the 'B' end 28 standard class seats are provided. These vehicles were heavily rebuilt from their days on the Waterloo-Weymouth line when they housed a large luggage van.* **CJM**

Right Bottom: *Marshalled between each driving car and the central MBC coach is a Trailer Standard Open (TSO). The vehicle at the 'A' end seats 76, while the one located at the 'B' end seats 66. The low-density 2+2 seating layout is used throughout. All Class 442s are finished in a non-Southern style, having a blue body with a wide mid-height white band and a deep red band at cantrail height. Originally the sets were branded Gatwick Express, but today just the word 'Express' is retained. Vehicle No. 71855 is shown.* **CJM**

Number range:	444001-444045
Introduced:	2003-2004
Built by:	Siemens Transportation SGP, Austria
Formation:	DMSO+TSO(A)+TSO(B)+TSRMB+DMCO
Vehicle numbers:	DMSO - 63801-63845
	TSO(A) - 67101-67145
	TSO(B) - 67151-67195
	TSRMB - 67201-67245
	DMCO - 63851-63895
Vehicle length:	77ft 3in (23.57m)
Height:	12ft 1½in (3.7m)
Width:	8ft 9in (2.74m)
Seating:	Total - 35F/299S
	DMSO - 76S
	TSO(A) - 76S
	TSO(B) - 76S
	TSRMB - 47S
	DMCO 35F/24S
Internal layout:	2+2S, 2+1F
Gangway:	Throughout
Toilets:	TSO, TSRMB - 1
Weight:	Total - 221.8 tonnes
	DMSO - 51.3 tonnes
	TSO(A) - 40.3 tonnes
	TSO(B) - 36.8 tonnes
	TSRMB - 42.1 tonnes
	DMCO - 51.3 tonnes
Brake type:	Air (regenerative)
Bogie type:	Siemens SGB5000
Power collection:	750V dc third rail
Traction motor type:	1TB2016-0GB02 3-phase
Output:	2,682hp (2,000kW)
Max speed:	100mph (161km/h)
Coupling type:	Outer - Dellner 12, Inner - Semi-auto
Multiple restriction:	444 and 450
Door type:	Single-leaf sliding plug
Total number in traffic:	45
Construction:	Aluminium
Special features:	Air conditioned, PIS
Owner:	Angel Trains
Operator:	South West Trains

Fact File

As part of the replacement order for South West Trains to withdraw slam door stock, a fleet of 45 five-car 'Desiro' express sets was ordered.

Painted in SWT 'white' main line livery, these are the 'Rolls-Royce' of the 'Desiro' build, fitted with low-density 2+2 seating with single-leaf sliding plug doors feeding cross vestibules at the coach ends, rather than opening directly into passenger saloons.

Sets are fully air conditioned and have a small buffet counter at one end of the TSRMB attached to the DMCO vehicle.

Sets are deployed on Waterloo-Southampton-Bournemouth-Weymouth services as well as fast Waterloo to Portsmouth duties.

All sets are based at the purpose-built Siemens maintenance facility at Northam, Southampton. The sets are fully compatible with Class 450s but the two types are rarely operated together. ■

Below: *Set No. 444022 of the 45 strong South West Trains five-car main line fleet used on the Waterloo to Bournemouth, Weymouth and Portsmouth routes. The trains DMSO is nearest the camera in this view at Fratton.* **CJM**

Above: *The South West Trains modernisation and replacement of slam-door stock saw a massive order placed with Siemens for its 'Desiro' stock. This included 45 five-car main line sets for long distance journeys. Painted in Stagecoach/SWT white and blue livery, the sets seat 35 first and 299 standard class passengers. With its DMCO nearest the camera, set No. 444015 passes Millbrook. The DMCO of these sets is booked to be at the London end.* **Antony Christie**

Right Middle Upper: *Two Trailer Standard Open (TSO) vehicles are coupled adjacent to the DMSO driving car, each seating 76 in the 2+2 style and have a toiler compartment in each vehicle. Exterior entrance is by a single sliding plug door feeding a transverse vestibule. Vehicle No. 67128 is illustrated at Eastleigh.* **CJM**

Right Middle Lower: *Coupled to each DMCO vehicle is a TSRMB, a trailer standard with a small buffet counter/shop at one end. These vehicles also house a pantograph well at the inner end in case of retro-fitting for 25kV ac operation. Vehicle No. 67230 is illustrated at Southampton.* **CJM**

Right Bottom: *The Class 444 interiors are luxurious compared with some modern multiple unit stock. The first class area of the DMCO coach seats 35 in the 2+1 layout with each seat having a reading light, power outlet and a table, either of the fixed or fold down type. The other end of the DMCO coach has seats for 24 standard class passengers. This view is looking towards the driving end transverse vestibule.* **CJM**

Traction Recognition

Sub-class:	450/0	450/5
Number range:	450001-450042, 450071-450127	450543-450570
Former number range	-	450043-450070
Introduced:	2002-2007	As 450/5 2008-2009
Built by:	Siemens Duewag, Germany, and Siemens SGP, Austria	Siemens Duewag, Germany, and Siemens SGP, Austria
Modified by:		Bournemouth SWT depot
Formation:	DMSO(A)+TCO+TSO+DMSO(B)	DMSO(A)+TCO+TSO+DMSO(B)
Vehicle numbers:	DMSO(A) - 63201-242/271-300/701-710/901-917	DMSO(A) - 63243-63270
	TCO - 64201-242/271-300/851-860/921-937	TCO(A) - 64243-64270
	TSO - 68101-142/171-200/801-810/901-917	TSO(B) - 68143-68170
	DMSO(B) - 63601-642/671-700/751-760/921-937	DMSO(B) - 63643-63670
Vehicle length:	66ft 9in (20.4m)	66ft 9in (20.4m)
Height:	12ft 1½in (3.7m)	12ft 1½in (3.7m)
Width:	9ft 2in (2.7m)	9ft 2in (2.7m)
Seating:	Total - 24F/242S + 13 tip up	Total - 24F/216S + 11 tip up
	DMSO(A) - 70S	DMSO(A) - 64S
	TCO - 24F/32S + 4 tip up	TCO(A) - 24F/32S + 4 tip-up
	TSO - 61S + 9 tip up	TSO(B) - 56S + 7 tip up
	DMSO(B) - 79S	DMSO(B) - 64S
Internal layout:	2+2F/2+2 & 2+3S	2+2F/2+2 & 2+3S
Gangway:	Throughout	Throughout
Toilets:	TCO - 1, TSO - 1	TCO - 1
Weight:	Total - 172.2 tonnes	Total - 171.9 tonnes
	DMSO(A) - 48.0 tonnes	DMSO(A) - 48.0 tonnes
	TCO - 35.8 tonnes	TCO - 35.8 tonnes
	TSO - 39.8 tonnes	TSO(B) - 39.8 tonnes
	DMSO(B) - 48.6 tonnes	DMSO(B) - 48.6 tonnes
Brake type:	Air (regenerative)	Air (regenerative)
Bogie type:	Siemens SGP SF5000	Siemens SGP SF5000
Power collection:	750V dc third rail	750V dc third rail
Traction motor type:	4 x 1TB2016 0GB02 three-phase	4 x 1TB2016 0GB02 three-phase
Output:	2,682hp (2,000kW)	2,682hp (2,000kW)
Max speed:	100mph (161km/h)	100mph (161km/h)
Coupling type:	Outer - Dellner 12, Inner - Semi-auto	Outer - Dellner 12, Inner - Semi-auto
Multiple restriction:	444 and 450	444 and 450
Door type:	Bi-parting sliding plug	Bi-parting sliding plug
Total number in traffic:	99	28
Construction:	Aluminium	Aluminium
Owner:	Angel Trains	Angel Trains
Operator:	South West Trains	South West Trains
Special features:	Air conditioned, CCTV, PIS	Air conditioned, CCTV, PIS
Sub-class variations:	Standard unit	High Capacity sets

Left: *The South West Trains outer-suburban slam door replacement stock was a fleet of 127 four-car Class 450 'Desiro' sets, painted in Stagecoach/SWT outer-suburban blue livery. The Class 450/0 sets seat 24 first and 242 standard class passengers. A batch of high-capacity sets, Class 450/5 are also in use which have fewer standard class seats but extra standing room with an overall seating for 24 first and 216 standard class passengers. Standard Class 450/0 set No. 450011 approaches Hersham with a service to Waterloo. The set's DMSO(A) coach is leading.* **CJM**

The replacement outer-suburban stock for South West Trains, ordered to replace slam-door VEP and CIG stock, consists of a batch of 127 four-car Siemens-built 'Desiro' units.

These bi-parting sliding door sets, with doors opening into the main seating area, are set out for 2+2 and 2+3 high-density occupation but to a high standard. Carpeting is fitted throughout and first class accommodation is provided in the 2+2 mode in the intermediate TCO vehicle, separated from the remainder of the coach by sliding doors.

Sets operate throughout the SWT area and are allocated to purpose-built depot facilities at Northam, Southampton.

All units are finished in SWT outer-suburban blue livery.

By 2008 a need arose for extra standard class accommodation on the 'Windsor Line' services from Waterloo. To meet this, a fleet of 28 units was modified by Bournemouth depot, removing the first class seating from the TCO and altering standard class seating to increase capacity. These sets were reclassified as 450/5 and identified as High Capacity or HC sets

Changes to deployment saw the first class returned to these sets in 2013-14 with the high capacity modifications remaining in the standard class, thus the sets retained their Class 450/5 classification. ∎

Above: *Class 450 front end layout, also applicable to Class 444. A: High-level marker light, B: Front gangway door, C: White marker light, D: Headlight, E: Red tail light, F: Lamp bracket, G: Air warning horn, H: Emergency air supply, I: Dellner 12 coupling, J: Obstacle deflector plate.* **CJM**

Below: *The Class 444 and 450 fleet are all allocated to purpose-built maintenance facilities at Northam, on the outskirts of Southampton, where all levels of service and repair work are carried out. In addition sets are stabled at many locations including Clapham Junction, Wimbledon, Woking, Farnham, Fratton, Basingstoke and Bournemouth. Led by its DMSO(A) vehicle seating 70 in the 2+2 and 2+3 style, set No. 450006 is seen on the up slow line at Woking. All sets are painted in SWT blue livery.* **CJM**

Electric Multiple Units

Above: *The Class 450 sets can operate with up to three sets coupled together in passenger service, giving a maximum seating figure for a 12-car formation of 72 first class and 726 standard class seats. An eight-car formation, led by set No. 450125, approaches Vauxhall with a Basingstoke service.* **CJM**

Left: *Class 450 Trailer Standard Open (TSO). On Class 450/0 sets these seat 61 standard passengers in the 2+2 and 2+3 style.* **CJM**

Below: *Class 450 Trailer Composite Open (TCO).These seat 24 first and 32 standard passengers and have a small guard's office in the middle. First class is identified by the blue dots above window height.* **CJM**

Above: *The Class 450 'Desiro' has a good quality interior with good high-back seating, with the airline seats offering fold down tables. An electronic passenger information system is fitted to give real time information. First class seating is in blue and standard in red moquette.* **CJM**

Below: *A fleet of 28 Class 450/5 'HC' or High-Capacity sets is in service; these were modified from 450/0s by removing the first class and altering the standard class seating to reduce the number of seats while increasing standing positions. These were modified for the Waterloo 'Windsor Line' services. In 2013-14, following introduction of ten-car Class 458 stock, the Class 450/5s have regained their first class seating (24 seats) but retain their lower standard class capacity. The sets have lost their HC branding, but have retained their Class 450/5 numbering. Set No. 450552 (450052) is seen at Southampton.* **CJM**

Electric Multiple Units

Sub-class:	455/7	455/8	455/9
Number range:	455701-455750	455801-455874	455901-455920
Introduced:	1984-1985	1982-1984	1985
Refurbished:	2003-2007	2003-2008	2004-2007
Built by:	BREL York	BREL York	BREL York
Refurbished by:	Bombardier Ashford	(Southern) Alstom Eastleigh (SWT) Bombardier Ashford	Bombardier Ashford
Formation:	DTSO(A)+MSO+ TSO+DTSO(B)	DTSO(A)+MSO+ TSO+DTSO(B)	DTSO(A)+MSO+ TSO+DTSO(B)
Vehicle numbers:	DTSO(A) - 77727-77811 (odds) MSO - 62783-62825 TSO - 71526-71568 DTSO(B) - 77728-77812 (evens)	DTSO(A) - 77579-77725 (odds) MSO - 62709-62782 TSO - 71637-71710 DTSO(B) - 77580-77726 (evens)	DTSO(A) - 77813-77852 (odds) MSO - 62826-62845 TSO - 71714-71733 DTSO(B) - 77814-77852 (evens)
Vehicle length:	DTSO - 65ft 0½in (19.83m) MSO/TSO - 65ft 4½in (19.92m)	DTSO - 65ft 0½in (19.83m) MSO/TSO - 65ft 4½in (19.92m)	DTSO - 65ft 0½in (19.83m) MSO/TSO - 65ft 4½in (19.92m)
Height:	DTSO/MSO - 12ft 1½in (3.7m) TSO - 11ft 6½in (3.58m) (ex-Class 508)	12ft 1½in (3.7m)	12ft 1½in (3.7m)
Width:	9ft 3¼in (2.82m)	9ft 3¼in (2.82m)	9ft 3¼in (2.82m)
Seating:	Total - 236S + 8 tip-up	Total - Southern 307S,+ 3 tip-up SWT 236S + 8 tip-up Southern sets:	Total - 236S + 9 tip-up
	DTSO(A) - 50S + 4 tip up MSO - 68S TSO - 68S DTSO(B) - 50S + 4 tip up	DTSO(A) - 74S MSO - 84S TSO - 75S + 3 tip up DTSO(B) - 74S South West Trains sets: DTSO(A) - 50S + 4 tip up MSO - 68S TSO - 68S DTSO(B) - 50S + 4 tip up	DTSO(A) - 50S + 4 tip up MSO - 68S TSO - 68S DTSO(B) - 50S + 5 tip up
Internal layout:	2+3	2+3	2+3
Gangway:	Throughout	Southern - Within set, SWT -Throughout	Throughout
Toilets:	Not fitted	Not fitted	Not fitted
Weight:	Total: 133.4 tonnes DTSO(A) - 30.8 tonnes MSO - 45.7 tonnes TSO - 26.1 tonnes DTSO(B) - 30.8 tonnes	Southern - 149.1 tonnes SWT - 131.7 tonnes Southern sets: DTSO(A) - 33.6 tonnes MSO - 47.9 tonnes TSO - 34.0 tonnes DTSO(B) - 33.6 tonnes South West Trains sets: DTSO(A) - 29.5 tonnes MSO - 45.6 tonnes TSO - 27.1 tonnes DTSO(B) - 29.5 tonnes	Total - 131.8 tonnes DTSO(A) - 30.7 tonnes MSO - 46.3 tonnes TSO - 28.3 tonnes DTSO(B) - 26.5 tonnes
Brake type:	Air (Westcode)	Air (Westcode)	Air (Westcode)
Bogie type:	DTSO - BREL BT13 MSO - BREL BP27 TSO - BREL BX1	DTSO - BREL BT13 MSO - BREL BP20 TSO - BREL BT13	DTSO - BREL BT13 MSO - BREL BP20 TSO - BREL BT13
Power collection:	750V dc third rail	750V dc third rail	750V dc third rail
Traction motor type:	4 x EE507 of 250hp	4 x EE507 of 250hp	4 x EE507 of 250hp
Horsepower:	1,000hp (746kW)	1,000hp (746kW)	1,000hp (746kW)
Max speed:	75mph (121km/h)	75mph (121km/h)	75mph (121km/h)
Coupling type:	Outer - Tightlock, Inner - Bar	Outer - Tightlock, Inner - Bar	Outer - Tightlock, Inner - Bar
Multiple restriction:	Class 455 and 456	Class 455 and 456	Class 455 and 456
Special features:	CCTV	CCTV	CCTV
Door type:	Bi-parting sliding	Bi-parting sliding	Bi-parting sliding
Total sets in traffic:	43	74	20
Construction:	Steel (TSO - Aluminium)	Steel	Steel
Owner:	Porterbrook	Eversholt, Porterbrook	Porterbrook
Operator:	South West Trains	Southern, South West Trains	South West Trains

Introduced from 1982 as inner-suburban stock on the Southern Region, the '455s' were originally used on the Western section; later a batch was transferred to the Central section to replace older stock.

Three batches of Class 455 were built. The first 74 (4558xx) units have a rugged front end, while the later 43 and 20 (4557xx and 4559xx) units have a rounded front end top design.

The 43 members of Class 455/7 were built as three-car sets and were augmented to four by the insertion of the TSO vehicles originally formed in the Class 508 units which operated on the Southern when first built.

Upon privatisation the '455s' were split between Eversholt and Porterbrook and all sets are now refurbished.

The Porterbrook sets operated by South West Trains have had one of the most radical refurbishments, which has rendered what many think is a brand new train.

Sets operated by Southern received modified front ends during refurbishment, with the central gangway door being sealed for passenger use and a large air conditioning module inserted in its centre lower section. Revised light clusters were also fitted.

Sets are allocated to Selhurst (Southern) and Wimbledon (South West Trains). ■

Above and Below: *The main South West Trains suburban unit is the Class 455, seating 236 passengers in a four-car set. The 43 Class 455/7 sets each have one different design TSO in their formation. These were originally Class 508 vehicles retained by the former Southern Region when the 508s were transferred to MerseyRail. The 455/7s were built as three-car sets ready to take the displaced vehicles. These cars are recognisable by having a different body profile. Set No. 455734 is seen in the above view and TSO No. 71547 showing its different profile and window design below. This vehicle was originally in Class 508 set No. 508022.* **CJM**

Above: *The original batch of Class 455s delivered was the Class 455/8 which had the earlier design of cab profile, with roof mounted horns. Today South West Trains has a fleet of 28 Class 455/8s, which operates in a common pool with the Class 455/7 and Class 455/9 units. The Class 455/8s seat 236 standard class passengers in the 2+3 style. Set No. 455866 is seen on the up slow line approaching Wimbledon.* **Antony Christie**

Left Top: *The third tranche of Class 455s, classified as 455/9 for South Western section use, are now operated by South West Trains. These 20 sets used the later style of streamlined cab roof and had revisions to their interior saloon ventilation. Today, these 20 sets together with 28 of the Class 455/8s and the 43 Class 455/7s form one core fleet for Waterloo route suburban services allocated to Wimbledon. Set No. 455905 is seen at Guildford.* **CJM**

Left Middle: *Power for the Class 455 fleet comes from an intermediate Motor Standard Open (MSO) which has both BP20 or BP27 bogies powered giving a total of 1,000hp (746kW). The South West Trains MSO vehicles seat 68 in the 2+2 and 2+3 style, with large 'stand-backs' by external door positions to allow room for standing passengers. MSO No. 62836 from set No. 455911 is illustrated. Note the body end power jumper receptacle for operation on depot trolley wire systems.* **CJM**

Right: *Class 455/8 Southern refurbished front end layout. The refurbishment at Alstom Eastleigh of the 46 Class 455/8s operated by Southern made a number of significant changes to the DTSO vehicles. The original gangway door was sealed up as part of a cab improvement package which included the fitting of air conditioning, while the original light clusters are replaced with new style units. Front end equipment - A: Air warning horns, B: Route/destination indicator, C: Former gangway door now housing cab air conditioning, D: Main reservoir pipe (yellow), E: Multiple control jumper cable, F: Multiple control jumper socket, G: Cab air vent, H: White marker/red tail light, I: Headlight, J: Tightlock coupling, K: Drumswitch box (controls multiple working), L: Lamp bracket. General equipment positions are the same for the Class 455s operated by South West Trains.* **CJM**

Above: *Southern operates a fleet of 46 four-car Class 455/8s, based at Selhurst for suburban or Metro operations. The sets have been given major refurbishment since BR days and now sport a slightly revised front end. Seating in the 2+3 style is for 307 standard class passengers. No first class or toilets are provided. Set No. 455833 is seen passing Honor Oak Park.* **CJM**

Right Middle: *The intermediate TSO vehicle in the Southern operated Class 455s seats 75 in the high-density 2+3 style. All sets are finished in Southern grey and two-tone green livery. Door control buttons are provided for passenger use both inside and out. Vehicle No. 71637 is illustrated from set No. 455819. The TSO vehicles of the Southern Class 455s are not formed in sets in numerical order.* **CJM**

Right Bottom: *The intermediate Motor Standard Open (MSO) vehicle on the Southern operated Class 455s seats 84 in the high-density 2+3 style. Each power bogie houses two EE507 dc traction motors, with control equipment housed in between bogie underslung boxes. MSO No. 62727 is illustrated from set No. 455819.* **CJM**

Class 456

Number range:	456001-456024
Introduced:	1990-1991
Built/rebuilt by:	BREL York
Formation:	DMSO+DTSO
Vehicle numbers:	DMSO - 64735-64758
	DTSO - 78250-78273
Vehicle length:	65ft 0½in (19.83m)
Height:	12ft 4½in (3.77m)
Width:	9ft 3in (2.82m)
Seating:	Total - 113S + 5 fold down, 15 perches
	DMSO - 59S + 8 perches
	DTSO - 54S + 5 fold down + 7 perches
Internal layout:	2+2
Gangway:	Within set
Toilets:	Not fitted
Weight:	Total - 72.5 tonnes
	DMSO - 41.1 tonnes
	DTSO - 31.4 tonnes
Brake type:	Air (Westcode)
Bogie type:	Powered - BREL P7
	Trailer - BREL T3
Power collection:	750V dc third rail
Traction motor type:	2 x GEC507-20J of 250hp
Horsepower:	500hp (370kW)
Max speed:	75mph (121km/h)
Coupling type:	Outer - Tightlock, Inner - Bar
Multiple restriction:	Class 455 and 456
Door type:	Bi-parting sliding
Total sets in traffic:	24
Construction:	Aluminium
Owner:	Porterbrook
Operator:	South West Trains

Fact File

To allow the operation of two-, six- or ten-car formations, Network SouthEast ordered a fleet of 24 two-car Class 456 sets from BREL York Works which were delivered in 1990-91.

As these sets were to operate alongside the Class 455s on SouthCentral services it was surprising that end gangways were not fitted. However, this omission did allow a full width driving cab to be installed, in many ways resembling the Class 319.

With accommodation for 152 standard class passengers in the 2+3 facing mode, these sets were allocated to Selhurst and used on their own, in pairs or to augment '455' stock on suburban routes.

A change came in 2014 when the sets were withdrawn by Southern following introduction of new Class 377/6 stock. The sets were then leased to South West Trains to allow a '10-car' railway to operate on the Waterloo Windsor lines. Sets were refurbished in line with the Class 455s at Wolverton Works and entered service from summer 2014. The refurbishment has seen a reduction of seating to just 113 per two-car set using the low-density 2+2 style.

Originally the sets were painted in NSE livery, but after privatisation and overhaul at Wolverton Works in 2006-07 Southern green and white livery was standard.

After transfer to South West Trains their suburban red colours were applied as sets were refurbished. ■

Left: *Class 456 front end layout and equipment. 1: Digital destination and route indicator, 2: Forward facing camera, 3: Main reservoir air pipe, 4: Multiple control jumper cable, 5: Multiple control jumper receptacle, 6: Headlight, 7: Joint white marker and red tail light, 8: Tightlock coupling, 9: Air warning horns. Set No. 456003, the first refurbished for South West Trains is illustrated.* **Antony Christie**

Above: *The 24 two-car Class 456 sets are now based on South West Trains at East Wimbledon, and operate as either two-car sets on low-density routes or in multiple with Class 455s to allow six- or ten-car trains to operate on the 'Windsor Lines' from Waterloo. Set No. 456003 is seen from its DMSO end, identifiable by the underframe carrying an array of equipment boxes.* **Antony Christie**

Right Upper: *The Class 456 Driving Trailer Standard Open (DTSO) vehicles have much less equipment mounted on the underframe. Passenger access is by two pairs of bi-parting doors on each vehicle, with a separate sliding-plug door for the driving cab.* **Antony Christie**

Right Middle: *Following transfer to South West Trains, all sets have been fully refurbished by Wolverton Works, bringing the passenger area in line with the SWT Class 455 stock. High-back 2+2 seating is now provided with several fold down seats in door pocket positions. Seating in the DMSO is for 59, while in the DTSO, 54 fixed seats are provided plus five fold down.* **Antony Christie**

Right Bottom: *When the Class 456 sets were built at York, it was agreed to install a full width driving cab, based on the previously-built Class 319 stock, this provided a pleasing cab environment, with the driving position on the left side and a guards position to the right. On the driver's side, the brake controller is on the left and the master switch and power controller on the right. A recent fitting, towards the middle of the illustration, is GSM-R radio equipment.*
Antony Christie

Electric Multiple Units

Class 458 'Juniper'

Sub-class	458/0	458/5
Number range:	458001-458030	458501-458536
Alpha code:	4-JOP	5-JUP
Introduced:	1999-2002	As 458/0 - 1999-2002
Modified:		2013-2014
Built by:	Alstom, Birmingham	
Modified by:		Wabtec Doncaster & Wabtec Loughborough
Formation:	DMCO(A)+TSO+MSO+DMCO(B)	DMSO(A)+TSOL+TSOL+MSO+DMSO(B)
Vehicle numbers:	DMCO(A) - 67601-67630	DMSO(A) - 67601-67630, 67904-67917*
	TSO - 74001-74030	TSOL - 74401-08, 74411-18, 74421-28, 74431-38,
		74441-42, 74451-52
		TSOL - 74001-74030, 74443-74448
	MSO - 74101-74130	MSO - 74101-74130, 74453-74458*
	DMCO(B) - 67701-67730	DMSO(B) - 67701-67730, 67902-67918*
Vehicle length:	DMCO - 69ft 6in (21.16m)	DMCO - 69ft 6in (21.16m)
	TSO, MSO - 65ft 4in (19.94m)	TSOL, MSO - 65ft 4in (19.94m)
Height:	12ft 3in (3.77m)	12ft 3in (3.77m)
Width:	9ft 2in (2.80m)	9ft 2in (2.80m)
Seating:	Total - 24F/255S + 6 tip-up	Total - 271 or 286S
	DMCO(A) - 12F/63S	DMSO(A) - 60S
	TSO - 54S + 6 tip up	TSOL - 42 or 54S
	MSO - 75S	TSOL - 53 or 56S
	DMCO(B) - 12F/63S	MSO - 56S
		DMSO(B) - 60S
Internal layout:	2+2F, 2+3S	2+2, 2+3
Gangway:	Throughout	Throughout
Toilets:	TSO, MSO - 1	TSOL, MSOL - 1
Weight:	Total - 169.5 tonnes	Total - 204.3 tonnes
	DMCO(A) - 46.4 tonnes	DMSO(A) - 46.4 tonnes
	TSO - 34.6 tonnes	TSO - 34.6 tonnes
	MSO - 42.1 tonnes	TSO - 34.8 tonnes
	DMCO(B) - 46.4 tonnes	MSO - 42.1 tonnes
		DMSO(B) - 46.4 tonnes
Brake type:	Air (regenerative)	Air (regenerative)
Bogie type:	Alstom ACR	Alstom ACR
Power collection:	750V dc third rail	750V dc third rail
Traction motor type:	6 x Alstom of 361hp (270kW)	6 x Alstom of 361hp (270kW)
Horsepower:	2,172hp (1,620kW)	2,172hp (1,620kW)
Max speed:	100mph (161km/h)	75mph (121km/h)
Coupling type:	Outer - Tightlock, Inner - Semi-auto	Outer - Dellner 12, Inner - Semi-auto
Multiple restriction:	Within class only	Within class only
Door type:	Bi-parting sliding plug	Bi-parting sliding plug
Special features:	Air conditioned, PIS	Air conditioned, PIS
Number in traffic:	30	36
Construction:	Steel	Steel
Owner:	Porterbrook	Porterbrook
Operator:	South West Trains	South West Trains
Notes:	Sets being reformed as 5-car units with modified Class 460 vehicles	458531-458536 are rebuilds of Class 460 units * vehicles not in order

Left: *Five-car Class 458/5 TSOL No. 74446, rebuilt from an original Class 460 Gatwick Express vehicle. These 'new' Class 458 vehicles seat 56 standard class passengers in the 2+2 and 2+3 configuration. The vehicle also has a toilet compartment. The Class 458s, now downgraded to 75mph operation and used for outer suburban work on the Waterloo 'Windsor' lines, are painted in Stagecoach/SWT blue livery.* **CJM**

Fact File

The four-car Alstom 'Juniper' outer-suburban units for South West Trains could rate as some of the ugliest ever built. If this fleet and the Class 334 or 460 are compared, it clearly shows that the demand by SWT for an end gangway left a most unpleasing exterior design.

Introduced from 2000, but not without problems, this fleet soon fell out of favour with the operators and by 2005 most were sidelined in favour of the new 'Desiro' product range.

A decision was then made that the entire fleet would be returned to owner Porterbrook from the end of 2006.

However, following the re-awarding of the SWT franchise to Stagecoach, all 30 sets were returned to full operational condition and brought up to the latest standards, including upgrading of both first and standard class seating areas.

In 2011 it was announced that a full rebuild of the 458 stock was to be undertaken, extending each set to five coaches and forming six additional sets, using vehicles from the stored Class 460 Gatwick Express units.

The rebuild contract was done by Alstom at Wabtec, with the new sets entering service in 2014. New front ends were fitted and the sets converted to all standard class occupancy. The sets are now finished in SWT blue livery. ■

Above: *Two of the original four-car Class 458 'Juniper' sets at Wimbledon depot; these sets are due for rebuilding to five-car sets in 2014-15.* **CJM**

Right: *New front end for the modified Class 458/5 fleet with a new more pleasing appearance. A: Air warning horns behind grilles, B: High-level marker light, C: Forward facing camera, D: Dual red tail/ white marker light, E: Headlight, F: Front gangway door, G: Anti-climber plate, H: Dellner coupling, I: Electrical connection box.* **CJM**

Below Right: *The new interior of the Class 458/5 sets uses high-back seating in a mix of 2+2 and 2+3. Above seat luggage racks are provided and rather obtrusive yellow grab poles are positioned throughout the train.* **CJM**

Sub-class:	465/0	465/1	465/2
Number range:	465001-465050	465151-465197	465235-465250
Year introduced:	1991-1993	1993	1991-1993
Year modified:	-		
Built by:	BREL/ABB York	BREL/ABB York	Metro-Cammell, Birmingham
Modified by:	-		
Formation:	DMSO(A)+TSO+	DMSO(A)+TSO+)	DMSO(A)+TSO+
	TSOL+DMSO(B)	TSOL+DMSO(B	TSOL+DMSO(B)
Vehicle numbers:	DMSO(A) - 64759-64808	DMSO(A) - 65800-65846	DMSO(A) - 65734-65749
	TSO - 72028-72126 (even Nos.)	TSO - 72900-72992 (even Nos.)	TSO - 72787-72817 (odd Nos.)
	TSOL - 72029-72126 (odd Nos.)	TSOL - 72901-72993 (odd Nos.)	TSOL - 72788-72818 (even Nos.)
	DMSO(B) - 64809-64858	DMSO(B) - 65847-65893	DMSO(B) - 65784-65799
Vehicle length:	DMSO - 68ft 6½in (20.89m)	DMSO - 68ft 6½in (20.89m)	DMSO - 68ft 6½in (20.89m)
	TSO, TSOL - 65ft 9¾in (20.06m)	TSO, TSOL - 65ft 9¾in (20.06m)	TSO, TSOL - 65ft 9¾in (20.06m)
Height:	12ft 4½in (3.77m)	12ft 4½in (3.77m)	12ft 4½in (3.77m)
Width:	9ft 3in (2.81m)	9ft 3in (2.81m)	9ft 3in (2.81m)
Seating:	Total - 348S	Total - 348S	Total - 348S
	DMSO(A) - 86S	DMSO(A) - 86S	DMSO(A) - 86S
	TSO - 90S	TSO - 90S	TSO - 90S
	TSOL - 86S	TSOL - 86S	TSOL - 86S
	DMSO (B) - 86S	DMSO (B) - 86S	DMSO (B) - 86S
Internal layout:	2+3 high density	2+3 high density	2+3 high density
Gangway:	Within set	Within set	Within set
Toilets:	TSOL - 1	TSOL - 1	TSOL - 1
Weight:	Total - 133.6 tonnes	Total - 133.6 tonnes	Total - 133.6 tonnes
	DMSO(A) - 39.2 tonnes	DMSO(A) - 39.2 tonnes	DMSO(A) - 39.2 tonnes
	TSO - 27.2 tonnes	TSO - 27.2 tonnes	TSO - 27.2 tonnes
	TSOL - 28 tonnes	TSOL - 28 tonnes	TSOL - 28 tonnes
	DMSO(B) - 39.2 tonnes	DMSO(B) - 39.2 tonnes	DMSO(B) - 39.2 tonnes
Brake type:	Air (regenerative)	Air (regenerative)	Air (regenerative)
Bogie type:	Powered - Adtranz P3	Powered - Adtranz P3	Powered - SRP BP62
	Trailer - Adtranz T3	Trailer - Adtranz T3	Trailer - SRP BT52
Power collection:	750V dc third rail	750V dc third rail	750V dc third rail
Traction motor type:	8 x Hitachi asynchronous	8 x Hitachi asynchronous	8 x Alsthom G352AY
Horsepower:	3,004hp (2,240kW)	3,004hp (2,240kW)	3,004hp (2,240kW)
Max speed:	75mph (121km/h)	75mph (121km/h)	75mph (121km/h)
Coupling type:	Outer - Tightlock,	Outer - Tightlock,	Outer - Tightlock,
	Inner - Semi-auto	Inner - Semi-auto	Inner - Semi-auto
Multiple restriction:	Class 465 and 466	Class 465 and 466	Class 465 and 466
Door type:	Bi-parting sliding plug	Bi-parting sliding plug	Bi-parting sliding plug
Total sets in traffic:	50	47	16
Construction:	Aluminium	Aluminium	Aluminium
Owner:	Eversholt	Eversholt	Angel Trains
Operator:	SouthEastern Trains	SouthEastern Trains	SouthEastern Trains
Sub-class differences:	BREL/ABB phase 1 train	BREL/ABB phase 2 train	Metro-Cammell built train

Electric Multiple Units

Left: *The mainstay of SouthEastern suburban train operations is a fleet of Class 465 'Networker' EMUS, introduced by Network SouthEast to replace slam door stock. Four sub-classes now exist. All sets are painted in SouthEastern white and blue livery. The Class 465/0s were built by BREL York in 1991-93 and are the phase 1 sets. Today, the fleet seat 348 passengers in the 2+2 and 2+3 style. One toilet is provided in the TSO at the 'B' end of the train. No. 465029 is illustrated. Since introduction a revision to the front end has been made to try and stop 'train surfing' by eliminating flat surfaces.* **CJM**

465/9	
465901-456934	
1991-1993	
2005	
Metro-Cammell, Birmingham	
Wabtec, Doncaster	
DMCO(A)+TSOL+	
TSO+DMCO(B)	
DMC0(A) - 65700-65733	
TSOL - 72719-72785 (odd Nos.)	
TSO - 72720-72786 (even Nos.)	
DMCO(B) - 65750-65783	
DMCO - 68ft 6½in (20.89m)	
TSO, TSOL - 65ft 9¾in (20.06m)	
12ft 4½in (3.77m)	
9ft 3in (2.81m)	
Total - 24F/302S	
DMCO(A) - 12F/68S	
TSO - 76S	
TSOL - 90S	
DMCO (B) - 12F/68S	
2+2F/2+3S	
Within set	
TSOL - 1	
Total - 138.2 tonnes	
DMCO(A) - 39.2 tonnes	
TSOL - 30.3 tonnes	
TSO - 29.5 tonnes	
DMCO(B) - 39.2 tonnes	
Air (regenerative)	
Powered - SRP BP62	
Trailer - SRP BT52	
750V dc third rail	
8 x Alsthom G352BY	
3,004hp (2,240kW)	
75mph (121km/h)	
Outer - Tightlock,	
Inner - Semi-auto	
Class 465 and 466	
Bi-parting sliding plug	
34	
Aluminium	
Angel Trains	
SouthEastern Trains	
Modified with first class	

Modernisation of the Kent suburban network took place in the 1990s with Network SouthEast ordering four-car EMUs from BREL and Metro-Cammell. These were of the same general body design as the Class 165 DMU fleet and became known as the 'Networker' fleet.

In total, 147 four-car sets were built in three batches: 97 by BREL/ABB and 50 by Metro-Cammell. The sets were very similar but with detail differences, mainly involving the original interiors.

A protracted delivery followed many technical issues, but the fleet soon revolutionised rail travel on the Kent inner and outer-suburban network, introducing driver-only operation, rapid acceleration and comfortable train interiors.

Originally all sets were painted in NSE colours, but following privatisation and operation by Connex and later SouthEastern Trains these operators' liveries have been applied.

Thirty-four of the original Metro-Cammell build were extensively rebuilt in 2005 for longer distance services. First class seating was provided in each driving car and a total refurbishment of the interior made. These sets were reclassified 465/9.

Members of Class 465/0, 465/1 and 465/2 are allocated to Slade Green depot, while the 465/9 batch are allocated to Gillingham. All units have pressure ventilation.

In recent years refurbishment has been carried out and by 2014 the latest SouthEastern white, blue and black livery is carried. ∎

Right Above: *The original BREL-built Class 465/0 and 465/1 sets have now been re-equipped with Hitachi traction equipment and the lower section bodyside skirts have been removed from the motor cars, as demonstrated of this view of DMSO No. 65836. These vehicles have a seating capacity of 86.* **CJM**

Right Below: *The intermediate trailer vehicles still retain their lower body skirts. In this view we seen TSOL No. 72925 from a Class 450/1 BREL phase 2 set. The TSOL vehicles seat 86, four seats fewer than a non-toilet fitted vehicle.* **CJM**

Electric Multiple Units

Above: *Clearly showing the very open underframe now sported by the original BREL units, phase 2 set No. 465190 is seen approaching Lewisham.* **CJM**

Left: *Networker Class 465 and 466 front end equipment positions. A: Destination/route indicator, B: Lamp cluster - from the outer edge this consists of a white marker light, headlight and a red tail light, C: Revised front fairing with angled top to stop train-surfing (handrails have also been removed), D: Tightlock coupling, E: Electrical and pneumatic connections behind roll-cover door.* **CJM**

Right: *The Metro-Cammell built 'Networker' sets of Class 465/2 and 465/9 still retain their full train length skirts which does improve the overall look of the trains. Painted in an earlier version of SouthEastern livery set No. 465249 is recorded at London Bridge.* **Antony Christie**

Below Middle: *The Class 465 interior is based on high-density 2+3 seating and is a mix of group and airline style. Above seat luggage racks and a passenger information system are fitted. As the Class 465s do not have full air conditioning, opening hopper windows are fitted throughout.* **Antony Christie**

Below: *In 2005, 35 Class 465/2 sets were rebuilt by Wabtec, Doncaster, with first class accommodation in both driving cars and were reclassified as 465/9. These sets were for longer distance commuter duties. Set No. 465907 is shown carrying full SouthEastern white and blue livery. The first class seating area is located in both driving cars directly behind the driving cab. Total seating on a Class 465/9 is for 24 first and 302 standard class passengers.* **Antony Christie**

Number range:	466001-466043
Introduced:	1992-1994
Built by:	GEC-Alstom, Birmingham
Formation:	DMSO+DTSO
Vehicle numbers:	DMSO - 64860-64902
	DTSO - 78312-78354
Vehicle length:	68ft 6½in (20.89m)
Height:	12ft 4½in (3.77m)
Width:	9ft 3in (2.81m)
Seating:	Total - 168S
	DMSO - 86S
	DTSO - 82S
Internal layout:	2+3 high density
Gangway:	Within set
Toilets:	DTSO - 1
Weight:	Total - 72 tonnes
	DMSO - 40.6 tonnes
	DTSO - 31.4 tonnes
Brake type:	Air (regenerative)
Bogie type:	Powered - Adtranz P3
	Trailer - Adtranz T3
Power collection:	750V dc third rail
Traction motor type:	4 x Alstom G352AY of 375hp (280kW)
Horsepower:	1,500hp (1,120kW)
Max speed:	75mph (121km/h)
Coupling type:	Outer - Tightlock, Inner - Semi-auto
Multiple restriction:	Class 465 and 466
Door type:	Bi-parting sliding plug
Total sets in traffic:	43
Construction:	Aluminium
Owner:	Angel Trains
Operator:	SouthEastern Trains

Fact File

For low patronage branch line use and to augment formations to either six or ten cars, a batch of 43 two-car 'Networker' sets was built by GEC-Alstom at Washwood Heath, Birmingham, in 1992-94. These sets are basically a two-car version of the Class 465/2 breed, except that one DMSO does not have traction equipment and is a Driving Trailer Standard Open. These vehicles also house a small toilet compartment (the only 'Networker' driving cars so fitted).

All sets are allocated to Slade Green and are painted in South Eastern Trains white, blue and black livery. The units can be seen throughout the SET operating area; all have now had their original front handrails removed and are fitted with anti-surfer angled plates above the buffer beam, in a similar manner to the Class 465s. ■

Electric Multiple Units

Below: *The SouthEastern with such high patronage has operated 10-car trains at peak periods for many years and when the modernisation by NSE took place 43 two-car 'Networkers' were ordered from Alstom. These sets also allowed shorter trains to be deployed on lesser used branch lines. The sets are now all refurbished and the majority painted in SouthEastern white, blue and black livery. The cab roofs have been modified to include a cab air conditioning system. Set No. 466003 is seen from its Driving Trailer end, a vehicle which seats 82.* **Antony Christie**

Above: *Viewed from its Driving Motor vehicle, set No. 466019 is seen at Denmark Hill leading a train towards London. These DMSO vehicles are the same as on the Alstom-built Class 465/2 sets. The front ends have been modified to eliminate flat surfaces to stop train-surfing.* **Antony Christie**

Below: *The Class 466 interior is identical to the Class 465 stock, the only exception being the Driving Trailer Standard vehicle which has a toilet compartment, the only 'Networker' driving cars to do so. Seating is in the 2+3 layout with above seat luggage racks and a passenger information system.* **Antony Christie**

Number range:	(483)002-(483)009 (last three digits carried)
Former number range:	Ex-LUL 1938 stock
Introduced originally:	1938
Introduced to Isle of Wight:	1989-1990
Built by:	Metro-Cammell
Rebuilt by:	BRML Eastleigh
Formation:	DMSO(A)+DMSO(B)
Vehicle numbers:	DMSO(A) - 122-129
	DMSO(B) - 224-229 (not in order)
Vehicle length:	DMSO - 52ft 9in (16.15m)
Height:	9ft 5½in (2.88m)
Width:	8ft 8½in (2.65m)
Seating:	Total - 82S
	DMSO(A) - 40S
	DMSO(B) - 42S
Internal layout:	2+2, bench
Gangway:	Within set, emergency end doors
Toilets:	Not fitted
Weight:	Total - 54.8 tonnes
	DMSO(A) - 27.4 tonnes
	DMSO(B) - 27.4 tonnes
Brake type:	Air (Auto/EP)
Bogie type:	LT
Power collection:	660V dc third rail
Traction motor type:	4 x Crompton Parkinson/GEC/BTH LT100
Horsepower:	670hp (500kW)
Max speed:	45mph (72.5km/h)
Coupling type:	Wedgelock
Multiple restriction:	Within type only
Door type:	Bi-parting and single sliding
Total sets available:	6 (only four in use at any time)
Construction:	Steel
Owner:	South West Trains
Operator:	South West Trains - Isle of Wight

Fact File

The railway system on the Isle of Wight has always been a little world of its own, and today the remaining railway which operates from Ryde Pier Head to Shanklin is no exception.

Electrified by BR Southern Region in the mid-1960s to rid steam traction from the Island, no normal railway stock could be used due to gauge clearances. To provide 'new' trains BR purchased a fleet of redundant 1927 tube stock and rebuilt this for use on the isolated network.

This stock became life-expired in the late 1980s and Network SouthEast purchased more 'modern' tube stock, dating from 1938! This was rebuilt into twin power-car sets which either operate in two- or four-car formations.

Sets are allocated to Ryde St Johns depot; they have LU-style group and longitudinal seats with crew-operated sliding doors.

Livery is mock London Transport red. ■

Electric Multiple Units

Above: *The Island Line, operated by Stagecoach as part of South West Trains, is a unique operation in many ways, its rolling stock fleet being no exception. Currently a fleet of six two-car ex-London Transport 1938 tube stock is in use. These are the oldest trains currently in National Rail daily service. Painted in mock-London Transport red livery the sets are based at Ryde St Johns Road depot. Set No. 006 is seen at Ryde St Johns Road station.* **Darren Ford**

Above: *The seating is a mix of facing and longitudinal, with the same style of decor as once used on London Underground. The vehicles sport a period wood finish on the upper inner bodywork. Seating per car is for either 40 or 42 depending on if you are in an 'A' or 'B' car.* **CJM**

Right: *The driving cabs of the Class 483 stock were fully refurbished when the sets were overhauled for NSE in 1989-90, but the facilities can best be described as 'basic' The main master switch and power controller is the handle on the right with the turned wooden knob, while in the middle is the electro-pneumatic and Westinghouse brake controller. Set No. 004 is illustrated.* **CJM**

Number range:	507001-507033
Introduced:	1978-1980
Built/rebuilt by:	BREL York/Alstom Eastleigh
Formation:	BDMSO+TSO+DMSO
Vehicle numbers:	BDMSO - 64367-64399
	TSO - 71342-71374
	DMSO - 64405-64437
Vehicle length:	BDMSO/DMSO - 64ft 11½in (19.80m)
	TSO - 65ft 4¼in (19.92m)
Height:	11ft 6½in (3.58m)
Width:	9ft 3in (2.82m)
Seating:	Total - 186S + 6 tip up
	BDMSO - 56S + 3 tip up
	TSO - 74S
	DMSO - 56S + 3 tip up
Internal layout:	2+2
Gangway:	Within set (emergency end doors)
Toilets:	Not fitted
Weight:	Total - 98 tonnes
	BDMSO - 37 tonnes
	TSO - 25.5 tonnes
	DMSO - 35.5 tonnes
Brake type:	Air (EP/rheostatic)
Bogie type:	BX1
Power collection:	700-750 V dc third rail
Traction motor type:	8 x GEC G310AZ of 110hp (82.12kW)
Horsepower:	880hp (657kW)
Max speed:	75mph (121km/h)
Coupling type:	Outer - Tightlock, Inner - Bar
Multiple restriction:	Class 507 and 508/1 only
Door type:	Bi-parting sliding
Total number in traffic:	33
Construction:	Body - aluminium, Frame - steel
Special features:	CCTV
Owner:	Angel Trains
Operator:	MerseyRail

Fact File

A derivative of the BR 1972-design high-density suburban EMU is this fleet of Class 507s.

Designed and equipped for the MerseyRail electrified network around Liverpool, the sets were originally of the high-density layout, but following refurbishment under the Merseytravel banner sets now sport 2+2 low-density interiors.

When built, units were painted in standard blue and grey BR livery; this later gave way to MerseyRail yellow and sets are now finished in Merseytravel silver grey and yellow.

Refurbishment at Eastleigh Works in recent years has seen revised front ends fitted with new headlight and marker lights.

All sets are allocated to Birkenhead depot and operate in a common pool alongside the Class 508/1 stock. ∎

Electric Multiple Units

Left Below: *The 33 Class 507 dc EMUs together with the Class 508s operate the MerseyRail electric services in and around Liverpool. Based at Birkenhead North these three-car sets have been fully refurbished since original introduction in the 1970s, with a much improved passenger environment. Painted in grey and yellow promotional livery, set No. 507031 is illustrated at Freshfield.* **John Binch**

Right: *Class 507 and 508 front end layout, showing the present refurbished condition. When first introduced these sets had a front end the same as the Class 313, 314 and 315 stock. A: High-level marker light, B: Air warning horns, C: Destination and route indicators, D: Emergency front (tunnel) door, E: Headlight, F: Dual white marker/red tail light, G: Tightlock coupling, H: Manual uncoupling arm, I: Drum switch, J: Emergency air connector.* **John Binch**

Below: *When originally introduced the Class 507s had high-density 3+2 seating using the standard 1970s low-back seats. Today the interior is much improved with high-back 2+2 seating throughout with a real time passenger information system. As these sets do not have air conditioning opening hopper windows are fitted.* **John Binch**

Number range:	508103-508143
Former number range:	508003-508043
Originally built:	1979-1980
Introduced:	As 508/1 - 1984-1985
Originally built:	BREL York
Refurbished by:	BRML Eastleigh
Formation:	DMSO+TSO+BDMSO
Vehicle numbers:	DMSO - 64651-64691
	TSO - 71485-71525
	BDMSO - 64694-64734
Vehicle length:	DMSO - 64ft 11½in (19.80m)
	TSO - 65ft 4½in (19.92m)
Height:	11ft 6½in (3.58m)
Width:	9ft 3in (2.82m)
Seating:	Total - 186S + 6 tip-up
	DMSO - 56S + 3 tip up
	TSO - 74S
	BDMSO - 56S + 3 tip up
Internal layout:	2+2
Gangway:	Within set,
	emergency end doors
Toilets:	Not fitted
Weight:	Total - 99.3 tonnes
	DMSO - 36.0 tonnes
	TSO - 26.7 tonnes
	BDMSO - 36.6 tonnes
Brake type:	Air (Westcode/rheostatic)
Bogie type:	BX1
Power collection:	750V dc third rail
Traction motor type:	8 x GEC G310AZ
Horsepower:	880hp (657kW)
Max speed:	75mph (121km/h)
Coupling type:	Outer - Tightlock
	Inner - Bar
Multiple restriction:	Class 507 and 508/1
Special features:	CCTV
Door type:	Bi-parting sliding
Total sets in traffic:	27
Construction:	Body - aluminium
Owner:	Angel Trains
Operator:	MerseyRail

Fact File

These 43 sets were originally introduced on BR Southern Region in 1979. They were transferred to the Liverpool area in 1984, but left one TSO vehicle on the Southern for reformation in Class 455 stock.

Eventually it was decided that all 43 sets were not needed for Liverpool operations and 16 units were stored. These were later returned to traffic, 12 with Connex South Eastern (later SouthEastern Trains) and three with Silverlink (later London Overground).

The SouthEastern sets were taken out of service in 2008-10 and stored, pending Angel Trains finding a new lease operator. The three Silverlink sets were removed from traffic on London Overground and disposed of in 2013.

All Mersey sets have now been refurbished and have revised front ends. The sets are allocated to Birkenhead and operate in a common pool with Class 507s. ■

Below: *Today just 27 of the original fleet of 43 Class 508s remain in service, all working with MerseyRail, based at Birkenhead North alongside the Class 507 fleet. Some sets remain stored, but it is unlikely that any new operator will come forward for them sets. Painted in MerseyRail silver and yellow, set No. 508139 is illustrated. The two driving cars of the '508s' each seat 56 passengers.* **Antony Christie**

Above: *The revised front ends given to the Class 508s during their last refresh overhaul made a major difference in appearance, made even more noticeable by painting a black egg shape around the light clusters. Set No. 508104 is illustrated. When originally built and introduced on the Southern Region at Wimbledon in 1979, this set was a four-car unit and numbered 508004.* **Antony Christie**

Right Middle: *As with the Class 507s, the Class 508s have received major interior refurbishment and upgrading, to such a level that it would be hard to imagine the original interior style. With high-back 2+2 seating, angled vestibule panels and a state-of-the-art passenger information system, these are some of the better suburban EMU interiors in the country.* **Antony Christie**

Right Bottom: *The Class 508 intermediate vehicle is a TSO, seating 74 is the 2+2 style. Two pairs of bi-parting passenger operated sliding doors are on each side of each vehicle.* **John Binch**

Sub-class:	700/0 (8-car) RLU	700/1 (12-car) FLU
Number range:	700001-700060	700101-700155
Introduced:	2015-2019	2015-2019
Built by:	Siemens Duewag, Germany	Siemens Duewag, Germany
Formation:	P T P T T P T P	P T P P T T T T P P T P
Vehicle numbers:	See below	See below
Train length:	528ft 2in (162m)	794ft 0in (242m)
Vehicle length:	66ft 9in (20.4m)	66ft 9in (20.4m)
Height:	To be advised	To be advised
Width:	9ft 2in (2.8m)	9ft 2in (2.8m)
Floor height:	43.3in (1.1m)	43.3in (1.1m)
Seating:	Total - 427 (by Fainsa of Spain)	Total - 666 by Fainsa of Spain)
	Details to be advised	Details to be advised
Internal layout:	2+2 Metro and commuter	2+2 Metro and commuter
Gangway:	Within set	Within set
Toilets:	Three per train	Five per train
Weight:	Total - 278 tonnes	Total - 410 tonnes
	Details to be advised	Details to be advised
Brake type:	Air (regenerative)	Air (regenerative)
Bogie type:	Siemens SGP SF7000	Siemens SGP SF7000
Power collection:	25kV ac overhead & 750V dc third rail	25kV ac overhead &750V dc third rail
Power output:	3.3Mw	5.0Mw
Traction motor type:	To be advised	To be advised
Output:	To be advised	To be advised
Wheel diameter:	32.3in (820mm)	32.3in (820mm)
Max speed:	100mph (161km/h)	100mph (161km/h)
Coupling type:	Outer - Dellner 12, Inner - Semi-auto	Outer - Dellner 12, Inner - Semi-auto
Multiple restriction:	Within class	Within class
Door type:	Bi-parting sliding pocket	Bi-parting sliding pocket
Construction:	Aluminium	Aluminium
Special features:	Automatic Train Operation (ATO)	Automatic Train Operation (ATO)
	Remote diagnostics	Remote diagnostics
Sub class variations:	8-car set	12-car set

Class 700 vehicle numbering.

DMCO:	401001-401060, 412001-412060
	401101-401155, 412101-412155
PTSO:	402001-402060, 411001-411060
	402101-402155, 411101-411160
MSO:	403001-403060, 410001-410060
	403101-403155, 404101-404155
	409101-409155, 410101-410155
TSO:	406001-406060, 407001-407060
	405101-405155, 406101-406155
	407101-407155, 408101-408155

Left: *An artist's impression of how the new Siemens Class 700 breed of Thameslink EMUs will look. The drawing has used South West Trains Surbiton station as its base, a station and route not on the Thameslink operation.* **Siemens**

The Class 700 has been given to the design of electric multiple unit procured by the Department for Transport (DfT) for the expanded Thameslink franchise which will include much of the First Capital Connect and Southern operations.

In 2011 Siemens was awarded preferred bidder status, following a protracted procurement process and final close of contract, with the delivery of the first fully tested train expected in 2015.

The £1.6 billion contract to manufacture and provide maintenance depots for the stock was agreed in mid-2013 with construction of both depots and trains commencing immediately.

A fleet of 60 eight-car and 55 twelve-car trains is being built, and expected to enter service between 2016 and 2018.

Purpose built depot facilities are being constructed at Hornsey and Three Bridges.

The first complete train was being tested in Germany in summer 2014. ∎

Sub-class:	800/1	800/2
Number range:	800101-801136 (Prov)	800201-800212, 800301-800310 (Prov)
Introduced:	2017 onwards	2017 onwards
Formation:	DPTS+M1S+M3S+M1C+DPTF	DPTS+M1S+M2S+TPS+M2S+ T2S+M3C+M1F+DPTF
Train length:	528ft 2in (162m)	528ft 2in (162m) & 794ft 0in (242m)
Vehicle length:	Driving - 83ft 4in (25.45m)	Driving - 83ft 4in (25.45m)
	Intermediate - 82ft 0in (25.0m)	Intermediate - 82ft 0in (25.0m)
Width:	8ft 10in (2.7m)	8ft 10in (2.7m)
Seating:	Total - 45F/270S,	Total - 101F/526S or Total - 45F/270S,
	DPTS - 56S, M1S - 88S, M3S - 88S	DPTS - 48S, M1S - 88S, M2S - 88S TPS - 88S, M2S - 88S
	M1C - 30F/38S, DPTF - 15F	T2S - 88S, M3C - 30F/38S M1F - 56F, DPTF - 15F
Internal layout:	2+1F, 2+2S	2+1F, 2+2S
Gangway:	Within set	Within set
Toilets:	DPTS-1, M1S-2, M3S-2, DPTF-1	DPTS-1, M1S-1M2S-2, TPS-2, M1F-2, DPTF-1
Brake type:	Air (regenerative)	Air (regenerative)
Power:	25kV ac overhead or on board diesel	25kV ac overhead or on board diesel
Diesel type:	MTU 12V 1600 R80L at 700kW	MTU 12V 1600 R80L at 700kW
Diesel output:	938hp (700kW) per engine	938hp (700kW) per engine
Max speed:	125mph (201km/h)	125mph (201km/h)
Coupling type:	Outer - Dellner 12, Inner - Semi-auto	Outer - Dellner 12, Inner - Semi-auto
Multiple restriction:	Within class (two sets only)	Within class (two sets only)
Door type:	Single leaf sliding plug	Single leaf sliding plug
Construction:	Aluminium	Aluminium
Special features:	Remote diagnostics, ATP	Remote diagnostics, ETCS
Train family:	Hitachi 'A' Train	Hitachi 'A' Train
Sub-class variations:	5-car set for Great Western	5 and 9-car set for East Coast

Sub-class:	801/1	801/2
Number range:	801101-801121(Prov)	801201-801243 (Prov)
Introduced:	2017 onwards	2017 onwards
Formation:	To be confirmed	To be confirmed
Train length:	794ft 0in (242m)	794ft 0in (242m)
Vehicle length:	Driving - 83ft 4in (25.45m)	Driving - 83ft 4in (25.45m)
	Intermediate - 82ft 0in (25.0m)	Intermediate - 82ft 0in (25.0m)
Width:	8ft 10in (2.7m)	8ft 10in (2.7m)
Seating:	Total - 101F/526S	Total - 101F/526S
	DPTS - 48S, M1S - 88S, M2S - 88S, TPS - 88S	DPTS - 48S, M1S - 88S, M2S - 88S, TPS - 88S
	M2S - 88S, T2S - 88S, M3C - 30F/38S,	M2S - 88S, T2S - 88S, M3C - 30F/38S, M1F - 56F
	M1F - 56F, DPTF - 15F	DPTF - 15F
Internal layout:	2+1F, 2+2S	2+1F, 2+2S
Gangway:	Within set	Within set
Toilets:	DPTS-1, M1S-1, M2S-2, TPS-2, M1F-2,	DPTS-1, M1S-1, M2S-2, TPS-2, M1F-2,
	DPTF-1	DPTF-1
Brake type:	Air (regenerative)	Air (regenerative)
Power:	25kV ac overhead	25kV ac overhead
Aux diesel type:	MTU 12V 1600 R80L at 700kW	MTU 12V 1600 R80L at 700kW
Diesel output:	938hp (700kW)	938hp (700kW)
Max speed:	125mph (201km/h)	125mph (201km/h)
Coupling type:	Outer - Dellner 12, Inner - Semi-auto	Outer - Dellner 12, Inner - Semi-auto
Multiple restriction:	Within class (two sets only)	Within class (two sets only)
Door type:	Single leaf sliding plug	Single leaf sliding plug
Construction:	Aluminium	Aluminium
Special features:	Remote diagnostics, ATP, ETCS	Remote diagnostics, ETCS
Train family:	Hitachi 'A' Train	Hitachi 'A' Train
Sub-class variations:	9-car set for Great Western	9-car set for East Coast

Electric Multiple Units

Fact File

In summer 2012 Agility Trains signed a contract with the Department for Transport (DfT) to design, build, finance and maintain 596 new carriages for the Great Western and East Coast Main Lines as part of the Intercity Express Programme.

Hitachi Rail Europe and John Laing are the main shareholders of Agility Trains and in summer 2013 an additional contract for the provision of an extra 270 carriages for the East Coast was placed, bringing the total number of vehicles ordered to 866.

Great Western will operate 36 five-car Class 800 dual mode and 21 nine-car electric Class 801 sets.

The East Coast will operate 22 five-car and 43 nine-car sets, both operators having a mix of electric and bi-mode trains.

Pre-production sets are to be built by Hitachi in Kasado, Japan, with the remainder built at a new Hitachi plant at Newton Aycliffe. ■

HST Vehicles

Type:	TSMB (GN2G)	TRFB (GN1G)	TRSB (GK2G)	TRFB (GK1G)
Number range:	40101-40119	40204-40231	40402-40434	40700-40757
Former range:	42xxx	404xx	40xxx	403xx
Introduced:	Orig: 1976-1980	Orig: 1976-1977	Orig: 1976-1977	Orig: 1978-1982
	TSMB – 2009-2010	TRFB – 1986	TRSB – 1986	TRFB – 1987
Built by:	BR Derby	BR Derby	BR Derby	BR Derby
Seating:	70S	23F	33S	17F
Speed:	125mph (201km/h)	125mph (201km/h)	125mph (201km/h)	125mph (201km/h)
Brake type:	Air	Air	Air	Air
Heating:	Electric	Electric	Electric	Electric
Bogie type:	BT10	BT10	BT10	BT10
Length:	75ft 0in (22.86m)	75ft 0in (22.86m)	75ft 0in (22.86m)	75ft 0in (22.86m)
Height:	12ft 7in (3.84m)	12ft 7in (3.84m)	12ft 7in (3.84m)	12ft 7in (3.84m)
Width:	9ft 2in (2.79m)	9ft 2in (2.79m)	9ft 2in (2.79m)	9ft 2in (2.79m)
Weight:	33.7 tonnes	36 tonnes	36 tonnes	38 tonnes
Owner:	PT	AN	PT	PT, AN
Operator:	GW	GW	GC	EM, EC, GW
Notes:				

Type:	TRB (GN1G)	TF (GH1G)	TS (GH2G)	TGS (GJ2G)
Number range:	40900-40904	41003-41206¤	42003-42409¤	44000-44101
Former range:	400xx, 404xx	-	-	-
Introduced:	Orig: 1976-1979	1976-1982	1976-1982	1980-1982
	TRB - 2003			-
Built by:	BR Derby	BR Derby	BR Derby	BR Derby
Seating:	23F	40-48F*	68-84S*	61-71S*
Speed:	125mph (201km/h)	125mph (201km/h)	125mph (201km/h)	125mph (201km/h)
Brake type:	Air	Air	Air	Air
Heating:	Electric	Electric	Electric	Electric
Bogie type:	BT10	BT10	BT10	BT10
Length:	75ft 0in (22.86m)	75ft 0in (22.86m)	75ft 0in (22.86m)	75ft 0in (22.86m)
Height:	12ft 7in (3.84m)	12ft 7in (3.84m)	12ft 7in (3.84m)	12ft 7in (3.84m)
Width:	9ft 2in (2.79m)	9ft 2in (2.79m)	9ft 2in (2.79m)	9ft 2in (2.79m)
Weight:	36 tonnes	33 tonnes	33 tonnes	34 tonnes
Owner:	FG	AN, PT, FG	AN, PT, FG	AN, PT, FG
Operator:	GW	GW, XC, EC, EM, GC	GW, XC, EC, EM, GC	GW, XC, EC, EM, GC
Notes:		* Depending on operator	* Depending on operator	* Depending on operator
		¤ Some rebuilt from Mk3 hauled stock	¤ Some rebuilt from Mk3 hauled stock	

Above: *First Great Western has a fleet of 108 HST Trailer First vehicles allocated to Laira and Old Oak Common depots. These vehicles have seating for 48 in the low-density 2+1 style. One toilet is provided on each vehicle. Car No. 41166 is illustrated.* **CJM**

Coaching Stock

TRFB (GL1G)

40800-40811
400xx, 404xx
Orig: 1976-1979
TRFB – 1986
BR Derby
17F
125mph (201km/h)
Air
Electric
BT10
75ft 0in (22.86m)
12ft 7in (3.84m)
9ft 2in (2.79m)
38 tonnes
PT
GW, EC

TCC (GH3G)

45001-45005
12xxx loco-hauled
Orig: 1975-1977
TCC - 2005-2006
Orig: BR Derby /
Rebuilt: Wabtec Doncaster
30F/10S
125mph (201km/h)
Air
Electric
BT10
75ft 0in (22.86m)
12ft 7in (3.84m)
9ft 2in (2.79m)
35 tonnes
PT
XC
Rebuilt from
Mk3 hauled stock

Right and Right Lower: *East Coast operates a small HST fleet for non-electrified main line services, especially those north of Edinburgh; 16 buffet cars, 31 Trailer Firsts, 71 Trailer Standards and 15 Trailer Guards Standards are based at Edinburgh Craigentinny. In the upper view is Trailer Standard No. 42192, a vehicle seating 76 in the 2+2 layout. Below is Trailer First No. 41098, this seats 48 in the 2+1 style with each seat having a table and above seat lighting. Vehicles are mainly painted in white with grey/silver ends and East Coast branding.* **CJM**

Above: *A total of 224 HST Trailer Standards are operated by FGW, with a number of different seating layouts, depending of their position in train make-ups. No. 42284 is shown. These vehicles seat between 68 and 84 and have two toilets, one at each end.* **CJM**

Above: *One TS from each FGW HST set has been modified and fitted with a disabled person's accessible toilet and a disabled seating area. These are recognisable on the outside by revised bodywork. Vehicle No. 42302 is illustrated.* **CJM**

Left Top: *Six different types of HST buffet car are in service. On First Great Western the TSRMB, TRFB, TRB type can be found. In this view we see Trailer Restaurant First Buffet No. 40207 from the catering end and counter side. Originally the two slats in the upper bodywork would have been windows but these have been plated over in recent years. These vehicles seat 23 first class passengers in the 2+1 style. Note that the non-passenger service door is painted in body colour.* **CJM**

Left Middle Upper: *Five Trailer Restaurant Buffet (TRB) vehicles are on the books of FGW allocated to Laira. These vehicles seat 23 first in the 2+1 layout. No. 40904 is illustrated from the passenger saloon end.* **CJM**

Left Middle Lower: *Interior of First Great Western HST TF vehicle showing the 2+1 seating layout, using high quality leather covered seats and glazed mid vehicle length dividers. Luggage racks are provided above seats and luggage stacks are located at coach ends. Power supply sockets are located by each seat, but no individual down lights are provided.* **CJM**

Coaching Stock

Left Bottom: *East Coast Trailer First, showing a very different passenger environment, still retaining the 2+1 style but with different style seats, moquette and tables. On these vehicles the mid-vehicle screen is solid rather than glazed.* **Nathan Williamson**

Right Top: *CrossCountry Trains introduced HSTs on its busiest routes from 2005-06 and operates enough Mk3 coaches to form five passenger rakes, although usually only three or four are in service at one time. First class seating in the 2+1 style is provided by a fleet of five TF vehicles, three of which were rebuilt from loco-hauled stock. Car No. 41193 is seen at Newton Abbot.*
Antony Christie

Right Middle: Upper *Five Trailer Guards Standard vehicles are on the books of CrossCountry; three are owned by Angel Trains and two by Porterbrook. Viewed from its guard's end car No. 44021 is seen at Taunton.*
Antony Christie

Right Middle Lower: *Standard class seating is provided by 25 Trailer Standard coaches, each seating 82 in the 2+2 style. One toilet is provided in each vehicle. TS No. 42369 is illustrated. This vehicle was rebuilt from former loco-hauled vehicle No. 12050.* **Antony Christie**

Below: *Open Access operator Grand Central operates a fleet of 21 HST vehicles with usually two HST sets in traffic. All its TF and TS vehicles are rebuilds from ex-Mk3 loco hauled stock. TRSB No. 40433 is seen with its catering facilities at the far end of the vehicle. The near end has seating for 33 standard class passengers, but is usually used to provide a catering service.* **CJM**

Coaching Stock

Left Top: *The interior of the Grand Central-operated HST stock has a very American theme and is pleasing to the eye. For passengers wanting something to do during their journey, printed board games are located on the tables. Vehicle No. 42408 is illustrated.* **Nathan Williamson**

Left Middle Upper: *Stagecoach East Midlands Trains operates a sizeable fleet of HST vehicles on its core St Pancras to Derby, Sheffield and Nottingham route. All vehicles have been refurbished and sport the EMT white 'main line' livery. Ten TRFB catering vehicles are on the books, providing a full at-seat meal service in first class and catering in standard. No. 40756 is illustrated from its saloon end which has 17 first class seats in the 2+1 layout.* **Antony Christie**

Left Middle Lower: *Standard class accommodation is provided by a fleet of 41 Trailer Standards and 11 TGS coaches. The TS cars seat 74 in the 2+2 style, while the TGS design seats 63. TS No. 42329 is illustrated.* **Tony Christie**

Below: *In 2014, a former East Midlands Trains HST set was transferred to East Coast; it was still sporting EMT livery but with full East Coast branding. This livery is shown by TS No. 42205 at London King's Cross.* **Antony Christie**

Type:	RSB (AG2J)	FO (AD1J)	FOD (AD1J)	FO (AD1J)
Mark:	4	4	4	4
Number range:	10300-10333	11201-11299	11301-11330	11401-11430
Former range:	-	11xxx, 12xxx	11xxx	11xxx
Introduced:	1989-1992	1989-1992	1989-1992	1989-1992
Built by:	Metro-Cammell	Metro-Cammell	Metro-Cammell	Metro-Cammell
Seating:	30S	46F	42F	46F
Speed:	140mph (225km/h)	140mph (225km/h)	140mph (225km/h)	140mph (225km/h)
Brake type:	Air	Air	Air	Air
Heating:	Electric/6	Electric/6	Electric/6	Electric/6
Bogie type:	BT41	BT41	BT41	BT41
Length:	75ft 0in (22.86m)	75ft 0in (22.86m)	75ft 0in (22.86m)	75ft 0in (22.86m)
Height:	12ft 7in (3.84m)	12ft 7in (3.84m)	12ft 7in (3.84m)	12ft 7in (3.84m)
Width:	9ft 2in (2.79m)	9ft 2in (2.79m)	9ft 2in (2.79m)	9ft 2in (2.79m)
Weight:	43 tonnes	42 tonnes	40 tonnes	42 tonnes
Operator:	EC	EC	EC	EC
Notes:				

Type:	FO (AD1J)	TSOE (AI2J)	TSOD (AL2J)	TSO (AC2J)
Mark:	4	4	4	4
Number range:	11998-11999	12200-12232	12300-12331	12400-12538
Former range:	10314 &10316	-	-	-
Introduced:	1989-1992	1989-1992	1989-1992	1989-1992
Built by:	Metro-Cammell	Metro-Cammell	Metro-Cammell	Metro-Cammell
Seating:	46F	76S	68S	76S
Speed:	140mph (225km/h)	140mph (225km/h)	140mph (225km/h)	140mph (225km/h)
Brake type:	Air	Air	Air	Air
Heating:	Electric/6	Electric/6	Electric/6	Electric/6
Bogie type:	BT41	BT41	BT41	BT41
Length:	75ft 0in (22.86m)	75ft 0in (22.86m)	75ft 0in (22.86m)	75ft 0in (22.86m)
Height:	12ft 7in (3.84m)	12ft 7in (3.84m)	12ft 7in (3.84m)	12ft 7in (3.84m)
Width:	9ft 2in (2.79m)	9ft 2in (2.79m)	9ft 2in (2.79m)	9ft 2in (2.79m)
Weight:	41 tonnes	39.5 tonnes	39.4 tonnes	40 tonnes
Operator:	EC	EC	EC	EC
Notes:				

Type:	DVT (NZ)
Mark:	4
Number range:	82200-82231
Introduced:	1988-1989
Built by:	Metro-Cammell
Seating:	-
Speed:	140mph (225km/h)
Brake type:	Air
Heating:	Electric/6
Bogie type:	SIG
Length:	75ft 0in (22.86m)
Height:	12ft 7in (3.84m)
Width:	9ft 2in (2.79m)
Weight:	43.5 tonnes
Operator:	EC
Notes:	

Right: *Outer end of East Coast Mk4 Trailer Standard Open End (TSOE). Main equipment items are - A: Red rear tail lights, B: Sealed up observation window, C: Sealed up communicating door, D: Pullman rubbing plate, E: Brake pipe (red), F: Main reservoir pipe (yellow), G: Train supply jumper socket, H: Buck-eye coupling (lowered position), I: Control jumper, J: Train supply jumper cable.* **Derek Porter**

Coaching Stock

Left Top: *Each East Coast Mk4 set has one Trailer Standard Open Disabled in its formation. This vehicle has 68 standard class seats, a disabled access toilet and a disabled seating area suitable for the parking of a wheelchair. Vehicle No. 12329 is illustrated at Doncaster.* **CJM**

Left Middle: *Catering facilities in the East Coast Mk4 fleet are provided by 30 RSB vehicles. These coaches have full kitchen and buffet facilities at one end and a saloon for 30 standard class passengers at the other. The vehicle is usually located between the first and standard class coaches. Coach No. 10332 is seen at Doncaster.* **CJM**

Left Lower: *First class seating on Mk4 trains is provided by a fleet of FO vehicles seating between 42 and 46 depending on layout and the provision of disabled facilities. Each Mk4 set has three first class vehicles coupled at the London end of the train between the DVT and buffet car. Vehicle No. 11280 is seen in a consist at Doncaster.* **CJM**

Below: *At the loco end of each Mk4 rake is a Trailer Standard Open End (TSOE) vehicle. This coach has no gangway connection at one end (coupled to the loco). TSOE vehicles are otherwise a standard TS vehicle with seating for 76 in the 2+1 style. TSOE No. 12231 is seen coupled to a Class 91 at London King's Cross.* **Antony Christie**

Coaching Stock

Above and Right: *A fleet of 31 Mk4 DVTs provide the remote driving facility to the Class 91 powered Mk4 sets. These have a full width driving cab with the remainder of the vehicle for luggage. In the upper view we see East Coast liveried No. 82204, while right we see Flying Scotsman promotional branded DVT No. 82205. Both:* **CJM**

Below: *Mk4 first class interior showing the luxury 2+1 seating layout and decor.*
Nathan Williamson

Coaching Stock

Type:	RFB (AJ1G)	GFW (AJ1F)	RMB (AN2G)	SLEP (AU4G)
Mark:	3a	3a	3a	3a
Number range:	10200-10259	10271-10274	10401-10406	10501-10617
Former range:	405xx HST		12xxx TSO	-
	10xxx, 11xxx	102xx series		
Introduced:	1975-1979	As GFW - 2012	1975-1977	1981-1983
Built by:	BR Derby	BR Derby	BR Derby	BR Derby
Seating:	18F-24F*	30F	52S	12 Comps
Speed:	110mph (177km/h)	110mph (177km/h)	110mph (177km/h)	110mph (177km/h)
Brake type:	Air	Air	Air	Air
Heating:	Electric/14	Electric/14	Electric/6	Electric/7
Bogie type:	BT10	BT10	BT10	BT10
Length:	75ft 0in (22.86m)	75ft 0in (22.86m)	75ft 0in (22.86m)	75ft 0in (22.86m)
Height:	12ft 9in (3.89m)	12ft 9in (3.89m)	12ft 9in (3.89m)	12ft 9in (3.89m)
Width:	8ft 11in (2.71m)	8ft 11in (2.71m)	8ft 11in (2.71m)	8ft 11in (2.71m)
Weight:	39.8 tonnes	40.1 tonnes	37 tonnes	41 tonnes
Operator:	PT, CD, DB	CD	PT	PB, CD, DB
Notes:	* Depending on style	Plug door fitted		

Type:	TSO (AC2G)	FO (AD1H)	BUO (AE1H)	DVT (NZ)
Mark:	3a	3b	3b	3b
Number range:	12005-12181	11064-11101	17173-17175	82101-82152
	§12602-12619			82301-82309
Former range:	-	-	-	-
Introduced:	1975-1977	1985	1986	1988
Built by:	BR Derby	BR Derby	BR Derby	BR Derby
Seating:	70-85S*	48F	36F	
Speed:	110mph (177km/h)	110mph (177km/h)	110mph (177km/h)	110mph (177km/h)
Brake type:	Air	Air	Air	Air
Heating:	Electric/6	Electric/6	Electric/5	Electric/5
Bogie type:	BT10	BT10	BT10	T4
Length:	75ft 0in (22.86m)	75ft 0in (22.86m)	75ft 0in (22.86m)	75ft 0in (22.86m)
Height:	12ft 9in (3.89m)	12ft 9in (3.89m)	12ft 9in (3.89m)	12ft 9in (3.89m)
Width:	8ft 11in (2.71m)	8ft 11in (2.71m)	8ft 11in (2.71m)	8ft 11in (2.71m)
Weight:	34.3 tonnes	36.5 tonnes	36 tonnes	45 tonnes
Operator:	PB, CD, CD, ST	CG,PT	PT	PB, CD, DB
Notes:	* Depending on style			
	§ Plug door fitted			

Below: *A large number of Mk3 passenger vehicles are still in service, working over a wide variety of routes. Arriva Trains Wales maintains two sets for its Cardiff-Holyhead business train. One vehicle in this pool is RFB No. 10259, illustrated from its catering corridor side at Newport. The far end of the coach has four bays of first class seating.* **CJM**

SLE/SLED (AQ4G)	FO (AD1G)
3a	3a
10647-10734	11005-11058
-	-
1980-1985	1975-1976
BR Derby	BR Derby
SLE 13 Comps, SLED 11 Comps	47F-48F
110mph (177km/h)	110mph (177km/h)
Air	Air
Electric/11	Electric/6
BT10	BT10
75ft 0in (22.86m)	75ft 0in (22.86m)
12ft 9in (3.89m)	12ft 9in (3.89m)
8ft 11in (2.71m)	8ft 11in (2.71m)
42-43 tonnes	34.3 tonnes
PB, DB, VS	PB, DB

Above: *Arriva Trains Wales operates six TSO vehicles (12176-12181), rebuilt from FO stock. No. 12176 is illustrated. These vehicles are owned by Arriva and allocated to Cardiff Canton.* **CJM**

Right Middle: *First Great Western's sleeper operating between London and Penzance has a requirement for six loco-hauled Mk3 non-sleeping car vehicles, three TSOs and three BFOs. The TSOs are set out with first class style 2+1 interiors and now seat just 43 using a first class interior design. TSO No. 12100 is seen coupled to an FGW Class 57/6 at Plymouth.* **Antony Christie**

Right Lower: *A fleet of 11 Mk3 sleeper vehicles is on the books of FGW. No. 10584 is seen from its compartment side.* **Nathan Williamson**

Below: *The First ScotRail Caledonian sleeper pool is based at Inverness depot and consists of 53 sleeping vehicles of three different designs. SLEP No. 10605 is shown from its compartment side. This coach has 12 sleeping berths and one pantry for the preparation of drinks and snacks.* **Antony Christie**

Coaching Stock

Left Top: *One of the most adventurous recent modifications to Mk3 stock has been the fitting of sliding plug doors to the Chiltern Trains fleet. Plug door fitted No. 12615. This is a TSO vehicle seating 72 in the 2+2 style and is viewed at Banbury.* **CJM**

Left Middle Upper: *Refurbished interior of a Chiltern Railways 'Business Zone' Mk3, showing the very pleasing interior design using 2+1 seating and small glazed screens by each seating bay.* **Antony Christie**

Left Middle Lower: *The Greater Anglia franchise operates a sizeable fleet of Mk3 vehicles for its loco-hauled London Liverpool Street to Norwich route. In terms of livery the fleet is in something of a transition with some vehicles in National Express colours, some in blue and others in the new Greater Anglia white. RFB No. 10216 is illustrated; these vehicles have catering at one end and 24 first class seats at the other.* **Antony Christie**

Right Bottom: *Arriva Trains Wales at Cardiff operates two Mk3 DVTs on the Cardiff-Holyhead route, although only one is usually in use at a time and the other lays spare at Cardiff Canton. These vehicles were refurbished by Brush. Vehicle No. 82308 is shown, a DVT which has now been transferred to Chiltern and is to be fitted with a generator.* **CJM**

Below: *In National Express grey and white colours with Greater Anglia branding, TSO No. 12132 is seen passing Stratford; with 2+2 seating these coaches seat 80 in mainly airline style. A toilet compartment is provided at both ends.* **CJM**

Coaching Stock

Above: *Greater Anglia operates a fleet of 15 Mk3 DVTs, and these usually operate at the Norwich end of formations. No. 82107 is shown.* **CJM**

Right: *Seven modified Mk3 DVTs, fitted with generators, are operated by Chiltern. These vehicles have a grille in place of the leading van door and an underslung fuel tank for the diesel generator. The generator is mounted directly behind the cab area. No. 82302 is illustrated at Banbury. The luggage van and guards office remain at the inner end.* **CJM**

Coaching Stock

Type:	PKF (AP1Z)	PFP (AQ1Z)	PFB (AR1Z)	RFB (AJ1F)
Mark:	2	2	2	2f
Number range:	504-506	546-553	586	1200-1260
Former range:	-	-	-	32, 33 & 34xx
Introduced:	1966	1966	1966	1973-1975
Built by:	BR Derby	BR Derby	BR Derby	BR Derby
Seating:	-	36F	30F	25F or 26F
Speed:	100mph (161km/h)	100mph (161km/h)	100mph (161km/h)	100mph (161km/h)
Brake type:	Air	Air	Air	Air
Heating:	Electric/6	Electric/5	Electric/4	Electric/6
Bogie type:	B5	B4	B4	B4
Length:	66ft 0in (20.12m)	66ft 0in (20.12m)	66ft 0in (20.12m)	66ft 0in (20.12m)
Height:	12ft 9½in (3.9m)	12ft 9½in (3.90m)	12ft 9½in (3.90m)	12ft 9½in (3.90m)
Width:	9ft 3in (2.82m)	9ft 3in (2.82m)	9ft 3in (2.82m)	9ft 3in (2.82m)
Weight:	40 tonnes	35 tonnes	37-39 tonnes	37-38 tonnes
Operator:	WC	WC	WC	HS, DM, CD
Notes:				

Type:	TSO (AC2Z)	SO (AD2Z)	TSO (AC2A)	TSO (AC2B)
Mark:	2	2	2a	2b
Number range:	5148-5222	5229-5249	5276-5419	5453-5491
Former range:	-	-	-	-
Introduced:	1965-1967	1966	1967-1968	1969
Built by:	BR Derby	BR Derby	BR Derby	BR Derby
Seating:	64S	48S	62-64S	62S
Speed:	100mph (161km/h)	100mph (161km/h)	100mph (161km/h)	100mph (161km/h)
Brake type:	Vacuum	Air or Vacuum	Air	Air
Heating:	Electric/4	Electric/4	Electric/4	Electric/4
Bogie type:	B4	B4	B4	B4
Length:	66ft 0in (20.12m)	66ft 0in (20.12m)	66ft 0in (20.12m)	66ft 0in (20.12m)
Height:	12ft 9½in (3.90m)	12ft 9½in (3.90m)	12ft 9½in (3.90m)	12ft 9½in (3.90m)
Width:	9ft 3in (2.82m)	9ft 3in (2.82m)	9ft 3in (2.82m)	9ft 3in (2.82m)
Weight:	32 tonnes	32 tonnes	32 tonnes	32 tonnes
Operator:	WC, HS	WC, WT	RV, WT, DB	WC
Notes:				

Left Top: *One of the largest operators of loco-hauled passenger stock is West Coast Railway, based at Carnforth. This company is the operator of a large number of charter trains and is a self contained Train Operating Co (TOC). In this view we see 1966-built Mk2 Standard Open (SO) No. 5249 painted in BR Southern Region green livery.* **Antony Christie**

Right: *First ScotRail as part of the Caledonian Sleeper trains has two Mk2f RFO vehicles Nos. 1210 and 1220 on its roster providing day seating and lounge facilities of overnight services. Vehicle 1220 is pictured at London Euston.* **Antony Christie**

Left Bottom: *Mk2f TSO No. 5991 is owned by Railfilms and operated in The Statesman luxury charter train. It is painted in traditional umber and cream Pullman livery. The vehicle is shown at Penzance.* **Antony Christie**

Coaching Stock

RSS (AN2F)	FO (AD1D)	FO (AD1E)	FO (AD1F)
2f	2d	2e	2f
1800	3174-3188	3223-3275	3277-3438
5970	-	-	-
1973	1971-1972	1972-1973	1973-1975
BR Derby	BR Derby	BR Derby	BR Derby
24S	42F	36-42F*	42F
100mph (161km/h)	100mph (161km/h)	100mph (161km/h)	100mph (161km/h)
Air	Air	Air	Air
Electric/12	Electric/5	Electric/5	Electric/5
B5	B4	B4	B4
66ft 0in (20.12m)	66ft 0in (20.12m)	66ft 0in (20.12m)	66ft 0in (20.12m)
12ft 9½in (3.90m)	12ft 9½in (3.90m)	12ft 9½in (3.90m)	12ft 9½in (3.90m)
9ft 3in (2.82m)	9ft 3in (2.82m)	9ft 3in (2.82m)	9ft 3in (2.82m)
33 tonnes	34 tonnes	32-35 tonnes	34 tonnes
WC	VS, RA	RV, RA, VS, HS, DB,	HS, DR, DB, CD, RV,
		* Depending on style	

TSO (AC2C)	TSO (AC2D)	TSO (AC2E)	TSO (AC2F)
2c	2d	2e	2f
5569	5631-5740	5745-5906	5908-6183
-	-	-	-
1969	1971	1972-1973	1973-1975
BR Derby	BR Derby	BR Derby	BR Derby
62S	58S	58-64S*	62-64S*
100mph (161km/h)	100mph (161km/h)	100mph (161km/h)	100mph (161km/h)
Air	Air	Air	Air
Electric/4	Electric/5	Electric/5	Electric/5
B4	B4	B4	B4
66ft 0in (20.12m)	66ft 0in (20.12m)	66ft 0in (20.12m)	66ft 0in (20.12m)
12ft 9½in (3.90m)	12ft 9½in (3.90m)	12ft 9½in (3.90m)	12ft 9½in (3.90m)
9ft 3in (2.82m)	9ft 3in (2.82m)	9ft 3in (2.82m)	9ft 3in (2.82m)
32 tonnes	33 tonnes	33 tonnes	33 tonnes
WC	DB, HS	HS, CG, AW, WC	HS, RV, AW, WC, CG, DM, DB, DR
		* Depending on style	* Depending on style

Type:	TSOT (AG2C)	RLO (AN1F)	RFB (AN1D)	BSOT (AH2Z)
Mark:	2c	2f	2d	2
Number range:	6528	6700-6708	6720-6724	9101-9104
Former range:	5592	32, 33xx	56, 57xx	9398 & 9401
Introduced:	1969	1973-1974	1971	1966
Built by:	BR Derby	BR Derby	BR Derby	BR Derby
Seating:	55S	25F	30F	23S
Speed:	100mph (161km/h)	100mph (161km/h)	100mph (161km/h)	100mph (161km/h)
Brake type:	Air	Air	Air	Vacuum
Heating:	Electric/4	Electric/5	Electric/5	Electric/4
Bogie type:	B4	B4	B4	B4
Length:	66ft 0in (20.12m)	66ft 0in (20.12m)	66ft 0in (20.12m)	66ft 0in (20.12m)
Height:	12ft 9½in (3.90m)	12ft 9½in (3.90m)	12ft 9½in (3.90m)	12ft 9½in (3.90m)
Width:	9ft 3in (2.82m)	9ft 3in (2.82m)	9ft 3in (2.82m)	9ft 3in (2.82m)
Weight:	32.5 tonnes	33.5 tonnes	32 tonnes	31 tonnes
Operator:	WC	HS	HS, DB	HS, WC
Notes:				

Type:	BSO (AE2F)	DBSO (AF2F)	BUO (AE4E)	FK (AA1A)
Mark:	2f	2f	2e	2a
Number range:	9513-9539	9704-9713	9800-9810	13440
Former range:	-	95xx	57, 58xx	-
Introduced:	1974	1974	1972-1973	1968
Built by:	BR Derby	BR Derby	BR Derby	BR Derby
Seating:	32S	30S	31S	42F
Speed:	100mph (161km/h)	100mph (161km/h)	100mph (161km/h)	100mph (161km/h)
Brake type:	Air	Air	Air	Vacuum
Heating:	Electric/5	Electric/5	Electric/4	Electric/4
Bogie type:	B4	B4	B4	B4
Length:	66ft 0in (20.12m)	66ft 0in (20.12m)	66ft 0in (20.12m)	66ft 0in (20.12m)
Height:	12ft 9½in (3.90m)	12ft 9½in (3.90m)	12ft 9½in (3.90m)	12ft 9½in (3.90m)
Width:	9ft 3in (2.82m)	9ft 3in (2.82m)	9ft 3in (2.82m)	9ft 3in (2.82m)
Weight:	34 tonnes	34 tonnes	33.5 tonnes	33 tonnes
Operator:	DR, HS, RV, AW, DB	HS	HS	WC
Notes:				

Left Top: *Of the huge number of Mk2 passenger coaches of various types and marks introduced from the mid-60s a handful still remain in service, mainly with the smaller charter operators. Mk2a BFK No. 17080 is owned by Railfilms Ltd and operated in The Statesman luxury train. It is painted in lined Pullman colours and is shown from its van end at Penzance.*
Antony Christie

Left Bottom: *First ScotRail still maintains a small fleet of Mk2 RLO stock for use with its Caledonian Sleeper operation. To provide a lounge car for the overnight service 11 Mk2e BUO vehicles were modified from TSO vehicles and now sport a serving area and between 25 and 31 unclassified seats. No. 6703 is shown.*
Robin Ralston

Coaching Stock

BSO (AE2Z)	BSO (AE2C)	BSO (AE2D)	BSO (AE2E)
2a	2c	2d	2e
9419, 9428	9440-9448	9479-9494	9496-9509
-	-	-	-
1969	1970	1971	1972
BR Derby	BR Derby	BR Derby	BR Derby
31S	31S	22-31S*	28-32S*
100mph (161km/h)	100mph (161km/h)	100mph (161km/h)	100mph (161km/h)
Air	Air	Air	Air
Electric/4	Electric/4	Electric/5	Electric/5
B4	B4	B4	B4
66ft 0in (20.12m)	66ft 0in (20.12m)	66ft 0in (20.12m)	66ft 0in (20.12m)
12ft 9½in (3.90m)	12ft 9½in (3.90m)	12ft 9½in (3.90m)	12ft 9½in (3.90m)
9ft 3in (2.82m)	9ft 3in (2.82m)	9ft 3in (2.82m)	9ft 3in (2.82m)
32 tonnes	32 tonnes	33 tonnes	33 tonnes
DRS	WC	DR, HS, DM, DB	HS, DM, AW, CG
		* Depending on style	* Depending on style

BFK (AB1A)	GEN (AX5B)	BFK (AB1D)	BSK (AB5C)
2a	2b	2d	2c
17056-17102	17105	17159-17168	35511
14056-14102	14105, 2905	14159-14168	14130/17130
1967-1968	1977	1971-1972	1969
BR Derby	BR Derby	BR Derby	BR Derby
24F	-	24S	-
100mph (161km/h)	100mph (161km/h)	100mph (161km/h)	100mph (161km/h)
Air	Air	Air	Air
Electric/4	Electric/5	Electric/5	Electric/4
B4	B5	B4	B4
66ft 0in (20.12m)	66ft 0in (20.12m)	66ft 0in (20.12m)	66ft 0in (20.12m)
12ft 9½in (3.90m)	12ft 9½in (3.90m)	12ft 9½in (3.90m)	12ft 9½in (3.90m)
9ft 3in (2.82m)	9ft 3in (2.82m)	9ft 3in (2.82m)	9ft 3in (2.82m)
32 tonnes	46 tonnes	33.5 tonnes	32.5 tonnes
RV, RA, HS, WC	RV	DR, VS, WC	RA

Above: *Direct Rail Services operates a sizeable passenger fleet, mainly used for charter operations. However, some Mk2a BSOs are used as flask escort vehicles. These have been modified with special surveillance equipment and have had their brake van end corridor connections removed. These vehicles do not operate within the charter fleet and are used exclusively with the flask train No. 9428 is shown nearest the camera.* **Nathan Williamson**

Type:	RF (AJ11)	RKB (AK51)	RBR (AJ41)	RMB (AN21)
Number range:	325	1566	1651-1730, 1953-1961	1813-1882
Former range:	2907	-	-	-
Introduced:	1961	1960	1960-1961	1960-1962
Built by:	BR Swindon	Cravens	Pressed Steel/BRCW BR Swindon	BR Wolverton
Seating:	24F	3F	11-21 chairs*	44S
Speed:	100mph (161km/h)	100mph (161km/h)	100mph (161km/h)	100mph (161km/h)
Brake type:	Air	Air	Air	Air
Heating:	Electric/2	Electric/1	Electric/2	Electric/3
Bogie type:	B5	B5	B5, COM	COM
Length:	64ft 6in (19.65m)	64ft 6in (19.65m)	64ft 6in (19.65m)	64ft 6in (19.65m)
Height:	12ft 9½in (3.90m)	12ft 9½in (3.90m)	12ft 9½in (3.90m)	12ft 9½in (3.90m)
Width:	9ft 3in (2.82m)	9ft 3in (2.82m)	9ft 3in (2.82m)	9ft 3in (2.82m)
Weight:	34 tonnes	41 tonnes	37-39 tonnes	37-38 tonnes
Operator:	VS	VS	RV, DR, DB, RA, SR, VS, WC	RV, WC, SR
Notes:			* Depending on style	

Type:	GEN (AX51)	FK (AA11)	BFK (AB11)	SK (AA21)
Number range:	6311-6313	13229-13321	17015-17018	18756-18862
Former range:	From NDA	-	14015-14018	24756-24862
Introduced:	1956-1958	1959	1961	1961-1962
Built by:	Pressed Steel, Cravens	BR Swindon	BR Swindon	BR Derby
Seating:	-	42F	24F	64S
Speed:	100mph (161km/h)	100mph (161km/h)	100mph (161km/h)	100mph (161km/h)
Brake type:	Air	Dual	Dual/vacuum	Dual/vacuum
Heating:	-	Electric/3	Electric/2	Electric/4
Bogie type:	B4	B4/COM	COM	COM
Length:	57ft 0in (17.37m)	64ft 6in (19.65m)	64ft 6in (19.65m)	64ft 6in (19.65m)
Height:	12ft 9in (3.88m)	12ft 9½in (3.90m)	12ft 9½in (3.90m)	12ft 9½in (3.90m)
Width:	9ft 3in (2.82m)	9ft 3in (2.82m)	9ft 3in (2.82m)	9ft 3in (2.82m)
Weight:	37.5 tonnes	33-37 tonnes	36 tonnes	36 tonnes
Operator:	DB, WC, VS	SR, WC	RV, VI	WC
Notes:				18806 rebuilt as TSC

Left Top: *The good old Mk1 passenger carriage can still be found, mainly operating for the charter businesses and not forgetting the preservation groups. Painted in mock BR chocolate and cream livery, Mk1 RMB mounted on Commonwealth bogies is shown at Bristol while engaged in 'Torbay Express' steam duties in 2013. This vehicle is operated by the DB-S charter section.* **CJM**

Left Bottom: *Mk1 RBR No. 1671 is operated by Riviera Trains, another significant player in the private rolling stock charter marker. This vehicle sports Commonwealth bogies and is also painted in mock Western Region chocolate and cream livery. It is viewed from the corridor side at the catering end.* **Antony Christie**

Coaching Stock

- (AU51)	FO (AD11)	TSO (AC21)	GEN (AX51)
2833-2834	3066-3150	3766-5044	6310
-	-	-	975325 (81448)
1964	1955-1963	1953-1962	1958
BR Derby	BR Doncaster, Swindon BRCW	BR York, Wolverton	Pressed Steel
Staff accom	42S	64S	-
100mph (161km/h)	100mph (161km/h)	100mph (161km/h)	125mph (201km/h)
Air	Air/Dual	Air/Dual	Air
Electric/2	Electric/3	Electric/4	-
COM	B4, COM	COM, B4	B5
64ft 6in (19.65m)	64ft 6in (19.65m)	64ft 6in (19.65m)	57ft 0in (17.37m)
12ft 9½in (3.90m)	12ft 9½in (3.90m)	12ft 9½in (3.90m)	12ft 9in (3.88m)
9ft 3in (2.82m)	9ft 3in (2.82m)	9ft 3in (2.82m)	9ft 3in (2.82m)
37 tonnes	33-36 tonnes	33-37 tonnes	42 tonnes
WC, RV	RV, SR, WC, JH	WC, SR, RV	RV
			Former HST generator

BCK (AB31)	BSK (AB21)	RK (AK51)
21241-21272	35185-35469	80041-80042
-	-	1690 & 1646
1961-1964	1959-1963	Orig: 1960, RK 1989/2006
BR Swindon, Derby	BR Wolverton	Pressed Steel
12F/18S or 12F/24S	24S	-
100mph (161km/h)	100mph (161km/h)	100mph (161km/h)
Dual	Dual	Dual, Air
Electric/2	Electric/2	Electric/2
COM	B4/COM	COM
64ft 6in (19.65m)	64ft 6in (19.65m)	64ft 6in (19.65m)
12ft 9½in (3.90m)	12ft 9½in (3.90m)	12ft 9½in (3.90m)
9ft 3in (2.82m)	9ft 3in (2.82m)	9ft 3in (2.82m)
36-37 tonnes	33-37 tonnes	39 tonnes
SR, RV, WC	SR, RV, WC	RV, DR

Right Top: *Owned and operated by Riviera Trains, this Mk1 BCK No. 21272 is painted in chocolate and cream colours and is a dual brake, electric heat example. The side corridor vehicle has a brake van at the near end followed by the guard's office and five compartments (two for first class and three for standard class) and a toilet at the far end. It is mounted on Commonwealth bogies.*
CJM

Right Bottom: *Mk1 BSK 35469. This vehicle with four side corridor fed compartments is operated by Riviera Trains and in painted in 'blood and custard' colours. The brake van at the far end has been rebuilt to accommodate a generator for train supply.*
Nathan Williamson

Traction Recognition

Coaching Stock

Above: *Standard 64 seat Mk1 TSO, owned by Riviera and mounted on Commonwealth bogies. This vehicle like many in charter use has had the middle set of passenger doors sealed up.* **CJM**

Right: *Operated by West Coast Railways, this FO No. 3128 carries the identity 99371* Victoria. *This 42 seat 2+1 coach is set out for luxury land cruise dining with table lamps. The vehicles centre door has been sealed and is used as a serving area.* **Antony Christie**

Left: *A number of Mk1 brake fitted vehicles have been adapted as steam locomotive support coaches, providing seating for staff and a store area for supplies. One of these is West Coast Railway BSK No. 35322, which carries the identity 99035. It is seen on the rear of a charter at Burton Salmon.*
Antony Christie

Right: *An unusual Mk1 vehicle operated by West Coast, officially as a steam loco support vehicle, is NNX No. 80204 which was previously used for Royal Mail traffic and modified from BSK 35297. It now has a large stowage van, a guard's space, a further stowage area fed by roller shutter doors and one seating compartment. The coach is seen acting as an HST barrier vehicle in this view.* **CJM**

Coaching Stock

Number	Type	Depot	Livery	Operator	Use
2903 (11001)	AT5G	ZN	ROY	NRL/DBS	HM The Queen's Saloon
2904 (12001)	AT5G	ZN	ROY	NRL/DBS	HRH The Duke of Edinburgh's Saloon
2915 (10735)	AT5G	ZN	ROY	NRL/DBS	Royal Household Sleeping Coach
2916 (40512)	AT5G	ZN	ROY	NRL/DBS	HRH The Prince of Wales's Dining Coach
2917 (40514)	AT5G	ZN	ROY	NRL/DBS	Kitchen Car and Royal Household Dining Coach
2918 (40515)	AT5G	ZN	ROY	NRL/DBS	Royal Household Coach
2919 (40518)	AT5G	ZN	ROY	NRL/DBS	Royal Household Coach
2920 (17109)	AT5B	ZN	ROY	NRL/DBS	Generator Coach and Household Sleeping Coach
2921 (17107)	AT5B	ZN	ROY	NRL/DBS	Brake, Coffin Carrier and Household Accommodation
2922		AT5G	ZN	ROY	NRL/DBS	HRH The Prince of Wales's Sleeping Coach
2923		AT5G	ZN	ROY	NRL/DBS	HRH The Prince of Wales's Saloon

Left: *Based at Wolverton Works, the UK Royal Train, which can be used by HM The Queen or Prince Charles, consists of 11 Mk2/Mk3 vehicles but the operational train can consist of anything from five to eight vehicles. It is usual that the two brake vehicles 2920 and 2921 accompany all moves. This view shows generator brake vehicle 2920 from its brake/generator end.* **Antony Christie**

Below: *The Prince of Wales' saloon No. 2923 is a purpose-built Mk3 for Royal use; it was built at Derby and transferred to Wolverton Works for fitting out. The Prince of Wales cypher is on the far end, and the vehicle is seen passing Dawlish.* **Antony Christie**

Coaching Stock

Left: *Built as Hastings line buffet vehicle 60755, this vehicle was converted into the Southern Region General Manager's saloon and remained allocated to Stewarts Lane until privatisation. The vehicle is now owned by Network Rail and kept at the RTC Derby and used as a route inspection vehicle. It has Blue star compatible remote control. In more recent years it has received modified front ends with Group Standard light clusters. The vehicle is painted in Southern multiple unit green livery and numbered 975025.* **Antony Christie**

Right: *Network Rail New Measurement Train vehicle 977993, rebuilt from HST TGS No. 44053, is fitted with a non-power collection pantograph for inspection of overhead line equipment. With its pantograph in the stowed position, the coach is seen from its pantograph end.* **Antony Christie**

Below: *Network Rail No. 977983, rebuilt from FO 3407, is used as a Hot Box Detection Coach. This image clearly shows the end modifications carried out and installation of test train jumper cables.* **Antony Christie**

Departmental Stock

Right and Below: *Network Rail No. 977985 is a rebuild from Mk2f TSO No. 6019 and is used as a laser vehicle on the Derby-based Structure Gauging Train (SGT). Since its passenger days the coach has received major modifications and test train high level jumpers on the coach ends. At one end a huge protruding laser reader is located, which requires an extended coupling to attach to a semi-permanently coupled support vehicle.* **Antony Christie**

Below: *Another part of the Structure Gauging Train is former Southern Region/NSE 4CIG MBS No. 63284. This coach has received some major structural changes from its passenger days, including a generator at one end (the former guard's van) and new window openings and underside equipment. It is hardly recognisable that this was once a passenger vehicle on South London commuter routes.* **Antony Christie**

Below: *Six Mk2f DBSO vehicles are on the books of Network Rail, based at Derby to provide remote driving facilities for test trains. Some of these vehicles have received major structural and technical changes. No. 9703 is illustrated from its cab end. The original front gangway door on this example has been totally removed and plated over. Note that no screw coupling is carried on the draw hook.* **Antony Christie**

Above: *A fleet of barrier/translator vehicles is operated either by TOCs or lease companies to enable the hauling of multiple unit stock fitted with either Dellner or Tightlock couplings. To operate the translator equipment and to enable train brakes to operate the translator vehicles require an electric train supply feed. Translator No. 6379, owned by Porterbrook and painted in all-over blue livery, is seen coupled between a Class 47/7 and a SWT Class 458/5 unit.* **CJM**

Above and Right: *Classified as 960, this three-car ex-Class 117 set is formed of three driving cars, although the middle vehicle has lost its cab. It is allocated to Chiltern Railways at Aylesbury for sandite and water jetting, to keep running rails clear of leaf debris during the leaf-fall season. The set is painted in green with a small yellow warning panel and these two views show the set stabled at Aylesbury. Both:* **Antony Christie**

Traction Recognition

Right Top: *Fitted with 'trip-cock' apparatus on its near bogie, former Class 121 'Bubble' No. 55022 still remains at Aylesbury and is officially used for route learning and leaf-fall rail cleaning duties. It is painted in BR blue and grey livery with Chiltern branding. This vehicle received a number of modifications when it operated as a sandite set.*
Antony Christie

Right Middle: *Three former Gatwick Express GLV Class 489 vehicles are owned by Network Rail to act as de-icing vehicles for third rail routes. The three vehicles are usually kept at Eastleigh when not in use and normally GBRf supplies traction to operate the vehicles. All three are seen in this illustration on a test run near Folkestone.*
Brian Stephenson

Below: *As part of the Class 150/1 build programme at BREL York, two extra vehicles were built which were shipped to the Railway Technical Centre, Derby, and built as a state-of-the art track assessment train. One coach is basically a Class 150 passenger coach, while the other equipment vehicle has only a few side windows and ventilation grilles for onboard generators. Today, the two-car set is operated by Network Rail, painted in yellow livery and traverses much of the UK rail system on a scheduled basis. It is seen passing Dawlish.* **CJM**

Arriva Trains Wales

Name	Alpha Code	Stock Types	Visibility
Cardiff	CF	142, 143, 150/2, 153, 158, CS	Partly visible from main line
Chester	CH	175	From passing trains
Machynlleth	MN	158	From passing trains

C2C

Name	Alpha Code	Stock Types	Visibility
East Ham	EM	357/0, 357/2	From passing trains

Chiltern Railways

Name	Alpha Code	Stock Types	Visibility
Aylesbury	AY	01/5, 121, 165/0, 168/0, 168/1, 168/2, 172/1, 960, CS	Partly visible from station

CrossCountry Trains

Name	Alpha Code	Stock Types	Visibility
Central Rivers (Burton)	CZ	220, 221	From passing trains
Edinburgh Craigentinny	EC	43, CS	From passing trains
Tyseley	TS	170/1, 170/3, 170/5, 170/6	From passing trains

East Coast

Name	Alpha Code	Stock Types	Visibility
Bounds Green	BN	91, CS	From passing trains
Edinburgh Craigentinny	EC	43, CS	From passing trains

East Midlands Trains

Name	Alpha Code	Stock Types	Visibility
Derby	DY	08, 222/0, 222/1	From passing trains
Neville Hill (Leeds)	NL	08, 43, CS,	From passing trains
Nottingham Eastcroft	NM	153, 156, 158,	From passing trains and station

Left: *East Midlands Trains Derby Etches Park depot, purpose-built to handle the fleet of Class 222 stock used on the St Pancras to Sheffield and Nottingham lines. Set No. 222018 is seen receiving attention.* **CJM**

Eurostar

Name	Alpha Code	Stock Types	Visibility
Forest (Brussels)	FF	373/1 (plus Belgian stock)	Partly visible from main line
Le Landy (Paris)	LY	373/2 (plus French stock)	Partly visible from main line
Temple Mills (London)	TI	08, 373/0 (374)	Not viewable from passing trains

First Capital Connect

Name	Alpha Code	Stock Types	Visibility
Bedford	BF	319/2, 319/3, 319/4, 377/5	Partly visible from passing trains
Hornsey	HE	313/0, 313/1, 317/3, 321/4, 365,	From passing trains
Selhurst	SU	319/0, 319/2	Partly visible from passing trains

Below: *The First Capital Connect depot on the Great Northern route is located at Hornsey, where all levels of work can be undertaken. Three Class 365s Nos. 365514, 365532 and 365534 are seen inside the main shed.* **CJM**

First Great Western

Name	Alpha Code	Stock Types	Visibility
Bristol St Philips Marsh	PM	08, 150/1, 150/2, 158/0, 158/9	Not viewable from passing trains
Exeter	EX	143, 150/1, 150/2, 153,	Visible from station
Laira	LA	08, 43	From main line passing trains
Landore	LE	08, 43	Partly visible from main line
Old Oak Common	OO	08, 43, 57, 180, CS	From passing trains on FGW
Penzance	PZ	08, CS	From main line passing trains
Reading	RG	150/0, 165, 166	From main line passing trains

First Hull Trains

Name	Alpha Code	Stock Types	Visibility
Crofton	XW	180	Not viewable from passing trains

First ScotRail

Name	Alpha Code	Stock Types	Visibility
Corkerhill	CK	156,	From passing trains
Inverness	IS	158, CS	From passing trains and station
Haymarket	HA	158, 170/3, 170/4	From passing trains
Glasgow Shields	GW	314, 318, 320, 334, 380/0, 380/1	From passing trains

Depots

First TransPennine Express

Name	Alpha Code	Stock Types	Visibility
Ardwick	AK	185	From passing trains
Crofton	XW	170/3	Not viewable from passing trains

Grand Central

Name	Alpha Code	Stock Types	Visibility
Heaton	HT	43, 180, CS	From passing trains

Greater Anglia

Name	Alpha Code	Stock Types	Visibility
Norwich Crown Point	NC	90, 153, 156, 170/2, CS	Partly visible from main line
Ilford	IL	315, 317/5, 317/6, 317/8, 321/3, 321/4 360/1, 379	From passing trains

Below: *Operated by Greater Anglia, the large depot at Ilford looks after all the GA fleet of electric multiple units. Adjacent to the Greater Anglia depot is a large Bombardier workshop equipped for coaching stock and multiple unit attention.* **CJM**

Heathrow Express & Heathrow Connect

Name	Alpha Code	Stock Types	Visibility
Old Oak Common HEX	OH	332, 360/2	From passing trains

London Midland

Name	Alpha Code	Stock Types	Visibility
Northampton	NN	321/4, 350/1, 350/2, (350/4)	From passing trains
Soho	SI	08, 323	From passing trains
Stourbridge Junction	SJ	139	From station
Tyseley	TS	08, 150/1, 153, 170/5, 170/6, 172/2, 172/3	From passing trains

London Overground

Name	Alpha Code	Stock Types	Visibility
New Cross	NX	378/1, 378/2	From passing trains
Willesden	WN	09/0, 172/0, 378/2	From passing trains

Depots

MerseyRail

Name	Alpha Code	Stock Types	Visibility
Birkenhead	BD	507, 508/1	From passing trains

Northern Rail

Name	Alpha Code	Stock Types	Visibility
Allerton	AN	156,	From passing trains
Heaton	HT	142, 156,	From passing trains
Longsight	LG	323	From passing trains
Newton Heath	NH	142, 150/1, 150/2, 158/0	From passing trains
Neville Hill (Leeds)	NL	144, 153, 155, 158/0, 158/9, 321/9, 322	From passing trains

South West Trains

Name	Alpha Code	Stock Types	Visibility
Northam	NT	444, 450	From passing trains
Ryde (IOW)	RY	483	Visible from station
Salisbury	SA	158, 159/0, 159/1	Visible from station
Wimbledon	WD	455/7, 455/8, 455/9, 458/0, 458/5	From passing trains

Right: *The main depot operated by South West Trains for non-'Desiro' stock is at Wimbledon, where a large complex of maintenance and stabling sidings can be found. The main workshops are located towards the Earlsfield end of the site. Here two Class 455s, Nos. 455872 and 455718, receive attention. The depot is also responsible for maintenance of Class 458 stock and stabling of 'Desiro' sets.* **CJM**

SouthEastern

Name	Alpha Code	Stock Types	Visibility
Ashford	AD	395	Visible from station
Ramsgate	RM	375/3, 375/6, 375/7, 375/8, 375/9	Visible from station
Slade Green	SG	376, 465/0, 465/1, 465/2, 465/9, 466	From passing trains

Southern

Name	Alpha Code	Stock Types	Visibility
Brighton	BI	08, 73, 313/2, 377/1, 377/2, 377/4, 377/6	From passing trains and station
Selhurst	SU	171/7, 171/8, 377/1, 377/2, 377/3, 377/4, 455/8, 456	Partly visible from passing trains
Stewarts Lane	SL	442	Visible from SouthEastern services

Virgin Trains West Coast

Name	Alpha Code	Stock Types	Visibility
Central Rivers (Burton)	CZ	221	From passing trains
Manchester International	MA	390	From passing trains
Wembley	WB	CS	From passing trains

Depots

Colas

Name	Alpha Code	Stock Types	Visibility
Rugby	RU	56, 66/8	From passing trains
Washwood Heath	ZE	47/7, 56	Not viewable from passing trains

DB-Schenker - EWS

Name	Alpha Code	Stock Types	Visibility
Alizay (France)	AZ	66/0	From passing trains
Bescot	BS	08, CS	From passing trains
Crewe Electric	CE	67, 90, 92, CS	Partly visible from passing trains
Doncaster	DR	08, 09	From passing trains
Eastleigh	EH	08, 58, CS	From passing trains
Poznan (Poland)	PN	66/0	From passing trains
Toton	TO	08, 09, 58, 59/2, 60, 66/0, CS	From passing trains

Direct Rail Services

Name	Alpha Code	Stock Types	Visibility
Carlisle Kingmoor	KM	20, 37/0, 37/4, 37/5, 37/6, 47/4, 47/7 57/0, 57/3, 66/3, 66/4, CS	From passing trains
Crewe Gresty Bridge	CG	68	From passing trains

Left: *Direct Rail Services operates a sizeable facility at Crewe Gresty Bridge, where all DRS classes can be found. The depot is the official home of the Class 68s. In this view we see three eras of DRS traction lined up at the shed, Class 37/6 No. 37610, Class 66/3 No. 66303 and Class 68 No. 68002.* **CJM**

Europorte-GBRf

Name	Alpha Code	Stock Types	Visibility
Cardiff	CF	08	From passing trains
Coquelles (France)	CQ	92	From passing trains
Dollands Moor	DM	92	From passing trains
Peterborough	PG	20, 66/7,	From passing trains
St Leonards	SE	73/1, 73/2	From passing trains

Freightliner

Name	Alpha Code	Stock Types	Visibility
Crewe LNWR	CP	86/6, 90/0	From passing trains
Leeds Midland Road	LD	66/5, 66/6, 66/9, 70	From passing trains
Southampton	SZ	08	From passing trains

Ian Allan

BOOK & MODEL SHOPS

We have four specialist interest Book and Model Shops across the country in London, Manchester, Birmingham and Cardiff. All our outlets provide a one-stop shop for enthusiasts and cater for every transport specialism, whether modern or historic. As well as books, we also offer an exhaustive range of top quality models and accessories.

We offer a unique combination of expertise and personal service, friendly and knowledgeable staff, a comprehensive stock and a Special Order service.

SUPPORT YOUR LOCAL INDEPENDENT BOOKSELLER!

MANCHESTER
5 Piccadilly Station Approach
Manchester
M1 2GH
Tel: 0161 237 9840
E-mail: manchester@ianallanpublishing.co.uk

LONDON
45/46 Lower Marsh
Waterloo, London
SE1 7RG
Tel: 020 7401 2100
E-mail: waterloo@ianallanpublishing.co.uk

BIRMINGHAM
12 Ethel Street
Birmingham
B2 4BG
Tel: 0121 643 2496
E-mail: bcc@ianallanpublishing.co.uk

CARDIFF
31 Royal Arcade
Cardiff
CF10 1AE
Tel: 029 2039 0615
E-mail:cardiff@ianallanpublishing.co.uk

OPENING HOURS
Monday-Friday 9.00am-5.30pm • Saturday 9.00am - 5.00pm • Sunday and Bank Holidays - Closed

www.ianallanpublishing.com

ALSO OF INTEREST

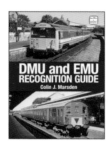

DMU AND EMU RECOGNITION GUIDE
Colin J. Marsden

This companion volume to *Traction Recognition* is a meticulously detailed guide to the historic rolling stock operated by BR and covers the complete diesel and electric fleet with over 390 pages of comprehensive and up to date material. An essential reference for modern scene enthusiasts.

Hardback | 210 x 150 mm | 392 pages | 978 0 7110 3740 3 | £25.00

RAIL GUIDE 2014
Colin J. Marsden

The *abc Rail Guide* has become quickly established as a must-have annual publication for the current scene railway enthusiast and is a traditional combined volume for the modern age. Listings are by user, with details of every locomotive and carriage used by that operator. Included are running numbers, depot, livery, owner, operator and name, if it carries one.

Author Colin Marsden constantly revises the content and presentation in the light of comments from readers and users. The 2014 edition is completely updated with a wholly new illustrative selection of colour photographs and maps.

Hardback | 210 x 150 mm | 304 pages | 978 0 7110 3771 7 | £20.00

LONDON UNDERGROUND ROLLING STOCK GUIDE
Ben Muldoon

This new numbers guide to all the rolling stock in the current London Underground fleet is what every dedicated LU enthusiast has long been waiting for. Produced in the ever popular Ian Allan 'abc' pocket book style, it provides a complete listing of the stock numbers of each vehicle operating on Underground lines as well as battery locomotives and maintenance vehicles, with the listing grouped under individual Underground lines, together with a representative selection of photographs.

Paperback | 210 x 150 mm | 96 pages | 978 0 7110 3807 3 | £13.50

AVAILABLE NOW
- From our website at **www.ianallanpublishing.com**
- From our Mail Order Hotline on 0844 245 6944
- From all good book retailers and our specialist bookshops in London, Cardiff, Birmingham and Manchester

Ian Allan PUBLISHING

HEAT WAVE

Contents

Haydn Middleton

Story illustrated by
Leo Hartas

Before Reading

In this story

 Alex

 Sarah

Tricky words

- watering
- hosepipe
- louder
- remind
- whispered
- through
- soaked
- siren

Introduce these tricky words and help the reader when they come across them later!

Story starter

Alex and Sarah care about the environment. They are members of a green kids' club, and they are always looking for ways to encourage people to 'think green'! One summer there was a hosepipe ban because there had been no rain for three weeks. Alex and Sarah were in the library, using the Internet to find out about ways to save water.

Turn Off That Tap!

Alex and Sarah were using the Internet to find out about ways to save water. "Look at this," said Alex. "It says people should *always* use watering cans to water their gardens. Not just when there is a hosepipe ban."

On their way home Sarah said,
"We should check that people
are not using their hosepipes."
"How can we tell?" asked Alex.
"Look out for green grass!"
said Sarah.

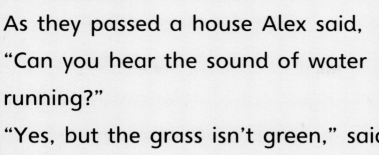

As they passed a house Alex said, "Can you hear the sound of water running?"

"Yes, but the grass isn't green," said Sarah. "Perhaps the people don't know they have left a tap running."

"Then we should tell them," said Alex.

Alex and Sarah went up to the house. The sound of water running got louder. They saw an outside tap on the side of the house. Fixed to the tap was a hose. The hose ran round to the back of the house.

"Do you think it's OK to go round the back of the house?" asked Sarah.

"We've got to remind them about the hosepipe ban," said Alex. "It's really important to save water."

When they got round to the back of the house, they saw a man with the hosepipe. He was filling plastic bottles with water. The man hadn't heard them. The noise of the running water was too loud.

"What is he doing?" whispered Alex.

"He seems to be washing empty plastic bottles," said Sarah.

"Why would he be doing that?" asked Alex.

"I don't know," said Sarah.

9

"Well, if we really want to be green we should remind him about the hosepipe ban," said Alex.

"OK," said Sarah.

They took a step towards the man.

But then Sarah looked through the window of a garden shed.
She could see more plastic bottles.
These bottles were full of water.
"I know what he's doing," whispered Sarah, "and he's not just breaking the hosepipe ban!"

What do you think the man is doing with the bottles?

Just then the man looked up. He saw Alex and Sarah standing by the shed. "Hey, you kids, clear off!" shouted the man.

"Remind him about the hosepipe ban," said Alex.

"Excuse me ..." Sarah began.

But the man turned the hose on her. She was soaked through!

"We've got to call the police," gasped Sarah as they ran to the front of the house. "He's cheating by selling tap water as bottled water!"

13

Sarah quickly called the police. But as she was giving them the man's address, the man turned the hose on her again. He blasted her mobile phone right out of her hand! He looked very angry indeed.

"You nosey kids!" shouted the man
and he charged at them.
But he forgot he was holding the
hosepipe. He tripped over it and
fell flat on his face!

At that moment Alex and Sarah heard the sound of a police siren.

"I think we've done more than just save water today," said Sarah as she picked up her mobile.

"Another victory for the greens!" said Alex.

Quiz

Text Detective

- Why was the man filling the plastic bottles?
- Do you think it was wise of Alex and Sarah to go round the back of the house?

Word Detective

- **Phonic Focus:** Identifying and spelling word endings
  Page 15: Find three past tense verbs ending with 'ed'.
  What sound does each 'ed' ending make?
  (shouted, ed; charged, d; tripped, t)
- Page 9: Find a word that means 'spoke quietly'.
- Page 9: Find two adjectives that describe the bottles.

Super Speller

Read these words:

always   important   charged

Now try to spell them!

HA! HA! HA!

Q Why did the woman give the man a bucket of water?

 A He was collecting for the swimming pool!

17

Find out about

• Why the Earth's weather is getting warmer

Tricky words

• weather
• dangerous
• warmer
• gases
• carbon dioxide
• breathe
• methane
• scientists

Introduce these tricky words and help the reader when they come across them later!

Text starter

The Earth's weather is slowly getting warmer. Many scientists believe *we* have something to do with it! When we burn fuel we make a gas called carbon dioxide. The carbon dioxide cannot escape into the atmosphere but clings around the Earth like a huge sky blanket. This causes global warming.

Warming Up

Do you like sunny weather?
Would you like it to be sunny
every day?
It sounds nice, but did you know
that it could be dangerous if the
Earth got any warmer?

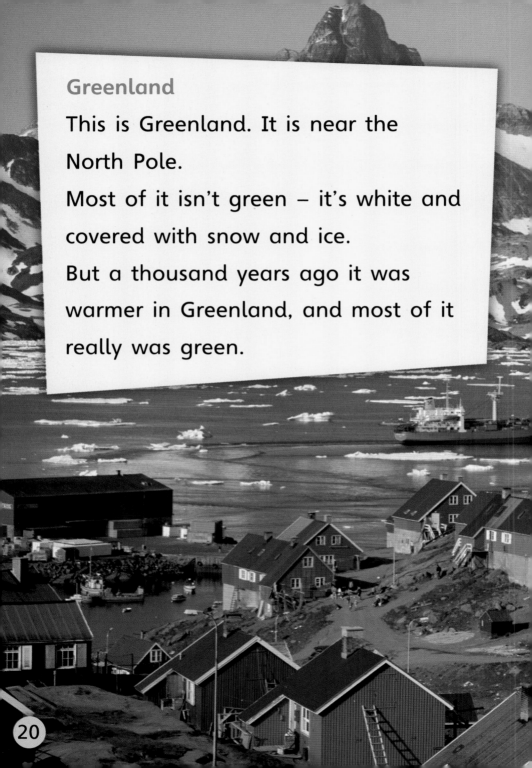

Greenland

This is Greenland. It is near the North Pole.

Most of it isn't green – it's white and covered with snow and ice.

But a thousand years ago it was warmer in Greenland, and most of it really was green.

Now the weather is getting warmer again. The ice in Greenland will melt if the Earth keeps heating up.
This might make Greenland greener, but it would not be good for the rest of the Earth.

Does warmer weather matter?

If the weather keeps getting warmer, the snow and ice at the North and South Poles will melt into the oceans. Polar bears and penguins would have to find new places to live!

If all the ice in Greenland melted, the oceans would rise by seven metres!

If the snow and ice melt, there will be much more water in the oceans. Some of this water would spill onto the land and cause dangerous floods. Some cities and islands would be under water!

Why is the Earth getting warmer?

We are making it warmer!

How?

When we burn fuel like coal, oil and petrol, gases escape into the sky.

The gases stay there like a sky blanket around the Earth.

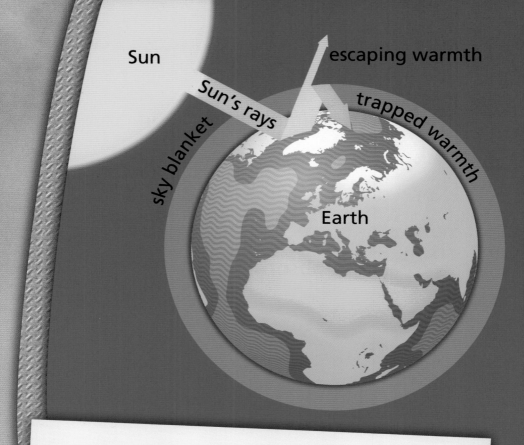

Sun

escaping warmth

Sun's rays

trapped warmth

sky blanket

Earth

The sun's rays warm the Earth. In the past, some of that warmth bounced back up into Space.

Now the sky blanket stops most of the warmth from bouncing back up into Space and the warmth is trapped.

So our weather gets warmer.

Carbon dioxide gas

People and animals breathe in oxygen and breathe out carbon dioxide. Plants and trees breathe in carbon dioxide and breathe out oxygen. So trees can absorb carbon dioxide.

But we have cut down too many trees. There aren't enough left to absorb all the carbon dioxide we are making. So the extra carbon dioxide goes up into the sky blanket and makes the weather even warmer.

Methane gas

The sky blanket also has lots of methane in it. Where does all that methane come from?

When we put rubbish in landfill sites, it slowly rots away. This makes methane.

But methane does not only come from rubbish. Cows also make methane when they burp or break wind.
This happens when people do it too!

One cow makes enough methane each day to fill 140 big plastic bottles!

The future

All over the Earth people are making too much carbon dioxide, and cows and rubbish are making too much methane.

So the sky blanket is getting thicker and thicker and the Earth is getting hotter and hotter.

Does it matter? YES!

If the ice and snow at the Poles melts, then parts of the world will flood. Other parts might become deserts because it will be too hot for plants to grow. Some animals may die out. Scientists think this could happen in the next hundred years!

Quiz

Text Detective

- Why is the Earth getting warmer?
- How do you think people could stop the Earth from warming up?

Word Detective

- **Phonic Focus:** Identifying and spelling word endings
  Page 30: Find two different adjectives with 'er' endings. What are the root words? *(thick, hot)*
- Page 21: Find a word that means the opposite of 'freeze'.
- Page 31: Why is there an exclamation mark at the end of the last sentence?

Super Speller

Read these words:

warmer   **enough**   **water**

Now try to spell them!

HA! HA! HA!

Q Why do cows have bells?

A Because their horns don't work!